# FEMINIST PERSPECTIVES
# ON HEALTH CARE LAW

Cavendish
Publishing
Limited

London • Sydney

# FEMINIST PERSPECTIVES ON HEALTH CARE LAW

Edited by
**Sally Sheldon** and **Michael Thomson**
both of the Law Department, Keele University

Cavendish
Publishing
Limited

London • Sydney

First published in 1998 by Cavendish Publishing Limited, The Glass House, Wharton Street, London WC1X 9PX, United Kingdom.

Telephone: 44 (0) 171 278 8000     Facsimile: 44 (0) 171 278 8080

E-mail: info@cavendishpublishing.com

Visit our Home Page on http://www.cavendishpublishing.com

Sheldon, Sally

Feminist perspectives on health care law. – (Feminist perspectives on law)

1. Medical laws and legislation – Great Britain 2. Feminist jurisprudence – Great Britain

I. Title II. Thomson, Michael

344.4'1'041'082

ISBN 1 85941 397 8

Printed and bound in Great Britain by Biddles Ltd, Guildford and King's Lynn

# SERIES EDITORS' PREFACE

*Anne Bottomley and Sally Sheldon*

This book is the first in a series of collections which gather together feminist perspectives on different areas of the law curriculum. There is now a large and ever-expanding body of literature on feminist perspectives on law. Many law departments teach courses under the title of 'women and law', 'gender and law', 'feminist perspectives on law' or (more adventurously) 'body politics and law'. The task which has inspired this series of books is to explore the contribution which feminists could make to an understanding of the foundational subjects of law and other popular optional subjects – to break out of the ghetto of the discrete third year option and infiltrate the mainstream of the law curriculum.

This refusal of 'ghettoisation' is also relevant within disciplines. For that reason, a scan down the contents list of this book might bring some surprises. Whilst this volume includes new perspectives on the kinds of subjects which have been of interest to feminists for some time, these sit alongside subjects which are *terra* (relatively) *incognita* including: administrative law, medical research, confidentiality, medical negligence, and death and dying. In all these cases, it is shown that a feminist perspective has something new to say. Moreover, the contributors to this volume would argue that feminism should not only be of interest to women. Rather, the lawyer who ignores the feminist critique will consequently have an impoverished understanding of the legal situation as it concerns both women and men.

The series editors would like to thank Cavendish Publishing for their support in producing this project and all our colleagues, in our own institutions and elsewhere, who have given us such encouragement and help in this project.

# FOREWORD

## IS THE PATIENT POSITION
## INEVITABLY FEMALE?

*Katherine O'Donovan*

Feminist jurisprudence has altered the way in which some traditional areas of the legal curriculum are researched, taught and understood. Can it do the same for health care law? The essays in this collection suggest that the answer is yes. This answer is not confined to the 'reproductive ghetto',[1] that is to issues of gender and physical differences, of particular female conditions, of uteri and ovaries. Broader issues of methodology, the constitution of the subject, the opening up of subject positions, analyses of concepts, are equally implicated, as is shown in this collection. For these reasons, and for many others, the collection is to be welcomed. It shows a variety of approaches, with new ways of asking questions about the relationship between law and the provision of health care. Noteworthy also is the breadth and variety of topics discussed, from posthumous pregnancies and clinical research to resource allocation and professional discipline.

This brief preface is an exploration of some paths which feminist analyses might follow. However, setting out on a journey requires us to know our starting point. So how is the subject named medical law, or health care law, constituted? Does it have an identity? Is there agreement regarding its nature and its boundaries?

In the introduction to his book, *Health Care Law*,[2] Jonathan Montgomery gently chides Kennedy and Grubb, the authors of the pioneering title *Medical Law*,[3] for 'an approach which begins from the work of doctors and works outwards'.[4] The doctor-centred approach is criticised as ignoring other health professionals, and as treating the clinical interaction between doctor and patient as the significant relationship, thus ignoring NHS structural and public health issues. Whilst these texts set themselves different parameters, neither book can claim to cover all the areas where those working in private and public medicine touch on the law in the course of their work. To be fair, it is doubtful whether a full account of the legal regulation of all aspects of health care and medical treatment can be given in one volume alone. There is space for alternative accounts, such as those contained in this book. Not only

---

1   Murphy, MT, 'Bursting binary bubbles: law, literature and the sexual body, in Morison, J and Bell, C (eds), *Tall Stories? Reading Law and Literature*, 1996, Aldershot: Dartmouth, pp 57–82, 70.

2   Montgomery, J, *Health Care Law*, 1997, Oxford: OUP.

3   Kennedy, I and Grubb, A, *Medical Law: Text with Materials*, 2nd edn, 1994, London: Butterworths.

4   Montgomery, *ibid*, p 1.

does this book provide alternative (competing and complementary) accounts but it also engages in the dialogue that Montgomery has begun regarding which aspects of health provision and their legal regulation are deemed worthy of study, and, perhaps more importantly, which are excluded.[5]

If, as Montgomery and Kennedy and Grubb accept with differing degrees of emphasis, the doctor-patient relationship is taken as a significant part of what is called health care/medical law, we can then ask how this relationship is constituted. Donald Black argues that the closer people are to one another, the less the law will be implicated in their relationships and dealings, and that the greater the distance is between persons, the more likely that the law will become involved.[6] If we apply this insight to a patient's involvement with a doctor, it becomes apparent that this is not primarily a legal relationship, nor is it seen as such by either party. The role of doctor can be analysed as following three paradigms: the classical, Hippocratic, collegial, benevolent, paternalist mode;[7] the scientific, experimental, mechanical mode; and the therapeutic alliance of doctor and patient mode. But even in this last, most patient-friendly mode, the inequality of the binary doctor-patient relationship cannot be disguised. This mutuality – if such it is – is not perceived as legally constituted. From the patient's vantage point it is constituted by a highly individualised need and dependence. As presented in medical education and practice, it is an ethical relationship governed from the doctor's viewpoint by collegiality and professional constraints.

Yet is there, in this inequality and dependence, an entry point for feminist analysis? The history of feminist jurisprudence offers examples of analysis of inequality in the very constitution of subject positions. Structural, constitutive, and masked inequalities have been exposed. This has occurred against a legal rhetoric of equality and difference which has been harnessed in the exposition of contradictory discourses. In the doctor-patient binary, legal discourse has not offered a model of equality. The positions are constituted as unequal in practice and discussion. The inevitability of this inequality is arguable. The introduction of the notion of the 'therapeutic alliance' signals a change. Investigation of patient subjectivity drawing on feminist methodology can open the way for insights into how power is placed in the doctor-patient relationship.

Current critiques of law's claim to be closed to the particulars of individual people owes something to feminist analysis. The critique of abstraction has various aspects: as reductionist, as denial of subjectivity, and of real persons as embodied and situated; as claiming neutrality but masking a gendered figure; and as containing an ideal type based on the imaginative projections of themselves by the powerful. In its constitution of abstract figures of patient

---

5    See Sheldon and Thomson, this volume.

6    Black, D, *The Sociological Imagination*, 1989, Oxford: OUP.

7    Jacob, J, *Doctors and Rules: A Sociology of Professional Values*, 1988, London: Routledge.

and doctor on a medical landscape, law cannot acknowledge a relationship beyond the mechanical. Yet the dissection of these figures can open up spaces for other possible relationships and alternative ways of structuring health care law. This can be an outcome of a feminist perspective and one of the paths such analysis might follow. Outlined below are some of the questions that theorists sensitive to gender may want to ask about the figures who constitute this binary relationship.

To point out that the figure of the doctor is constituted as the knower, whereas the patient simply waits passively, is obvious. Although critical work on the position of the doctor has begun,[8] the contradictory positioning of the patient has yet to be examined. Consent is placed as central to law and ethics in the treatment of patients. This is a reflection of the creation of the patient as a rational, choosing person, capable of choices and decisions. Consent is a paradigmatic aspect of autonomy. Yet brief thought reveals it to be placed in an ambivalent relationship to 'the best interests of the patient', also upheld as an ethical part of the doctor's duty. The ideals of the classical mode of doctoring thus become confused with respect for individual patients' decisions.

Feminist analyses of the concept of consent in areas of criminal and family law throw the limitations of the concept as deployed in the discourse of law and medical ethics into relief. Yet such analogies have not been heard as part of legal arguments regarding medical consent. Exclusionary reasons of boundary maintenance have been given as reasons for excluding such comparisons. Perhaps the underlying reason, however, is the instability of the concept, as revealed in feminist analysis.

When the concept of consent, as it has been elucidated within commercial law, is compared with consent in tort, criminal, family and health care law, we find many varieties of legal consent. In criminal rape cases, consent is gendered and is surrounded by stereotyped assumptions.[9] The discourse of consent in family law concerns voluntary unions in which consent is eternal, and is gendered in so far as one partner consents to give up her autonomy, and therefore her future ability to consent.[10] Medical ethics as taught in medical schools, and as written up in the press, concerns 'informed consent', containing a notion of information about risks and consequent choices. The reality is somewhat different, given the power relations involved. In any case the courts have their own version of this, which omits the word 'informed'.[11] Commercial law, in which the paradigmatic economic rational chooser reigns, offers opportunities to the legal subject to change his mind after giving

---

8    Thomson, this volume.

9    See Duncan, S, 'Disrupting the surface of order and innocence: towards a theory of sexuality and the law' (1994) 2 FLS 3.

10   O'Donovan, K, *Family Law Matters*, 1993, London: Pluto Press.

11   See Foster, this volume.

consent. Paradoxically, commercial consent is permissive about hesitation containing 'cooling-off' periods. The conclusion is that the concept of consent has to be understood in the context of the figures that are constructed in the history and landscape of particular legal areas. Consent in health care law must be understood in the context of assumptions about trust and healing.

One of the strengths of feminist jurisprudence has been its method of 'sexing the subject.'[12] This involves a methodology of deconstruction of stereotyped associations of gender and characteristics. Feminists, however, do not accept such associations as substantive, and reject the implied 'essentialism' involved. Certain traits have been identified as feminine, such as emotion, the body, the other, the private sphere; by contrast masculinity is defined in terms of reason, mind, self, the public sphere. The figure at the heart of the legal discourse about the patient is open to similar identification. This figure is feminised in its passivity, powerlessness, bodily weakness. A major issue to be addressed is the person who is seen under the term 'patient'. To what extent does illness or disease lessen my ability to make choices and to claim autonomy? Jennifer Nedelsky gives a picture of autonomy as interactive, accepting that just as my consciousness engages in a continuous relationship with my body, so too do I interact with other autonomous beings.[13] This promises a form of analysis which rejects a 'mind/body' dualism, but offers a way of seeing the 'therapeutic alliance'. As already stated, such an alliance must necessarily allow space for the perspectives of both parties.

Evidence-based medicine has established that certain medical procedures, for example episiotomies, are unnecessary. This is to be welcomed as a scientific approach which is empirical in the full sense of looking to results and consequences. However, it is not subject-based in the sense of allowing entry to the perspective of the subject. Elements of the 'body as machine' approach to patient research remain. Feminist jurisprudence has opened the way for demands for the perspectives of legal subjects to be incorporated in law in various ways, practical, professional, conceptual and emotional. This can apply to all those concerned in the patient's quest for health, and should not be limited as a 'patient-centred' approach.

As can be deduced from this brief comment, I believe that there is room for new ways of seeing many aspects of health care law. These will enrich our perspectives in whichever contact we have with health care provision. For these reasons, I warmly welcome this timely collection.

---

12   Naffine, N and Owen, R, *Sexing the Subject of Law*, 1997, Sydney: Law Book Company.

13   Nedelsky, J, 'Meditations on embodied autonomy' (1995) 2 Graven Images 159. See Stychin, this volume, for elaboration of a relational concept of autonomy and its application in the health care context.

# ACKNOWLEDGMENTS

The majority of the essays in this volume were presented at a two day workshop held at Keele University in April 1997. We would like to thank all the contributors for the strong spirit of mutual endeavour with which they approached the workshop. This has helped to make this volume the kind of collective exercise which is truly rewarding and often sadly lacking in a Research Assessment Exercise driven world. We would also like to express our gratitude to the members of the audience for their encouraging, insightful and constructive involvement. Thanks must also go to the Departments of Law and Philosophy and Cavendish Publishing for their sponsorship of this event.

The inspiration for this series of books was Anne Bottomley's and thus we owe her a debt of gratitude for enabling us to set out on this project. Anne's energy, her enthusiasm and her sound feminist insight continues to be of great help to both of us in various ways and at various times. Kathryn Hague has provided efficient editorial assistance, often under pressure, and always with good humour. Jo Reddy has been an enthusiastic editor whose commitment to the Feminist Perspectives series in general, and this volume in particular, has been unstinting.

Finally we would like to thank our colleagues at Keele Law Department. It remains a supportive, stimulating and happy place to work.

*Sally Sheldon*
*Michael Thomson*
*April 1998*

# CONTRIBUTORS

**Hazel Biggs** lectures at the University of Kent, Canterbury. Her research interests are in medical law, criminal law and feminist legal theory and she has published in each of these areas. Her recent work has focused on death, dying and euthanasia and she is currently researching into the legal, medical and ethical implications of surrogacy and the new reproductive technologies.

**Jo Bridgeman** is a lecturer in the Centre for Legal Studies at the University of Sussex. Her research interests are law and women's health, and feminist perspectives on law. She is interested in the law's engagement with the female body, particularly in relation to body image and contraception. She is co-author (with Susan Millns) of *Feminist Perspectives on Law: Law's Engagement with the Female Body* (1998).

**Katherine de Gama** is a lecturer in law at Keele University. Her subject areas are medical law and ethics, criminal law and women and the law. Her research interests include the legal and medical regulation of reproduction and decision making about death and dying.

**Eileen Fegan** has lectured in legal foundations and jurisprudence at Lancaster, Oxford and, currently, Cardiff University. She has published papers on feminist legal theory and Canadian abortion litigation. She is at present conducting empirical research into women's experiences of abortion decision making.

**Philip Fennell** is Reader in law at the University of Wales, Cardiff, where he teaches medical law and European Community law. He was a member of the Mental Health Act Commission from 1983–89. He is co-author of Gostin and Fennell, *Mental Health: Tribunal Procedure* (1992) and his book entitled *Treatment without Consent: Law, Psychiatry and the Treatment of Mental Disorder since 1845*, was published in 1996.

**Peggy Foster** is a senior lecturer in social policy at the University of Manchester. She is the co-author (with Jennifer Dale) of *Feminists and State Welfare* (1986) and author of *Women and The Health Care Industry: An Unhealthy Relationship?* (1995). She is currently working on women and contraception and welfare professionalism in the late 1990s.

**Marie Fox** teaches law at the University of Manchester. Her main research interests are in health care law and criminal law. She is co-author (with Jean McHale) of *Health Care Law: Text and Materials* (1997).

**Jonathan Montgomery** is Reader in health care law at the University of Southampton. He is author of *Health Care Law* (1997), *Health Care Choices: Making Decisions with Children* (1996) with Priscilla Alderson, and *Nursing and the Law* (1989) with David Carson. He has also co-edited the *Encyclopaedia of Health Services and Medical Law*. He is a non-executive director of the Southampton Community Health Services NHS Trust and Chair of the Southampton Joint Research Ethics Committee.

**Derek Morgan** teaches at the University of Wales, Cardiff. He is a member of the British Medical Association's Medical Ethics Committee, has chaired two of its committees on medical law reform and contributed to numerous reports and publications.

**Thérèse Murphy** teaches law at the University of Nottingham. Her chapter was completed whilst on sabbatical leave at Harvard Law School in 1997 and she would like to thank all those who helped to make her visit such an exhilarating one. Special thanks go to Professor Martha Minow, Professor David Kennedy and the other members of the 1996–97 Graduate Program, and Stella Rozanski and the Feminist Project.

**Katherine O'Donovan** is Professor of Law at the University of London. She teaches medical law to both law and medical students at Queen Mary and Westfield College and St Bartholomew's Hospital. An editor of *Social and Legal Studies*, she has been writing of feminist jurisprudence since the 1970s.

**Sally Sheldon** is a lecturer in law at Keele University. She is author of *Beyond Control: Medical Power and Abortion Law* (1997) and has published widely in the area of health care law.

**Carl Stychin** currently teaches at Keele University, but will take up a professorship in law and social theory at the University of Reading in 1998. He writes primarily in the area of legal theory, with a particular focus on gender and sexuality. He is the author of *Law's Desire: Sexuality and the Limits of Justice* (1995), *A Nation by Rights: National Cultures, Sexual Identity Politics, and the Discourse of Rights* (1998), and co-editor (with Didi Herman) of *Legal Inversions: Lesbians, Gay Men, and the Politics of Law* (1995).

**Michael Thomson** is a lecturer in law at Keele University. His research interests are primarily in the areas of health care law and literature. He is the author of *Reproducing Narrative: Gender, Reproduction and the Law* (1998).

**Celia Wells** is Professor of Law at the University of Wales, Cardiff, where she has taught and researched in law since 1986. Her research has mainly focused on criminal law, in particular the criminal liability of corporations (*Corporations and Criminal Responsibility*, 1993). More recently, Celia Wells has published a study of the law relating to disasters (*Negotiating Tragedy*, 1995), which reflects her interest in issues of risk and blame. With Nicola Lacey, she is co-author of *Reconstructing Criminal Law*, which adopts an explicitly feminist perspective.

**Noel Whitty** teaches public law, law and society, and health care law at Keele University. He is co-editor (with Sue Millns) of the forthcoming *Feminist Perspectives on Public Law* (Cavendish Publishing, 1999).

# CONTENTS

# Contents

# Contents

# TABLE OF CASES

# TABLE OF LEGISLATION

# TABLE OF ABBREVIATIONS

| | |
|---|---|
| AC | Appeal Cases |
| All ER | All England Law Reports |
| | |
| BMJ | British Medical Journal |
| BMLR | Butterworths Medico-Legal Reports |
| | |
| Cal Rptr | Californian Law Reporter |
| | |
| DLR | Dominion Law Reports |
| | |
| F | Federal Reporter |
| Fam LR | Family Law Reports |
| FCR | Federal Court Reports |
| FLR | Family Law Reports |
| FLS | Feminist Legal Studies |
| FSR | Fleet Street Reports |
| F Supp | Federal Supplement |
| | |
| Ga App | Georgia Appeal Reports |
| | |
| JLS | Journal of Law and Society |
| JSWFL | Journal of Social Welfare and Family Law |
| | |
| LR QB | Queen's Bench Law Reports |
| LS | Legal Studies |
| LQR | Law Quarterly Review |
| | |
| Med L Rev | Medical Law Review |
| Med LR | Medical Law Reports |
| MLR | Modern Law Review |
| | |
| NJ | Newfoundland Judgments |
| NLJ Rep | New Law Journal Reports |
| NW | North Western Reporter |

| | |
|---|---|
| Obs and Gyn | Obstetrics and Gynaecology |
| OJLS | Oxford Journal of Legal Studies |
| | |
| P | Probate and Divorce Law Reports |
| P&C | Property and Compensation |
| | |
| QB | Queen's Bench |
| | |
| SDNY | Southern District New York |
| SE | South Eastern Reporter |
| SJ | Solicitors Journal |
| SLS | Social and Legal Studies |
| SW | South Western Reporter |
| | |
| Wis L Rev | Wisconsin Law Review |
| WLR | Weekly Law Reports |
| WWR | Western Weekly Reports |

# CHAPTER ONE

# HEALTH CARE LAW AND FEMINISM: A DEVELOPING RELATIONSHIP

*Sally Sheldon and Michael Thomson*

Ten years ago, the title *Feminist Perspectives on Health Care Law* would have been guaranteed to alienate at least as many of those with an interest in law as it would have attracted. To the traditional lawyer, whose eye was caught as he[1] scanned the shelves for the latest edition of Winfield and Jolowicz on *Tort* or Smith and Hogan on *Criminal Law*, it would have been a point of irritation on (at least) two grounds. First, no doubt, he would have been sceptical about the merits of even recognising health care (or medical) law as a discrete subject for study. Indeed, flicking through the pages of Smith and Hogan, the traditionalist might well have reflected that no such subject as health care law exists. Subjects such as abortion are included in the pages before him, (reassuringly located alongside related criminal offences under the title of 'homicide'). Likewise, he would have known that in Winfield and Jolowicz, he would have found discussion of the leading cases regulating medical malpractice alongside other non-medical cases, under such generic headings as 'professional standards'. 'Health care law', he might have concluded, is nothing more than a collection of cases and statutes which might each be better located within one of the core subjects of law: crime, administrative law, equity, property, contract and – in particular – tort law.[2]

Second, our traditionalist may have subscribed to the opinion – still widely voiced in the corridors of law departments across the country (although less often committed to paper) – that feminism has very little of interest to say about law at all.[3] And if the relevance of feminism were conceded, this was

---

1   We have deliberately chosen to nominate this straw traditionalist as 'he' in order to highlight a particular gendered subject position. It should be of interest to the reader to note how the contributors to this collection deliberately employ and deploy different formulations of 'he', 'she', and 'he or she' to make or enforce different arguments and perspectives.

2   Along with European Community law, these are now described as the 'foundational subjects'. Although these subject groupings may often be viewed as objective or inevitable, as Bottomley points out, the construction of the 'foundational' subjects which must form the core of an exempting law degree are the result of much negotiation and contention. See Bottomley, A, 'Exploring foundational subjects', in *Feminist Perspectives on the Foundational Subjects of Law*, 1996, London: Cavendish Publishing, p 4. Another frequent misapprehension about health care law is that it is only concerned with medical negligence.

3   This kind of resistance to feminist legal scholarship might have two strands: first, it might be argued that theoretical analysis is irrelevant to law outside of jurisprudence courses (Smart calls this the 'black-letter' constituency) and secondly, it might be asserted that law in more developed countries has transcended a sexual bias and thus is not in need of feminist critique (the 'liberal constituency'). See Smart, C, *Law, Crime and Sexuality: Essays in Feminism*, 1995, London: Sage, p 186.

likely to be accepted only within the confines of a jurisprudence course or with regard to what are perceived to be 'women's issues' – rape, abortion, sexual harassment, pornography, sexual discrimination and so on. How can there be a feminist perspective on the core of the health care law curriculum? What is there to be said about topics such as medical research, medical negligence, allocation of resources in health care, confidentiality and euthanasia?

It is to be hoped that a close examination of this volume might go some way to shaking the confidence of the traditionalist in both of these views. The contributions to it demonstrate the rich diversity of feminist perspectives and the various insights which they can offer into the workings of law. And whilst reproduction and its legal regulation continues to raise new issues which are particularly pressing for feminists, the book also brings insights to terrain which is less familiar for feminist analysis. Further, the contributions provide clear evidence that health care law has earned its place as a subject on the law curriculum. Indeed, we would contend that it is not merely true to say that the subject matter of health care law can be treated as a separate discipline, rather, we would make the stronger claim that it must be so treated, if the rules which form its subject matter are to be adequately understood. It is these two claims which will be explored in this introduction to the volume.

Before going on to make these arguments in more detail, though, we would like to pause for a moment to consider the nature of the doubts which we have ascribed to our straw traditionalist. Both of his concerns, it seems to us, stem from the same problem They both raise issues of inclusion and exclusion, of what counts as 'real' law, 'real' knowledge and 'real' legal scholarship, of what is appropriate to be taught or researched in the law school and of what has no place there. In a volume which was a precursor to the series of which this book forms part, Anne Bottomley speaks of 'the construction of these narratives, their partiality and their violence towards the excluded'.[4] The choices made in structuring a law curriculum and in developing teaching practice are all fiercely political ones which the cloak of tradition helps to present as natural, objective and rational.[5] This argument might be illustrated by some explanation of why we feel that it is important to treat health care law as a subject in its own right.

---

4    *Op cit*, fn 2, p 1.

5    See Kennedy, D, 'Legal education as training for hierarchy', in Grigg-Spall, I and Ireland, P (eds), *The Critical Lawyers' Handbook*, London: Pluto Press, pp 51–61. Furthermore, the birth of the Research Assessment Exercise has meant that choices made by individual researchers are increasingly open to external scrutiny and may carry funding implications for their departments.

# HEALTH CARE LAW

Ian Kennedy has argued the case for treating medical law (which he describes as the 'law concerning the interactions between doctors and patients')[6] as a subject in its own right:

> There are common issues which permeate all the problems and the doctor-patient relationship: respect for autonomy and self-determination in the context of consent, truth-telling and confidences, respect for dignity, respect for life, and respect for justice. All these ethical precepts run through the area involved. But the issues still tend to be seen in terms of traditional legal categories; for example, as problems of family law, tort law, or contract law in the area of private law, or as problems of administrative law, constitutional law, or criminal law in the area of public law. This prevents them from being understood as problems having certain things in common which mark them off from others. And, until that happens, I do not think that we are going to have a coherent approach to the emerging problems in medical law, an approach which recognises these common themes and seeks to develop a body of doctrine which has coherence and some internal consistency.[7]

As Kennedy argues, health care law involves certain themes and concepts which must be grasped before one can understand what is happening in the areas under consideration. To take an example: as Carl Stychin demonstrates in this volume, the issues of abortion, surrogacy and female genital surgery are all closely and intricately linked in involving consideration of autonomy and to what extent, and in what form, it can and should be recognised. Without understanding the importance of this underlying concern, one will not fully understand what is at stake in these areas and, as Kennedy asserts, there can be no coherent approach to the legal (or extra-legal) resolution of them.

Further, whilst we would agree with Kennedy in noting the importance of these ethical precepts in providing some unity to health care law, we would also cite a further unifying feature which owes more to sociology: the acceptance of the claims of medical professionalism.[8] Deference to medical opinion runs throughout health care law. It can, for example, be seen clearly in the recent spate of forced Caesarean cases, in the power which law accords to

---

6   Kennedy, I, *Treat me Right: Essays in Medical Law and Ethics*, Oxford: Clarendon Press, p 3. We will come on to our reasons for choosing the different title of 'Health Care Law' below.

7   *Ibid*. See a similar argument in Kennedy, I and Grubb, A, *Medical Law: Text with Materials*, 1994, London: Butterworths, p 3.

8   See Montgomery, J, 'Medicine, accountability, and professionalism' (1989) 16 JLS 319. Judicial deference to medical discretion can be understood as a result of the existence of different and important policy considerations which the judges must take into account when determining medical cases, which will not concern them elsewhere: eg, fear of defensive medicine, a perceived need to protect the medical relationship, the perception of medicine as altruistic practice, the belief that medicine is art as well as science and so on. Equally it can be understood as resulting from a gendered fraternity of interests between doctors and judges; see Sheldon, this volume.

mental health professionals, and in the regulation of professional malpractice, abortion and access to infertility services.[9] As Michael Thomson demonstrates in this volume, the construction of the figure of the doctor as a responsible and respectable man who can be trusted to do his best for his patients has had a notable effect on his standing in court. And as Katherine O'Donovan has noted in a different context, '[o]ld stories can retain a powerful hold. Stories affect the creation of law and its application. Such laws remain with us and mediate our perception of realities and truths. The stories influence what we see and what we can see.'[10] Judicial and parliamentary deference to the stories which have been told about the medical man and medical science can be seen as recurrent themes throughout the history of health care law.[11] And they run like leitmotifs through the essays in this volume.

It is not just the coherence of the law regulating medical practice which is at stake here, however. Without understanding the importance of context, one cannot understand the precedent value of medical decisions to future cases in the non-medical context. In other words, the special pull of various factors in the medical context may be absent elsewhere and accordingly the outcome may be different. An interesting example of this is the regulation of professional negligence. Professional negligence is governed by the *Bolam* test which states that the professional will not be liable in negligence if he has acted in accordance with a responsible body of opinion within that profession. However, judges have been far more confident in intervening in non-medical contexts to hold that such a body of opinion may itself be wrong.[12] Health care law principles are at once part of health care law and part of some other area of law. The health care lawyer thus needs to be able to wear two hats at once – to locate a problem within the rules of, say, tort law and simultaneously to understand it from within the context of health care law.[13]

This classification of a discrete law subject with reference to substance rather than procedure may be more familiar to feminist scholars than to other lawyers. In a book published 10 years ago, Tove Stang Dahl, a pivotal figure in the Norwegian 'women's law' project, noted that:

[t]he feminist perspective establishes a systematic cross-section through existing rules of law in order to perceive otherwise unnoticed connections of

---

9   See, respectively: Wells, this volume; Fegan and Fennell, this volume; Montgomery, this volume; Sheldon, this volume; Sheldon, S, '"Subject only to the discretion of the surgeon concerned": the judicial protection of medical discretion' (1996) 5 SLS 95; and Millns, S, '"A judgment which goes beyond the purely medical": the reproductive revolution and access to fertility services', in Bridgeman, J and Millns, S (eds), *Law and Body Politics*, 1995, Aldershot: Dartmouth. See also, generally, *op cit*, fn 8, Montgomery.

10  O'Donovan, K, 'Marriage: a sacred or profane love machine?' (1993) 1 FLS 75, p 90.

11  Thomson, M, *Reproducing Narrative: Gender, Reproduction and Law*, 1998, Aldershot: Dartmouth.

12  'Re Herald of Free Enterprise: appeal by Captain Lewry' (1987) *The Independent*, 18 December; *Edward Wong Finance Co Ltd v Stokes and Masters* [1984] AC 1296.

13  The role of the *Bolam* test in medical negligence cases, and medical practice more generally, is considered by Sheldon, this volume.

significance for all individuals, but especially and directly to women. This means that we in women's law attach greater weight to law's systematizing function, and thereunder its concept formation and theory construction, in comparison to what is usual in law.[14]

Stang Dahl suggests new ways of determining which phenomena 'hang together' and questions the acceptance of traditional legal boundaries and categories. She speaks of the development of the 'law of birth' which is 'built upon a long row of fragmented rules which especially concern pregnant and childbearing women. It is due to the fact that these fragments are gathered and seen in context that the concept of 'birth law' originates.'[15] For Stang Dahl, 'women's law' is built on new concepts: equal status law, birth law, housewives' law, paid-work law. This categorisation might be seen as taking its starting point in common sense intuition about the law and its organisation. These categories reflect popular experience. In this sense, focusing on 'health care law' rather than subsuming discussion of the cases into books on tort, contract, public law or equity, might be seen as beginning to challenge law's own exclusionary structures, to reformulate the organisation of principles under headings which do not immediately confound and exclude the reader with no knowledge of law. The adoption of this category itself might be seen as part of a feminist legal project of breaking down exclusionary structures and beginning a process of the deprivatisation of knowledge. In this sense, many of the health care law textbooks currently available claim to be accessible to the non-lawyer.[16]

This kind of attempt at the reorganisation of legal knowledge does bring its own problems. One of the challenges of learning (and teaching) health care law, is that one must become a 'Jacqui of all trades', having command of the basic principles of all areas of law (with the related danger of being 'mistress' of none). This is not unlike the challenge which is familiar to feminist lawyers, of being able to approach a problem both from the perspective of the traditional lawyer and also to step outside of that paradigm to bring specifically feminist understandings to bear. The health care lawyer must think through a specific issue both in the context of health care law and in the context of the body of rules (for example, tort) within which it is more traditionally located. She must understand the implications of/for both contexts.

Finally, it is worth noting why we have chosen the title of 'health care law' rather than the more traditional 'medical law'. The rationale for this decision

---

14 Stang Dahl, T, *Women's Law*, 1987, Oslo: Norwegian University Press, p 27 (references omitted).

15 *Ibid*, p 35 (references omitted).

16 Of the texts currently available, Mason, JK and McCall Smith, RA, *Law and Medical Ethics*, 4th edn, 1994, London: Butterworths; Montgomery, J, *Health Care Law*, 1997, Oxford: OUP; and Brazier, M, *Medicine, Patients and the Law*, 2nd edn, 1992, London: Penguin, come closest to realising this intention.

has been convincingly explained by Jonathan Montgomery, who begins his own *Health Care Law* with a citation from Kennedy and Grubb's *Medical Law: Text and Materials*. The latter explain that medical law is 'essentially concerned with the relationship between doctors (and to a lesser extent hospitals and other institutions) and patients'. Montgomery comments that this is an approach which begins from the work of doctors and works outwards, seeing the clinical interaction between doctor and patient as the paradigm.[17] He argues that, while this is clearly an important part of health care law, to restrict the subject's scope to issues raised in the clinical medical context would exclude a number of important areas of law, because, *inter alia*, doctors are not the only health professionals and the delivery of health care in the United Kingdom is primarily the responsibility of the National Health Service.[18] Montgomery's contribution to this volume furthers this project. His analysis of the differing structures of professional regulation between doctors and other health care workers casts light not only on the role which gender has played in structuring such regulation, but also calls into question the traditional pre-eminence of the medical/doctor model.

This expansion of the project of health care law, and its refusal to collude with the hierarchy implicit in focusing on doctors alone, can itself be seen as a feminist project. The issue is one of what (and whom) are worthy of consideration. In such a light, the definition and delimitation of the subject matter can be clearly seen to be a political choice. Medical law, for many years, has focused on the decisions made by doctors (who are, as Thomson shows below, constructed in the legal imagination as male) and has ignored the legal position of other professional groups such as nurses, occupational therapists and physiotherapists (who are predominantly made up of women and have often been constructed in the legal imagination as little more than doctors' handmaidens).[19] Part of the projects of feminism and of the construction of a subject called 'health care law' must be to reveal, to interrogate and to challenge these exclusions. With the diversity of health care topics addressed in this volume – most notably those that move beyond the relationship between doctor and patient, for example the chapters on experimentation by Fox, death and dying by Biggs, resource allocation by Whitty and professional regulation by Montgomery – this volume embraces this need to include the currently excluded and, in so doing, to engage with the defining of this subject. At the same time, however, we cannot ignore the fact that feminism

---

17   *Op cit*, fn 16, Montgomery, p 1.

18   See Montgomery in this volume on the structuring of professional relationships between nurse and doctor, and Whitty in this volume on State, Area Health Authority and NHS Trust obligations in the provision of health care.

19   Montgomery, J, 'Doctors' handmaidens: the legal contribution', in Wheeler, S and McVeigh, S (eds), *Law, Health and Medical Regulation*, 1992, Aldershot: Dartmouth.

continues to face its own battle to be recognised as having a voice in the design of the law curriculum.

## FEMINIST PERSPECTIVES

In the introduction to their *Health Care Law: Text and Materials*, Jean McHale and Marie Fox (with John Murphy) explain that:

> One persistent problem that can easily be overlooked is the role of gender in debate about health care law. Many of the most contentious areas of health care law raise issues that cannot be seen as gender-neutral. Abortion is clearly a more personal issue for the pregnant woman than for anyone else. Many of the developments in reproductive technology impact more directly on women than men. However, gender issues are not confined to questions about the patients involved. Feminist ethics has highlighted the extent to which the dominant traditions of health care ethics have often stressed independence and autonomy at the expense of recognising the social world in which we live. We need to consider how far our approaches to moral thinking have blinkered our understanding of the problems as well as illuminating them.[20]

The approach taken by these writers is the exception rather than the rule. There is no other textbook currently available in the UK which engages in any depth with feminist writing on health care law. This would seem in large part to be explained by two factors. The first of these is the view which we ascribed to our traditionalist lawyer above: that feminism can have nothing of interest to say about law. Anne Bottomley has exposed this problem in the following terms:

> Courses which use feminist material are too often simply subject areas deemed to be about women – most obviously family law. Even in these courses, when standard texts do refer to feminist material it is often introduced with a health warning against taking the argument too far. Courses using feminist materials are usually taught by women, taken by women, and are presumed by our colleagues to be simply about women. A lecture on feminism may be given on other courses but is often seen as 'a lecture' and given by a woman lecturer invited in. The so-called core courses still ignore (with some notable exceptions) the rich seam of material available that would raise key issues usually rendered invisible in the subject area.[21]

Fully in keeping with Bottomley's argument, a review of the existing medical law textbooks gives the impression that feminist perspectives have had no serious impact on this part of the legal academy. Thus, whilst Derek Morgan's

---

20  McHale, J and Fox, M with Murphy, J, *Health Care Law: Text and Materials*, 1997, London: Sweet & Maxwell, p 4.

21  Bottomley, A, 'Feminism: paradoxes of the double bind', in Grigg-Spall, I and Ireland, P (eds), *Critical Lawyers' Handbook*, 1992, London: Pluto Press, pp 22–30 (references omitted).

chapter in this volume clearly exposes the rich vein of feminist scholarship which exists regarding reproduction and its legal regulation, such literature receives little mention in the core texts.[22]

A brief perusal of how these books deal with abortion – the issue which McHale and Fox rightly cite as one of more personal importance to women – might serve to illustrate this point. Only in McHale and Fox's own book is any serious attempt made to draw upon the substantial feminist literature in this area. Mason and McCall Smith's *Medical Ethics and Law* is more typical of the norm. Their chapter on abortion is broken down into the following sections: the evolution of the law, the Abortion Act 1967, the rights of the foetus and other people's rights ('other people' here includes doctors, nursing staff and others involved, and the father), abortion and the incompetent, reduction of multiple pregnancies and selective reduction. The only mention of the significance of abortion services to women is in the introduction to the chapter, where the authors note in passing that attitudes to abortion depend on one's views on the foetal right to life versus the woman's right to control her own body. Indeed, according to the authors, the major significance of abortion, given the abrogation of a central tenet of the Hippocratic oath, is its effect on the medical ethos.[23]

And even where the relevance of feminist perspectives have been admitted into lectures and seminars dealing with reproduction, this will often be the end of the story. Few health care lawyers, for example, will ever have asked themselves why so many of the cases dealing with medical malpractice seem to involve female plaintiffs (particularly those concerning flawed consent).[24] Is this just a coincidence? Is the need to provide adequate information to patients more routinely disregarded where those patients are female? Are cases where the plaintiff is female more likely to reach the courts? Whilst an adequate answer to this question is the subject for another paper, it is worthy of note that this paper has yet to be written.

It might be argued that the criticism of law texts for their failure to engage with feminist perspectives is disingenuous and that the problem here is actually a more wide-ranging one, as the criticism set out should really be aimed at black-letter law teaching in general which excludes consideration of anything but the text of the law itself. This is in part true. Yet in recent years, lawyers have become increasingly open to broader perspectives and a

---

22  The textbooks most widely in use in British universities at this time include *op cit*, fn 7, Kennedy and Grubb; *op cit*, fn 16, Montgomery; *op cit*, fn 20, McHale and Fox with Murphy *op cit*, fn 16, Brazier; and *op cit*, fn 16, Mason and McCall Smith.

23  *Op cit*, fn 16, Mason and McCall Smith.

24  See *Sidaway v Bethlem RHG* [1985] 1 All ER 643; *Blyth v Bloomsbury HA* [1993] 4 Med LR 151; *Gold v Haringey HA* [1987] 1 FLR 125; *Chatterton v Gerson* [1981] 1 All ER 257; *Devi v West Midlands RHA* (1981) unreported (CA).

commitment to socio-legal teaching is not uncommon in law schools. It seems that the resistance to feminism is more than this.

## FEMINIST PERSPECTIVES ON HEALTH CARE LAW

If the identity of health care law as a discrete subject is open to debate, the existence of feminism as a discrete and unified political or theoretical movement is scarcely less so. In recent years, feminists have found it far easier to talk about diversity and difference than unity and shared political goals. The present collection takes its strength from this eclecticism and diversity, incorporating a broad range of different perspectives and theoretical frameworks. The chapters cut across the various 'schools' which have been outlined by those writers who have sought to impose some conceptual order on this mass of material. Some chapters reach conclusions which may challenge the common sense of the feminist reader. In this sense, the volume is a clear statement that feminist thought refuses any confinement to the formulaic.

Yet at the same time, there is a clear sense of shared endeavour in the contributions to this volume. One common concern is with the (lack of) realisation of the ethical principles which according to the above citation from Kennedy, are supposedly at the core of health care ethics and law: justice, dignity and, most importantly, autonomy.

The concern with justice is clearest in the contributions to the volume made by Noel Whitty and Marie Fox. Whitty provides a close analysis of the allocation of resources in health care, locating this within a political context in order to challenge any perception of neutrality or justice in the way in which allocation decisions are made. As Whitty shows, the process of locating law in a broader context is in itself a political move, because it denies the law's objectivity and impartiality. The feminist context – with its focus on gender – is just one possibility. In several of the chapters, although perhaps most clearly in Whitty's, this blends with consideration of other factors and other aspects of inclusion and exclusion. Whitty's work again reveals that a feminist analysis is not only of interest to women. Marie Fox's concern is with clinical research trials. As she notes, concern with the injustice of women's under-representation in these trials has led to feminist assertions of women's right to participate in them. Fox sounds a cautious note, raising various problems with such uncritical assessment of the benefit of clinical research.

Kathy de Gama's chapter provides the most obvious engagement with the failure to recognise or to protect women's dignity. What of the dignity of the brain-dead pregnant woman, kept alive as an incubator for her foetus? Locating the ventilation of brain-dead pregnant women within a broader context of the medical regulation of women's bodies, de Gama reveals the sinister overtones of this practice. And, by examining it alongside the *Blood* case (regarding extraction of sperm from a comatose man), she clearly exposes the difference accorded to men's and to women's dignity. As de Gama shows, the reality of the ventilated foetal incubator is not that of a 'sleeping beauty', rather it is that of a multiply intubated body, slowly decomposing.

However, it is the concern with autonomy in the medical context which is the theme which most closely concerns the majority of the chapters in this book. This preoccupation with (and problematisation of) autonomy is perhaps not surprising in such a collection. The issue of autonomy is of central concern in the health care arena where patients encounter nurses, doctors and other health care professionals in a position of vulnerability. This makes autonomy of central concern to all. Yet autonomy poses a still more difficult and thorny issue for feminists. It is women's autonomy which is most frequently denied, most routinely ignored in the medical context as in many others.[25] Yet, at the same time, feminists have shown a resistance to the pursuit of autonomy as an end it itself, questioning the validity of the very ethical framework within which it is prioritised.

Nonetheless, a first point of concern raised by the chapters of this volume is that the law fails to accord due protection to women's autonomy, or provides it less protection than is accorded to that of men. In an examination of consent to treatment, Peggy Foster challenges the rhetoric of documents like *The Patient's Charter*, and argues that the lofty ideals espoused in it and in cases like *Re T* have had little impact in practice.[26] Foster analyses screening campaigns and assesses the scant consideration paid to informed consent within them. She finds that the information given to women is misleading, biased or incomplete. Marie Fox expresses similar concern at the inadequacy of procedures ensuring the validity of patient consent in the context of clinical research. This failure to recognise patient autonomy fully is juxtaposed against the authority and power of the doctor. The legal entrenchment of such authority emerges clearly in Sally Sheldon's chapter on medical negligence. As Sheldon argues, the law has left the determination of the standard of care expected of medical professionals to be determined by medical professionals themselves, thus further entrenching their professional power, and this can only operate to the detriment of patient autonomy. For Sheldon, this judicial failure to intervene is damaging for all, but for women more than for men.

But is full recognition of autonomy what women really need? Celia Wells, Jo Bridgeman and Hazel Biggs all draw on different areas of law and distinctive theoretical perspectives to challenge any unconditional answer in the affirmative. Wells is troubled by an unproblematic recourse to the notion of autonomy by those who criticise the judges' decisions to authorise doctors

---

25   See, Foster, P, *An Unhealthy Relationship: Women and the Healthcare Industry* 1995, Milton Keynes: Open University Press.

26   *Re T* [1992] 4 All ER 649.

to perform non-consensual Caesarean sections. She questions whether the death of a woman in childbirth or a full-term foetus through refusal of treatment can really be seen as raising a relatively simple question of autonomy versus paternalism. Likewise, Bridgeman re-examines the case law which has evolved around the non-consensual treatment of children, again refuting any simplistic reduction of the issue at stake to such a formula. Drawing on the work of Carol Gilligan and Robin West, Bridgeman suggests that the child should be seen as located within a web of relationships which will influence the decisions which are made regarding her care. Finally, Hazel Biggs raises a related concern which should be heard within the current debate regarding the possible decriminalisation of euthanasia. Against the 'progressive' tide in favour of reform, Biggs asks what the effects of this will be on women who may have different life experiences and different expectations of old age. Would the decriminalisation of active voluntary euthanasia really be a positive step towards securing their autonomy? Or would it create new pressures which would restrict women's choices in new and dangerous ways?

However, a powerful critique of the failure of autonomy as the appropriate heuristic in understanding the ethical issues at stake, does not mean that feminists necessarily want to reject any recourse to it. Despite her critique of the law regulating reproduction, de Gama ultimately refuses to jettison autonomy. However flawed, she reasons, it may yet be the best tool currently on offer. For de Gama, a strategic use of autonomy is necessary to avoid falling into the familiar dangers of paternalism. Fegan and Fennell display similar pragmatism. Their chapter offers a chilling and cogent exposition of the treatment which women have received for perceived mental health problems, treatment often received precisely because their autonomy is denied. Fegan and Fennell outline the long list of law's failures to offer adequate protection to these women and provide ample illustration of the injuries which they have suffered in the name of psychiatric 'help'. Yet they are ultimately unwilling to reject wholesale either psychiatry or recourse to law. Like de Gama, they argue for local, *ad hoc* strategies of resistance. Such strategies might involve using law or relying on considerations of autonomy. Equally, they might not.

Other contributors to the volume suggest reconceptualising autonomy in a way which may be more sensitive and more acceptable to feminists. Carl Stychin is concerned with the development of a relational concept of autonomy, which would suggest new ways forward in the protracted debates regarding abortion, surrogacy and female genital modification. More specifically, he argues for an understanding which sees autonomy as grounded in the connectivity and interdependence of bodies. He concludes that whilst this may not provide easy answers in these debates, it may at least provide a better set of questions.

Yet this concern with justice, dignity and autonomy is perhaps most explicit, and most broadly applied, in Derek Morgan's contribution. Morgan provides a framework through which we may understand feminisms' accounts of reproductive technologies. In so doing he calls for a recovery *of the person as a whole* who has been banished by the biomedical model. This recognition of the need to recover the individual person and the physical and social environment in which she or he is located is implicit in many of the other chapters, for example those by Biggs, Bridgeman and de Gama.

It is not just a substantive focus on women which concerns feminism, however, but also a concern with methodology. As such, the contributors to this volume are united not just in a substantive endeavour, but also in a theoretical one. And in recent years feminism has shown an increased concern with theory and with the foundations of 'feminist knowledge'. As Derek Morgan neatly paraphrases the feminist mantra, 'the personal is theoretical'. An important part of a feminist methodology is a mistrust in the impartiality of knowledge and a profound sense of the standpoint from which one is speaking. This has led both to a challenging of 'mainstream' knowledge as 'malestream' knowledge (as is particularly clear in Marie Fox's critique of scientific rationality) and a certain methodological self-consciousness which is most obvious in Wells' explicit awareness of her own partiality and the clear location of her argument within her own lived experience. Likewise, Morgan begins with a clear statement of his own subject position and the limitations which this imposes on what he can claim to say with any authority. Other chapters place a focus on the need to include accounts of women's lived experiences. Hazel Biggs draws on the biographies of women who have experienced caring for the dying. Bridgeman and de Gama both use Robin West's work on female experience as characterised by 'connection' to others.

Whatever the differences in approach between the chapters of this volume, what becomes clear throughout is that an understanding of health care law that ignores the questions which feminists have raised (and the tentative answers which some have begun to offer) would be partial and flawed. However, as Marx famously said, the point is not to understand the world but to change it. Whilst these two endeavours are not easily separated, some chapters in this volume do go beyond critique and offer some suggestions for resistance and reform. These range from the concrete (see, for example, Foster's suggestions regarding screening campaigns) to the conceptual (see Stychin, Bridgeman, Whitty and Thomson). The focus throughout is on the small scale, the tentative, the *ad hoc* (see especially Fegan and Fennell). Thérèse Murphy, for example, suggests the liberatory power of talk and locates her strategy within the law regulating health care confidentiality. She argues that the values of trust, faithfulness and loyalty which are privileged within confidentiality may provide the basis for more meaningful dialogue within health care.

Bringing this introduction to an end with that contribution in mind leaves us at a point which recognises a more wide-ranging ambition of this collection. Whilst firmly located within health care law a number of the chapters attempt to reach beyond these disciplines. In other words, for some contributors the specific strategies that are called for have more 'global' possibilities. Thomson's call to rewrite the doctor, for example, might be seen as part of a broader strategy to cleave women from their over-determined bodies and hence to realign gender relations within a social system which is not predicated on sexual difference. Murphy's focus on confidentiality provides a case study in the creation of true talk which convinces of the possibilities of meaningful communication. She urges a revival of interest in the intimate and steers us towards a communicative ethics. A feminist engagement with health care becomes an argument and model for a truly participatory democracy.

## CONCLUSION

To end, let us return to our straw traditionalist who came back, out of curiosity, to the title which had earlier caught his eye. Perhaps he may have bought it – for a number of reasons he may have wanted it visible on his shelves. He may even have read it. What would we want such a reader – indeed any reader – to gain from committing their time and energies to this volume? Readers such as our traditionalist, we would hope, may come away having reassessed the place of health care law as a discrete area of study. We may even hope that the place of feminist perspectives in the legal academy may be strengthened. The diversity, depth and rigour of the analysis presented within the chapters cannot be ignored. For the majority of those who will open this volume – those who need no convincing as to the merits of health care law or feminist perspectives – we hope that the collection will add to their knowledge, affirm their belief in the value of feminist engagement with law, and, not least, be an engaging and provocative read.

# CHAPTER TWO

# 'A RESPONSIBLE BODY OF MEDICAL MEN SKILLED IN THAT PARTICULAR ART ...': RETHINKING THE *BOLAM* TEST

*Sally Sheldon*[1]

But the law's standard is, in effect, set by the medical profession. If a doctor can show that his advice, or his treatment, reached a standard of care which was accepted by a respectable and responsible body of medical opinion as adequate, he cannot be made liable in damages if anything goes wrong. It is a totally medical proposition erected into a working rule of law ...[2]

## INTRODUCTION

The plaintiff who brings an action in medical negligence faces a number of obstacles including practical problems in establishing causation (which are particularly onerous in the medical context),[3] evidential problems in proving what went wrong,[4] and jurisprudential problems in establishing that her doctor has fallen below the appropriate standard of care. Furthermore, those claims which look likely to overcome these hurdles are likely to be headed off by the medical defence organisations which, in the interests of their members, are keen to prevent the establishment of unfavourable precedents.[5] In this chapter, I will focus on the third of these hurdles: the standard of care and, specifically, the operation of what has become known as the *Bolam* test.[6] According to *Bolam v Friern Hospital Management Committee*, a doctor will be deemed not to have acted negligently where he has acted in accordance with a practice accepted as proper by a responsible body of medical opinion. There is already a substantial body of critique of the *Bolam* test. However, this has been

---

1   I would like to thank Michael Thomson, Tony Dugdale, Carl Stychin and Steve Wilkinson for their comments on an earlier draft of this paper. I would also like to thank Jonathan Montgomery for directing me towards the Wendy Savage case.

2   Lord Scarman, 'Law and medical practice', in Byrne, P (ed), *Medicine in Contemporary Society*, 1987, London: King Edward's Hospital Fund for London, p 134. The desire for conformity with a 'respectable' body of opinion speaks to the importance of reputation in medical practice.

3   See, for example, *Wilsher v Essex AHA* [1986] 3 All ER 801: the plaintiff's eye condition could have been caused by any one of five factors, only one of which was caused by the defendant's negligence.

4   It has been argued that the adversarial system militates against a full investigation. There is also the problem of obtaining expert witnesses prepared to testify against another doctor. See Brazier, M, *Medicine, Patients and the Law*, 1992, London: Penguin, p 221.

5   See especially Montgomery, J, 'Medicine, accountability, and professionalism' (1989) 16 JLS 319.

largely framed in gender-neutral terms in a way which denies any significance to the fact that the development of medical practice and standards have been activities which have been mainly carried out by men, while the majority of consumers of health care are women.[7] I will argue that the conflation in *Bolam* of what constitutes *accepted* practice with what should be deemed to be acceptable practice should be a point of special interest and concern to feminist lawyers for two reasons. Firstly, I will argue that it is impossible to understand fully the development of the *Bolam* principle outside a context of gender. Secondly, I will argue that the impact of *Bolam* is disproportionate in the effect which it has on men and on women. Before going any further, however, it is necessary to sketch out in slightly more detail how the *Bolam* test operates.[8]

## THE *BOLAM* TEST

... the law imposes the duty of care but the standard is a matter for medical judgment.[9]

In order to found an action in negligence, a plaintiff must show that the defendant owed her a duty of care, that the defendant failed to reach the required standard in the exercise of that care and that that failure caused injury to the plaintiff. The standard of care expected of a doctor is determined by reference to what has become popularly known as the *Bolam* test which provides that: 'a doctor is not guilty of negligence if he has acted in accordance with a practice accepted as proper by a responsible body of medical men skilled in that particular art'.[10] Whilst in non-professional negligence cases, the court will hear evidence from expert witnesses for defendant and plaintiff and then reach its own conclusions as to whether the necessary standard of care has been met, for professionals the position is rather different. Once the court is convinced that two (or more) different schools of thought exist within the profession, it seems that all the defendant must do is show that he has acted in accordance with one of them, subject to the caveat that such a school must constitute a 'responsible body of opinion'.[11]

---

7    See Foster, P, *Women and the Health Care Industry: An Unhealthy Relationship?*, 1995, Milton Keynes: Open University Press, p 2.

8    For a more detailed account, see Jones, M, *Medical Negligence*, 1996, 2nd edn, London: Sweet & Maxwell.

9    *Sidaway v Bethlem RHG* [1985] AC 871, *per* Lord Scarman, p 881.

10   *Bolam, per* McNair J at 587. This is also the standard required of other health care professionals, although the court may be less reluctant to determine what constitutes negligence in the case of other professional groups, see Montgomery, J, *Health Care Law*, 1997, Oxford: OUP, p 176.

11   In contrast to current convention regarding the use of gendered pronouns, I have referred to the doctor throughout as 'he'. Part of my argument is that, in the legal consciousness, the doctor remains a male figure. To adopt gender-neutral pronouns in this context would merely obscure this fact.

And although the courts have talked of the need for compliance with a 'substantial' body of opinion, it is now clear that 'substantial' does not simply refer to numbers: the issue cannot be determined simply by counting heads.[12]

Whilst there are a number of cases outside the medical context where the courts have intervened to deem an accepted practice to be negligent,[13] there are very few cases in the medical context where this has happened since the *Bolam* judgment.[14] It is true that there has been some anti-*Bolam* activity in the lower courts over the last few years, where having followed an accepted practice has not automatically exculpated a medical defendant.[15] However, a close reading of these judgments reveals that they are more properly understood as involving a challenge to the integrity of medical witnesses or the existence of a practice.[16] Jonathon Montgomery has argued that *Hucks v Cole*,[17] which is normally taken to be the strongest judicial statement against *Bolam*, is authority for the need to scrutinise the reasoning of medical expert witnesses rather than encouragement for the courts to override the considered opinion of responsible medical experts that a practice is reasonable.[18] Montgomery also cites the later case of *Ratty v Haringey HA* as authority for the proposition that once the credibility of witnesses is established, their evidence should be accepted without further questioning.[19]

The strongest anti-*Bolam* stance to be found in a judgment of an appeal court occurs in *Joyce v Wandsworth HA*. Roch LJ, sitting in the Court of Appeal, stated that the trial judge would have stated the law incorrectly if he had only referred to accepted clinical practice. The judge's statement of the law was only correct because he had added '[p]rovided that clinical practice stood up to analysis and was not unreasonable in the light of medical knowledge at the time'.[20] However, the Court of Appeal failed to consider the incompatibility of this statement with earlier binding precedent and, as such, its authority must be unclear. And further, as Montgomery notes, 'even if there is now some ground for believing that the courts may, as a matter of law, intervene by setting standards for the medical profession, it is clear that they are very reluctant to do so'.[21] What is clear, then, is that in practice, the *Bolam* test remains largely unchallenged.

---

12  See *Hills v Potter* [1984] 1 WLR 641 and *DeFreitas v O'Brian and Connolly* [1995] 6 Med LR 108.

13  'Re Herald of Free Enterprise: appeal by Captain Lewry' (1987) *The Independent*, 18 December; *Edward Wong Finance Co Ltd v Stokes and Masters* [1984] AC 1296.

14  For such a decision which predates *Bolam*, see *Clarke v Adams* (1950) 94 SJ 599.

15  *Smith v Tunbridge Wells HA* [1994] 5 Med LR 334, p 339, *Gascoigne v Ian Sheridan & Co* [1994] 5 Med LR 437, *Joyce v Merton and Sutton and Wandsworth HA* [1995] 6 Med LR 60.

16  See *op cit*, fn 10, Montgomery, pp 169–76.

17  (1960); [1994] 4 Med LR 393.

18  *Op cit*, fn 10, Montgomery, p 173.

19  [1994] 5 Med LR 413. See *op cit*, fn 10, Montgomery, p 175.

20  *Joyce v Merton Sutton and Wandsworth HA* (1993) 27 BMLR 124, p 144.

21  *Op cit*, fn 10, Montgomery, p 176.

*Bolam* has been considered by the House of Lords only three times: *Whitehouse v Jordan*,[22] established *Bolam* as the bedrock of the medical negligence action, a place which was later confirmed by *Sidaway v Bethlem RHG and others*[23] and *Maynard v West Midlands RHA*.[24] It is these three decisions, and particularly *Whitehouse* and *Sidaway*, which will form the focus of the present work. The cases show the importance of *Bolam* across all areas of medical negligence, respectively establishing it as the relevant test for the standard of care in negligent treatment, disclosure of information prior to treatment, and diagnosis. How the *Bolam* test operates in practice can be clearly illustrated by a brief consideration of their facts.

In *Whitehouse*, a claim was brought on behalf of a baby, Stuart Whitehouse, who was born brain-damaged following a difficult and protracted delivery. Mr Jordan, the senior registrar in charge of the birth, attempted a trial labour, making five or six attempts to move the baby by forceps. Finally, he discontinued these attempts and proceeded swiftly and, by all accounts, efficiently to deliver the baby by Caesarean section. Stuart Whitehouse, acting through his father, alleged that his brain damage resulted from the continued attempts to deliver by forceps and that Mr Jordan had persevered in those attempts beyond the point where a competent obstetrician would have desisted. He argued that Mr Jordan was negligent in not proceeding sooner to delivery by Caesarean. The opinions of the expert witnesses were divided. However because, at the end of the day, the plaintiff was not able to prove that Mr Jordan had not acted in accordance with a practice which was deemed to be acceptable by a 'responsible body of medical opinion', his action failed.

In *Sidaway*, a patient sued her doctor on the basis that the operation to which she had agreed involved two specific risks over and above the risk inherent in any surgery under general anaesthesis – damage to a root nerve and damage to the spinal cord. The latter risk, which was assessed as less than 1%, materialised, leaving her partially paralysed. She alleged that her surgeon had never told her of this risk and that, had she known of it, she would never have agreed to surgery. The courts found that her surgeon had acted in accordance with a practice accepted as proper by a responsible body of medical opinion in failing to warn of these particular risks and therefore was not liable.[25]

---

22  [1980] 1 All ER 650 (CA); [1981] 1 All ER 267 (HL).

23  [1984] 1 All ER 1018 (CA); [1985] 1 All ER 643 (HL).

24  [1985] 1 All ER 635 (HL).

25  Several possible caveats were entered to this rule *obiter dicta*, but these have not been followed, see *Blyth v Bloomsbury HA* [1993] 4 Med LR 151, denying that a doctor has a duty to disclose information when asked specific questions about a certain risk, and *Gold v Haringey HA* [1988] QB 481 rejecting the suggestion that the *Bolam* standard applies only to therapeutic treatments.

In *Maynard*, the plaintiff alleged that the consultants who had treated her were negligent in carrying out an exploratory operation to determine whether she was suffering from Hodgkin's disease (which resulted in damage to her vocal cords) before obtaining the results of a test for tuberculosis, which would have rendered the operation unnecessary. Again, the defendant consultants were able to show that a responsible body of medical men skilled in that particular art would have acted as they had done and consequently they were found not to be liable in negligence.

## Criticism of the *Bolam* test

The *Bolam* standard has thus assumed tremendous importance in the regulation of the medical profession in the UK, forming the basis for actions in all areas of medical negligence. Moreover, its significance has also extended into other areas of medical law, the Court of Appeal suggesting that *Bolam* can, in certain circumstances, even have a role to play in establishing causation.[26] As such, it is scarcely surprising that it has provoked a good deal of academic interest and critical comment. Lawyers have been predictably sceptical of allowing doctors to determine what is essentially a standard of *legal* liability.[27] Ian Kennedy and Andrew Grubb, for example, question whether the test confuses *description* (explaining what the current state of common medical practice is) with prescription (determining minimal standards for what acceptable medical practice ought to be). Is it not unusual, they ask, for the court to allow a particular group to prescribe what the law should be?[28]

Taking this kind of critical commentary as my starting point, I want to ask two further, related questions which involve situating *Bolam* in a context of gendered power relations. First, if it is true that *Bolam* does confuse description with prescription, what explanation can we deduce for such a confusion? In other words: why has the law developed in this way and what does locating *Bolam* in a context of gender add to our understanding of its evolution? Secondly, what particular problems does the *Bolam* test's conflation of description with prescription – of *accepted* with *acceptable* practice – pose for women?

---

26  A doctor must show that there was an accepted medical practice which included an omission to act, and that he acted in accordance with it. This is the rule from *Bolitho v City and Hackney HA* (1992) 13 BMLR 111. For criticism, see Hobhouse LJ in *op cit*, fn 20, *Joyce*, p 156, Kennedy, I and Grubb, A, *Medical Law: Text with Materials*, 1994, London: Butterworths, p 492.

27  See Montrose, JL, 'Is negligence an ethical or a sociological concept?' (1958) 21 MLR 258; *op cit*, fn 10, Montgomery; *ibid*, Kennedy and Grubb, p 460; Robertson, G, '*Whitehouse v Jordan* – Medical negligence retried' (1981) 44 MLR 457; Jones, M, 'Doctor knows best?' (1984) 100 LQR 355.

28  *Ibid*, Kennedy and Grubb, p 460.

## LEGAL AND MEDICAL PRACTICE: WHY THE *BOLAM* STANDARD?

That the professional skills of doctor and lawyer may sometimes lead to conflict is a matter for regret but it should not diminish the high mutual respect and esteem that the two professions have long shared.[29]

The appeal court judges who decided *Whitehouse*, *Sidaway* and *Maynard* provide some arguments in support of the adoption of the *Bolam* standard. In doing so, they draw on a 'common sense' view of the world which, I will argue, is partial and draws on their lived experience as professional men.[30] First, they cite the importance of reputation and the need to defend the good name of the medical man as a member of a respectable and responsible profession. In *Whitehouse*, for example, Lawton LJ goes so far as to cite Lord Denning's conclusion from an earlier decision that in a case involving an attack on the reputation of a medical man: '[t]he more serious the allegation the higher degree of probability that is required'.[31] Secondly, the courts note that medicine is a specialist body of knowledge, not easily amenable to being understood, or judged, from the outside. Consequently, medical practice is not readily susceptible to being second-guessed by those untrained in specialist thinking. It is not merely a science, but also an art.[32] Thirdly, they point out that doctors are motivated by altruistic reasons and as such it would scarcely be a just reward to penalise them every time they make an error.[33] Fourthly, the courts argue that it would be disruptive of medical practice and the doctor-patient relationship as we currently know it to encourage medical negligence claims. This rests on a view of the medical relationship as properly characterised by a power imbalance. As Dunn LJ explains in *Sidaway*:

> The evidence in this case showed that a [decision in favour of the plaintiff] would be damaging to the relationship of trust and confidence between doctor and patient, and might well have an adverse effect on the practice of medicine. It is doubtful whether it would be of any signficant benefit to patients, most of

---

29  *Op cit*, fn 8, Jones, p xii.

30  See Graycar, R, 'The gender of judgments: an introduction', in Thornton, M (ed), *Public and Private: Feminist Legal Debates*, 1992, Oxford: OUP, p 276: 'Common sense ... can masquerade as knowledge and is both dangerous and difficult to unmask and dislodge because some element of accuracy is usually present' (citations omitted).

31  Lawton LJ in *Whitehouse*, p 659, citing *Hornal* [1956] 3 All ER 970, p 973; [1957] 1 QB 247, p 258. The natural corollary of this would suggest that the more serious the degree of injury suffered by the plaintiff, the higher the burden of proof she will face before she can obtain any damages!

32  This view is clearly seen in the expert evidence of Sir John Dewhurst offered in *Whitehouse* on behalf of Mr Jordan and accepted by the court, cited by Lord Denning MR, p 657.

33  As Lord Denning MR explains with characteristic frankness: 'Medical science has conferred great benefits on mankind, but these benefits are attended by considerable risks ... We cannot take the benefits without taking the risks ... Doctors, like the rest of us, have to learn by experience; and experience often teaches in a hard way' *Roe v Minister of Health* [1954] 2 QB 66, p 83.

whom prefer to put themselves unreservedly in the hands of their doctors. This is not ... 'paternalism', to repeat an evocative word used in argument. It is simply an acceptance of the doctor-patient relationship as it has developed in this country.[34]

And finally, the courts make frequent reference to fears of defensive medicine. If doctors feel that they are likely to be sued, their professional practice will be driven by these concerns, rather than being focused purely on acting in the best interests of the patient.[35]

It is not necessary here to discuss the merits of these arguments. What I would like to highlight, however, is the partiality of the judicial vision in these cases. The judges fail to consider equally compelling policy arguments which would have tended towards rather different conclusions. First, they pay little or no attention to the need to compensate victims of medical misadventure. Secondly, they ignore the potential role of negligence liability in raising standards and in deterring bad practice. Thirdly, they fail to consider the patient's particular vulnerability in the medical relationship and the greater confidence which would be inspired by the knowledge of adequate legal protection if anything goes wrong. Fourthly, they fail to consider whether doctors who, as a group, are granted such high status and remuneration, must be held to the highest standards.[36] Finally, it is interesting to note that the existence of liability insurance has not played a role here in making the courts more sympathetic to plaintiffs (as it has in many other contexts).

What is important to note here is that the choice of the policy factors which the courts use to justify their decisions is precisely that – a *choice*. Why is it that the judges prioritise one set of policy considerations to the complete occlusion of the others? I would argue that this is best understood within a context of class, race and gender, where the judges naturally identify with the position of the doctor as a fellow professional. This is not surprising: judges and doctors share the same socio-economic space within society. Judges will probably have similar career aspirations and expectations to doctors and are likely to have family and friends who are doctors and thus should have a clear understanding of their concerns. What becomes clear on a close reading of these cases are the very different reactions to doctor and patient.[37]

---

34  *Sidaway v Bethlem RHG* [1984] 1 All ER 1018 (CA), *per* Dunn LJ, pp 1030–31.

35  See, for example, *ibid, per* Browne-Wilkinson LJ, p 1035; Dunn LJ, p 1030; Lord Diplock, p 657; *Whitehouse v Jordan* [1980] 1 All ER 650 (CA), *per* Lawton LJ, p 659.

36  This parallels the argument made by Wells, this volume.

37  The case which is heard in a law court employs a construct carefully designed to play on the sympathies of judge and, where appropriate, the jury. In an action in medical negligence, the image of the doctor will often be the work of the Medical Defence Union.

# IMAGES OF DOCTOR AND PATIENT

The way in which the doctor is perceived in all three cases under discussion is strikingly similar. This comes out most clearly in *Whitehouse v Jordan*. Mr Jordan is referred to as a 'very able and promising'[38] young obstetrician of near consultant status, of 'highest skill and repute'.[39] The specialist unit where he worked was one which was 'held in the highest regard by the medical profession'.[40] He shows clear dedication to his work. We hear that, although officially off duty at the time Mrs Whitehouse went into labour at 11.30 pm he was upstairs working on a research project.[41] Mrs Whitehouse, on the other hand, is cast as a 'distraught'[42] young mother who was a 'difficult, nervous and at times aggressive patient'[43] with an 'instinctive revulsion against her vagina being examined'.[44] It is this, we find implicitly suggested several times, which was responsible for some of the problems which arose later on, her 'obdurate attitude' having created a lack of information regarding the dimensions of her birth canal.[45] Mrs Whitehouse seems to have a problem with accepting the authority of her doctors and was in a 'condition of lack of confidence in the medical procedure'.[46] When the tragic outcome of the birth becomes apparent, she is bitter and irrationally blames the hospital despite the fact that everything possible was done for her. Donaldson LJ notes that:

> It is no criticism of Mrs Whitehouse to say that she was so emotionally involved, so bitter, so convinced that Mr Jordan was to blame, and had had so long to mull over the traumatic events of the birth, that it would have been remarkable if she had been an objective and reliable witness on any crucial matter.[47]

It is this construction of Mrs Whitehouse which is later used in discounting her story of the birth (although a part of her account had been accepted, albeit

---

38  *Whitehouse v Jordan* [1980] 1 All ER 650 (CA), *per* Lord Denning MR, p 653.

39  *Ibid, per* Lord Donaldson, p 662.

40  *Ibid, per* Lord Denning MR, p 653.

41  *Ibid, per* Lord Denning MR, p 656.

42  *Ibid, per* Lawton LJ, p 658.

43  *Whitehouse v Jordan* [1981] 1 All ER 267 (HL), *per* Lord Wilberforce, p 271.

44  *Ibid*, fn 38, *per* Lord Denning MR, p 653.

45  *Ibid*, fn 43, *per* Lord Edmund-Davies, p 276. See also Lord Denning MR, p 653 (CA) and Lord Wilberforce, p 271 (HL). Lord Wilberforce adds 'to be fair' that Mr Jordan was not greatly handicapped by this as, by the time he arrived, Mrs Whitehouse was under epidural anaesthetic and he was able to examine her vaginally.

46  *Ibid, per* Lord Wilberforce, p 273.

47  *Ibid*, fn 38, p 666. Similarly, Lord Denning MR notes that: 'Naturally enough [the baby's] mother is greatly distressed. She toils day and night for him. The saddest part of it is that she blames it all on the hospital and particularly on Mr Jordan, the surgeon who delivered the child': *Whitehouse*, p 653 (CA). See also Lord Wilberforce, p 273 (HL): 'She had been in labour for nearly 24 hours; recorded as distressed; there had been vomiting; she was, for understandable reasons connected with her family, intensely anxious and tense; she was in a condition of lack of confidence in the medical procedure.'

in a largely modified form, by the trial judge). On the basis of these polarised images of the two parties, the young, dedicated, skilled professional man and the distraught, obdurate, expectant mother with a fear of intimate examination, it is no surprise that, whilst the judges express sympathy for Mrs Whitehouse, it is clearly easier for them to feel *empathy* for Mr Jordan.

This identification of the judges with the position of Mr Jordan is especially clear in the judgment of Lord Denning:

> the [trial judge] required Mr Jordan to come up to 'the very high standard of professional competence that the law requires'. That suggests that the law makes no allowance for errors of judgment. That would be a mistake. Else there would be a danger, in all cases of professional men, of their being made liable whenever something goes wrong. Whenever I give a judgment, and it is afterwards reversed by the House of Lords, is it to be said that I was negligent? That I did not pay enough attention to a previous binding authority or the like? Every one of us every day gives a judgment which is afterwards found to be wrong. It may be an error of judgment but it is not negligent. So also with a barrister who advises that there is a good cause of action and it afterwards fails. Is it to be said on that account that he was negligent?[48]

Although the phrase 'errors of judgment' has been subject to criticism,[49] the general tenor of Lord Denning's argument is very much in keeping with the arguments made by the other judges. What is interesting here is Lord Denning's understanding of the action against Mr Jordan as an attack on professional men in general, including Lord Denning himself. As Denning himself had put it in an earlier case, the doctor's 'professional reputation is as dear to him as his body, perhaps more so, and an action for negligence can wound his reputation as severely as a dagger can his body'.[50] Thus, as Sheila McLean explains, 'because the medical man has a status and a position to preserve we are invited to maintain that status unless absolutely forced, in extreme circumstances, to criticise or condemn.'[51]

No doubt this identification with the 'professional man' is strengthened by a sense that law, like medicine, is a specialised body of knowledge not easily amenable to comprehension by the lay person who should therefore not hazard to judge when a mistake has been made and further that judges, like doctors, are high-minded and selfless, being essentially engaged in an altruistic service.

As is clear from the judges' description of Mrs Whitehouse, there is no similar intuitive empathy for the patient. In *Sidaway*, we see one of their

---

48  *Op cit*, fn 38, *per* Lord Denning MR, p 658.

49  *Op cit*, fn 43, *per* Lord Edmund-Davies, p 276; Lord Fraser, p 281; and Lord Russell, p 284. See also *op cit*, fn 27, Robertson.

50  *Hatcher v Black* (1954) *The Times*, 2 July.

51  McLean, S, 'Negligence – a dagger at the doctor's back?', in Robson, P and Watchman, P (eds), *Justice, Lord Denning and the Constitution*, 1981, Farnborough: Gower, p 109.

Lordships explaining why the verdict they have handed down to Mrs Sidaway would not be appropriate had the patient been someone more like one of their Lordships:

> ... when it comes to warning about risks, the kind of training and experience that a judge will have undergone at the Bar makes it natural for him to say (correctly) it is my right to decide whether any particular thing is done to my body, and I want to be fully informed of any risks there may be involved of which I am not already aware from my general knowledge as a highly educated man of experience, so that I may form my own judgment whether to refuse the advised treatment or not. No doubt, if the patient in fact manifested this attitude by means of questioning, the doctor would tell him whatever it was the patient wanted to know; but we are concerned here with volunteering unsought information about risks ...[52]

Mrs Sidaway is thus characterised precisely by her *difference* to their Lordships and it is this difference which here underlies the refusal to recognise any right to information. Although the judges admit to having no knowledge of her character, they are clearly not giving her the benefit of any doubt. Lord Diplock notes that: 'We know nothing of the emotional idiosyncracies of the plaintiff, Mrs Sidaway (the patient), even in ordinary health let alone under stress of ill-health and the prospects of waiting for surgical treatment ...'[53]

And without any evidence regarding what was actually said by Mr Falconer, the doctor, to Mrs Sidaway, or Mrs Sidaway's own mental state, Lord Templeman feels able to conclude that, 'Mr Falconer may reasonably have taken the view that Mrs Sidaway might be confused, frightened or misled by more detailed information which she was unable to evaluate at a time when she was suffering from stress, pain and anxiety'.[54]

Notwithstanding the fact that Mr Falconer is unable to give any evidence regarding what information he gave to Mrs Sidaway, the trial judge feels able to dismiss Mrs Sidaway's evidence that Mr Falconer did not examine her. Mr Falconer died before Mrs Sidaway's case was heard and the judges were left to build up their own image of him. This bears striking similarities to the the picture drawn of Mr Jordan (with some obvious differences dictated by the fact that Mr Falconer was at the end of his career whilst Mr Jordan was just beginning his). The construction is that of a 'distinguished neuro-surgeon',[55] 'a careful and compassionate man', who was 'experienced, competent, conscientious and considerate in his practice and in his attitude to his patients'.[56] Mr Ross, one of the surgeons in the *Maynard* case is similarly

---

52  *Sidaway v Bethlem RHG* [1985] 1 All ER 643 (HL), *per* Lord Diplock, p 659. The later case of *Blyth v Bloomsbury HA* [1993] 4 Med LR 151 closed this caveat, making it clear that the doctor owed no additional duty to give more information to the more inquisitive or assertive patient.

53  *Sidaway*, p 655.

54  *Ibid*, p 664.

55  *Ibid, per* Lord Scarman, p 645.

56  *Ibid, per* Lord Templeman, p 663. See also Lord Donaldson, p 1020 (HL).

described as a 'careful, skilful, highly experienced consultant' with a 'cautious approach'.[57]

Moreover, whilst it has been seen that the goodwill of the altruistic medical personnel is routinely assumed, the same is not true for the plaintiffs. The judges were content to assert that Mrs Sidaway might merely have been 'confused'. The Whitehouses fare less well:

> Ever since the child was born, [Mrs Whitehouse] and her husband have sought an inquiry. They invoked the aid of the press, the media and their member of Parliament. When an inquiry was refused, she obtained legal aid to press the case against the hospital and the surgeon ... In this case two of the most eminent obstetricians in the country have given evidence against the surgeon: and two equally eminent have given evidence for him. Eminent counsel have been engaged to press the case against him: and counsel equally eminent to defend him. The expense must have been colossal. All borne on both sides by the taxpayers of this country.[58]

The Whitehouses are seen as engaged in a futile and obsessive quest, regardless of the expense to the public purse. This ignores an alternative construction of this chain of events. It is, after all, only when the Whitehouses are refused an inquiry that they resort to the courts. And this might be construed as the action of dedicated parents trying to ensure fair play and to obtain adequate money to maximise the quality of life of a beloved and damaged son. Lord Denning MR argues that, in any case, money is not what is needed by Mrs Whitehouse:

> Let it not be thought that I am wanting in sympathy for the mother. It is a most grievous thing for her. But it is not a thing which will be cured by money damages. Everyone will rally round to help her as they have already done during these last 10 years. She should be grateful for all that has been done for her without laying blame on the doctors.[59]

In jurisprudential terms, this statement is striking for its complete dismissal of the established basis of compensation in negligence law. It is also noteworthy for its confinement of Mrs Whitehouse and the problems now facing her family to the private sphere. According to the court, Mrs Whitehouse must seek to meet the needs of her son through her own caring work and the help provided through informal support networks, rather than seeking the financial assistance which would allow her to pass on some of this work to professional carers.

What this analysis has sought to reveal is that the policy arguments advanced by the courts are based on a stereotypical, idealised vision of the medical relationship and that these arguments serve to occlude other visions. There is a choice as to where the loss should be allowed to fall which seems

---

57  *Maynard v West Midlands RHA* [1988] 1 All ER 635, p 641.

58  *Whitehouse v Jordan* [1980] 1 All ER 650 (CA), p 653

59  *Ibid, per* Lord Denning MR, p 658.

importantly influenced by the judges' identification with the doctors involved. This identification would seem to be importantly influenced by a shared background, in which gender (along with other factors such as class and race) plays an important role.

Having spent some time unpacking the 'common sense' notions which underpin the *Bolam* test, in the rest of this paper I will move on to a brief critical examination of its effects in practice. I will argue that the impact of *Bolam* is disproportionate: that its effects are more serious for women, whether that be the female patient or the female doctor who tries to bring feminist values to her work.

## THE *BOLAM* TEST, WOMEN AND MEDICAL PRACTICE

### The patient

A wealth of research has shown that women are likely to suffer the worst excesses of medical paternalism both in terms of the quotidian medical encounter and the more spectacular intervention.[60] There is also clear evidence to suggest that doctors show least respect for patient autonomy when their patients are women. Feminist research has shown that medical texts are often informed by characterisations of women as irrational, sexually passive, and maternal[61] and that it is precisely these constructions which have formed the basis for a perceived need for medical control.[62] Various historical studies have shown how medicine has policed femininity, ensuring female compliance with ideas of appropriate feminine behaviour through such draconian measures as ovariectomies[63] or committal to psychiatric institutions.[64] Likewise, medical science was pivotal to strategies for keeping women out of the universities, and in the home, in the 19th century and more

---

60  A clear critical overview of some of the mass of work in this area can be found in Lupton, D, *Medicine as Culture: Illness, Disease and the Body in Western Societies*, 1994, London: Thousand Oaks; New Delhi: Sage. See also *op cit*, fn 7, Foster; Davis, K, *Power Under the Microscope: Towards a Grounded Theory of Gendered Relations in Medical Encounters*, 1988, Amsterdam: Foris Publications.

61  Scully, D and Bart, P, 'A funny thing happended to me on the way to the orifice: women in gynecology textbooks' (1973) 78 *American Journal of Sociology* 1045; Merchant, C, *The Death of Nature: Women, Ecology and the Scientific Revolution*, 1980, San Francisco: Harper and Row; Easlea, B, *Science and Sexual Oppression*, 1981, London: Weidenfeld and Nicolson; Martin, E, *The Woman in the Body: A Cultural Analysis of Reproduction*, 1987, Milton Keynes: Open University Press.

62  Sheldon, S, '"Who is the mother to make the judgment?": constructions of woman in English abortion law' (1993) 1 FLS 3.

63  Scully, D, *Men Who Control Women's Health: The Miseducation of Obstetrician-Gynecologists*, 1980, Boston: Houghton Mifflin Company.

64  This was practised well into this century under the Mental Defective Act 1913 for unmarried mothers on the grounds of moral imbecility or feeble-mindedness. See also Fegan and Fennell, this volume.

recently, it has been equally implicated in excluding women from certain (traditionally male) industries on the grounds of foetal protection.[65] Although the claims and methods of medical science seem (by and large) to be far less dramatic in recent years, at times evidence of the same pattern of medical enforcement of appropriate female behaviour is still clearly visible.[66] Furthermore, women use health services more frequently than men and thus, it has been argued, are more subject to routine, daily medical control.[67] If this is so, then it will be women who are most injured by the law's failure to provide any adequate redress for iatrogenic injury and by the legal refusal to play a more active role in laying down standards.

The most furious indictments of medical practice in recent years have been provoked by instances of obstetric and gynaecological practice. It is perhaps in obstetrics and gynaecology that the gulf between what the doctor believes to be in the woman's best interests, and what she herself believes, may be greatest. The potential for conflict is clear in the series of recent cases involving enforced Caesarean sections.[68] Litigation has also arisen from cases of allegedly 'scalpel happy' doctors performing unwanted hysterectomies, ovariectomies and abortions on women who had consented to a quite different operation.[69] The courts, in some instances, have been seen to concur with a view that deems a woman incapable of making her own decisions when she is pregnant or in labour and that the doctor is best placed to make these decisions on her behalf.[70]

In fact a large quantity of feminist research into health care practice has focused precisely on the gulf between what is currently *accepted* medical practice and what should be deemed to be *acceptable*. Feminists also have convincingly argued that medical practice is not always guided primarily by the interests of the patient, but is also influenced by the working conditions

---

65  Thomson, M, *Reproducing Narrative: Gender, Reproduction and Law*, 1998, Aldershot: Dartmouth.

66  See Hudson, D, 'You can't commit violence against an object: women, psychiatry and psychosurgery', in Hanmer, J and Maynard, M (eds), *Women, Violence and Social Control*, 1987, Hampshire: Macmillan, pp 110–21; Roberts, H, *The Patient Patients: Women and their Doctors*, 1985, London: Pandora Press, p 33.

67  Barrett, M and Roberts, H, 'Doctors and their patients: the social control of women in general practice', in Smart, C and Smart, B (eds), *Women, Sexuality and Social Control*, 1978, pp 41–64, London, Henley and Boston: Routledge and Kegan Paul; Gardner, K, 'Well women clinics: a positive approach to women's health', in Roberts, H (ed), *Women, Health and Reproduction*, 1981, pp 129–43, London: Routledge, pp 130–31; Roberts, *ibid*; Davis, K, *Power under the Microscope: Towards a Grounded Theory of Gender Relations in Medical Encounters*, 1988, Amsterdam: Foris Publications.

68  See Wells, this volume; Widdett, C and Thomson, M, 'Justifying treatment and other stories' (1997) 5 FLS 77; and Thomson, M, 'After Re S' (1994) 2 Med L Rev 127.

69  See Sheldon, S, '"Subject only to the attitude of the doctor concerned": judicial protection of medical discretion' (1996) 5 SLS 93. See also Foster, Wells, Fegan and Fennell, this volume.

70  See Fegan and Fennell, this volume.

and the occupational concerns of the professional groups in question.[71] In a recent book, Peggy Foster has conducted a wide-ranging survey of some of the iatrogenic effects of modern medicine for female patients.[72] Foster concludes that modern medical practice is not influenced exclusively by concern for the well-being of the patient; other factors can also be important. Her particular focus is on the financial incentives in medical practice which can lead to the widespread use of unnecessary, often high technology procedures and the significant negative effects that this can have for women.

Whilst it would obviously be unfair to convict medical science on the weight of the above evidence without allowing a case to be presented for the defence, what is relevant here is that the law has no way of recognising this research, which is declared inadmissible before the start of the trial. The judicial forum has always been more open to certain voices and certain knowledges.[73] In this case, it is not so much that the medical voice is prioritised over other accounts. Rather, it is permitted to silence any other completely. Judicial endorsement of the professional standard is an endorsement of this control. Because the judiciary takes accepted practice to be, by that fact alone, acceptable, any broader critique, feminist or other, of such practice can have no purchase in this formula.

This has had particularly startling effect in the case of duties of disclosure as seen in *Sidaway*. Notwithstanding the lip service paid to the importance of informed consent in documents such as *The Patient's Charter*, the relevant test of what information a doctor must give to a patient is to be determined by the doctor, regardless of questions asked and whether the operation is therapeutic or not.[74] It also means that in cases such as *Maynard* or *Whitehouse*, the courts refuse the opportunity to scrutinise common practice and to declare it to be unacceptable. This is still more worrying given the challenge posed by the work of writers such as Foster to the courts' assumption that altruism and beneficence are the primary motivating forces which guide medical practice.[75]

## The doctor

Within the medical profession, although there is equality of pay and terms and conditions of service, one finds that women doctors are poorly represented at the top of the profession ... They are under-represented in teaching hospitals so

---

71 See particularly, Thomson, M, *Reproducing Narrative: Gender, Reproduction and Law*, 1998, Aldershot: Dartmouth.

72 *Op cit*, fn 7, Foster.

73 This has been a recurrent theme in the work of Carol Smart. See particularly Smart, C, *Feminism and the Power of Law*, 1989, London and New York: Routledge.

74 See *Blyth* and *Gold*, above. The legal failure to intervene to ensure adequate disclosure of information to allow the patient to make fully informed decisions can only have contributed to the very low standards which often operate in practice, see Foster this volume.

75 *Op cit*, fn 7, Foster.

that female students may lack role models. For example, there is not one professor of obstetrics and gynaecology who is a woman ... [76]

The *Bolam* test may also pose a second significant problem for women. Much feminist research has denounced mainstream medical practices as *male*stream practices in the sense that they have been developed by men and incorporate certain gendered assumptions.[77] It may be that it is not only female patients who are likely to suffer as a result of this, but also those women who attempt to challenge these standards 'from the inside'. In this sense, some commentators have reported the difficulties of bringing feminist values to bear in their work.[78]

Wendy Savage has more direct experience of this problem than most doctors. Savage is a London consultant gynaecologist and obstetrician, who was suspended from her post in 1985 pending an investigation into her practice and five cases with which she had dealt. The most serious of these cases involved a decision to allow one of her patients to have a trial labour notwithstanding the fact that her baby was in the breech position and would almost inevitably need to be delivered by Caesarean section. Savage's decision was influenced by her belief in the psychological importance for a woman to experience for herself that vaginal delivery was impossible. Following a full investigation, she was eventually exonerated completely. A major motivation for the investigation into her competence seems to have been her failure to conform to mainstream (malestream) standards of medical practice. Savage describes the problem in the following way:

> I and many of my supporters saw my suspension as part of the continuing struggle about who controls childbirth, and it was on this ground that we chose to fight ... at a deeper level, I knew that this battle was about the way doctors relate to and work with each other, and about the fact that I am not a member of the 'establishment' and saw no reason to conform to the medical profession's unwritten, but well understood 'party line', especially if I thought this was not in the interests of patients.[79]

Some support is lent to Savage's interpretation of events by the comments of a senior obstetrician made at the time of the inquiry: 'She should have been a good and agreeable girl and made sure she got on with her colleagues. If she had played her cards right she would have found being a woman was to her advantage and her male colleagues might have been prepared to do her more favours.'[80]

---

76  Savage, W, *A Savage Enquiry: Who Controls Childbirth?*, 1987, London: Virago, p 141.

77  See particularly Emily Martin, *op cit*, fn 61, and the extensive work of Ann Oakley on this subject, particularly Oakley, A, *Subject Woman*, 1981, Oxford: Martin Robertson; and Oakley, A, *The Captured Womb: A History of the Medical Care of Pregnant Women*, 1984, Oxford: Blackwells.

78  *Ibid*, Savage.

79  *Ibid*, Savage, p xvi.

80  (1986) *The Sunday Times*, 9 March, cited in *ibid*, Savage, p xv.

It would seem to me that this does not merely suggest that female doctors should adopt an appropriately 'feminine' demeanour with regard to their senior colleagues but also that they should defer to their opinions and established procedures in a way that will obviously impact on their practice and dealings with patients. Savage's medical practice was informed by the feminist values which she brought to her work, which implied certain conclusions regarding the respective roles of women and doctors in the birthing process. Her practice drew more on this than the developed malestream practices around birth which, some have argued, are often influenced more by considerations of making life easier for the doctor than at improving the birthing experience for the pregnant woman.[81] There was no evidence to suggest that her practice posed any greater risk to her patients than any other and the investigation into it did not arise as a result of complaints made by her patients. Savage was eventually exonerated completely.

Savage ends her account of the investigation by outlining six broad issues which she saw as being raised by her suspension and the subsequent inquiry. One of these was the problem of how to define incompetence in a specialty like obstetrics where there is a wide spectrum of opinion about the way to look after pregnant women. Savage's question is slightly different from the present inquiry – incompetence (as she notes) depends on a continuing state of affairs whilst an action in negligence normally focuses on an isolated incident. Nonetheless, the issue which she raises does have significant resonances for the present work: 'What is acceptable practice as far as the professional is concerned? Does this differ from what women think is acceptable practice? ... How much of accepted practice (based on opinion and current working methods) is *acceptable* practice ... ?'[82]

The standard currently adopted by the law is the practice (or, more accurately, those practices) condoned by a 'responsible body of opinion' within the medical establishment, the upper echelons of which are still dominated by men and male standards. The failure of the law to intervene to examine the accepted practice standard leaves no potential to challenge the status quo. As was seen above, this may have harmful effects for female plaintiffs. What emerges from the Savage case is that the standard may also be dangerous for those doctors who, like Savage, attempt to introduce more woman-centred practices. Whilst the *Bolam* test has been cited as being protective of doctors and set on doctors' terms, it is essential to realise that those are the terms of the higher echelons normally not reached by women and only rarely reached by those who openly challenge conventional values.[83]

---

81  See *op cit*, fn 77, Oakley, 1984.

82  *Op cit*, fn 76, Savage, p 179, italics in original.

83  For a detailed historical account of the problems faced by women aspiring to progress in the medical profession, see Witz, A, *Professions and Patriarchy*, 1992, London and New York: Routledge.

Savage quotes a leader in the *British Medical Journal* which talks of the 'tendency of the medical profession to run like an Edwardian gentleman's club'.[84] She adds:

> Women find it difficult to be members of this club and remain true to their ideals. Yet unless they take their place in this medico-political committee structured world they, like hundreds of male doctors who don't like the system, will continue to find themselves not fulfilling their potential and working in a profession that increasingly is not giving patients what they want and, I believe, have a right to expect in the latter part of the 20th century.[85]

*Bolam* may be protective of a plurality of practices, but if the acceptable range of such a plurality is dictated by the medical profession, the law relinquishes control over what should properly be included within it. The words of Lord Scarman, which formed my starting point, indicated the need for conformity not just with a 'responsible' body of opinion, but with one which is also 'respectable', that is, one which conforms to certain norms and values. We have seen that these norms and values remain dictated by the medical profession's upper echelons.

## CONCLUSIONS

> It can be seen that English malpractice law is not ... generally able to render the health professions accountable to their patients and clients. Usually tort law aims to establish objective standards that define where a reasonable balance is to be drawn between risks and benefits. In the health care context, that balance is drawn by the professions and merely policed by the courts. Consequently, the deterrent effect of the law is weak. It certainly cannot contribute to raising professional standards. It is further diluted by the fact that health professionals will rarely find themselves liable to pay any damages that are awarded out of their own pockets.[86]

An important part of any feminist engagement with law must be challenging law's 'common sense' view of the world and revealing the assumptions upon which it is predicated.[87] As was seen above, the assumptions which have informed medical negligence law include a reluctance to tarnish a doctor's professional reputation, an acceptance of medicine as a body of specialist knowledge, an assumption of altruism as the motivating force in medical practice, a reluctance to disrupt the smooth working of the medical relationship by the facilitation of litigation, and a fear of defensive medicine. I

---

84  *Op cit*, fn 76, Savage, p 148.

85  *Op cit*, fn 76, Savage, p 148.

86  *Op cit*, fn 10, Montgomery, p 189.

87  *Op cit*, fn 30, Graycar; and Conaghan, J, 'Tort law and the feminist critique of reason', in Bottomley, A (ed), *Feminist Perspectives on the Foundational Subjects of Law*, 1996, London: Cavendish Publishing, pp 48–49.

have argued that the prioritisation of these policy factors is underpinned by the judges' identification with the defendant doctors involved. The conflicting considerations which are thereby occluded are a sense of the patient's particular vulnerability, a subjugation of the needs of medical accident victims who must rely, like Mrs Whitehouse, on friends and family to 'rally round', the potential deterrent effect of holding doctors liable and a consequent raising of professional standards, and finally damage to medical relationships through inadequate remedies for wronged parties.

Within the framework established by *Bolam*, the judges intervene to correct only the most flagrant excesses. The reduction of the normative (legal) question of *acceptability* to the essentially empirical question of whether a particular procedure is *accepted* means that, in practice, doctors will be allowed to do what doctors normally do. This judicial recognition of expertise has been seen to rest firmly on a gendered solidarity, a fraternity of interests. And whilst this abdication of authority to the medical profession is one which should concern us all, I have argued that it is of particular significance for women. The power of the male-dominated, higher echelons of the medical professions is entrenched and those doctors who fail to conform to its values may receive scant protection from the law. Further, if the action in negligence does have any useful role to play in influencing medical behaviour or in protecting victims from the actions of tortfeasors, or for compensating those who are injured when something goes wrong, then this role is likely to be doubly important for women. Correlatively, its failure to perform these roles adequately will be doubly harmful.

# CHAPTER THREE

# PROFESSIONAL REGULATION: A GENDERED PHENOMENON?

*Jonathan Montgomery*

## INTRODUCTION

The pursuit of professionalism has been a conscious strategy for many of the predominantly female groups of health workers. The self-images of the professions stress their specialist knowledge base, their altruistic values and the legitimacy of their claim to self-regulation.[1] This has proved attractive to nurses seeking to establish their credibility as a graduate profession, or at least one trained through higher education establishments, and enhance their status in the health services.

The less vaunted aspect of professional status is the dominant position that it gives in the division of labour. From this position, professionalism provides a form of occupational closure in which the professionals themselves define what they should do and how they should do it, protected from outside scrutiny.[2] The framework of occupational power is mediated through social acceptance that professionals should be the judge of their own competence and the aims of their work, through their control over education and access to professional work, and through the insulation of their systems for remuneration and management from their actual work for individual patients.

Each of these pillars of professional status is reflected in the legal rules that govern the practice of the health professions. Litigation is dominated by the *Bolam* test, which, at least as interpreted by the higher courts, precludes detailed scrutiny of professionals' standards.[3] Instead, it provides a reinforcement of existing professional practice. Health professionals are subject to the discipline of their statutory governing bodies, but this once again leads to a form of self-regulation, because the membership of those bodies is drawn almost exclusively from within the professions. Those statutory bodies are able to restrict access to the profession by establishing educational requirements, requiring registration before individuals can work

---

1 Friedson, E, *Profession of Medicine: A Study in the Sociology of Applied Knowledge*, 1970, New York: Dodd Mead.

2 Johnson, T, *Professions and Power*, 1972, London: Macmillan.

3 Montgomery, J, 'Medicine, accountability and professionalism' (1989) 16 JLS 339; Montgomery, J, *Health Care Law*, 1997, Oxford: OUP, pp 169–76; see Sheldon, this volume.

in the professions, and reserving the power to strike off the register those who do not live up to their requirements. So far as remuneration and management are concerned, the position of the health professions varies. Within the British NHS, doctors have remained highly successful at maintaining national pay scales unrelated to individual job descriptions and performance. They have also been able to resist managerial interference in their clinical freedom. Nurses have been subject to a rather more volatile employment environment.

The role of gender in professional regulation can easily be masked by a formal analysis of this sort set out above. The profession of medicine established its modern form through the legal guarantee of a range of privileges under the Medical (Registration) Act 1858. This regime effectively barred women from the profession because of their exclusion from the educational establishments that provided the qualifications that had now become prerequisite for entry. The Act itself used the gender-neutral language of 'persons', but the universities, royal colleges and teaching hospitals were less enlightened. Witz shows how a series of strategies were then followed, ultimately successfully, to win women access to the privileges that were guaranteed by the legislation.[4] These gained for women membership of a profession whose shape had been determined by men. The battle was fought over the agenda of the inclusion or exclusion of women rather than the nature of the profession itself.

Witz also discusses how a number of other health occupations have pursued professional status. She shows how medical men reacted to these projects in a number of ways. Sometimes, the tactic was to accept the aspirations of the emerging profession to autonomous status, but to demarcate and limit the scope of its practice so as to neutralise the threat to the power of medicine. Sometimes, doctors sought to limit the autonomy of the emerging professions by subordinating their practice to medical control.

Interestingly, however, Witz shows that the response of the doctors was not uniform. Discussing responses to midwives' drive to registration, she contrasts the support of obstetricians for the midwives and the opposition of general practitioners. For the former, an autonomous, but limited, and subordinate, profession of midwifery enabled the obstetricians to concentrate on providing services for the rich without becoming responsible for the provision of maternity care to the masses. By securing involvement in the governing bodies of midwifery and the training of midwives, obstetricians could obtain control over the range of maternity care without having actually to deliver it unless it was convenient and financially advantageous to do so. From the perspective of the general practitioners, the prospect of a profession of registered midwives looked rather different. It would provide a group of competitors who might rob them of business. General practitioners were not opposed to the idea of registration for a predominantly female profession,

---

4    Witz, A, *Professions and Patriarchy*, 1992, London: Routledge.

they supported those nurses who were seeking it. They opposed the particular manifestation of it for reasons that were essentially economic.

Witz argues that the support of general practitioners for nurse registration had its roots in a tension between the 'ordinary ranks' of the medical profession and the powerful elite body of physicians and surgeons who dominated the profession. She suggests that there was an affinity between the cause of the generalist doctors in securing more influence within their own profession and the creation of a populist, grass roots form of a self-regulated profession in nursing.[5] This sort of tension, within the profession and between specialists and generalists, continues to arise in the health professions. The constitution of the General Medical Council (hereafter the GMC) was altered after the Merrison report to make it more accountable to representatives of the profession.[6] The United Kingdom Central Council for Nursing, Midwifery and Health Visiting (hereafter the UKCC) saw similar changes following the Nurses, Midwives and Health Visitors Act 1992, with the introduction of direct elections to the Council. Previously elections had been made to four National Boards, and those Boards had nominated members to the Council. These democratic changes reduced the ability of the elite professional establishments to dictate to the rank and file of ordinary practitioners.

The tension between the centralised regulatory power exercised by the professional establishments and the freedom of individual practitioners to determine the way in which they intend to practise is the principal concern of this chapter. Witz has shown how struggles for professionalism are intertwined with broader issues of gender within civil society.[7] It is not that professionalism is a male-dominated concept, nor that professionalisation is necessarily a battle between gender groups, but that the workings of these concepts cannot be understood without reference to issues of gender. Both the male dominance of medicine from the second half of the 19th century and the need for nurses and midwives to establish a registration system can be linked with the move of health care from a predominantly domestic sphere to an occupation in the market-place.[8] Professionalisation is a strategy for securing power in the employment market.

This chapter examines aspects of the regulatory systems of medicine, a predominantly male profession, and nursing, midwifery and health visiting, three predominantly female professions brought together under a single statutory body. It argues that while the systems seem to follow a single constitutional pattern, there are in fact subtle differences in the ways in which the governing bodies have exercised their powers over the members of the professions. While there is now considerable cross-fertilisation between the

---

5   *Op cit*, Witz, fn 4.

6   *Report of the Committee of Inquiry into the Regulation of the Medical Profession*, 1975, London: HMSO, Cmnd 6018.

7   *Op cit*, Witz, fn 4.

8   Stacey, M, *The Sociology of Health and Healing*, 1988, London: Unwin Hyman.

models of professional regulation, I shall argue that the thrust of medical regulation has been to preserve the individual autonomy of doctors, while the steer given by the UKCC has been more corporatist, seeking greater uniformity of values and practice.

I shall consider how far this difference can be attributed to the gendered division of health labour. I shall examine two main aspects of this. First, the possibility that there may be a distinctively feminine conception of 'professionalism' emphasising corporate responsibility over individual autonomy. This would mirror the differences in approaches to moral reasoning identified by Carol Gilligan.[9] Second, it may be that the form of professional registration is shaped by the economic and social position in which the female occupations find themselves. Witz argues convincingly that it is erroneous to conceive of professionalisation as a uniform strategy, and shows how it is more illuminating to think of individual professional projects, in which particular professional groups adopt strategies that will succeed, given the limits and possibilities of their position.[10] This historical specificity is likely to lead to different outcomes for those groups whose professional regulation emerges from a position of social and economic strength, as was the case with the male profession of medicine, than for those groups where social and economic power has to be fought for, as the female professions have had to do.

## REGULATING THE PROFESSIONS

The general framework for professional regulation is common to all the health professions. Work as a professional is restricted to those whose names are entered on a register maintained by a statutory body. Conditions of entry are established which are primarily concerned with educational qualifications, standards of which are usually laid down by the profession. Continued registration is subject to the jurisdiction of the professional body to remove the names of people who are unfit to practise, whether by reason of ill-health or misconduct. The professional bodies also have statutory powers in relation to the giving of guidance on standards of practice. These professional bodies thus have a pivotal role to play in determining the character of professional regulation. Although the general pattern just set out holds for all the health professions, there are important differences between them that illuminate the questions being explored in this paper.

---

9    Gilligan, C, *In a Different Voice*, 1982, Cambridge, Mass: Harvard University Press.
10   *Op cit*, Witz, fn 4.

## Entry to the profession

In the case of medicine, an approved qualification provides the basis for provisional registration, which can be converted into full registration following a year's employment as a house officer (ss 3, 10, 11 of the Medical Act 1983). Registration is a matter of 'entitlement' once the necessary qualifications have been obtained. The General Medical Council has relatively little control over individual entrants to the profession. It can determine the nature and content of the medical curriculum, and in theory it also determines which institutions are trusted to deliver it. The exercise of this function has demonstrated a tension between the exercise of power by the purely vocational wings of the profession and those based in universities. Stacey describes the powerful influence of the 'old' universities in the GMC's Education Committee and shows how concerned the Committee was with interference in the autonomy of those institutions.[11] The regulatory function of the General Medical Council in relation to the approval of courses reflects confidence in, or weakness in respect of, the work of the medical schools.

The power of the ancient medical schools is reflected in drafting of the Medical Act 1983 and in the constitution of the General Medical Council itself. The statute sets out the list of institutions that are entitled to hold qualifying examinations (s 4). While the GMC's Education Committee is able to monitor standards in these institutions and to consider other worthy contenders for the training of doctors, the power to add to or subtract from the list of institutions offering qualifying examinations lies neither with the Committee, nor with the GMC, but with the Privy Council. Thus, the law guarantees these institutions the right to educate and train doctors, and ensures that there is ample opportunity for lobbying on their behalf if the status quo is challenged. The GMC's powers to influence the course of medical education are limited, making negotiation rather than prescription the necessary strategy.

The weakness of the General Medical Council's position can also be seen in its constitution. Almost one quarter of the membership of the Council is made up of appointees of the royal colleges (which play an important post-registration educational function) and of the universities. Thus, the educational bodies that are overseen by the Council have a significant voice within the organisation that regulates them as well as a strong position from which to resist unwanted pressure. This pattern is even clearer in the GMC's Education Committee. Here, the majority of the Committee must be formed by members appointed from the educational bodies. The function of the Education Committee is to provide a forum for the educators to reach a consensus on their work, not to impose any particular direction upon them from the wider profession.

---

11   Stacey, M, *Regulating British Medicine: The General Medical Council*, 1992, Chichester: Wiley.

It can be seen from this brief analysis that the regulatory framework for medical education is designed to ensure a balance of power between the co-ordinating tendencies of statutory bodies, pursuing strategies designed for application by the whole profession, and the decentralised interests of the educational institutions keen to preserve academic freedom. The statutory rights to hold qualifying examinations and the influential position of these institutions in the regulatory structure insulate them from central control. This is a feature of medical professonalisation that is not only important in relation to the self-regulatory dimension, but also crucial in protecting medical education from the managerial pressures that manifest themselves in a system of state medicine. The legally guaranteed position of the medical schools prevents the National Health Service from requiring them to educate doctors to meet immediate service needs. The NHS is not able to choose doctors trained in the way it desires because entry into the educational market is limited by statute, with any change controlled by the Privy Council.

If the regulatory regime of medicine serves to resist the centralisation of power and preserve the independence of the satellite institutions of the medical establishment, the position in relation to nursing, midwifery and health visiting is rather different. The power of the medical schools, and their location mainly in the 'ancient' and exclusively in the 'old' universities, predates that of the GMC. In contrast, the position of the higher education establishments which educate nurses, midwives and health visitors derives from the power of the UKCC. The move towards nurse education as opposed to training in the immediate skills of the occupations was only firmly established as a result of the UKCC's 'Project 2000'. As a result of this initiative, the majority of those qualifying in the professions under the UKCC's umbrella became students in higher education for the first time. Previously, only a minority of practitioners qualified with degrees in their profession. Also, as a result of 'Project 2000', colleges of nursing and midwifery moved from the NHS to the universities. At the same time there was a growing acceptance of the importance of making practice research-based, which has strengthened the interdependence between vocational training and higher education. Medicine had always taken its place in the universities, and was firmly entrenched there before the genesis of professional regulation. Nursing, midwifery and health visiting have won their stakes in higher education on the back of initiatives emerging from the professional bodies.

In medicine, the strength of the educational institutions ensured that the curriculum was not prescribed for them in detail. The rights of the institutions were inscribed in law, the content of the curriculum was extra-statutory. In nursing, midwifery and health visiting the converse is true. Under the Nurses, Midwives and Health Visitors Rules[12] the entry requirements for students

---

12   Nurses, Midwives and Health Visitors Rules Approval Order 1983, SI 1983/873.

and the skills that they are required to learn are prescribed by law. The rules contain detailed accounts of the objectives to be pursued in programmes for each of the three professions.

Thus, midwives (as an example) must undertake programmes of education enabling them to:

(a) appreciate the influence of social, political and cultural factors in relation to health care and health promotion;

(b) recognise common factors adversely affecting the well-being of mother and baby;

(c) assess, plan, implement and evaluate care within the sphere of midwifery to meet the physical, emotional, social, spiritual and educational needs of mother, baby and family;

(d) take action on their own responsibility, including seeking assistance when required;

(e) interpret and undertake care prescribed by a medical practitioner;

(f) use appropriate and effective communication skills with mothers and their families, with colleagues and with those in other disciplines;

(g) use relevant literature and research to inform practice;

(h) function effectively in a multi-professional team;

(i) understand the legislative requirements relevant to the practice of midwifery;

(j) understand ethical issues relating to midwifery practice, and the responsibilities which these impose;

(k) assign appropriate duties to others, supervising and monitoring such assigned duties.[13]

While the content of the self-definition of the professional role as seen by the regulatory body is of interest, the main point here is that such a definition has been produced at all. The drawing up of a single prescribed curriculum of this sort marks a distinction with the looser framework imposed by the GMC. It demonstrates a drive for uniformity and consistency that shows a greater desire for centralised leadership than medicine has accepted. That this leadership is legitimated by detailed legal prescription and not merely guidance under a statutory power reinforces the impression of firm government.

The circumscribed freedom of institutions educating nurses, midwives and health visitors to develop their own curricula has been compounded by their lack of security as suppliers of professional qualifications. Unlike the medical schools, colleges of nursing, midwifery and health visiting have no statutory right to hold examinations and confer qualifications. Their viability

---

13  Adapted from r 33 of the Nurses, Midwives and Health Visitors Rules.

is dependent on NHS authorities agreeing to sponsor students and support the clinical aspects of their programmes. Unlike the position with medical training, these authorities may, and do, decide to withdraw their support from educational institutions. Those institutions must therefore satisfy both the professional body which establishes and monitors standards, and the NHS authorities who hold the purse strings. The academic freedom of those who educate nurses, midwives and health visitors is therefore considerably more constrained than that of their medical counterparts.

There is also a further sting in the tail for individuals. Those who hold an approved medical qualification are thereby entitled to have their names entered on the register. Not so for nurses, midwives and health visitors. They must also satisfy the UKCC that they are of 'good character'.[14] While this may not be of enormous practical significance, and is not unique in the regulation of the health professions, it is of some symbolic importance. The UKCC is effectively reserving the right to refuse to register those whom the educators have accredited as suitable for the profession. The GMC is required to accept the decisions of the bodies conferring academic qualifications.

There is also a significant difference between the drafting of the statutes. The Medical Act 1983 uses the language of entitlement. Educational establishments are entitled to hold examinations and confer qualifications. Those holding such approved qualifications are 'entitled' to be entered on the register. The perspective adopted by the drafters is that of the individual doctor or autonomous university. The GMC's role is entirely passive, responding to the rights of those outside it. Contrast the wording of the Nurses, Midwives and Health Visitors Act 1997. Here the perspective is that of the professional body. An applicant to the UKCC 'shall be registered' if they satisfy the statutory criteria, a form of words describing the activity of the professional body, not the status of the applicant. This difference is not a matter of chronology (the Nurses, Midwives and Health Visitors Act 1979 used the same terms). Rather, it shows how the medical legislation is framed so as to set out the limits of regulatory power, while that governing nursing, midwifery and health visiting assumes sympathy with the regulators. The Medical Act 1983 displays suspicion of regulation, while the Nurses, Midwives and Health Visitors Act 1997 embraces it. It also reflects the gender differences in moral reasoning identified by Gilligan.[15] The language of rights and entitlement, with its acontextual atomisation of individuals' positions, can been seen as a masculinist feature of the legal framework. It assumes that disputes will arise in a confrontational manner and delineates the respective positions of the parties. The drafting of the Nurses, Midwives and Health Visitors Act 1997 assumes that the UKCC, the educational institutions and individual practitioners will usually co-operate with each other so that it is

---

14   Section 8(2) of the Nurses, Midwives and Health Visitors Act 1997.

15   *Op cit*, Gilligan, fn 9.

more important to set out what is expected than to describe the entitlements of parties should there be a dispute.

## Professional ethics

The identification by Gilligan of feminine emphasis on responsibilities rather than rights as the root of morality can be seen also in the way in which the professional bodies explain to practitioners the values expected of them. Both the UKCC and the GMC have a statutory power to issue advice to the professions on ethical conduct. Until very recently, these powers have been exercised in rather different ways. From its establishment under the Nurses, Midwives and Health Visitors Act 1979, the UKCC saw its task as establishing standards of good practice. It issued a Code of Professional Conduct for the Nurse, Midwife and Health Visitor, and a separate Midwife's Code of Practice. These documents set out the principles that were expected to guide the conduct of members of the profession. The latter is mainly a description of the legal rights and responsibilities of midwives, with little by way of moral evaluation of the law. The former is a bold statement of the values that members of the profession are expected to uphold. The Code begins by asserting that:

> Each registered nurse, midwife and health visitor shall act, at all times, in such a manner as to: safeguard and promote the interests of individual patients and clients; serve the interests of society; justify public trust and confidence and uphold and enhance the good standing and reputation of the professions.

In its subsequent clauses, the Code requires practitioners always to promote and safeguard the interests of patients/clients.[16] This goes beyond merely ensuring that their acts or omissions are not detrimental to patients/clients,[17] in that it aims to promote their interests, not merely to protect them. The UKCC also holds practitioners responsible for reporting situations where standards of care are compromised.[18]

The provisions of the Code give positive guidance on good practice. Although they are said to provide advice on the minimum action to be taken, they do in fact go much further.[19] The Code sets out the qualities that practitioners are supposed to embody, in a form that constitute aspirations as much as minimum standards. The drafting of Clause 1 has already been noted; with its aim of promotion being one that can only be aimed at and never realised, it will always be possible to promote patient/clients' well-

---

16  United Kingdom Central Council for Nursing, Midwifery and Health Visiting, *Code of Professional Conduct for Nurse, Midwife and Health Visitor*, 3rd edn, 1992, London: UKCC, Clause 1.

17  *Ibid*, Clause 2.

18  *Ibid*, Clauses 11–13.

19  United Kingdom Central Council for Nursing, Midwifery and Health Visiting, *Guidelines for Professional Practice*, 1996, London: UKCC, p 21.

being even further. Clause 3 requires practitioners to improve their professional knowledge and competence, a constant process of education, not a standard that can be reached and then ignored in the way that qualifications for entry to the register can be obtained without guaranteeing continued competence. Nor is the obligation limited to keeping up to date, as with the medical equivalent (see below). Nurses, midwives and health visitors are expected to work co-operatively with their patients, their clients and their professional colleagues.[20] The Code is about defining good practice rather than bad practice. Thus, it does far more than identify pitfalls and how to avoid them.

The tone of the UKCC's Code of Professional Conduct can be contrasted with the approach traditionally taken by the General Medical Council. Until recently, the GMC left questions of good practice to the non-statutory bodies such as the royal colleges and the British Medical Association. It was those bodies that usually issued advice to doctors on the ethical principles that should be brought to bear on their work. The main semi-official guide to medical ethics would have been the BMA's *Handbook of Medical Ethics* now superseded by the much more detailed *Medical Ethics Today* from the same body. The GMC's contribution was the 'Blue Book': *Professional Conduct and Discipline: Fitness to Practise*. This booklet, which was regularly updated, explained the disciplinary procedures, summarised the types of conduct that might lead to disciplinary proceedings, and gave guidance on standards of professional conduct and medical ethics. It did so in that order, and apparently with those priorities. Such concerns that the GMC displayed with the interests of patients were generated by outside pressure, not by the profession's desire to improve standards.[21]

In effect, the purpose of the 'Blue Book' was to help doctors keep out of trouble. It highlighted areas where disciplinary action might be taken, gave guidance designed to help doctors avoid the hazards, and explained how they would be dealt with if they failed to heed that advice. This is an approach that concentrates on the minimum standards of good practice, safeguarding patients from the worst doctors, but doing nothing to indicate what good practice is. Even the section on 'standards of professional conduct and on medical ethics' is characterised by such concerns. It explained the limits of acceptable relationships between doctors and patients. It explored how self-promotion could give rise to difficulties, including how 'publicity in newspapers or books or the radio or television ... has frequently attracted uninformed criticism of the doctor concerned, but in most instances has appeared on examination to be harmless'. Note the assumption that criticism is usually 'uninformed' and that if only the matter is looked at properly

20   United Kingdom Central Council for Nursing, Midwifery and Health Visiting, *Code of Conduct for the Nurse, Midwife and Health Visitor*, 3rd edn, 1992, London: UKCC, Clauses 5, 6 and 14.

21   Stacey, M, 'The General Medical Council and medical ethics' in Wiesz, G (ed), *Social Science Perspectives on Medical Ethics*, 1990, London: Kluwer.

(presumably by doctors on the GMC) it will soon become apparent that the doctor is blameless. The intention seems to be less to protect the public from doctors than to protect doctors from the public.

The UKCC's Code serves to define a set of professional values, emphasising what professionals should do and not what they should not do. The GMC, on the other hand, set out the limits to the rights of doctors to practise as they please. The contrast between these conceptions of what it means to be a professional mirrors the differences identified by Gilligan.[22] The guidance from the predominantly female professions displays a commitment to responsibility, stressing what is expected without regard to the sacrifices that it may require to deliver them. The individuality of each member of the profession is not highlighted. Rather the importance of working within relationships is stressed. Collaboration and co-operation,[23] and appropriate reporting to those in authority are emphasised.[24] Doctors are assumed to follow their own consciences unless something untoward occurs. The emphasis is then on resolving problems. The focus is on the process of accountability, how it operates and what practitioners will be expected to justify. Accountability is seen as a process for making individuals explain their behaviour to the professional body, not for the professional body to explain the responsibilities that come with being a doctor.

More recently, the GMC has altered its approach. In 1995 it published a series of four booklets, under the umbrella title of 'Duties of a Doctor'. In addition to specific booklets on confidentiality, AIDS, and advertising, there was a general statement of the principles underpinning good medical practice. This set out the expectations that doctors would make the care of patients their first concern, treat them politely and considerately, respect their dignity and privacy, listen to and respect their views, inform them in ways they can understand and respect their right to be fully involved in decisions about their care. The booklet also emphasised the obligations of doctors to keep their professional knowledge and skills up to date, recognise the limitations of their competence, be honest and trustworthy, respect and protect confidential information, make sure their personal beliefs do not prejudice patients' care, act quickly to protect patients from risk due to their own or colleagues' unfitness to practise, avoid abusing medical colleagues, and work with colleagues in patients' interests. Finally, doctors are reminded not to discriminate against patients and colleagues.

The importance of this new turn is that it aims to encourage a particular group of professional values that should foster not merely safe practice, but also good practice. The GMC's understanding of its role in regulating medical ethics has been transformed from that of policeman to priest. Formerly it

---

22  *Op cit*, Gilligan, fn 9.

23  United Kingdom Central Council for Nursing, Midwifery and Health Visiting, *Code of Professional Conduct*, 3rd edn, 1992, London: UKCC, Clauses 6 and 14.

24  *Ibid*, Clauses 8, 11–13.

appeared to be interested only in cases of serious disregard for standards of practice, when the focus was on the sanctions that could be applied to provide appropriate punishment and deterrence. The GMC now seeks to give moral guidance to the profession exhorting them to the good life. The language of the two documents is very different. In the 'Blue Book', the subject of the sentence is usually 'the doctor', emphasising the individual practitioner's place at the centre of activity. In *Good Medical Practice* the usual formulation of sentences is 'you must'. This is the language of leadership and instruction, reminiscent of the structure of the Ten Commandments.

It can be seen that the GMC has now adopted the role that the UKCC appropriated from the beginning. Regulation of medicine was initially concerned with delineating the boundaries of acceptable practice. It showed little interest in what went on so long as those boundaries were not breached. The UKCC's approach to regulation, on the other hand, has been to try to shape all professional practice, not merely that which appears suspect. In the past, only wayward doctors need have concerned themselves with the details of the GMC's views on medical ethics – for they were only relevant for those likely to break the mould. The ethics of individual doctors were primarily a matter for their own consciences. If there was a consensus as to the ethical values of the medical profession, it was implicit and certainly not derived from the views of the regulatory body. Nurses, midwives and health visitors were encouraged to conform to a single value system, a definition of what it means to be a member of one of those professions that is built as much out of an imposed conception of ethics as of technical skills.

## Professional discipline

There is one obvious difference between the jurisdictions of the UKCC and the GMC in respect of professional discipline. The GMC's concern is with 'serious professional misconduct' while the UKCC can invoke disciplinary sanctions when a practitioner is found guilty of 'professional misconduct' without the need to establish that a threshold of seriousness has been crossed. This suggests that the UKCC is keener than the GMC to become involved in disciplinary matters. It might also indicate a more punitive approach that seeks to control individual practitioners, although this does not necessarily follow. The UKCC might consider a wider range of cases than the GMC, but take a similar approach to sanctions (reserving serious sanctions for serious misconduct that would fall within the GMC's jurisdiction just as much as within that of the UKCC). How far this area of the professional bodies' work supports the idea that they take different approaches to the task of regulation needs to be explored in relation both to the definition of misconduct, and the sanctions that are applied.

Prior to the Medical Act 1969, the GMC had been required to consider whether the accused doctor had been guilty of 'infamous conduct in any professional respect'. The classic formulation of this test was that set out in *Allinson v General Council for Medical Education and Registration*:[25]

> ... something with regard to [the pursuit of his profession] which would be reasonably regarded as disgraceful or dishonourable by his professional brethren of good repute and competency ...

This is a formulation that concerns reputation rather than the standard of care. In *Bhattacharya v GMC*[26] this was made even more apparent with the offending conduct being described as having a tendency to debase or degrade the standing and reputation of the profession. The offence was less to put patients at risk than to let the medical profession down by departing from the gentlemanly standards of behaviour that were expected.

In 1969, the modern formulation of 'serious professional misconduct' was introduced. This may not have been intended to be anything more than a more modern form of words[27] but it can be seen as a move towards a more technical concern with the tasks of medicine rather than a gentlemanly morality.[28] Certainly, there emerged for the first time a regular pattern of cases coming before the Council involving neglect of patients, although sexual offences remained as prominent as before.[29] The judicial explanation of the new test eventually stressed standards of conduct rather than morality, *Doughty v General Dental Council*,[30] and it is now clear that a single act of malpractice can constitute serious professional misconduct if it falls 'deplorably short' of the standards patients are entitled to expect from their doctors: *McCandless v GMC*.[31] This final step also shows how the focus has changed from what doctors expect of each other to what patients are entitled to expect. The modern jurisdiction of the GMC is as concerned with failures in patient care as it is with social and sexual morality and a new set of procedures has been set up to tackle questions of competence that fall short of serious professional misconduct.

The professional discipline of nursing, midwifery and health visiting did not escape the preoccupation with social deviance. In 1915, a midwife was struck off the professional register for cohabiting with a man who was not her husband, *Stock v Central Board of Midwives*.[32] The early cases heard by the General Nursing Council's Disciplinary and Penal Cases Committee concerned conduct that had little to do with professional work and much to

---

25   [1894] 1 QB 750.
26   [1967] 2 AC 259.
27   Smith, RG, *Medical Discipline: The Professional Conduct Jurisdiction of the General Medical Council, 1858–1990*, 1994, Oxford: OUP.
28   Jacob, J, *Doctors and Rules: A Sociology of Professional Values*, 1988, London: Routledge.
29   *Ibid*, Smith, fn 27.
30   [1987] 3 All ER 843.
31   [1996] 1 WLR 168.
32   [1915] 3 KB 756.

do with theft, fraud and general immorality.[33] There was perhaps an earlier concern with standards of professional practice than was seen with medicine,[34] but this is not clearly manifest in the overall pattern of the disciplinary jurisdiction. Today, however, most of the work of the UKCC is focused on allegations concerning misconduct in the delivery of care, rather than sexual and social morality.

In 1995–96 the Professional Conduct Committee of the UKCC considered 552 practice-related allegations and 42 that were not practice-related. The three main categories of practice-related misconduct allegations were 'physical/verbal abuse of patients/clients', 'failure to keep accurate records or report incidents' and 'failure/inappropriate attention to basic needs'.[35] It is interesting to note that the General Medical Council would not usually be concerned with record-keeping or verbal abuse. Smith's study of the GMC disciplinary work identified no case that would come into any of these three categories in 1990, although there was a series of 'failure to visit' allegations in 1989 that might be considered comparable to the 'inadequate attention to basic needs' categories.[36] The professional regulation of nursing, midwifery and health visiting is concerned with more mundane details of day-to-day care than the GMC.

The more intense scrutiny provided by the UKCC also extends to the sanctions applied. Just over half of those accused of failing to keep proper records or of inattention to basic needs, and nearly 70% of those accused of abusing clients, were disciplined. These are cases where there would probably not even have been jurisdiction to discipline under the medical scheme, in which many cases do not result in penalties being applied.[37] The contrast between medicine on the one hand and nursing, midwifery and health visiting on the other is not merely a matter of the broader range of conduct considered, it is also manifest in the probability of disciplinary action being taken. In consonance with its interests in the principles of good practice, the UKCC has used its jurisdiction to oversee the way in which the profession practises, not merely to weed out, identify and exclude miscreants. Women have felt the impact of being subject to professional regulation more firmly than have men.

Of particular interest is the way in which the UKCC's use of its disciplinary powers demonstrates the pressures perceived to threaten the

---

33  Pyne, RH, *Professional Discipline in Nursing, Midwifery and Health Visiting*, 1992, Oxford: Blackwell Scientific Publications.

34  Pyne, RH, *Professional Discipline in Nursing: Theory and Practice*, 1981, Oxford: Blackwell Scientific Publications, pp 22–27, Appendix C.

35  United Kingdom Central Council for Nursing, Midwifery and Health Visiting, *Statistical Analysis of the Council's Professional Register, 1 April 1995 to 31 March 1996*, 1996, London: UKCC, Vol 5, p 17.

36  *Op cit*, Smith, fn 27.

37  *Ibid*.

status of the professions. First, this is apparent in relation to the autonomy of nursing from medicine; a long-standing tension that is reflected in legal structures governing relations between the professions.[38] In one case, the UKCC struck a nurse off the register for failing to respect the demarcation of management responsibilities between nursing and medicine. The nurse had wrongly administered an additional immunisation to a baby. Rather than report the incident to her nurse manager, the nurse explained her mistake to a doctor, and gained reassurance that there would be no lasting adverse effect, although the child's temperature might be raised for a while. She passed this information on to the mother. By this conduct, the nurse demonstrated that she was prepared to acknowledge her responsibility for the error and take the necessary steps to protect her patient. She did not seek to hide the mistake from the mother and she recorded in the notes that she had administered the wrong injection. However, the UKCC found that the nurse had been guilty of professional misconduct in three respects; failing to check the prescription, administering the wrong immunisation, and failing to report the mistake to the senior nurse or health visitor. The Professional Conduct Committee proceeded to remove her name from the register.

When the nurse appealed to the court, it was held that the decision was seriously flawed, *Hefferon v Professional Conduct Committee of the UKCC*.[39] There was no evidence to support the allegation that she had failed to check what immunisation was due. There was no evidence that there was any system requiring the nurse to report such an incident to the nurse manager. In the absence of such a system, no reasonable committee could have concluded that there had been misconduct. In relation to the mistake itself, Watkins LJ found that there had been a simple error, the nurse had shown the utmost frankness and had taken care to ensure that no real harm would come to the child. In his view no reasonable professional conduct committee could have concluded that there had been misconduct. In relation to sentence, the judge restricted his criticisms to procedural flaws. However, it is surprising that the Committee should have applied its most severe penalty in a case that the court did not even find to be misconduct. The difference between the Committee's perception of what was at stake and that of the courts is stark.

The most convincing explanation for the seriousness with which the UKCC took the incident relates to the manner in which the nurse in question departed from the expected role of nurses in the health care team. From the nursing perspective, she failed to accept her own professional hierarchy, preferring to rely on direct communication with a doctor. The UKCC has pushed very strongly the independence of nursing from medicine,

---

38  Montgomery, J, 'Doctors' handmaidens: the legal contribution', in McVeigh, S and Wheeler, S (eds), *Law, Health and Medical Regulation*, 1992, Aldershot: Dartmouth.
39  (1988) 10 BMLR 1.

championing the importance of nurses being managed by other nurses, who understand their professional skills. That position depends on clear lines of demarcation being drawn that were disregarded by nurse Hefferon. The fact that she took all the available steps to protect the individual patient did not prevent her falling foul of the UKCC because she betrayed her profession as a whole by accepting the authority of a doctor. The responsibility of conforming to the shared professional role of nurses overrode the freedom of individual action. It is hard to imagine the GMC taking such a view.

A second aspect of the disciplinary jurisdiction that is of interest is that of whistle blowing. The UKCC has advised practitioners that to fail to act 'knowing that a colleague or subordinate is improperly treating or abusing patients' is a ground for removal from the register.[40] Thus there is an expectation that nurses will act as a covert police force rooting out misconduct amongst their colleagues. The approach of the GMC is rather more circumscribed. There has long been a statement in the 'Blue Book' noting that doctors have 'a duty, where circumstances so warrant, to inform an appropriate body about a professional colleague whose behaviour may have raised a question of serious professional misconduct ...'. However, it appears as an exception to the general principle that 'it is improper for a doctor to disparage, whether directly or by implication, the professional skill, knowledge, qualifications or services of any other doctor ... and such disparagement may raise a question of serious professional misconduct'. Thus, doctors who sought to expose misconduct on the part of their colleagues risked themselves being found guilty of serious professional misconduct for doing so.

The ranking of the duty to raise concerns as a mere exception to the more general duty not to disparage colleagues makes it clear that the medical profession sees the vice of sullying the reputations of others as more serious than the need to bring wrongdoing to light. The new guidance, *Good Medical Practice*, does little to dispel this impression. There is now a clear statement of the duty to protect patients when a colleague's conduct or performance is a threat to them.[41] However, doctors are advised to act cautiously; doing their 'best to find out the facts' (implying that they may have misunderstood the situation because it is unlikely that there would be a real threat to patients), informing the employer or regulatory body 'if necessary' (implying that it will often not be) and being 'honest' in making comments (implying that the motives of whistle blowers may be suspect).[42] Further, there remains a conflicting obligation to preserve the reputation of other doctors:

---

40  United Kingdom Central Council for Nursing, Midwifery and Health Visiting, *... with a view to removal from the register ...?*, 1990, London: UKCC.

41  General Medical Council, *Good Medical Practice*, 1995, London: GMC, para 18.

42  *Ibid*, para 19.

... you must not make any patient doubt a colleague's knowledge or skills by making unnecessary or unsustainable comments about them.[43]

The GMC remains keen to protect individual doctors from criticism unless the case is compelling. It is the whistle blower's responsibility to seek to establish the facts before raising concerns. The UKCC advises its practitioners to raise concerns without this form of self-censorship.[44]

What can be seen from this analysis of the two disciplinary jurisdictions is that the regulation of medicine reserves its powers to deal with individuals who are regarded as deviating seriously from the norms of professional practice. The limitation of the jurisdiction to cases of 'serious' misconduct ensures that there is little continuity between the disciplinary cases and everyday dilemmas. The approach to whistle blowing suggests a suspicion that allegations of misconduct will be more often unfounded than true. The UKCC, on the other hand, examines a far broader range of allegations, there being no threshold of seriousness to overcome, and regards aspects of ordinary practice as firmly within its remit. It sees the disciplinary jurisdiction as a tool to disseminate its views on how nurses, midwives and health visitors should behave, publishing special guidance on what constitutes 'professional misconduct'[45] and encouraging practitioners to attend hearings before the Professional Conduct Committee for their educational value. For the UKCC, the disciplinary jurisdiction is another opportunity to define professional norms and encourage good practice; for the GMC it is merely a mechanism for punishing those who breach the code of medical honour.

The General Medical Council's tool for focusing on standards of practice rather than immorality is the newly implemented system for dealing with doctors who are alleged to be incompetent rather than wicked. The Medical (Professional Performance) Act 1995 amended the Medical Act 1983 to provide for control over doctors whose professional performance is found to be seriously deficient. Ultimately, this regulatory function is carried out by a new Committee on Professional Performance, which has the power to suspend a doctor's registration, or to impose conditions upon it. However, before this Committee exercises its jurisdiction, the doctor concerned will have been given an opportunity to undergo assessment to identify shortcomings and to undertake remedial action to rectify them. Only after a reassessment showing that the problems persisted, or that the doctor refused to take the opportunity to use the assessment process to avoid the more formal procedures, would the full machinery of performance review come into play. The system thus ensures that individual doctors faced with doubts over their competence have a chance to control their destiny. Regulations will also

---

43  *Op cit*, fn 41, General Medical Council, para 24.
44  *Op cit*, fn 19, UKCC, pp 21–22.
45  *Op cit*, fn 40, UKCC.

provide them with an opportunity to accept the difficulties and resign from the profession by requesting that their names be removed from the register.

These new procedures mark an important shift in the understanding of the requirements of self-regulation on the part of the medical profession. The President of the General Medical Council has argued that there has grown up a perception that the profession has failed to demonstrate that self-regulation is effective and responsive to criticism. He suggests that a more transparent system for accountability can ensure that doctors remain independent. Professional self-regulation, he says, needs to be seen as 'positive and helpful, part of continuing education, personal professional development, and quality assurance'.[46] He links with the new model of regulation the developing interest in making explicit the 'core values' of medicine, as illustrated by the changing format of ethical guidance (see above). This transformation of the nature of self-regulation, from an inward-looking set of club rules into a mechanism for reassuring the public that their faith in doctors is justified, is also a movement towards the model of regulation with which nurses, midwives and health visitors are familiar. It subordinates individual desire for self-direction to the need to secure the privileged position of the profession as a whole.

# CONCLUSION

It has been shown that there are affinities between the drafting of the documents produced by the UKCC, and even the statutory formulations put before Parliament, and the feminine ethic of caring identified by Gilligan. While medical regulation has assumed and affirmed the norm of autonomous individuals and institutions, the oversight of the predominantly female professions has recognised the interdependence of practitioners and assumed that conformity to professional norms can be expected. Individual doctors' rights to clinical freedom have been championed by the GMC. The predominantly female members of the professions of nursing, midwifery and health visiting have not seen the UKCC promoting individual freedoms so much as collective responsibilities. It could be suggested that the UKCC embodies a victory for a feminine ethic of responsibility over a masculinist hunger for power, albeit at the expense of individual autonomy.

The pursuit of professional status for the female professions examined in this chapter was less to do with establishing autonomy than with status. Until recently, medicine was able to rest on its historical laurels. It did not need to justify its professional privileges and professional registration was introduced to reconfigure the organisation of an already privileged occupation in such a

---

46   Irvine, D, 'The performance of doctors I: professionalism in a changing world' (1997) 314 BMJ 1540.

way as to resist the encroachment of rival groups of healers into its market. There was no need for logic to the rationale of medicine's professional status because it was never in question. The women who sought similar privileges for their occupations had to justify them. Thus, the expertise and high moral character of practitioners had to be demonstrated, not merely asserted. To be convincing, the professions had to show that they could guarantee the quality of registered practitioners. Witz has shown how the strategies used by women to achieve professional status were adapted to the circumstances in which they were seeking it. What is being suggested here is that once that status is achieved the mode of regulation must also be seen in relation to the pressures on the continued respect for the professions' calling.

The strong grip on the practice of nurses, midwives and health visitors developed by the UKCC was primarily a defence against those who argued that they were not truly professions and threatened to reduce their status (or frustrate the professional establishment's project to enhance it). While this took the form of a collectivist interpretation of professionalism that fits the responsibility ethic of feminine moral reasoning, it can be seen from the transformation of medical regulation that this is not the whole picture. In the modern bureaucratic division of health labour, medicine, as much as the other professions, is being forced to demonstrate that its practice is genuinely based on expert knowledge: hence the vogue for evidence-based medicine. So too, it needs to show that the claims to a high ethic of altruism, on which the profession's supposed contract with society is based, are well founded. Hence the production of concrete statements and guidance on the core values of medicine. The claim for continued self-regulation now needs to be sustained by a clear commitment to rooting out incompetence. Thus medicine has been forced to adopt a more feminine model of professional regulation by the changing nature of the context in which it carries out its work.

It can be seen that the experience of being a professional in the predominantly female professions of nursing, midwifery and health visiting has been more constraining than it has been for that of doctors. Professional status has not won for women the autonomy that it gained for men for so many years. Furthermore, the drive for greater professionalisation is now unlikely to deliver those benefits (if indeed they are to be desired). The nature of professional power now available to health workers in the UK, as doctors are discovering, requires subordination to socially determined roles reinforced by professional discipline.

# CHAPTER FOUR

# INFORMED CONSENT IN PRACTICE

*Peggy Foster*

## INTRODUCTION

Consent in the context of modern medicine is, according to Ian Kennedy 'an ethical doctrine about respect for persons and about power. It seeks to transfer some power to the patient in areas affecting her self-determination, so as to create the optimal relationship between doctor and patient ... namely a partnership of shared endeavour in pursuit of the clients' interests'.[1] This view of doctors and patients as partners in a shared endeavour is clearly a modern version of the doctor-patient relationship which can be set against the more traditional paternalistic 'doctor knows best' approach to medical decision-making.

When I first began investigating the doctor-patient relationship in the mid 1970s, I was surprised by the extent to which the patients I interviewed did not think that the question 'What do you want your doctor to do for you today?' was appropriate. Several of them answered crossly that it was solely up to their doctor to determine what they needed. One patient even told me that she would put her hand in the fire if that was what her doctor recommended. The twin concepts of informed consent and patient autonomy clearly had little meaning or relevance to patients such as her. Since the 1970s, however, much has changed and, in general, patients are no longer quite so in awe of medical expertise as they were. An explosion of medical literature written for patients, self-help groups, World Wide Web sites and articles in the popular press have all begun to create a much more medically literate general public. Meanwhile politicians have also increasingly challenged the traditional autonomy of the medical profession. For example, in 1991 John Major's *Patient's Charter* emphasised that the NHS should 'always put the patient first' and advised patients that they had a pre-existing right 'to be given a clear explanation of any treatment proposed, including any risks and any alternatives before you decide whether you will agree to the treatment'.[2]

---

1 Kennedy, I, *Treat Me Right: Essays in Medical Law and Ethics*, 1991, Oxford: Clarendon Press, p 178.
2 Department of Health, *The Patient's Charter*, 1991, London: HMSO.

On the one hand, therefore, the late 20th century can be seen as a time when patients' rights, including the right to medical information, were strengthened, while doctors' traditional authority diminished. On the other hand, however, the late 20th century has also witnessed a dramatic increase in the medicalisation of all our lives. When Ivan Illich wrote *Medical Nemesis* in the mid 1970s, even he could hardly have predicted the extent to which modern medicine would expand its tentacles to touch not just those who felt unwell but virtually all healthy adults.[3] In Britain healthy adult women between the ages of 21 and 65 now receive an invitation to cervical screening at least once every five years, and women between the ages of 50 and 65 are invited to have a mammogram once every three years. These two screening programmes alone clearly represent a major enterprise for the NHS and involve millions of women annually in a very new and experimental form of modern medicine which is generally welcomed as life-saving. The consensus view that screening saves lives, however, has tended to obscure the potential hazards of mass screening programmes. Whilst many feminists have fully supported the implementation of national cervical and breast-screening programmes, others have suggested that such programmes form part of a wider net of medical control and surveillance over women that actually reduces their overall autonomy and well-being.[4] In particular, critics of the cancer-screening programmes aimed at women have argued that their failure to take seriously the ethical and legal issue of informed consent is quite unacceptable and seriously affects women's autonomy in this area of their lives.

According to Tina Posner:

As autonomous adults, potential (screening) programme participants need accurate information about the possible benefits, risks and costs of the screening test and any subsequent intervention in order to weigh up the pros and cons for themselves in the context of their own lives and to give fully informed consent. It is the ethical responsibility of the medical personnel involved to provide this information and to minimise the risks and costs to the individual whether physical or psychosocial.[5]

References such as this to 'autonomous adults' beg the question 'what exactly does it mean to be an autonomous adult in relation to one's own health and health care?'. Clearly the concept of autonomy in relation to complex medical decision-making is fraught with difficulty. For example, how autonomous is a woman who refuses a particular type of medical intervention primarily because her overbearing husband insists that he will not allow her to have it?

3    Illich, I, *Medical Nemesis: The Expropriation of Health*, 1975, London: Marion Boyars.

4    Foster, P, *Women and The Health Care Industry: An Unhealthy Relationship?*, 1995, Buckingham: Open University Press.

5    Posner, T, 'Ethical issues and the individual woman in cancer screening programmes' (1993) 2(3) *Journal of Advances in Health and Nursing Care* 55.

Unfortunately, or perhaps fortunately, limitations of space mean that this ethical debate will not be pursued further here, and the principle of informed consent will be explored in relation to healthy women's participation in cancer-screening programmes without fully linking this issue to the related one of women's autonomy over their own bodies and medical decision-making.

In this chapter the legal status of the ethical principle of informed consent will be briefly examined before the lack of information currently given to women on the risks of cervical and breast-screening is documented. The barriers to giving patients more information about the risks of screening will then be explored before possible ways of overcoming these barriers are put forward.

## THE LAW ON PATIENT CONSENT TO MEDICAL INTERVENTIONS

The principle that a patient has a legal right to be given enough information to give informed consent to medical treatment first emerged in America in 1957 in the case of *Salgo*, when the court concluded, in a landmark judgment, that the doctor had a duty to disclose to the patient 'any facts which are necessary to form the basis of an intelligent consent by the patient to the proposed treatment'.[6] This definition is simply a broad expression of principle which does not necessarily help to resolve specific court cases, but it has now become a central part of medical ethics. Moreover in both the USA and Canada the legal test in relation to informed consent is now one of what the reasonable patient would want to know. Thus, according to the American courts in *Canterbury v Spence*,[7] doctors must tell their patients of any material risk inherent in a proposed line of treatment, and a risk is material when 'a *reasonable person* – in what the physician knows or should know to be the patient's position – would be likely to attach significance to the risk or cluster of risks in deciding whether or not to forgo the proposed therapy'. Likewise, for the Canadian Supreme Court in *Reibl v Hughes*,[8] emphasis was laid on the 'patient's right to know what risks are involved in undergoing or forgoing certain surgery or other treatment'. However, in this judgment the court did recognise a defence of 'therapeutic privilege' which justified a doctor withholding or generalising information about which he would otherwise be more specific if a particular patient might 'because of emotional factors, be

---

6   *Salgo v Leland Stanford Junior Board of Trustees* 317 P 2d 170 (Cal, 1957), per Bray J.
7   464 F 2d 772 (DC, 1972).
8   (1980) 114 DLR (3d) 1.

unable to cope with facts relevant to the recommended surgery or treatment'.[9]

In the UK the law regulating consent now takes its starting point the very strong statement of patient autonomy set out in the case of *Re T* (1992) which provides that every mentally competent adult has an inviolable right to determine what is done to his or her own body:

> An adult patient who ... suffers from no mental incapacity has an absolute right to choose whether to consent to medical treatment, to refuse it or to choose one rather than another of the treatments being offered ... This right of choice is not limited to decisions which others might regard as sensible. It exists notwithstanding that the reasons for making the choice are rational, irrational, unknown or even non-existent.[10]

Transgression of this general principle will give rise to two possible civil law actions: battery and negligence, although in recent years the battery action has been used very infrequently. However, in Britain, partly perhaps as a means of avoiding excess litigation against doctors, the courts have tended to be relatively conservative in their definitions of informed consent. A number of legal judgments in British courts have left the ball more in the doctors' court by accepting that a doctor can withhold certain information from a patient, even where the patient specifically asks for it if other responsible doctors would have done likewise.[11] In other words if a doctor conforms to a responsible body of medical opinion in deciding what to tell and what not to tell patients, he/she has discharged his/her duty properly according to the British courts, even if a reasonable patient might well be assumed to have wanted more specific information about the disadvantages or risks of the line of action the doctor took.

According to Ian Kennedy, the present state of law in the UK, and the reluctance of British judges to override medical autonomy in such matters, 'fails to give proper recognition to the ethical principle of respect for autonomy' which would involve giving the patient:

> ... all information material to the decision of whether to consent to a particular treatment. It sets a standard for disclosure which reflects the views of the doctor as to what the patient ought to know rather than what the patient may actually wish to know. It therefore favours paternalism, albeit subject to an ill-defined power of review, over autonomy at a time when paternalism is increasingly seen as morally unacceptable and when the law in other contexts is increasingly recognising and enforcing the civil rights of the citizens.[12]

Despite the lack of a radical lead from the British courts, several authorities on medical law strongly argue that the tide of opinion is running in the direction

---

9    (1980) 114 DLR (3d) 1.

10   [1992] 4 All ER 649, *per* Lord Donaldson MR.

11   *Sidaway v Bethlem RHG* [1985] 1 All ER 643. Also see Sheldon, this volume.

12   *Op cit*, fn 1, Kennedy, p 214.

of supporting the principle of patient autonomy. Diana Brahams has argued, for example, that 'it is up to us to persuade doctors to alter their practice so as to divulge more information routinely and bring their standards up to what a prudent patient would like to know – without intervention of law'.[13] The arguments put forward in the following sections of this chapter are an attempt to contribute to this enterprise.

# THE CURRENT LACK OF INFORMATION ON
# THE RISKS OF SCREENING

Supporters of cervical and breast screening appear to assume that taking part in these screening programmes is self-evidently a good thing and not in any way equivalent to consenting to something as invasive, painful and potentially risky as surgery. Because these tests are assumed to save lives, any 'minor' disadvantages associated with them are usually accepted, by both doctors and the general public, as a small price well worth paying for protection against the very real threat of invasive cancer. Supporters of cervical and breast-screening programmes have therefore paid little attention to the ethical imperative of informed consent, and most literature on these two types of medical screening fails to consider this issue in any way. There is a general tendency to regard the tests themselves as relatively quick and simple without acknowledging that a woman who agrees to an initial test is also inherently agreeing to further investigation and even treatment if that test proves positive. It is much easier to say no to an initial screening test than to say no to further investigation of a suspicious or positive test result. Any individual who consents to be screened is therefore unwittingly consenting to a complex and potentially painful and invasive series of medical interventions that are an inherent part of any screening package. Once a woman has accepted an invitation to be screened she is in effect stepping on to a ride which usually starts off gently but has the potential to turn into a terrifying rollercoaster. Once the patient has stepped on to that ride it becomes almost impossible for either her or her doctor to stop it in mid flow.

None of this complexity is clearly explained to women invited for cancer screening. The smear test, in particular, has been 'sold' to women as a very simple procedure that is – at worst – just a little uncomfortable and embarrassing. Some patient information leaflets produced by local health authorities have not even informed women that the test involves a vaginal examination. The latest leaflet on NHS breast screening produced by the Health Education Authority does warn women that 'many women find the test uncomfortable and some find it painful', but it goes on, reassuringly, 'if

---

13  Mason, JK and McCall Smith, RA, *Law and Medical Ethics*, 4th edn, 1994, London: Butterworths.

you do experience some pain, this should last no longer than the test – just a few minutes'.[14] Yet we now have research evidence that shows that, for a minority of women at least, having a smear test or mammogram can be a distressing experience in its own right before any consideration is given to the further risks of unnecessary investigations and treatment following these tests. For example, one survey of over 700 women who had attended for a mammogram found that 26% of respondents agreed with the statement that the test had been painful and 6.4% agreed with the statement that the experience had been distressing.[15] One woman has described her pain during a mammogram as 'excruciating' and commented that it lasted in both breasts 'for three or four days before gradually subsiding'.[16] A survey of women in Tower Hamlets in the late 1980s found that 54% of women who had had a smear test reported that it was 'painful or uncomfortable' and 46% found it 'embarrassing'.[17] Whilst for most women this discomfort and embarrassment may be relatively minor, the fact that the smear test involves a vaginal examination can be particularly distressing to some women, for example, women who have been sexually assaulted.

Although we lack quantitative evidence on the nature of the distress that some women claim to have experienced during a smear test, one recent article did cite the case of a woman with learning difficulties who became so distressed when cervical screening 'was contemplated' that the idea had to be abandoned. The authors of this article also noted the trauma sometimes experienced by women who have been sexually abused and who recall memories of that abuse whilst undergoing a smear test. One such patient, according to this article, actually fainted whilst having the test but was later able to have a satisfactory smear taken.[18] Another woman has commented in relation to her experience of smear tests, 'I am a rape victim and I don't think doctors have even thought about how traumatic intimate examinations can be for a woman like me'.[19]

As well as the pain, embarrassment and even distress associated with the initial tests, an even greater disadvantage to participants of cancer-screening programmes is the risk of receiving a false positive result. Even strong supporters of screening accept that all screening tests carry this risk and

14 Health Education Authority, *NHS Breast Screening: The Facts*, 1996, London: Health Education Authority.

15 Orton, M *et al*, 'Factors affecting women's response to an invitation to attend for a second breast cancer screening examination' (1991) 41 *British Journal of General Practice* 320–23, p 321.

16 McTaggart, L, *What Doctors Don't Tell You*, 1996, London: Thorsons, p 84.

17 Schwartz, M, Savage, W, George, J and Emohare, L, 'Women's knowledge and experience of cervical screening: a failure of health education and medical organisation' (1989) 11(4) *Community Medicine* 287.

18 Seamark, C, 'Why women do not present for cervical smears – observations from general practice' (1996) 22 *The British Journal of Family Planning* 50.

19 Neustatter, A, 'The screening crisis' (1992) *New Woman*, April, p 38.

research has demonstrated that the risk of receiving a false positive result from a smear test or mammogram is relatively high. For example, according to Wright and Mueller, 'about 5% of screening mammograms are positive or suspicious and of these 80–90% are false positives that cause much unnecessary anxiety and further procedures including surgery'.[20] One Swedish study monitored 352 women who were eventually given the all clear after a positive mammogram result. Between them these women had 'suffered' 1,112 visits to doctors, 307 biopsies and 90 in-hospital surgical biopsies.[21]

The problem of false positive results from smear tests is complicated by the lack of medical consensus over the meaning of minor cervical abnormalities. Whilst some experts see even minor abnormalities as potentially dangerous, others have claimed that most minor abnormalities are self-limiting and will never progress to threaten a woman's life. Those who see minor abnormalities as mainly harmless have therefore argued that cervical screening is currently unnecessarily identifying very large numbers of women as having a potentially serious medical problem. For example, according to those responsible for the Bristol cervical screening programme, 'during each round (of screening) in Bristol over 15,000 healthy women are incorrectly told that they are "at risk (of developing cervical cancer)", over 5,500 women are being investigated, with many also treated for a disease that would never have troubled them'.[22]

The costs of false positive screening results to those women who receive them are generally agreed to be very high. Women who have received a positive smear test result have described fearing that they were going to die and even planning their own funeral.[23] Researchers have also found that a substantial number of women recalled for further investigation following a false positive mammogram reading continue to suffer intense anxiety for months and even years.[24] Not only do women receiving a positive test result suffer the trauma of a temporary diagnosis of 'possible cancer', they also must usually go through a series of invasive tests and some will also be treated for a disease they did not actually have. Critics of mammography screening have

20  Wright, CJ and Mueller, CB, 'Screening mammography and public policy: the need for perspective' (1995) 346 The Lancet 29.

21  Lidbrink, E, Elfving, J, Frisell, J and Jonsson, E, 'Neglected aspects of false positive findings of mammography in breast cancer screening: analysis of false positive cases from the Stockholm trial' (1996) 312 BMJ 273.

22  Raffle, AE, Alden, B, Mackenzie, EFD, 'Detection rates for abnormal cervical smears: what are we screening for?' (1995) 345 The Lancet 1472.

23  Posner, T, and Veesey, M, Prevention of Cervical Cancer: The Patient's View, 1988, London: King Edward's Hospital Fund for London, p 44.

24  Lerman, C et al 'Psychological and behavioral implications of abnormal mammograms' (1991) 114 Annals of Internal Medicine 657–61.

even claimed that many women are now undergoing unnecessary mastectomies as a result of it.[25]

Leaflets designed to explain cervical and breast-screening programmes to potential participants fail to warn women adequately of these major risks. They do now state that the tests are not 100% accurate and the Health Education Authority's most recent leaflet on breast cancer screening does emphasise that being recalled does not necessarily mean a woman has cancer,[26] but this information is designed to reassure women rather than alert them to a major risk of the screening programme. Similarly, the 1996 Health Education Authority leaflet on 'Your Smear Test' does reassure women that 'often (abnormal) cells return to normal by themselves'[27] but it does not point out the risk of being treated unnecessarily. Nor does this leaflet adequately warn women that the rate of false negative results from smear testing may be very high. For example, a study of the screening histories of all women diagnosed with invasive cervical cancer in Britain in 1992 found that 47% of these women had been adequately screened according to the current national guidelines.[28] Similarly, critics of mammography screening have claimed that the false reassurance of a negative mammogram is another serious issue, since 10–15% of early breast cancers are missed by mammography.[29] This means that a significant minority of women who are reassured by a negative mammography result are actually already suffering from breast cancer. In some cases this may lead women to ignore other signs of early breast cancer and thus delay, rather than promote, early treatment of the disease.

The risks and limitations of cervical and breast screening, particularly the risk of false positive results, have been explored within the confines of medical journals, but women invited for screening are given virtually no information about these self-same risks and limitations. Those providing cervical and breast cancer-screening programmes do now sometimes acknowledge that women have the right to make fully informed decisions about their own health and health care. In 1994, for example the National Co-ordinating Network for the NHS cervical screening programme listed as one of its specific programme objectives 'to give women information about the benefits and limitations of the cervical smear test'.[30] They also argued that the fact that all screening programmes 'must have false positives and false

---

25 Skrabanek, P and McCormick, J, *Follies and Fallacies in Medicine*, 1989, Glasgow: Tarragon Press, p 102.

26 Health Education Authority, *NHS Breast Screening: The Facts*, 1996, London: Health Education Authority.

27 Health Education Authority, *Your Smear Test*, 1996, London: Health Education Authority.

28 Sasieni, PD *et al*, 'Estimating the efficacy of screening by auditing smear histories of women with and without cervical cancer' (1996) 73 *British Journal of Cancer* 1001.

29 *Op cit*, fn 20, Wright and Mueller, p 31.

30 National Co-ordinating Network, *Report of the First Five Years of the NHS Cervical Screening Programme*, 1994, Oxford: National Co-ordinating Network, p 8.

negatives ... should be made clearly available to women being offered screening'.[31] The Network did not, however, take on the responsibility for educating women in this way, primarily on the grounds that they believed that such information would be most appropriately given by primary care teams.

Another example of those responsible for screening programmes accepting the principle of informed consent can be found in an undated document entitled 'Sheffield Cervical Working Party's Guide For Smear Takers' which stated:

> Individuals, whatever their state of health, have the right to self-determination ... the service should be provided in such a way that women receive support to make informed decisions about their health, about the screening test, about treatment offered and about the ways in which they receive care. To achieve this, professionals must share knowledge and information with women and enable them to make informed choices.[32]

Yet the leaflet on the smear test produced by the same working party was particularly uninformative. It did not mention that some women find this test embarrassing and even painful. It did not suggest any alternative ways in which women might protect themselves from cervical cancer if they did not wish to undergo a smear test, nor did it give them any information about the relative risks of developing cervical cancer compared to the likelihood of receiving some type of positive smear test result.

Although more recent patient leaflets on smear tests and mammograms do tend to give women a little more information about the inaccuracies of these tests compared to leaflets produced several years ago, there is still a strong emphasis in patient leaflets on encouraging women to be tested on a regular basis. For example, the Health Education Authority's 1996 'NHS Breast Screening: The Facts' leaflet concludes with 'when you receive an invitation to go for screening do accept it. It's well worth it. Breast screening makes sense. It could save your life',[33] whilst its 1996 leaflet on NHS cervical screening states that the policy of testing all women between the ages of 20 and 64 at least once every five years 'has been recommended by medical professionals' and concludes 'regular smear tests are important. They pick up the early warning signals that could save your life'.[34]

Thus, to date, there appears to have been no real attempt by screening providers, either nationally or locally, to enable women to make up their own minds about screening on the basis of unbiased information about the costs as well as the benefits of screening. There has been no public acknowledgment

---

31  *Op cit*, fn 30, National Co-ordinating Network, p 5.
32  Sheffield Cervical Cytology Call and Recall Programme, 'A Guide for all Smear Takers', undated, p 5.
33  *Op cit*, fn 26, Health Education Authority.
34  *Op cit*, fn 27, Health Education Authority.

that an individual woman might make a rational choice to decline a screening test on the grounds that her own risk of cancer appears to be low compared to the risks of over-treatment inherent in current screening procedures. In the next section we will explore why the policy of informed consent is not being put into practice even by those screening experts who appear to accept it in principle.

## BARRIERS TO INFORMED CONSENT TO SCREENING

In this section we will explore three major barriers to informed consent to smear tests and mammograms: first, doctors' belief that these types of tests save lives; second, the managerial and financial incentives to screen as many women as possible and third, the reputations and high status of screening experts.

The belief held by the vast majority of health care providers that cancer screening saves women's lives appears to lead many of them to accept as ethically justified even quite coercive techniques to improve uptake of screening. Modern medicine prides itself on being based on good scientific evidence, yet the smear test has never been evaluated by a controlled trial designed to prove that the benefits of screening outweigh the costs. The evidence that cervical screening saves lives is based on a decrease in the incidence of and mortality from cervical cancer in areas where screening has been introduced, but critics of screening point out that this evidence is unconvincing, since the rates of cervical cancer have also fallen in areas which have not benefited from an organised screening programme.[35] Nevertheless, in response to a questionnaire sent to over 500 GPs in the North West of England, 89% of respondents agreed with the statement 'I thoroughly agree with cervical screening'.[36] One GP, on reading a research report that stated that 44% of clinically invasive cancers of the cervix occurred in completely unscreened women, concluded 'any method that ensures screening and re-screening will take place automatically will contribute more than anything else to preventing invasive cancer of cervix'.[37]

In contrast to the smear test, a number of large, controlled trials have been conducted to test the efficacy of mammography screening. According to Wright and Mueller, four recent trials have failed to show a statistically significant reduction of deaths due to breast cancer for women at any age.[38] The widely quoted 30% reduction in mortality which is based on the results of

---

35   *Op cit*, fn 25, Skrabanek and McCormick.
36   Anderson, M, unpublished survey of GPs in the North West region, 1994.
37   Marshall, S, 'Any method to ensure screening is worthwhile' (1994) *Pulse*, 11 June, p 39.
38   *Op cit*, fn 20, Wright and Mueller.

some early trials is actually a relative reduction. It does not mean that the overall death rate from breast cancer could be reduced by a third even if take up rates of screening were very high.[39] Yet most screening providers cite as gospel the belief that for women over 50, regular screening can reduce breast cancer mortality by 30%.

Hundreds if not thousands of articles have now been published in medical journals world-wide, looking at ways to increase women's participation in cancer screening programmes, with titles such as 'Improving compliance with breast cancer screening in older women: results of randomised controlled trials'[40] and 'Can health education increase the uptake of cervical testing among Asian women?'[41] One article, entitled 'Breast cancer screening in older women: ethical issues',[42] typifies the general belief that screening is so self-evidently beneficial that doctors actually have a duty to persuade women to be screened. The author of this article claims that 'so much evidence has accrued about the efficacy of ... mammography ... that physicians are obligated to attempt to educate and persuade patients to have the screening done'.[43] She does accept that 'there should be no coercion involved'; however, she then argues that the reasons an older woman may give for not wanting screening procedures may seem 'silly or even crazy' and that the doctor should therefore 'persist in a gentle way in an attempt to persuade'. She goes on to suggest that where a patient is suffering from dementia 'a professional care giver could even give consent (for a mammogram) because the risk of the procedure is so minimal'.[44]

Several experts on cancer screening programmes have publicly announced that one of the key reasons for their disappointing impact on mortality rates is not any intrinsic weaknesses of the tests themselves but the problematic attitudes of women who fail to accept screening invitations. According to a headline in *The Times* in 1988, 'Women's fears may hinder scheme to fight breast cancer'. The article went on to cite the views of a Swedish specialist in breast cancer screening who believed that British women's 'ill-founded lack of confidence in medicine' was preventing them from seeking screening and that a campaign was needed aimed at changing these attitudes.[45]

---

39   Skrabanek, P, 'The debate over mass mammography in Britain: the case against' (1988) 297 BMJ 971–72.

40   Herman, CJ, Speroff, T and Cebul, R, 'Improving compliance with breast cancer screening in older women: results of randomised controlled trials' (1995) 155 *Archives of Internal Medicine* 717–22.

41   McAvoy, BR and Raza, R, 'Can health education increase uptake of cervical smear testing among Asian women?' (1991) 302 BMJ 333–36.

42   Cassel, C, 'Breast cancer screening in older women: ethical issues' (1992) 47 *The Journal of Gerontology* 126–30.

43   *Ibid*, p 126.

44   *Ibid*, p 127.

45   Prentice, T, 'Women's fears may hinder scheme to fight breast cancer' (1988) *The Times*, 11 November, p 6.

In 1990, when the results of a seven-year screening trial in Edinburgh produced a statistically insignificant gain in mortality rates, those responsible for the trial again blamed women's attitudes and their low attendance for the disappointing results and concluded 'a massive health education programme is required in the UK if attitudes are to change'.[46] Women's attitudes have also been blamed for the failure of the cervical screening programme to eradicate cervical cancer in Britain. For example, one cervical screening expert has blamed the 'complex attitudinal problem' of some women for the failure of the cervical screening programme to screen all those invited to have the test.[47]

Whilst most supporters of mammography simply exhort primary physicians to persuade their patients to accept mammography screening, cervical screening is encouraged through direct financial incentives to GPs to screen as many eligible patients as possible. Several of the GPs in a survey carried out in the North West admitted that their screening behaviour was being influenced by these financial incentives. One GP commented 'we are afraid of missing our targets, not missing a cancer', whilst another admitted 'I'm keen to do smears, but to be honest more for the targets than for benefit to patients'.[48] In 1990, a follow-up survey of two groups of GPs who had previously had high or low involvement with screening found that two-thirds of GPs in the low interest group had increased their cervical screening primarily as a response to financial incentives.[49]

The magazine *Financial Pulse*, which is distributed free to GPs, has advised doctors how to increase their earnings from their female patients by finding a medical reason for repeating a smear in a newly registered female who has already had a test in the last five years but not within general practice.[50] Such advice clearly verges on suggesting unnecessary repeat smear tests in order to boost their practice income. Another ethically suspect tactic for achieving screening targets, suggested by an article in *Update*, was to persuade some pensioners of the value of cervical screening even though 'in women more than 60 years old the procedure for taking smears can be both painful and yield insufficient material'.[51] Meanwhile an article in *Doctor* entitled 'Hit that target' reminded GPs that 'achieving the top target for ... cervical smears is not only good clinical practice but financially rewarding. And all practices are

46 Roberts, M *et al*, 'Edinburgh trial of screening for breast cancer: mortality at seven years' (1990) 335 *The Lancet* 245.

47 Dr Alistair Robertson, cited Lewis, C, 'GP cervical screening hits a ceiling' (1993) *Pulse*, 4 September, p 2.

48 *Op cit*, fn 36, Anderson.

49 Corney, R, 'Changes in preventive medicine among general practitioners' (1994) 24 *Health Trends* 139–42.

50 Blackburn, J, 'Women are key to high earnings' (1995) *Financial Pulse*, 22 February, p 45.

51 Mead, MG, 'How to achieve cervical cytology targets'(1989) *Update*, 1 December, p 1043.

capable of achieving these targets'.[52] GPs were then advised that it was essential to 'list and chase defaulters who have not responded (to an invitation for a smear test) within three months of the first invitation'.

There is also evidence that at least some GPs have followed such advice and put their female patients under considerable pressure to accept an invitation to a smear test. For example, according to Chomet and Chomet, some GPs have sent out cervical screening invitations to coincide with patients' birthdays and have sent them in the form of a 'congratulations card' offering a well woman check as a ' birthday present' and containing a definite appointment time which requires the patient to contact the practice either to confirm the appointment or to change the date. According to the authors of this article 'this invitation technique of a ready-booked appointment is more likely to trigger some kind of positive response than simply a recall invitation which the patient may put off indefinitely'.[53] Another article offering advice to GPs based on current 'good' practice suggested that 'reminders by telephone are more effective than standard letters' although the author does add 'but care must be taken not to coerce women against their will'.[54] The article then continued: 'Studies have shown that flagging the notes of non-attenders and offering them screening on an opportunistic basis increases uptake.'[55]

Although we have no research data on how women feel if they are contacted on several occasions with repeat invitations to attend for a smear test, sent very personal invitations to which they may feel obliged to reply, or even offered a smear test during a consultation for an unconnected medical problem, such tactics are clearly designed to put pressure on reluctant screening participants. The practice of 'opportunistic screening' is certainly unlikely to give the patient any time or private space to reflect on the benefits and risks of screening before deciding whether or not to proceed, particularly if the patient is actually having a vaginal examination for an unrelated reason at the time of the 'opportunistic' invitation.

Although most of the advice given to GPs on how to maximise their income from cervical screening is careful to avoid suggesting overtly coercive tactics, there have been occasional press reports of GPs threatening to cross cervical 'defaulters' off their practice lists. For example, in November 1990 the *Guardian* reported that one doctor, who stood to lose £1,300 if he did not reach his screening target, had threatened to strike 20 women off his list because they would not attend for a smear test.

---

52  Callen, D, 'Hit that target', *Doctor*, 12 October 1994, p 72.
53  Chomet, J and Chomet, J, 'Cervical screening in general practice: a "new" scenario' (1990) 300 BMJ 1505.
54  Austoker, J, 'Screening for cervical cancer' (1994) 309 BMJ 244.
55  *Ibid*, p 244.

Apart from the financial incentives attached to cervical screening, all health care providers involved in cancer-screening programmes currently have a strong incentive to increase levels of participation, since this is the key criterion being used to judge the success of these programmes. For example, the National Co-ordinating Network for the NHS Cervical Screening Programme has ruled out using the incidence of invasive cancer as an indicator of screening effectiveness on the grounds that there is a long time delay between screening and the development of invasive cancer and because cancer registrations are incomplete.[56] Nor do they accept that mortality from cervical cancer can be used as the primary indicator of the screening programme effectiveness. Having ruled out using outcome measures to judge the national cervical screening programme, the co-ordinating committee focuses on the proportion of eligible women being adequately screened as one of its key evaluative criteria. The national target they have set is that 80% of eligible women aged 25–64 should have had an adequate smear within the preceding five years.[57] This sets a benchmark for local health authorities, some of which have set themselves even higher targets in terms of coverage.

When national or local targets are reached, everyone involved can give themselves a pat on the back. When a report by the National Co-ordinating Network for the cervical screening programme revealed that coverage of cervical screening had almost quadrupled in five years, the Chairwoman of the NCN, Dr Elaine Farmery, commented 'it's a tremendous achievement on the part of GPs and their primary health care teams'.[58] As far as the national breast-screening programme is concerned, those running the national programme emphasised from the start the need to achieve at least 70% uptake amongst women between the ages of 50 and 64. To achieve this goal, one of their key objectives was 'to promote positive attitudes towards breast screening and uptake of the service'.[59] As Cribb and Haran have pointed out, 'it would not be surprising if this resulted in unintended pressures on freedom of choice'.[60] The strong emphasis which those running the breast screening programme place on uptake is illustrated by the front cover of the British National Programme's 1996 Annual Review which featured the phrase 'a dramatic increase in just one year from 72% to 77% of women accepting the invitation for screening'.[61]

56  National Co-ordinating Network, *Assuring the Quality and Measuring the Effectiveness of Cervical Screening*, 1994, Oxford: National Co-ordinating Network, p 13.

57  *Ibid*, p 18.

58  Bingham, K, 'GPs praised for fall in cervical cancer deaths' (1994) *GP*, 15 October, p 2.

59  Cribb, A and Haran, D, 'The benefits and ethics of screening for breast cancer' (1991) 105 *Public Health* 66.

60  *Ibid*.

61  NHS Breast Cancer Screening Programme, *Review 1996*, 1996, Sheffield: NHS Breast Cancer Screening Programme.

Whilst most health care providers may well be primarily motivated by a desire to save lives, regardless of any other sorts of incentives to screen, much of the information on the benefits of screening on which they base their active support for screening comes from experts who have made their reputations in developing these pioneering programmes. Without wishing to accuse the medical profession of being peculiarly motivated by self-interest, it is important at least to note the element of empire-building which may contaminate the motives of screening enthusiasts. Before she herself died of breast cancer, Maureen Roberts, a former clinical director of the Edinburgh breast-screening project, wrote a very brave review of her own work in which she questioned whether mammography screening was the best way to tackle breast cancer. In this review Roberts commented:

> The current national screening programme seems prestigious and has consequently attracted many good people who want to set up a high quality service ... It is possibly in danger of becoming a highly technological service. There is also an air of evangelism, few people questioning what is actually being done. Are we brainwashing ourselves into thinking that we are making a dramatic impact on a serious disease before we brainwash the public? ... I hope very much that pressure is not put on women to attend. The decision must be theirs and a truthful account of the facts must be made available to the public and the individual patient. It will not be what they want to hear ... the currently expressed or strongly implied statement that if women attend for screening everything will be all right is not acceptable.[62]

Unfortunately Maureen Roberts' plea for women to be given more accurate information appears to have gone unheeded by those responsible for screening programmes, perhaps partly because so many reputations would now be at stake if women were to decide on the basis of more accurate information that they were more likely to be harmed than saved by taking part in these programmes. Finally, we should also briefly note that although most cancer screening in Britain is provided free of charge through the NHS, medical screening is nevertheless akin to an industry which not only employs large numbers of workers, some on very high rate of pay, but also presumably generates significant profits for those companies supplying all the equipment needed to take and then process the tests.

## THE WAY FORWARD

One simple way to reduce the possibility of coercive pressure being placed on women who may be reluctant to be screened would be to abandon input targets and stop measuring the success of breast and cervical screening programmes primarily according to their coverage. Supporters of screening

---

62   Roberts, M, 'Breast screening: time for a rethink' (1989) 299 BMJ 1154.

would claim that abandoning all national and local targets in terms of the coverage of these programmes would seriously jeopardise the outcome of screening in terms of its key goal of reducing overall mortality from breast and cervical cancer. This claim must be taken seriously by all those who have criticised screening enthusiasts for overriding the autonomy of healthy individuals 'for their own ultimate good'. The view of many medical ethicists, however, is that such a paternalistic approach to patients is outdated and unethical. According to a number of critics of mass screening programmes, the rights of the individual patient to make an informed choice about whether or not to be screened should not be sacrificed in the interests of the greater good of women as a whole, particularly when the actual size of that greater good is far from clear. Therefore, even at the expense of a slight increase in mortality from cancer, critics of the current screening programmes argue that there is an ethical imperative to give individual women more accurate information about the risks to them of undergoing screening.

Abandoning national and local targets on screening uptake would certainly provide a much less coercive framework for screening and enable women to say no to any invitation for a test without coming under such pressure from screening providers worried about missing their targets. Unfortunately, policy makers and screening providers are all so wedded to measuring their success in terms of these targets that it is very difficult to imagine a major change of policy away from targets in the foreseeable future, particularly as any such change would be greeted by howls of protest from all those convinced that it was primarily a cost-cutting exercise which would endanger women's health.

A less radical change to screening policy would be to keep national targets in terms of identifying eligible women and inviting them to be screened, but to build in the safeguard of allowing women to opt out. At present, statistics on the proportion of eligible women screened give no information on the numbers of women who have received their invitation, understood it and still declined it for reasons best known to themselves. In particular the targets for cervical screening do not currently allow GPs to include recorded refusals in their returns. Women who are recorded as having declined an invitation to be screened, for whatever reason, should be counted in rather than out of any targets set. Women not wishing to be screened for cervical cancer should certainly not have to identify themselves as 'virgins' or 'sexually abused' or any other category which some screeners now accept as legitimate 'excuses' for missing a smear test.[63] Being granted medical permission to opt out of screening without being further pursued or persuaded is hardly the same as being given the right to fully informed consent to screening, but it would

---

63  See, for example, Seamark, C, 'Why women do not present for cervical smears – observations from general practice' (1996) 22 *The British Journal of Family Planning* 50–52.

nevertheless be a significant advance on the current situation in terms of respecting individuals' autonomy in relation to preventive medicine.

Another step forward in screening policy would be to ensure that patient leaflets on the smear test and mammograms included some brief information on alternative approaches to cancer prevention in order to give all women a more genuine choice of action. The current emphasis on screening as the key to reducing the incidence of cervical cancer completely ignores primary prevention strategies that might prevent women from contracting the sexually transmitted agent that is now believed to cause most cases of cervical cancer. The latest Health Education Authority patient information leaflet on cervical screening, for example, fails to tell women that using a barrier method of contraception might well be an effective alternative way of preventing cervical cancer,[64] particularly for those women who find smear tests painful and/or distressing. Unfortunately there is, as yet, no very firm evidence that any particular primary prevention strategy such as a change in diet can actually protect women from breast cancer,[65] despite some health education experts advising women to switch to a low-fat diet. Nevertheless leaflets on breast cancer screening could suggest that women who decide not to attend for mammogram screening could still take steps to protect themselves from advanced cancer by reporting any changes in the appearance or feel of their breasts to their GP without delay.

The above policy changes could be implemented by the Department for Health without any legal intervention. However, screening is politically popular, since women have been led to believe that it saves their lives. According to John Warden, a parliamentary lobby journalist, Norman Fowler 'knew he was on to a winner with MPs (to say nothing of the women's vote)' when he announced the government's plans for a nation-wide breast-screening service just before a general election in 1987.[66] Any national or government decision to reduce the scope of cervical and breast screening would probably be interpreted by the popular press as an outrageously mean attack on women's health care rights and thus prove very unpopular with the electorate. Not only are politicians reluctant to take the politically unpopular step of reducing any type of medical service, they are also, understandably, strongly influenced by current expert medical opinion. In recent years, more and more resources have been poured into health promotion and prevention programmes with only the occasional voice raised to suggest that the whole enterprise might be a late 20th century version of the emperor's new clothes. Although there is a significant and by no means tiny band of critics of modern

---

64    *Op cit*, fn 26, Health Education Authority.

65    See Hulka, B and Stark, AT, 'Breast cancer: cause and prevention' (1995) 346 *The Lancet* 884.

66    Warden, J, 'Prevention is politically popular' (1987) BMJ 657.

medicine who speak out against the futility and dangers of the ever-increasing medicalisation and medical control of women's lives, the voice of these critics is consistently drowned out by media portrayals of yet another life-saving medical breakthrough.

If those running the NHS are unlikely to put the principle of informed consent before the objective of maximising the coverage of cancer-screening programmes and if individual doctors who are sceptical of the benefits of screening nevertheless feel obliged to follow national policy in this area, we are left with the possibility of using the legal system to force through a change of policy on the information given to women about the cancer-screening programmes. However, it seems a very remote possibility that an individual woman harmed by unnecessary treatment following a false positive result from a cervical smear or mammogram will take her case to court, since a woman in this position is highly unlikely to realise that her treatment has been unnecessary. A woman given a cone biopsy after a 'suspicious' smear test result and colposcopy examination is far more likely to assume that modern medicine has saved her life than to question whether the diagnosis of 'pre-cancerous' changes was correct and the subsequent treatment really necessary. Similarly, a woman treated for carcinoma *in situ* of the breast, whether ductal or lobular, is not going to know that the experts do not yet know the best way to treat these small cancers[67] and that therefore many women may be receiving unnecessary radiotherapy and/or chemotherapy . Ironically, it is far more likely that doctors will be sued for failing to follow up positive test results than for unnecessarily treating a woman with a false positive result. One GP, for example, agreed to pay £200,000 damages awarded by the High Court to the family of a woman who died from cervical cancer after a failure to refer her for further investigation and treatment following a positive smear test result.

Given the complexity of the meaning of a false positive result in relation to cervical and breast screening, it seems likely that those wishing to strengthen individuals' rights to full information in screening programmes will have to rely on a knock-on effect from a legal judgment involving the issue of informed consent to another type of medical intervention. If British judges were unambiguously to endorse the principle that informed consent to surgery must be based on the rule that the doctor must give 'that information which a reasonable patient in the particular patient's position would wish to know',[68] rather than what responsible doctors decide would be in the best interests of the patient, the case for more information to be given to patients in all areas of modern medicine would be strengthened. It would certainly support the argument that all women invited for cervical and breast screening

---

67   *Op cit*, fn 61, NHS Breast Cancer Screening Programme, p 6.
68   *Op cit*, fn 1, Kennedy, p 215.

should have an enforceable right to know the potential risks as well as the benefits of their participation in what are, after all, experimental programmes.

As Peter Skarabanek and James McCormick have pointed out, the right of very sick patients asked to participate in clinical trials to be given full information about the risks of those trials is now legally well established, whilst the rights of healthy individuals taking part in screening programmes have been relatively ignored.[69] Yet surely healthy individuals who are approached by health care experts to use a particular medical service should have at least the same, if not greater, legal rights to full and accurate information about their medical options than sick individuals who approach medical experts seeking their help. If this argument is accepted by most lawyers, doctors and members of the public then the day must surely come when all healthy individuals will be given a clear legal right to be informed of the potential risks and limitations of any type of screening programme which is offered to them on an unsolicited basis. When this day comes, screening providers who fail to point out these limitations will lay themselves open to possible legal claims by those individuals who are persuaded to have a distressing test, further painful investigations, and even treatment, to prevent a disease which they then find out they did not have, never had, and in all likelihood probably never would have, without any form of medical intervention whatsoever.

---

69   Op cit, fn 25, Skrabanek and McCormick, p 109.

# CHAPTER FIVE

# FEMINIST PERSPECTIVES ON MENTAL HEALTH LAW

*Eileen V Fegan and Philip Fennell*

## INTRODUCTION

This chapter is an attempt to develop a practical feminist politics of mental health law. While all feminist analyses of psychiatry share the common aim of improving the management of women's mental ill-health, our concern is to foster a position vis à vis psychiatry and law which offers the best scope for the development of political action under existing institutional conditions. Earlier feminist analyses which portray psychiatry as a monolithic instrument serving uniformly to repress women and subjugate their 'true' nature have attracted increasing dissatisfaction due to their nihilistic implications and utopian ideals. It has thus become necessary to consider more constructive ways of responding to the observation that women's interests are not adequately represented in the current mental health care system.

In the preliminary section, the development of the feminist critique of psychiatry will be traced, paying attention to concerns raised by the often barbaric historical treatment of women by the psychiatric profession. It will then be argued that, although understandable, traditional feminist responses rejecting psychiatric intervention altogether have not led to any substantial (statistical) improvement in women's mental health, nor in their material position under the legislative regime.[1] The key focus throughout the following analysis of pressing contemporary questions surrounding the diagnosis and aetiology of women's mental illness, and of the administration of pyschotropic and surgical treatments without consent, will be on how such improvements may best be achieved. The practically oriented approach which develops, therefore, represents a significant shift away from the reliance upon a universalising theoretical framework, and incorporates more specific analyses of the gender implications of a number of contemporary legal and psychiatric practices, asking how each of these might be confronted and engaged with in a way which actually *benefits women*.

---

1   Whilst there are many issues relating to women's criminal responsibility, most notably the availability of the defence of provocation and the forced reliance on medical defences such as diminished responsibility, space does not permit their consideration here, and our focus will be on civil admissions.

## FEMINIST CRITIQUES OF PSYCHIATRY

Although the Mental Health Act 1983 applies equally to women and men, and regardless of ethnic origin, a superficial examination of mental health statistics would suggest that women are more prone to mental ill-health than men.[2] Evidence has also emerged that male patients of Afro-Caribbean ethnicity are more likely to be detained under its provisions, and once detained are more likely to be detained in conditions of security. Feminist and transcultural critiques of psychiatry have traditionally occupied similar political space in their denial that this reflects actual morbidity. Both deny a 'natural' correlation between femininity and minority ethnic status and actual incidence of mental disorder. Both draw attention to the causal connections between the experience of racism or patriarchy and mental pathology.

Indeed, feminist critiques of psychiatry produced during the 1960s and 1970s concentrated primarily on displacing the notion that the consistent over-representation of women confirmed patriarchal views of women as inherently unstable, irrational and prone to hysteria. Phyllis Chesler's *Women and Madness*, published in Britain in 1974, is an early example of a polemical work primarily aimed at accounting for the high incidence of diagnosed female mental disorder in terms of the social oppression of women. In so doing Chesler portrays the central project of psychiatry as the maintenance of patriarchal domination. Elaine Showalter's 1988 work develops this analysis, highlighting a disturbing

> ... equation between femininity and insanity which goes beyond statistical evidence ... [W]omen, within our dualistic systems of language and representation, are typically situated on the side of irrationality, silence, nature, and *the body*, while men are situated on the side of reason, discourse, culture and the mind.[3]

Showalter, too, portrays women's high rate of mental disorder as a product of their confining social roles and ironically, as a by-product of their mistreatment by a male-dominated and 'possibly misogynistic' psychiatric profession.[4] An important factor in the apparent over-representation of

---

2   Total admissions to mental illness specialities in England for 1994–95 show that of 216,240 admissions, 113,340 (approximately 53%) were women, and 101,870 (approximately 47%) were men. There are no reliable national statistics on ethnicity, age and social class in relation to psychiatric admissions.

3   Showalter, E, *A Female Malady: Women, Madness and English Culture 1830–1980*, 1987, London: Virago, pp 3–4 (emphasis added). Moreover, she considers the extent and persistence of this alliance overwhelming: 'While the name of the symbolic female disorder may change from one historical period to the next, the gender asymmetry of the representational tradition remains constant. Thus, madness, even when experienced by men, is metaphorically and symbolically represented as feminine: a female malady.' Ussher, J, *Women's Madness: Misogyny or Mental Illness?*, 1991, London: Harvester Wheatsheaf, p 20, further suggests that the association of femininity with weakness of mind and moral ineptitude is also a cross-cultural phenomenon.

4   *Ibid*, Showalter, p 3.

women is described by Goudsmit as the 'psychologisation of women's health problems – emphasis on psychological factors in illness where there is little or no evidence to justify it', where women who present complaining of physical symptoms are diagnosed as having a psychiatric problem and offered anti-depressant or tranquillising medicine, only to be found later to have a genuine physical complaint.[5]

Barnes and Maple summarise the extensive evidence showing that women are more often identified as being mentally ill than men, arguing that it is possible to understand this by reference to the circumstances of women in a male-dominated society.[6] They also argue that the question of what is defined as mental ill-health may also be a function of that domination, and the perpetuation of patriarchal attitudes in modern psychiatry, and indeed in general medicine. They would accept that psychiatry can reinforce sexual stereoptypes and repress women. Their analysis is less polemical than Chesler's and draws back from her contention that the maintenance of patriarchal dominance is the central project of psychiatry, even though it may be an incidental result of its activities.

Historical analysis of psychiatry provides ample evidence to support a theory based on the willing and knowing complicity of individual psychiatrists and other doctors in patriarchal dominance, and in locating the causes of women's insanity in female sexuality. A classic example of the latter is Dr Isaac Baker Brown, who wrote a book in 1866 concluding, from 'long and frequent observation' that 'a large number of affections peculiar to females depended on loss of nerve power and that this was produced by peripheral irritation arising originally in some branches of the pudic nerve, more particularly, the incident nerve supplying the clitoris'. During the 1860s and 1870s theories linking insanity to masturbation in both sexes enjoyed great credence. Baker Brown's solution, for his female patients, was clitoridectomy using surgical scissors, in his view 'more effective and humane' than the method favoured by many of his contemporaries, namely cauterisation with caustic substances. His book reported the results of 48 operations carried out in his London surgical home over a seven-year period, and refers also to a 'much larger number of cases occurring in private practice' which he was obliged to omit. In describing the favourable results of his activities, Baker Brown's case studies refer variously to women 'becoming in every respect a good wife', 'moving in high society and being outwardly admired,' and being restored to the society of family and friends.[7] Baker

5    Goudsmit, EM, 'All in Her Mind! Stereotypic Views and the Psychologisation of Women's Illness', in Wilkinson, S and Kitzinger, C (eds), *Women and Health: Feminist Perspectives*, 1994, London: Taylor and Francis, pp 7–12. See also Medawar, C, *Power and Dependence: Social Audit on the Safety of Medicines*, 1992, London: Social Audit.

6    Barnes, M and Maple, NA, *Women and Mental Health: Challenging the Stereotypes*, 1992, London: Venture Press, p 11.

7    Baker Brown, I, *On the Curability of Certain Forms of Epilepsy, Catalepsy and Hysteria in Females*, 1866, London: Hardwicke.

Brown was deprived of his fellowship of the Obstetrical Society, tantamount to being struck off, for carrying out these operations without consent from the women, their husbands, or their 'natural protectors'. Blistering by caustic substances continued to be widely used for at least another decade.

Psychosurgery continued to be widely practised in the United Kingdom in the 1940s and 1950s before the development in 1954 of neuroleptic drugs for schizophrenia. It is irreversible. A Ministry of Health survey of 10,365 patients who underwent the operation between 1942 and 1954 showed that 6,338 were women. Sixty-four percent of the patients had a diagnosis of schizophrenia, 25% had affective disorders and the rest had other diagnoses. Women were in the majority in all three categories.[8] The proponents of psychosurgery offer prime examples of psychiatrists claiming success when they have 'assisted' women to fit in with male oppression. The 1972 edition of William Sargant and Elliot Slater's standard British psychiatric text on physical treatments discusses the usefulness of psychosurgery in cases of reactive depression where 'irremediable environmental factors' are involved:

> A depressed woman, for instance, may owe her illness to a psychopathic husband who cannot change and will not accept treatment. Separation may be the answer, but is ruled out by other ties ... Patients of this type are often helped by anti-depressant drugs. But in the occasional case where they do not work, we have seen patients enabled by a leucotomy to return to a difficult environment and cope with it in a way which had hitherto been impossible.[9]

With such an ancestry it is understandable why earlier feminist observers sought to challenge modern psychiatry's self-perception as an authoritative discourse and a legitimate form of medical practice.

However, reflecting developments in other fields of feminist scholarship,[10] more recent analyses of psychiatry are moving away from the radical rejection of psychiatry as a discipline which exists primarily to maintain patriarchal dominance over women, toward more pragmatic efforts to develop a feminist politics of mental health with greater potential for reform. Central to Chesler's analysis, and that of other feminists, is that women's psychopathology is explicable in terms of the sex roles imposed by patriarchal society, and that psychiatry has been a willing accomplice in that process. A noted critic of this approach is Hilary Allen. She takes issue with three central conditions of early feminist analyses: the refusal to recognise any inherent vulnerability of women to psychiatric morbidity – without which it is assumed that such analysis could not be feminist; an explanation of women's psychopathology in

---

8   Fennell, P, *Treatment Without Consent: Law, Psychiatry and the Treatment of Mentally Disordered People Since 1845*, 1996, London: Routledge, p 138.

9   Sargant, W and Slater, E, *Introduction to Physical Treatments in Psychiatry*, 5th edn, 1972, Edinburgh: Livingstone, pp 105–06.

10  See Smart, C, *Feminism and the Power of Law*, 1989, London: Routledge; and Fegan, E, '"Ideology" after "discourse": a re-conceptualisation for feminist analyses of law' (1996) 23 JLS 173, for an appreciation of this 'post-structuralist' approach in feminist legal theory.

terms of overarching conditions to which, in principle, all women are assumed to be subject – without which it is assumed the analysis could not be theoretically adequate; and the attribution of patriarchal blame – without which it is assumed the analysis could not be political.[11]

In criticising Chesler and others, Allen does not in any way deny the need 'to break the long silence over the unspoken "she" of psychiatry and expose to feminist attention the wards and waiting rooms full of women who lurk behind the bland "he" of psychiatric textbooks'.[12] But she sees little value in attributing the over-representation of women in various diagnostic categories, such as, typically, depressive illness, to 'little more than femininity writ large'. The theorisation of women's depression, hysteria, anorexia, etc, as simply 'the perversely self-destructive exaggeration of those debilitating traits in which femininity is seen to inhere: dependency, self-effacement, emotionality, triviality, timidity, passivity',[13] amounts to nothing short of an ultimately damning acknowledgment of women as victims of a seemingly insurmountable patriarchal order.

Allen's critique would not deny that there is ample evidence of a pervasive sexism within psychiatry and in medicine generally, but to construe the *raison d'être* of all psychiatric treatment as the further enforcement of a debilitating femininity, that which initially occasioned the psychiatric intervention, she argues, is ultimately disempowering for women.[14] Thus, Allen's main quarrel with traditional feminist analysis lies in its attempts to provide overarching analysis. In her view it is not possible to explain all women's mental disorder in terms of material or ideological oppressions of women, that women's mental illness is explicable wholly in terms of over-conformity to, or rebellion against, stereotyped feminine roles. There must be space for a feminist politics, whether or not women are inherently more vulnerable than men to mental disorder, whether or not women's psychopathology can be theorised from the material or ideological oppression of women, and 'whether or not the patriarchy is to blame'.[15]

Allen would not deny that certain forms of distress can be explained by material or ideological oppression of women. A classic example is anorexia nervosa, which is said to be found in 1–3% of adolescent and young adult females. Anorexia is far more prevalent in industrialised societies where there

---

11   Allen, H, 'Psychiatry and the construction of the feminine', in Miller, P and Rose, N (eds), *The Power of Psychiatry*, 1986, London: Polity Press, pp 85–111.

12   *Ibid*, p 87.

13   *Ibid*, p 92.

14   *Ibid*, pp 92–93. Allen adds, '[s]mall comfort for women that Chesler's analysis denies any "essential" mental pathology of women, born of any "essential" femininity: the socially engendered pathology, born of a socially engendered femininity, seems almost equally ineluctable. All that seems to have shifted is the locus of responsibility for this unfortunate state of affairs from an inescapable nature to an inescapable patriarchy'.

15   *Ibid*, pp 108–09.

is an abundance of food and where, especially for females, attractiveness is linked to being thin.[16] Immigrants from cultures where the disorder is rare who immigrate to cultures where it is prevalent have been found to develop anorexia as thin body ideals are assimilated. Eating disorders may be triggered by stressful life events, but there is overwhelming evidence that they emanate from societal images of female attractiveness. Susan Bordo argues that anorexia is a cultural phenomenon linked to the particular situation of women in modern Western culture, which idealises both control of the mind over the body and the slenderness of women to such an extent that women who do not conform to the dominant, thin and well-toned images of feminine beauty are considered lacking in some fundamental respects.[17] Whilst acknowledging that many women do accept and indeed willingly participate in the creation of these very images (often making substantial economic and status gains as a result),[18] it remains difficult to accept psychiatric theories which claim a purely biological cause for eating disorders in a culture which feeds women on a daily basis with blatant and subliminal messages that only 'a perfect body will be rewarded by success in both their professional and personal lives'.

The international diagnostic manuals ICD-10[19] and DSM-IV[20] both contain categories of disorder which have been linked to women's biological make-up, but which can also be linked to societally imposed role expectations. The risk of severe post-natal depression (post-partum onset mood disorder) with psychotic symptoms is said to be from one in 500 to one in 1000 deliveries, with a much higher incidence of non-psychotic depression involving suicidal ideation, profound and uncontrollable guilt at not feeling 'how a new mother should feel'.[21] The question of how much of the aetiology of this disorder is explicable in terms of women's biology, and how much in such role expectations, remains largely unanswered. Yet the risks of suicide, self-harm and harm to the neonate may often lead to compulsory detention and treatment. A biological explanation of the disorder, coupled with an urgency to have the woman 'functioning normally as a mother' might dictate

---

16   American Psychiatric Association, *Diagnostic and Statistical Manual of the American Psychiatric Association* (DSM-IV), Washington DC: American Psychiatric Association, p 542.

17   Bordo, S, 'Anorexia nervosa: psychopathology as the crystallisation of culture', in Diamond, I and Quinby, L (eds), *Feminism and Foucault*, 1988, Boston: Northeastern University Press, pp 88–114.

18   As an important rider to Bordo's arguments, see Davies, K, 'Remaking the she devil: a critical look at feminist approaches to beauty' (1991) 6 *Hypatia* 21, who cautions against the view that all women's attempts to improve their appearance are necessarily (over)determined by oppressive cultural constructions of feminine beauty, since this depends upon a conception of women as 'devoid of agency', one which, we would agree, is ultimately destructive to the development of an empowering feminist theory and politics.

19   World Health Organisation, *International Classification of Diseases of the World Health Organisation* (ICD-10), Berne: World Health Organisation.

20   *Ibid*, fn 16, American Psychiatric Association.

21   *Ibid*, p 386.

that treatment take the form of drugs and electro-convulsive therapy, whereas a more long-term approach based on a conception of the aetiology grounded in societal role expectations might dictate a more psychological and psychotherapeutic approach (which would itself need to be free of sexism, racism, age and class bias).

Conversely, ignorance of the biological basis of women's mental disturbance may lead to deprivation of liberty and possibly invasive and inappropriate psychiatric treatment. A classic area for attention by feminists should be the treatment of pre-menstrual tension or syndrome. The DSM-IV states that studies report that pre-menstrual syndrome, variously defined, occurs in between 20–50% of women. The most severe category of pre-menstrual disorder is pre-menstrual disphoric disorder which produces the classic symptoms of depressive illness, including feelings of hopelessness, marked anxiety and tension, marked sudden sadness and sensitivity to rejection, persistent marked anger or irritability, increased interpersonal conflicts, possibly involving violence, decreased interest in everyday activities, and difficulty in concentrating. Yet, despite the recognition of PMS as producing psychiatric symptoms, there is evidence to show that women may receive a diagnosis of another mental disorder such as manic depressive psychosis, and be inappropriately admitted to secure psychiatric wards as a result. A recent study of 50 women in Whitchurch Hospital in Cardiff showed that women who had been diagnosed as manically depressed and showed violent behaviour underwent a dramatic improvement on the onset of menstruation. The women in the study, conducted by two psychiatric nurses, reported that their psychiatrists were unwilling to accept a menstrual link with their psychological symptoms.[22] The treatment of PMS is in a limbo between psychiatry and obstetrics and gynaecology. It can be treated by hormones or hormone analogue treatment. A leading specialist, Professor O'Briene, runs one of only two psycho-endocrine clinics in the UK for women with PMS. He is quoted in the press as having said that '[t]here are few gynaecologists who take PMS seriously because they say it is a psychiatric disorder and there are few psychiatrists who take it seriously because they say it is a hormonal disorder. No single speciality has taken on responsibility for dealing with this disorder'. So whilst certain forms of mental distress can be theorised in terms of women's material and ideological oppression, to account for all women's disorders in this way, in Allen's words, serves to 'distort the field of feminist attention'. Because legal definitions of mental illness and mental disorder are very broad and leave great discretion to psychiatrists, a woman with PMS who is behaving violently might be detained as suffering from a mental illness, or she might be detained under the catch-all 'any other disorder or disability of mind'.[23]

---

22  (1997) *The Western Mail*, 15 May.
23  Mental Health Act 1983, s 1.

Alternatively, if the cause of her behavioural symptoms was identified, she might receive treatment from an obstetrician without needing detention under mental health legislation. A denial of any link to female biology and a blindness to gender difference serve only to deny women access to effective therapy, and may even cause them to be detained as psychiatric in-patients when recognised treatment likely to benefit them could be provided by obstetricians, or even by alternative medicine.

To treat psychiatry and the psychiatric system as a homogeneous institution committed to reinforcing patriarchal oppression has the political consequence of rejecting it as a route to relief of women's mental distress, and the development of alternative women's therapies 'outside the psychiatric system'. This is unobjectionable for those lucky enough to be able to avail themselves of alternatives, and here, 'lucky' means financially well-off. However, it leaves undefended those women and members of minority ethnic communities who are caught up in the psychiatric system, either because they have access to, or know of, no alternative, or because they have been detained under the Mental Health Act. It is important to address the discrimination which afflicts these patients and to develop a feminist politics which addresses those factors already mentioned which militate against effective therapy. How can such a politics be developed in relation to the operation of mental health legislation?

## TREATMENTS AUTHORISED UNDER THE MENTAL HEALTH ACT 1983

### Detention

Almost 90% of non-offender psychiatric patients are admitted 'informally' without recourse to powers of detention. This does not necessarily mean that they have actively consented to admission. Informal patients include those who may not be capable of consenting to admission, who have not actively objected to it, or those who have chosen to enter hospital informally, knowing that if they do not, they will be 'sectioned'. The majority of informal admissions are women. Until very recently, the majority (55%) of compulsory admissions of non-offender patients to British psychiatric hospitals were women. In the early 1990s the gap narrowed, and by 1995–96 the proportion of women had fallen to 46%. Although compulsory admissions of women increased by almost 40% between 1990 and 1996, during the same period psychiatric detentions of males rose by 65%. We can only speculate as to possible explanations of these changes, but there may be social and material causes. Changes in the labour economy have caused more male unemployment and more women to become breadwinners, often through part-time work.

These developments may have led to men suffering the same pressures which hitherto have fallen primarily on women.

In order to be liable to psychiatric detention a person must be suffering from mental disorder, which is broadly defined in s 1 to include 'mental illness, psychopathic disorder, arrested or incomplete development of mind or any other disorder or disability of mind'. Mental illness is undefined in the legislation but it includes the psychotic illnesses (characterised by delusion or hallucination), most notably schizophrenia and manic depressive psychosis. It also includes depressive illnesses of all kinds, reactive depression, post-natal depression, the mental disorders of old age such as Alzheimer's Disease, and eating disorders such as anorexia and bulimia nervosa. 'Psychopathic disorder' means a persistent disorder or disability of mind which results in abnormally aggressive or seriously irresponsible conduct. Its broad ambit extends from the multiple rapist to the young woman patient who persistently harms herself. The diagnosis is rarely applied to non-offender patients and rarely applied to women. 'Arrested or incomplete development of mind' means learning disability, and the oblique 'any other disorder or disability of mind' encompasses other disorders from international diagnostic manuals not already included in the preceding categories.

Mental disorder of itself is not enough to justify detention, but nonetheless the criteria are broad. The disorder must be of a nature or degree which warrants detention in the interests of the person's health or safety or for the protection of others. Overt dangerousness to self or others is not required. A person may be detained on the paternalist grounds of necessity for his/her own health, and health includes mental health. An application for admission is made either by a specially qualified approved social worker, or the patient's nearest relative and, except in emergencies, must be supported by two medical recommendations, one from a doctor with special experience in the diagnosis or treatment of mental disorder.

Under Article 5 of the European Convention on Human Rights, no one may be subject to psychiatric detention, except in an emergency, unless there is objective evidence of a true mental disorder of a nature or degree warranting detention. We argue that this should entail a full assessment based on sensitivity to issues of gender, sexuality and ethnicity. The extent of psychiatry's blindness to these issues remains a significant problem in the admission process. The Whitchurch study of admissions of women with PMS who were given a diagnosis of manic depression is a classic example of the disastrous results which this can produce. The differences in rates of admission between men and women have been evident for many years, yet they remain largely unexplored in the psychiatric professional journals, apart from the odd article showing the therapeutic pitfalls of failing to take full case histories from women. The Mental Health Act Code of Practice provides only oblique references to the relevance of gender to admission assessments. It states that people being assessed for possible admission should receive respect and consideration of their individual qualities and diverse backgrounds – social, cultural, ethnic and religious – and should have their needs fully taken into account, although it is recognised that within available resources it may not always be possible to meet them. Those making the assessment should take into account, *inter alia*, the risk of making assumptions based on a person's sex, social and cultural background, or ethnic origin.[24] The Code of Practice is not law, but it may be referred to in legal proceedings, and explanations required for failure to follow its provisions.

A further issue is the treatment of lesbians and gay men. It is now more than 20 years since homosexuality was removed from the international psychiatric diagnostic manuals. Section 1(3) of the Mental Health Act states that no one shall be treated as suffering from mental disorder by reason only of sexual deviance. MIND (the National Association for Mental Health) has published a survey detailing the experiences of lesbian and gay men, which reports that many are living in a climate of fear, and are subject to physical assault, verbal abuse and discrimination when they use psychiatric services. Nearly three-quarters of those surveyed said they had suffered prejudice and discrimination and more than one in five suffered physical and sexual violence. More than half said that staff had used their homosexuality to explain their mental health problems.

There is an obvious need for the Royal College of Psychiatrists and the Central Council for the Education and Training of Social Workers to incorporate in their training special components on the importance of sensitivity to gender and sexuality in the assessment process. What are also needed are local small-scale studies of informal and compulsory psychiatric admissions which identify the psychiatric illnesses which women are diagnosed as suffering from, and whether the conditions justifying admission were own health, own safety or the protection of others. These studies need to take into account social class and ethnicity, so that an accurate picture of the epidemiology and causes of mental disorder may be attained, rather than the imperfect and incomplete one provided by national statistics.

# CONSENT TO TREATMENT

The common law is that every adult patient of sound mind has the right to refuse medical treatment, even if the consequence of the refusal will be his or her own death. This is so whether the reasons for the decision are rational, irrational, unknown or non-existent.[25] The right of bodily self-determination was described in 1904 in the US case of *Pratt v Davis* as 'the free citizen's first

---

24  Department of Health and the Welsh Office, Mental Health Act Code of Practice, 1993, paras 1.3 and 2.6.

25  *Re T* [1992] 4 All ER 649.

and greatest right, which underlies all others – the right to inviolability of his person; in other words, the right to himself'.[26] Or, we might add, 'herself', but would this be accurate? Is the right of self-determination available to a woman on the same terms as to a man? There are two circumstances where an adult may be treated without consent.

One is where she or he is detained under the Mental Health Act 1983. Until the 1970s, there was a widespread assumption amongst British psychiatrists that detained psychiatric patients, being by definition not 'free citizens', could be given treatment without consent. This assumption came under attack in the 1970s. The 1983 Act introduced new provisions in relation to consent to treatment for mental disorder, requiring consent for the most controversial treatments (psychosurgery and surgical hormone implants), and a second opinion if ECT or medicine for mental disorder is to be given without consent.[27] The other is where she or he lacks capacity at common law. The right of self-determination applies to adult patients who have the capacity to decide for themselves, prompting the question of when a person will be deemed to lack capacity. There is a presumption of capacity until shown to be incapable, which applies to all adults. It is for those alleging incapacity to demonstrate it according to legal criteria. The courts cannot force treatment on a capable adult, even in his or her best interests. Refusal for irrational reasons does not of itself amount to incapacity. However, it may be evidence of incapacity if the irrationality is the result of mental disorder, and the graver the consequences, the greater the capacity required.

In theory a woman has just as much right as a man to refuse treatment for irrational reasons, and in theory this applies across the medical spectrum. What is the position in practice?

## Treatment requiring consent under the 1983 Act

The 1983 Act provides that no one may be given psychosurgery or a surgical implantation of hormones for the reduction of male sex drive (female sex drive receives no equivalent protection) unless they have been independently certified to be capable of understanding its nature, purpose and likely effects and to have consented to it. Even then, the treatment may not proceed unless an independent second opinion doctor has certified that it ought to be given, having regard to the likelihood that it will alleviate or prevent deterioration in the patient's condition.[28] There has only been one referral for a surgical implant of hormones since 1983. The majority of cases have been for psychosurgery, with between 20 and 30 cases per year proceeding to

---

26   (1904) 37 *Chicago Leg News* 213; referred to in *Mohr v Williams* (1905) 104 NW 12, p 14.

27   *Op cit*, fn 8, Fennell, Chap 11.

28   Mental Health Act 1983, s 57.

operation. Between 1985 and 1993, 76 requests for psychosurgery second opinions were made involving males (including one hormone implant) and 135 for females. The figures are published by the Mental Health Act Commission without comment, and there is no indication that any research is under way as to why there might be such a preponderance of women.[29]

## Treatment without consent under the 1983 Act: ECT and medicines

Detained patients may be given treatment for mental disorder in the form of drugs or electro-convulsive therapy (ECT) without consent, subject to a system of second opinion safeguards set out in Part IV of the 1983 Act. In deciding whether to approve treatment, a second opinion doctor appointed by the Mental Health Act Commission (MHAC) applies the test of whether the treatment is likely to alleviate or prevent deterioration in the patient's condition and must consult a nurse and another person who have been professionally concerned with the patient's treatment. ECT has been in use in world psychiatry since its invention in 1938 by the Italians Cerletti and Bini. It is an established treatment for affective psychosis and depressive disorder, which are more prevalent in women. It is also used, albeit less frequently, in the treatment of schizophrenic psychosis. As any student of *Bolam v Friern Hospital Management Committee*[30] will know, the physical hazards of ECT are substantially reduced if it is given with muscle relaxants and an anaesthetic, but anaesthetics carry increased dangers for elderly patients. The risk of death has been estimated at 4.5 deaths per 100,000 treatments, which is low compared to the rate from overdoses of anti-depressant drugs.[31] The side effects of ECT include loss of memory which is usually temporary, but which may last for up to three months. However, some patients complain that they have never regained their memory properly.

Statistics produced by the Mental Health Act Commission show that women make up between 65% and 70% of second opinions for ECT whilst men are between 60% and 65% of the second opinions for medicines.[32] In a study of 1,009 second opinions carried out by Fennell in 1992, women were found to have proportionally more second opinions for ECT than men in all the largest diagnostic categories.[33] Many more women than men have second opinions for ECT. Substantial numbers of middle-aged and elderly women are being detained under the Mental Health Act and are having ECT in

---

29 Mental Health Act Commission, *First–Seventh Biennial Reports 1985–97*, London: HMSO.
30 [1957] 1 WLR 582.
31 Royal College of Psychiatrists, *The Use of Electro-Convulsive Therapy*, 1977, London: Royal College of Psychiatrists.
32 *Ibid*, Mental Health Act Commission.
33 *Op cit*, fn 8, Fennell, pp 196–200.

circumstances where they are either refusing or are unable to consent. A large proportion of the ECT work of second opinion doctors is for old people 'who have been detained because they cannot consent to ECT, even though they are already unprotestingly in hospital and the treatment is required because they are refusing food and fluids'. It might be said that the high numbers of older women reflect the fact that women live longer than men, and are more likely to suffer bereavement and social isolation, which are classic causal factors in these illnesses. It might also be said that the figures simply reflect the fact that it is a mainstream treatment for depressive disorders and that women are more often afflicted with these disorders than men. But this does not account for the fact that women tend to have ECT more than men even within diagnostic categories, whether or not they are illnesses for which ECT is a well-established and widely used treatment.

Opinion about ECT amongst those who have undergone it is deeply divided. Some patients say that it provides the only effective relief, whilst others say that it has done them harm. There is continuing controversy about the use of ECT with the very young and the elderly, with some doctors as well as survivors of the treatment asserting that it causes irreversible damage to the brain and mental function, whilst the bulk of the medical establishment insists that its use should not be ruled out on any age group on grounds that it may be essential to relieve acute depression.[34] We have already seen how feminist analysis of depression has built a convincing case for understanding its aetiology in the context of the effects of the ideological and material situation of women. Yet psychiatry still relies to a great extent on anti-depressants and ECT as the prime weapons against depression, with the effect that its underlying causes may remain unaddressed. Psychotherapy offers much more scope in this respect, but as an intensive, expensive and time-consuming process, it remains a peripheral form of treatment. The figures on the use of ECT on detained and non-consenting patients require further examination by a systematic long-term study of second opinions which is able to look at the circumstances in which the second opinion was sought, and which can shed light on the apparent over-representation of women.

## Physical treatment without consent

Part IV of the Mental Health Act applies only to treatment for mental disorder. If a detained patient is suffering from a physical disorder needing treatment, he or she has the right to refuse that treatment, provided he or she has capacity at common law to make a decision in relation to that treatment.

---

34  See Breggin, PR, *Electroshock: Its Brain Disabling Effects*, 1979, New York: Springer; Morgan, RF, *Electroshock: The Case Against*, 1991, Toronto: IPI Publishing; and Siddall, R, 'A Shock in the Dark' (1994) *Community Care* 26 May–1 June, pp 23–24.

Even psychiatric patients are entitled to the presumption of capacity, and it is for those alleging incapacity to demonstrate it. Whilst it is unwise to generalise from a small sample, it is noteworthy that the one case, *Re C*, where a detained patient's refusal of treatment for a physical disorder was upheld by the courts, involved a man. Mr C was a male schizophrenic patient aged 67, detained under the 1983 Act, who developed a gangrenous foot.[35] The hospital authorities wanted to amputate it. His refusal was upheld, even though it was possible that he would die without the amputation. The treatment was not for mental disorder and so s 63 did not come into play, even though the patient had a delusional belief that he was an internationally renowned surgeon who had successfully treated many patients with gangrene without operation. He believed that God and the good doctors would see him through without amputation. Thorpe J laid down the following common law test of capacity: A person must be capable of:

(a) understanding and retaining the relevant treatment information;

(b) believing it (ie their ability to believe it is not destroyed by the effects of mental disorder); and

(c) weighing it in the balance to make a choice.

Thorpe J held that the presumption of capacity had not been displaced, and upheld C's refusal. He was capable of understanding and retaining the treatment information, and 'in his own way' he believed it. At the time of writing Mr C is living on the south coast with both his feet. It is noteworthy that if Mr C had been refusing ECT he could have been given the treatment even if he was competent, subject to the approval of a second opinion doctor under s 58 that it was likely to alleviate or prevent deterioration in his condition. Treatment of a detained but competent patient without consent can be authorised by Part IV, provided the treatment is for mental disorder. Treatment for physical disorder is covered by common law.

However, the exclusion of physical treatments from the range of interventions which may be given without consent under Part IV has been significantly eroded by case law. No discussion of consent would be complete without reference to s 63 of the 1983 Act, in Lord Elton's words, included 'to put the legal position beyond doubt ... for the sake of the psychiatrists, nurses and other staff who care for these very troubled patients'.[36] It provides that any medical treatment for mental disorder not specifically identified under s 57 or s 58 of the 1983 Act as requiring a second opinion may be given to a detained patient without consent by or under the direction of the resident medical officer.

The key concept here is 'medical treatment for mental disorder' defined broadly to include 'nursing, and care, habilitation and rehabilitation under

---

35   *Re C (Adult: Refusal of Treatment)* [1994] 1 All ER 819.

36   *Hansard*, HL Deb, Ser 5, Vol 426, col 1064–65, 1982 (1 February).

medical supervision'. When faced with the criticism, which has since proved well founded, that s 63 might authorise a disturbingly wide range of interventions, Lord Elton emphasised that it was not intended to apply to 'borderline' or 'experimental' treatments but 'things which a person in hospital for treatment ought to undergo for his own good and for the good of the running of the hospital and for the good of other patients ... perfectly routine, sensible treatment'.[37]

Subsequent case law has made it clear that the section is not so confined. In *Re KB (Adult) (Mental Patient: Medical Treatment)* it was held that force-feeding a female detained patient suffering from anorexia nervosa can be 'treatment for mental disorder' covered by s 63.[38] Anorexia nervosa is viewed as a mental illness, and therefore force-feeding could be seen as a treatment of the symptoms of that disorder. Ewbank J said that relieving symptoms of the woman's disorder was just as much part of treatment as relieving the underlying cause.[39] In *B v Croydon HA*[40] the patient suffered from a borderline personality disorder (a form of psychopathic disorder) rather than anorexia (a form of mental illness), but the Court of Appeal held that s 63 applied to treatment directed at 'the symptoms or sequelae' of mental disorder just as much as to treatment directed to remedying B's core disorder, borderline personality disorder. This is characterised by low self-esteem and a compulsion to self-harm, and caused her compulsion not to eat. Ms B had been abused as a child and her personality disorder had its roots in her traumatic childhood. She had been treated by psychotherapy, which is the only effective treatment for such a disorder, but her therapist had changed jobs. She had written to the hospital authorities asking for psychotherapy and expressing her need to find out why she felt compelled to starve herself. Although the court authorised forcible feeding, she was transferred to another hospital and was not in the end forcibly fed. The case has engendered wide discussion amongst psychiatrists, with many arguing that to subject a victim of sexual abuse to a process whereby tubes are forcibly inserted into her body cannot fail to have adverse psychological effects.

The scope of treatment for mental disorder extended even more dramatically when s 63 was held to authorise the use of reasonable force to secure delivery of a baby by Caesarean section where the mother is a detained patient (*Tameside and Glossop Acute Services Trust v CH*).[41] The foetus was small for the gestational date, and the doctors feared placental failure. CH was receiving tranquillising drugs for her schizophrenia and it was felt that she needed to be given neuroleptic medication instead, which might have a

---

37   *Op cit*, fn 36, *Hansard*, col 1071.

38   (1994) 19 BMLR 144.

39   *Ibid*, p 146.

40   [1995] 1 All ER 683.

41   [1996] 1 FLR 762.

damaging affect on the foetus. It was therefore in the interests of her mental health that the pregnancy be brought to a swift conclusion to enable the new drug regime to start. Moreover, it was in the interests of her mental health that the baby be born alive, because otherwise she would blame the doctors, and this would exacerbate her schizophrenic illness. By this etiolated logic, Caesarean sections became treatments for mental disorder. It is evident from the reports of the case that all concerned were at pains to decide the case under the Mental Health Act rather than at common law, hence avoiding the possibility that force could be used on a non-detained patient. One of the grounds of deciding the case on the basis of s 63 rather than common law was that it was doubted whether reasonable force could be used under common law to impose the operation. In other words, the precedent could be confined to those who were detained under mental health legislation rather than extended to all women.

The line soon gave way. In *Norfolk and Norwich Healthcare (NHS) Trust v W*[42] it was held that where the mother lacks capacity but is not detained under the 1983 Act, reasonable force may be used to impose the treatment if it is necessary in her best interests. In *Rochdale Healthcare (NHS) Trust v C*[43] Johnson J authorised a Caesarean section under common law which was considered to be necessary within the hour if the foetus was to survive and risk of damage to the patient's health was to be avoided. Johnson J found the patient to be incapable of weighing up the information which she was given, the third element of the *Re C* test. He said this:

> The patient was in the throes of labour with all that is involved in terms of pain and emotional stress. I concluded that a patient who could, in those circumstances, speak in terms which seemed to accept the inevitability of her own death, was not a patient who was able properly to weigh up the considerations which arose so as to make any valid decision about anything of even the most trivial kind, still less one which involved her own life.

It would appear to curtail significantly the right of refusal for reasons which are irrational even if the consequences are one's own death, if acceptance of death's inevitability can be evidence destroying capacity.

In *Re L* a patient with a needle phobia was found to be suffering from a psychological affliction compelling her to act against medical advice with such force that her life would be in serious peril. In all these cases the courts emphasised that the decision was being taken in the mother's best interests, not those of the foetus. But it is always possible for the courts to find that it is in the mother's interests to uphold the foetus's interest in being born alive. In all these cases the women wanted the babies to be born alive, but for different reasons refused Caesareans.

---

42  [1996] 2 FLR 613.
43  [1997] 1 FCR 274.

In the latest case, *Re MB*, MB wanted a Caesarean, but could not consent to the anaesthetist's injection.[44] Here the risk of non-intervention to the foetus in terms of death or brain damage was about 50%, although there was little physical danger to the mother. Because of the risk to the foetus it was the practice to recommend that a breech presentation by the foot should always be delivered by Caesarean section. After the ultrasound scan Dr N explained to Ms MB the 50% risk of brain damage or death to the foetus of vaginal delivery, and she agreed to a Caesarean section. However, she had a needle phobia which led her to refuse the necessary anaesthetic injections. At 40 weeks pregnant, Ms MB was admitted to hospital on Friday 14 February. At 9.55 pm on 18 February 1997, Hollis J granted declarations over the telephone that it would be lawful for the consultant gynaecologist to operate to deliver the foetus by Caesarean section. Ms MB appealed to the Court of Appeal. The appeal was heard in open court at 11.00 pm on the same day, and the appeal was dismissed at 1.00 am the following day. MB then consented and the Caesarean proceeded. The Court of Appeal reserved their reasons and between judgment and the delivery of reasons the patient was examined by a psychiatrist to determine capacity.

It would seem that when the treatment decision is taken in the context of childbirth, a woman is much more at risk of being found incompetent. Sometimes this is for reasons connected with the process itself. Reassuringly, confusion, shock, fatigue, pain or drugs have all been held not of themselves to amount to incapacity. But all of them have been held to be capable of eroding capacity. It will be a fortunate women who does not hold all five of these unwelcome cards in her hand during childbirth. All five together may be deemed by some doctors to remove the right to respect for one's treatment decisions, and might result in a finding of temporary incompetence.

The most potent element in the cocktail however is the interests of the foetus, the forbidden ingredient, whose banishment is solemnly proclaimed by the law, but whose influence is everywhere. As in the previous cases, it was stressed in *Re MB* that the decision was to be taken in the mother's interests, not those of the foetus, but the courts could not make any decision if she had capacity to decide for herself. Until the moment of birth, the foetus has no rights which require its interests to be taken into account. But it is difficult to reconcile this banishment with the references to the foetus as 'the baby' and 'the unborn child' which pepper the narrative of Butler-Sloss LJ's judgment. More interesting are the references to Ms MB as 'the mother'. If 'the mother' wants the baby to be born alive, and even if she doesn't, then it will always be held to be in her best interests that this should happen, because otherwise she might suffer long-term psychological damage. The Court of Appeal in *Re MB* said that it *had* to be in the best interests of a woman carrying a full-term foetus, whom she wants to be born alive and healthy, that such a

---

44   (1997) 38 BMLR 175.

result should, if possible, be achieved. In MB's case there was psychiatric evidence vigorously supporting medical intervention as being in her best interests, that she was likely to suffer significant long-term damage if there was no operation and the child was born handicapped or died.

The test for incapacity laid down in *Re MB*[45] was as follows:

A person lacks capacity if some impairment or disturbance of mental functioning renders the person unable to make a decision whether to consent to or refuse treatment. Such inability to make a decision would occur when:

(a) the patient is unable to comprehend and retain the information which is material to the decision, especially as to the likely consequences of having or not having the treatment in question; or

(b) the patient is unable to use the information and weigh it in the balance as part of the process of arriving at a decision. If, as Thorpe J observed in *Re C*, a compulsive disorder or phobia from which the patient suffers stifles belief in the information presented to her, then the decision may not be a true one. As Lord Cockburn put it in *Banks v Goodfellow*,[46] '[o]ne object may be so forced upon the attention of the invalid as to shut out all others that might require consideration'.

In Ms MB's case the fear of needles prevented her from proceeding with the operation which she said she wanted. 'At the moment of panic ... her fear dominated all (the *Banks v Goodfellow* test).' 'At the actual point she was not capable of making a decision at all ... at that moment, the needle or mask dominated her thinking and made her quite unable to consider anything else.' She willed the end but could not accept the means. She was incapable of making any decision at all. She was at that moment suffering an impairment of her mental functioning which disabled her. She was temporarily incompetent. In the emergency, the doctors would be free to administer the anaesthetic if that were in her best interests.

In the cases to date, the women wanted the foetuses to be born alive, and in the needle phobia cases, they wanted to have a Caesarean to ensure that this happened. What if the mother is prepared to take the risk that the baby will be born dead or handicapped? This is a more difficult case. An irrational refusal will be upheld unless the irrationality is the result of mental disorder. Is this a decision which falls within the medical adaptation of the *Wednesbury* irrationality formula – 'so outrageous in its defiance of logic or of accepted moral standards that no sensible person who had applied his mind to the question to be decided could have arrived at it'? Even if a refusal is for irrational reasons, it will be upheld unless it is the result of mental disorder. Although not of itself amounting to incapacity, irrationality may be evidence of incapacity, for example because the irrational reason resulted from an irrational perception which was the result of mental disorder.

---

45  (1997) 38 BMLR 175, pp 186–87.

46  (1870) LR 5 QB 549, p 569.

There is great potential for overlap between irrationality and mental disorder. Both involve a cognitive and a moral dimension. Irrational decision-making in terms of outrageous defiance of logic or accepted moral standards can be viewed as key signs of mental disorder. Psychotic hallucinations or delusions are abnormal perceptions which outrageously defy logic. Irrational reasons resulting from delusional perceptions will be viewed as indicative of incapacity, because the irrational reason is induced by mental illness, as we can see from Lady Justice Butler-Sloss's example of someone thinking blood was poisoned because it is red. What of the moral component of irrationality, and indeed of mental disorder? A woman who says she does not wish to have a Caesarean in any circumstances, regardless of the risk to the foetus, will be met with disbelief – she cannot mean it, this cannot be what she really wants. If it is clear that this is what she really wants, questions will be asked about the rationality of her wishes. Do they outrageously defy accepted moral standards? What are accepted moral standards? The overwhelming social expectation bearing on pregnant women who have gone near to full term is that they should want what is best for the foetus. If they do not give paramountcy to the foetus' interests by refusing a Caesarean, the response is that it is not really what they want, that there must be something wrong with them mentally, and when they have come to their senses they will be thankful for having their refusal overridden. And if the outrageous defiance of moral or logical standards, the irrationality, stems from mental disorder it will not be upheld, but may be overridden.

Paradoxically, the exclusion of the foetus from legal status may actually strengthen the extent to which moral obligations to take account of its interests can be imposed on the mother, and women risk being thought 'unmaternally mad' if they do not succumb. The foetus has no legal status, no rights. What 'mother' in her right mind would fail to sacrifice herself for such a vulnerable creature? The weight of social and medical expectation would suggest that the sanity, and hence the capacity, of such a woman be questioned. Although allowed to be irrational and outrageously to defy accepted moral standards, where the survival of a foetus is concerned, outrageous defiance of accepted moral standards might also be viewed as a sign of a personality disorder, amounting to psychopathic disorder. Psychopathic disorder is a persistent disorder or disability of mind resulting in abnormally aggressive or seriously irresponsible conduct. Is it seriously irresponsible to refuse insistently a Caesarean regardless of the effect on the interests of the foetus?

How can a pregnant woman ensure that she is not subject to a forced Caesarean section, even if the life of the foetus will be at risk? At the time of delivery she may well be in a state of panic, she may well be under the influence of pain-killing drugs, and she may well appear indecisive, all of which, although not constitutive of incapacity, may be evidence tending to establish it. The only possibility would appear to be an advance refusal of treatment, made when the patient is competent and covering the circumstances which later arise. In many States in the USA, living-will legislation sets limits on the effectiveness of advance declarations made during the maker's pregnancy. Advance refusals of treatment are governed by common law in England, although the Law Commission report *Mental Incapacity* has recommended placing them on a statutory footing. The Law Commission recommended the creation of a statutory presumption that, unless there was an indication to the contrary, an advance refusal of treatment should not apply in circumstances where those having the care of the woman who made it consider that the refusal endangers the life of the foetus.[47] This would mean a refusal of a Caesarean would need to specify that it is intended to apply even if the life of the foetus is endangered.

The Court of Appeal made it clear that an application would only be entertained on the grounds that the patient was incapable, implying that the decision would be based on common law and that s 63 of the Mental Health Act would no longer be applied to these cases. But if there is an advance refusal made while competent which is intended to cover the circumstances which later arise, there would seem to be only one possible way of overcoming it. It may be overridden if the patient is detained under the Mental Health Act, and the Caesarean is a treatment covered by s 63, since a statutory regime will override the common law. The grounds for compulsory admission are wide. A woman could be admitted for assessment with treatment if she was suffering from mental illness, psychopathic disorder (personality disorder with abnormally aggressive or seriously irresponsible behaviour), learning disability (mental handicap) or any other disorder or disability of mind (which could include any phobias which appear in the international diagnostic manuals).

These cases raise the question of the scope of women's right of self-determination. Although the courts have resoundingly endorsed the right of competent women to refuse Caesareans, regardless of the interests of the foetus, their decisions have rendered the concept of incapacity so open-ended and have elided the interests of the mother with those of the foetus to such an extent, that the right of self-determination appears more rhetorical than real. It is interesting to note that traditionally, appeals to nature have been used to bring women into line, but in some of these cases women are being brought into line for wishing to let nature take its course rather than agreeing to medical intervention!

It might be objected to these arguments that women have the safeguard of a court hearing. At common law, if there is doubt about a woman's capacity, an application to the court will be necessary. In *Re MB*, the Court of Appeal heard the case in great haste and laid down guidelines as to how these difficulties might be avoided in the future. The court should be approached early in the pregnancy before the case becomes an emergency, to enable the

---

47   Law Commission, *Mental Incapacity*, Law Com No 231, 1995, London: HMSO.

parties, especially the 'mother', to be properly represented, and evidence to be heard, 'if appropriate', in an *inter partes* hearing. But it is inherently more likely that the women involved in these cases will not have been to ante-natal clinics before presenting at the end of pregnancy and resisting surgery or anaesthetic. The Court of Appeal said that 'there should in general be some evidence, preferably, but not necessarily, from a psychiatrist, as to the competence of the patient, if competence is in issue, and, time permitting, the person identified to give the evidence as to capacity should be made aware of the criteria for determining incapacity laid down in the judgment'. Despite this guidance, it is likely that many of these cases will be heard over the telephone, or in great haste, because of the urgency of the situation. Furthermore, women who do not want surgical intervention in their pregnancy but are aware that it might be forced on them will avoid ante-natal care totally, or at least wait until the last possible minute in order to avoid the possibility of a coerced Caesarean.

If a woman is detained under the Mental Health Act, it does not matter whether she is capable or not; the fact of detention will mean that a Caesarean can be authorised under s 63, if it is in the interests of her mental health. Women detained under the Mental Health Act are entitled to apply for review of their detention before a Mental Health Review Tribunal, which can order discharge if the preconditions of detention are not met. If a woman's detention is invalid, she cannot be treated under s 63. But a hearing takes some time to arrange, and it is unlikely that one could take place before the operation is carried out. In February 1997, Ms S challenged her detention under the Mental Health Act and the subsequent delivery of her baby by forced Caesarean, arguing that she had been treated as mentally disordered by reason of her refusal of a Caesarean section made during a visit to her GP. She had not been able to challenge her detention by seeking habeas corpus or appealing to a Mental Health Review Tribunal. A tribunal hearing could not be convened in time before the operation, and although Ms S had asked that the court order authorising the Caesarean be faxed to a solicitor so that she could challenge the treatment by habeas corpus, this had not happened. In this case, once the patient had been detained under the Mental Health Act, the 'safeguards against wrongful detention which would normally apply': appeal to a MHRT, or court application for judicial review, or habeas corpus, could not be implemented. She was not heard at the hearing, and the Caesarean went ahead without any effective review of the detention which formed the legal basis for the operation.[48]

It is only by stretching logic and the language of s 63 almost to breaking point that Caesareans can be viewed as treatment for mental disorder. The powers of psychiatric detention are operated by doctors and social workers, not courts. The processes of appeal following detention are largely ineffective

---

48   (1997) *The Independent*, 19 February.

in these cases. Psychiatric detention will trump an advance refusal made whilst capable and sufficiently clear in scope to cover the circumstances which later arise. The Official Solicitor has said that cases which come to his office will only proceed to court on the common law basis of incapacity rather than on the basis of s 63 of the 1983 Act. But there can be no guarantee that the courts will not proceed on the basis of s 63 if there is no alternative. Given these factors, if the right of self-determination is not to be completely eradicated, the Mental Health Act should be amended to provide that a Caesarean section shall not be regarded as a treatment for mental disorder. Then the question could be left to the common law which would decide on the basis of a finding of incapacity. As we have seen, this still leaves women at risk of forced Caesareans, but there at least a valid advance refusal would have to be recognised.

# CONCLUSION

The foregoing analysis has identified a number of sites for feminist political action in relation to mental health law. Because diagnosis of mental disorder may result in detention and forcible treatment, it is important to subject psychiatric diagnostic classifications to multiform feminist deconstruction in order to provide a more comprehensive and contextual understanding of women's mental ill-health. Just as there is no sole definable cause of women's apparent predisposition to psychiatric morbidity, neither is there a uniform prescription for how feminists ought to respond to it, nor of how we might best secure improvements in psychiatric, social and legal arrangements. Overarching analyses of psychiatry as an instrument of the patriarchy do little to help the post-natally depressed woman to whom the psychiatric services provide the only means to relieve her distress. Whilst it remains necessary to expose the partiality of psychiatric theories which anticipate female sexuality and biology as the indicator of all women's mental illness, thereby distracting attention away from other possible explanations which might be more beneficial to women,[49] an exclusive focus upon such deconstructive political efforts is insufficient to advance the need for gender sensitive medical research into areas which do have some physiological basis, such as pre-menstrual syndrome.

This is not to deny that further investigation into other possible social and environmental causes of women's mental illness, which 'challenge[s] the pre-eminence of medicine in understanding the origins of mental distress',[50] as in the case of anorexia, may lead to greater efforts to address the social, cultural

---

49  See Russell, D, 'Female bodies and food: a case of ethics and psychiatry' in Komesaroff, PA (ed), *Troubled Bodies: Critical Perspectives on Postmodernism, Medical Ethics and the Body*, 1995, Melbourne: Melbourne University Press, pp 222–34.

50  *Op cit*, fn 6, Barnes and Maple, p 1.

and economic factors underlying some of its manifestations. Indeed, recent research into the social bases of reactive depression suggests this approach is already recognised as fundamental in increasing social awareness about, and de-stigmatising, other predominantly 'female' disorders. However, as Allen argues, to adopt without question the assumption that a feminist analysis of psychiatry must 'account for the high incidence of diagnosed female pathology ... in terms that securely demonstrate its social aetiology in women's oppression',[51] no matter how well intended, offers little practical support for the disproportionately large number of women who make up the annual statistics. Since no universalising framework can account for or address the myriad of issues which impact upon the incidence, diagnosis and treatment of women's mental ill-health, it follows that any feminist strategy to improve their psychiatric care must be a multifaceted one, promoting immediate action in the areas that can be identified, while upholding a commitment to explore further those in which at present there is insufficient knowledge to base proposals for change.

Gender, race and class issues rarely find expression in legislation and case law, which are couched in universal language applying to all. However, awareness of gender and class is beginning to permeate 'soft law' such as the Code of Practice on the Mental Health Act 1983, in relation to assessment prior to compulsory admission. *The Patient's Charter for Mental Health Services* provides another example in relation to single-sex wards. Sexual harassment and sexual assault of women patients in mixed wards have become widely publicised in psychiatric journals, leading in some cases to a return to single-sex wards. *The Patient's Charter for Mental Health Services* entitles users to be told before they go into hospital whether it is intended to care for them in mixed-sex wards. In all cases they can expect single-sex washing and toilet facilities. Wishes to be cared for in single-sex wards are to be respected 'wherever possible', although the Charter recognises that there may be situations, especially emergencies, where a hospital cannot provide single-sex accommodation. The organisation, Women in Special Hospitals (WISH), has long argued against practices in the top security special hospitals whereby women were expected to socialise with male patients, many of whom were convicted sex offenders, as part of their joint rehabilitation. Whilst it may be difficult to achieve recognition of issues affecting women in legislation, a more effective strategy may be to press for reforms of codes and charters which have to be considered in applying the legislation, and which give patients some entitlements.

Beyond this, there is widespread feminist concern about the 'destructiveness of traditional approaches to women seeking psychiatric help'.[52] Respect for the autonomous treatment decisions of capable adults is a highly prized legal principle. A finding of incapacity, or detention under

---

51  *Op cit*, fn 11, Allen, p 87.
52  Smith, DE and David, SJ (eds), *Women look at Psychiatry*, 1975, Vancouver: Press Gang, p vi.

mental health legislation, can remove the right to that respect. In theory women and men are entitled to equal treatment under the law, but the force-feeding and Caesarean cases must lead us to question whether this is borne out in reality. In *B v Croydon*, B's own request for further psychotherapy instead of force-feeding did not even receive a reply from the hospital concerned, providing evidence of the persistent psychiatric (and legal) image of mentally distressed women as invariably irrational and unable to judge what is in their own 'best interests'. Contemporary case law resonates with echoes of 19th century notions of women needing decisions to be taken for them by 'their natural protectors', in this case the medical profession and the courts. The courts do not so readily intervene to protect men from their own decisions. And when one adds a foetus into the equation, the impulse to protect against self-determination becomes irresistible.

Consider the position of Mr C if he had been a pregnant women instead of a man with a gangrenous foot. What if she had a delusion that she was an internationally renowned gynaecologist who did not believe in Caesareans and had delivered many babies without recourse to surgery? What if she had believed that God and the good doctors would see her and the foetus through? If foetuses really have no legal status we would expect the result to be the same, but it would be most unlikely that a court faced with such a case would uphold such a refusal as competent. Feminist critiques of psychiatry emphasise the connection between the incidence of diagnosed mental disorder in women and the sense of loss of control over one's own life. Whilst autonomy cannot be treated as an absolute value, there can be no greater loss of control than the denial of autonomy in relation to one's own body. The Caesarean cases show that women are still at risk of having any behaviour which conflicts with 'accepted moral standards' attributed to an 'unstable psyche' by psychiatry and other powerful discourses, including law. We have suggested a practical legal reform of providing that treatment for mental disorder will not include Caesarean sections, but we also need to recognise that women, particularly pregnant women, though subject to the same rules on capacity, are likely to have them applied in a different way. In their case the concept of autonomy is modified and a finding of incapacity is more readily available. The rhetorical sleight of hand by which the pregnant woman's interests are conflated with those of her foetus must therefore be exposed and confronted. Only then will we be in a position to achieve Barnes and Maple's goal of a non-sexist mental health theory and practice which, in dismantling sex-based stereotypical notions of what constitutes 'normal' or healthy behaviour, would better serve the interests of both women and men in having their decisions and requests treated respectfully, and in being offered the psychiatric care they need.[53]

---

53   *Op cit*, fn 6, Barnes and Maple, p 9, note that men may be deprived of the potential benefits of mental health services because they are less likely to identify their problems and seek help for them in terms of mental distress.

# CHAPTER SIX

# BECAUSE WE CARE?
# THE MEDICAL TREATMENT OF CHILDREN

*Jo Bridgeman*

## INTRODUCTION

Whilst the cases within health care law are dominated by concerns with the extremes, where the spectre of death or sex stand near, the health care of ourselves and our children is more usually concerned with matters far more mundane. Considering both the ordinary and the extreme, this chapter explores legal responsibilities in relation to the health care of children from before birth to the age of majority and across the spectrum of medical intervention. Decisions made about health care on behalf of, and by, children are contemplated within the context of their relationships with those making the decisions and providing the care. Parental care enables children to develop from a position of dependence upon others for the provision of the basic requirements of good health to possessors of the skills necessary to take responsibility for their own well-being. At each stage parents and, when older, children negotiate with health care professionals to achieve the common aim of the good health of the child but, for reasons which I shall explore, not always in agreement as to the means or the ends of that goal. Parents may feel that they are being supervised by, rather than working with, professionals when carrying out their responsibilities in relation to the basic health care of their young child. Yet the surveillance and monitoring undertaken by professionals takes on a different guise with the initiation of legal action in the face of parental support for older children refusing their consent to treatment. That there may be disagreement between parents and professionals as to the appropriate treatment of the child (or whether to treat in the face of a refusal) should not mask the fact that both feel so strongly because, in different ways, they care. I suggest that insights may be gained into the different views of parents and professionals, the resort to legal advice and the conclusions reached by the courts in relation to whether the decision of an older child should be overridden in their best interests by examining the relationships between the child and those caring for her, whether as parent or professional. Drawing upon the work of Carol Gilligan and Robin West, I suggest that a feminist analysis may provide an explanation for decisions to provide medical treatment in the face of a refusal which may be experienced by the child as oppressive and, by identifying the reasons for those decisions, that an 'ethic of care' model of decision-making in relation to the medical treatment of children may be more appropriate than an approach based upon the abstract rights of the separate isolated individual. First, however, I want to locate decisions made by older children within the context of the care meted out to younger children and the insight which that provides into the relationships between parents and professionals.

## THE HEALTH OF CHILDREN

The medicalisation of everyday life has expanded the province of health care:

[A]n increasing emphasis on the prevention of disease, and on 'healthy' habits and lifestyles, shifts medicine into the lives of healthy people. Balanced diet, the amount of exercise taken, leisure activities, type of housing and heating, alcohol consumption, cigarette smoking, standards of cleanliness, body weight, all come under medical scrutiny in the name of disease prevention.[1]

In addition to the focus upon maintaining health, Agnes Miles identifies the development of medical technology and pharmaceutical products, the increase in professionals offering their expertise on aspects of everyday life and the classification as 'illness' of areas of life previously defined as deviant, such as crime or homosexuality, as features of the changing scope of health care.[2] Accompanying the shift to the prevention of illness is the imposition of responsibility upon individuals to ensure their own health.[3] Whilst mandated to take responsibility for our own health, women are also expected to ensure the health of their children. This responsibility commences before conception and remains throughout pregnancy, during which time women are expected to follow a healthy diet, to take regular moderate exercise and avoid toxins. During this time, the health of the mother and the development of the foetus are monitored, bringing women into contact with health professionals with whom she shares the goal of ensuring the well-being of her child (who at this stage is physically dependent upon her body). After birth and the physical separation of mother and child, the task of maintaining the health of children can be shared although, in many cases, the primary responsibility remains with the mother. In this role, she engages with a range of health care professionals who offer their help with, and supervision over, her performance of the task.[4]

---

1    Miles, A, *Women, health and medicine*, 1991, Milton Keynes: Open University Press, p 183.
2    *Ibid*, pp 183–84.
3    *Ibid*, p 183.
4    *Ibid*, p 201.

Supported after the birth by midwives and discharged into the care of primary health services,[5] the interrelationship between basic care and the health of children is apparent from birth. In their everyday care of children, ensuring cleanliness, the provision of a suitable diet and stimulation, a sense of security, stability and love, the basic requirements of physical and mental health are met by mothers: 'The underlying assumption of health professionals and lay people alike is that the general welfare of the family is the mother's business.'[6] Ensuring the health and well-being of their children demands that mothers develop skills both in negotiating the health care system when taking children for developmental checks or vaccinations and in making assessments of the need for medical aid for common childhood illnesses or accidental injury. In the everyday fulfilment of their responsibilities in ensuring the health of their children, mothers work with health professionals in a mutually dependent relationship in pursuance of a common goal. Yet, the sense that these duties are being performed under the surveillance of health professionals is an enduring one. Jane Lewis and Fennella Cannell quote Ferdinand Mount:

> Our feelings are mixed even in the case of the most helpful of all public visitors. The District Health Visitor, who visits mothers with babies, is often sweet and sensitive and genuinely useful. But – and it is an inescapable, embarrassing But – they cannot help being continually aware that she is there as an inspector as well as an advisor. Her eye roams the room and the baby for evidence of dirt, neglect, even brutality. This kindly middle-aged body has at her ultimate disposal a Stalinist array of powers.[7]

With young children who lack sufficient understanding and intelligence to make decisions regarding health care, the legal duty is upon parents[8] to give or refuse their consent according to their determination of the course of action which is in the best interests of the child. The law permits parents to consent to both everyday health care and to more extraordinary treatments, covering the range of intervention from the weighing and measuring of new-borns, vaccination against common childhood illness, the setting of broken limbs, to invasive treatment for leukaemia or a liver transplant. Further, parents may

---

5    See Montgomery, J, *Health Care Law*, 1997, Oxford: OUP, pp 395–96, 406–07.

6    *Op cit*, fn 1, Miles, p 203.

7    Mount, F, *The Subversive Family*, 1983, p 174, quoted by Lewis, J and Cannell, F, 'The politics of motherhood in the 1980s: Warnock, Gillick and feminists' (1986) 13 JLS 321, p 323.

8    From here on, I shall refer to parents as opposed to mothers. Although I am aware of no research on the issue, I believe that where the child's medical condition is serious (rather than everyday health care) decisions about medical treatment are made jointly by parents. Thus, the problem moves from a 'mothering' one (which may be fulfilled by a person of either sex) to a 'parenting' one (denoting, for my purposes here, shared responsibility). Further, consent to medical treatment can be given by anyone with parental responsibility (which is not commensurate with biological parenthood), including the local authority where the child is in care, and anyone with a residence order relating to the child.

refuse their consent to medical treatment, proposed by a health care professional, in the best interests of their child. Where basic health care of the child is concerned, parents will seek the advice of the array of experts available to them until they are satisfied with the advice or treatment given. Where parental refusal is considered damaging to the child, the surveillance function may prove operative and the social services profession become involved.[9] However, disagreement between health care professionals and parents over proposed treatment for more serious conditions may be subject to scrutiny by the court who, if they disagree with the conclusion as to best interests reached by the parents, will give consent.[10]

The relationship between parents, health care professionals and the court in relation to the provision of medical treatment to children is portrayed by Lord Donaldson MR in *Re J* as a partnership:

> No one can dictate the treatment to be given to the child, neither court, parents nor doctors. There are checks and balances. The doctors can recommend treatment A in preference to treatment B. They can also refuse to adopt treatment C on the grounds that it is medically contra-indicated or for some other reason is a treatment which they could not conscientiously administer. The court or parents for their part can refuse to consent to treatment A or B or both, but cannot insist on treatment C. The inevitable and desirable result is that choice of treatment is in some measure a joint decision of the doctors and the court or parents.[11]

The partnership may not, however, be one of equals. Whilst parents have primary responsibility for the everyday health of children, their refusal to consent to treatment may be overridden by the court, yet the court will not require health care professionals to act against their clinical judgment to provide treatment at the behest of parents.[12]

Whilst providing care and making decisions for children, parenting also involves equipping children with the skills to care for and make decisions for themselves. The older child may have a view as to the medical treatment she is prepared to undergo for her condition, a view which may differ from that held by her parents or the health care professionals caring for her. The question of law is the validity of any consent or refusal to consent given by an

---

9   An unreasonable refusal to consent to medical treatment may amount to the offence of 'wilful neglect' contrary to s 1(1) of the Children and Young Persons Act 1933.

10  *Re R (A Minor) (Blood Transfusion)* [1993] 2 FLR 757; *Re O (A Minor) (Medical Treatment)* [1993] 2 FLR 149; *Re S (A Minor) (Medical Treatment)* [1993] 1 FLR 396 – in all three cases the court gave consent to treatment involving the use of blood products refused by the parents. In comparison, in *Re T (A Minor) (Medical Treatment)* [1997] 1 WLR 242, the Court of Appeal considered that the mother's refusal of consent to a liver transplant was not unreasonable. For discussion of the court's perception of her role in caring for her son see Fox, M and McHale, J, 'In Whose Best Interests?' (1997) 60 MLR 700.

11  *Re J (A Minor) (Wardship: Medical Treatment)* [1990] 3 All ER 930, p 934.

12  *Re J (A Minor) (Child in Care: Medical Treatment)* [1992] 3 WLR 507, p 516 *per* Lord Donaldson MR.

older child. Consent is the legal expression of the right of rational, free-thinking, self-interested, isolated, autonomous individuals to bodily integrity and self-determination. As with younger children, the everyday health care of older children is secured through a process of negotiation with professionals although, depending upon the understanding of the child, they may participate in the negotiation process. It is with the more serious conditions and decisions relating to the treatment of them, where the decision of the child is perceived to jeopardise their well-being, health or life, that judicial involvement enables us to explore the resolution of conflicts between child, parents and health professionals.

# MAKING/TAKING DECISIONS

## *Gillick*: the drift of autonomy

Section 8 of the Family Law Reform Act 1969 creates a presumption that children aged 16 or over are competent to give a valid consent, but does not address the ability of children under that age to give a valid consent or the relevance of parental consent where the child has attained competence. Both were raised in *Gillick v West Norfolk and Wisbech AHA*[13] which confirmed the developmental nature of autonomy so that children (under the age of 16) are permitted to give consent to medical treatment (rendering parental consent unnecessary) where they have 'sufficient understanding and intelligence to understand the nature and implications of the proposed treatment'.[14] Respect for the bodily integrity and self-determination of autonomous individuals, values central to western liberal democracies, and the concomitant right to give a valid consent to medical treatment extend to older children. Despite the confirmation of autonomy as the foundation of child consent to medical treatment, the courts since *Gillick* have been reluctant to accept the consequences of that conclusion in cases where children have refused consent to proposed medical treatment.

## Regretting *Gilllick*?

### *Avoiding autonomy*

The House of Lords in *Gillick* confirmed that a child could consent to medical treatment as long as she understood what was proposed. What a child is required to understand depends upon the circumstances, that is, her condition

---

13   [1986] 1 AC 112.
14   *Ibid*, see Lord Scarman, pp 188–89; Lord Fraser, p 169.

and the treatment proposed. Whilst adults merely have to understand 'in broad terms ... the nature of the procedure',[15] a child will have to have a greater understanding before she can give a valid consent.[16] A child who does not have sufficient understanding of what is proposed lacks the qualities of an autonomous individual. Then, irrespective of her views, treatment may be carried out on the basis of consent given in her best interests by anyone with parental authority. One way in which the court has enabled the decisions of older children which may lead to deterioration in their health, or even death, to be pushed aside is by a determination that the child does not possess sufficient understanding given the circumstances of their condition and the proposed treatment.

In *Re E (A Minor) (Wardship: Medical Treatment)*,[17] E was a 15-year-old Jehovah's Witness who, having recently been diagnosed as suffering from leukaemia, refused his consent to the conventional treatment which necessitated blood transfusions. He had been given an alternative course of treatment. In view of the evidence that the course adopted was not working as well as expected, the hospital authority sought leave to treat by the conventional means. Ward J concluded that E did possess the intelligence necessary to make some decisions for himself, but that 'there is a range of decisions of which some are outside his ability fully to grasp their implications'.[18] In his Lordship's view, treatment refusal came within this latter category, because he did not have sufficient understanding of:

> ... the pain he has yet to suffer, of the fear that he will be undergoing, of the distress not only occasioned by that fear but also – and importantly – the distress he will inevitably suffer as he, a loving son, helplessly watches his parents' and his family's distress ... He may have some concept of the fact that he will die, but as to the manner of his death and to the extent of his and his family's suffering I find he has not the ability to turn his mind to it, nor the will to do so.[19]

Requiring an understanding of the emotional pain which would be caused to your family as they helplessly watch you die and the pain to the self from the knowledge that you are the cause of their agony before being able to give a valid refusal to life-saving treatment suggests that a child will never be able to

---

15  *Chatterton v Gerson* [1980] 3 WLR 1003; which they must (1) take in and retain, (2) believe, (3) weigh up balancing risks and needs, in *Re C (Adult: Refusal of Treatment)* [1994] 1 WLR 290, p 292, *per* Thorpe J. See Fegan and Fennell, this volume, for more discussion of this case.

16  The judgments are not, unfortunately, very clear as to exactly what is required for a sufficient understanding. Lord Scarman focuses upon the social and personal issues, p 189, Lord Fraser upon the medical information which the doctor must provide, p 174; see Montgomery, J, 'Children as property?' (1988) 51 MLR 323, pp 337–38.

17  [1993] 1 FLR 386. E is referred to in the judgment as A. To avoid confusion I shall use the initial E.

18  *Ibid*, p 391.

19  *Ibid*. Ward J further doubted whether E had made a free choice, see p 393.

refuse in such circumstances.[20] Likewise, in *Re S (A Minor) (Medical Treatment)*,[21] S refused her consent to blood transfusions she had been receiving monthly since birth for thalassaemia. S was fed up and Johnson J considered that this made her susceptible to the influence of Jehovah's Witnesses (her mother having converted to the faith), although not to the extent that her will had been overborne; however, '[i]t does not seem to me that her capacity is commensurate with the gravity of the decision which she has made'.[22] Following *E*: 'It seems to me that an understanding that she will die is not enough. For her decision to carry weight she should have a greater understanding of the manner of the death and pain and the distress'.[23]

## *Overriding autonomy*

Whilst in the cases mentioned so far the courts have gathered arguments in support of a view that the expressed decision was not autonomous, another approach has been for the courts to override the autonomous refusal and give consent to the proposed medical treatment. The first occasion was *Re W (A Minor) (Medical Treatment: Court's Jurisdiction)*,[24] in which W, 16 years old and suffering from anorexia, had refused her consent to be moved to a different treatment centre, wishing to remain where she was currently being treated. Lord Donaldson MR looked to s 8(3) of the Family Law Reform Act 1969 which provides that consent which would have been effective but for the enactment of that section remains so. Hence, his Lordship concluded that where a competent child was refusing her consent, the court or anyone with parental responsibility could give it.[25] Destroying, in one foul judgment, any meaningful role for older children in decisions relating to their medical treatment.

Similarly, in *South Glamorgan County Council v W and B*,[26] Douglas Brown J gave consent to the psychiatric examination and assessment of A at a Family and Adolescent Unit for up to eight weeks and for the use of means to restrain her and keep her at that unit. A was 15 years old and her behaviour had become increasingly bizarre to the extent that she had lived as a recluse in her

---

20 The same might be said of adults. However, adults are not required to attain this level of understanding, for them assessment of competence is centred upon 'treatment information' see fn 15 above and accompanying text. Upon attaining majority, E refused his consent and subsequently died.

21 [1994] 2 FLR 1065.

22 *Ibid*, p 1076.

23 *Ibid*.

24 [1992] 3 WLR 758.

25 Which is, in the words of Lord Donaldson MR, 'the legal "flak jacket" which protects the doctor from claims by the litigious' and although '[a]nyone who gives him a flak jacket (that is, consent) may take it back ... the doctor only needs one and so long as he continues to have one he has the legal right to proceed' [1992] 3 WLR 758, p 767.

26 [1993] 1 FLR 574.

bedroom for some 11 months prior to the application controlling her family by giving orders which were carried out on her threats of self-harm or committing suicide.[27] Section 38(6) of the Children Act 1989 provides that a child who possesses sufficient understanding may refuse to submit to a psychiatric examination or assessment directed by the court in an interim order or interim supervision order. Further, Douglas Brown J was 'not prepared to find ... that she is "*Gillick* incompetent"'.[28] However, taking lead from *Re W*, Douglas Brown J concluded that the Children Act 1989 did not remove the powers of the court so that, despite her ability to make an autonomous decision, the court made the order for her to receive psychiatric assessment aware that, because of her wishes to the contrary, it might be necessary to use restraint to keep her there.[29]

In *W* and *South Glamorgan*, as in an increasing number of cases concerning competent adult patients,[30] the court overrode the decisions of autonomous individuals and in *E* and *S* by requiring a greater understanding concluded that the expressed decisions were not autonomous. Why?

# WHY CAN'T WE LET THEM DECIDE?

## The limits of autonomy

Margaret Brazier and Caroline Bridge argue that these cases, in which judges have given consent to medical treatment refused by older children, demonstrate a failure on the part of the judiciary to understand the concept of autonomy (as well as an unacceptable wish to avoid use of the Mental Health Act 1983). They suggest that the children in the above cases had not made autonomous decisions because of 'defects in reason'[31] and that, in the words of John Harris, 'paternalistic interference in the lives of others' may be 'justified by imperfections in the autonomy of people's choices'.[32] Identifying further qualifications to autonomous decision-making clearly provides an explanation for the cases in which the decisions of older children have been

---

27  [1993] 1 FLR 574, pp 578–79.

28  *Ibid*, p 582.

29  To the contrary, the Children Act 1989 could be considered to be a paradigmatic example of law as 'increasingly child-user-friendly, eager to listen to children and take their preferences into account whenever possible', Roche, J, 'Children's rights: in the name of the child' (1995) 17 JSWFL 281, p 282.

30  For a discussion of the use of court orders where pregnant women refuse to consent to intervention proposed by health professionals as an illustration of unwillingness to accept as autonomous decisions of adults perceived to present a risk of deterioration in health or death, see Wells, this volume.

31  Brazier, M and Bridge, C, 'Coercion or caring: analysing adolescent autonomy' (1996) 16 LS 84.

32  Harris, J, *The Value of Life*, 1985, London: Routledge, p 195.

overridden. However, it does not seem to me to be a fruitful enterprise, for we can in that way hypothesise autonomy out of meaningful existence.

The reason for doing so may be that the decisions of these older children to refuse consent are regrettable, posing as they do the risk of deterioration in health or even death. Despite seeming to have understanding of their condition and the proposed treatment suggesting that their decisions should be respected, they are still only children and should not be permitted to make decisions with potentially fatal consequences under the age of majority. The finality of a decision which may lead to death prompts paternalistic intervention preventing them from making irreversible decisions until adulthood. Ward J, in *Re E*, expressed the view that, '[t]hose of us who have passed beyond callow youth can all remember convictions we have loudly proclaimed which we now find somewhat embarrassing'.[33] Johnson J, in *Re S*, did not invoke his own experiences but limited his consideration to the medical evidence relating to refusal of treatment by teenagers suffering from long-term conditions. For example, Dr J said of his experiences with diabetics: 'I find that if I can hold a situation for a year or so, by the age of 17 or so their added maturity leads to a change in attitude.'[34] Lord Donaldson MR, in *Re W*, noted W's wish to retain some control and decide for herself when to increase her food intake and the consequences of acceding to it: 'That she might leave it too late, does not seem to have occurred to her.'[35]

If we, as a society, do place such value upon autonomy, surely an autonomous decision must be respected for its quality as such, no matter what the consequences:

> ... it is the autonomous choice of the patient and not the Hippocratic principle of beneficence which justifies the medical intervention. The judgment, competence and skill of the doctor are merely placed at the disposal of the patient should they so choose. In so far as this choice is not obtained or is obtained but not respected by the attending physician, the patient is (literally) treated as a mere means to the end of the doctor, be that end however beneficial or (medically) necessary.[36]

Whilst paternalism provides a justification for treating older children in our better judgment, it does not, in my view, provide a sufficient explanation.[37] It

---

33    *Op cit*, fn 17, *Re E*, p 393.

34    *Op cit*, fn 21, *Re S*, p 1072.

35    *Op cit*, fn 24, *Re W*, p 769.

36    Harrington, J, 'Privileging the medical norm: liberalism, self-determination and refusal of treatment' (1996) 16 LS 348, p 350.

37    Paternalism is defined by Tom Beauchamp and James Childress as 'the intentional overriding of one person's known preferences or actions by another person, where the person who overrides justifies the action by the goal of benefiting or avoiding harm to the person whose will is overridden': Beauchamp, TL and Childress, JF, *Principles of Biomedical Ethics*, 1994, New York: OUP, p 274. Fine, but if we are all isolated autonomous individuals valuing separation from and fearing invasion by others, what motivates us to act paternalistically?

simply does not sit with an autonomy-respecting approach, for autonomy, as John Harris points out, surely brings with it the right to make decisions the autonomous may later regret (or even not live to regret).[38] Further, I can find no explanation for why, simply because of their age, the autonomous decisions of children should paternalistically be overridden. What is the motivation behind paternalistic intervention? Why do we (as a society, as medical professionals, legal professionals or parents) want to intervene to prevent competent children from refusing medical treatment and running the risk of harm or death? As Margaret Brazier and Caroline Bridge argue: 'If society is not prepared to allow adolescents to court unfavourable outcomes in judgments relating to medical treatment, we should say so openly,'[39] and we should have clear explanations as to why.

## Relationships of care

The importance placed within western liberal democracies upon the bodily integrity and self-determination of the autonomous individual has already been noted. The cases considering the refusal of older children to consent to medical treatment demonstrate the limitations of this model, based as it is upon abstract individuals and the prioritisation of competing rights. What can be detected from the judgments is the extent to which the search for a legal basis upon which to provide the treatment is motivated by the circumstances of existing relationships, a sense of responsibility and sentiments of care and affection.[40]

The problems presented by children refusing consent to treatment, thereby risking their health or life, may be resolved by parents or those seeking to fulfil professional caring responsibilities in terms of the 'ethic of care' identified by Carol Gilligan, rather than on the basis of the abstract rights of the autonomous individual.[41] Central to the ethic of care which Carol Gilligan heard in the 'different voice' of the women in her study are the activity of caring, the process of communication and mutual dependence upon the maintenance of relationships.[42] Whilst the ethic of justice takes an adversarial approach, prioritising competing abstract rights, the ethic of care reasons through a 'network of connection, a web of relationships'.[43] The ethic of

---

38  *Op cit*, fn 32, Harris, p 199.

39  *Op cit*, fn 31, Brazier and Bridge, p 109.

40  An interesting comparison is *Secretary of State for the Home Department v Robb* [1995] 1 All ER 677 in which Thorpe J presents Robb as an abstract rights-bearing individual rather than situating the legal problem posed by his refusal to eat within the context of existing relationships.

41  Gilligan, C, *In a Different Voice: Psychological Theory and Women's Development*, 1993, Cambridge, Mass: Harvard University Press.

42  *Ibid*, p 30.

43  *Ibid*, p 32.

justice approach posits individuals as essentially separate autonomy seekers who experience any limitation imposed upon their autonomy as an invasion, whilst the ethic of care approach, based upon the connections between people, mandates the provision of care.[44] Individuals are not conceived of as separate, commonly respecting the autonomy of others but located within a web of relationships such that '[r]esponsibility now includes both self and other, viewed as different but connected rather than as separate and opposed'.[45] Robin West argues that the value placed within liberal democracies upon autonomy follows from the perception of the individual as first and foremost a separate being who then reaches out to make contact with others.[46] She argues that women are not principally separate but are primarily connected such that:

> The potential for material connection with the other defines women's subjective, phenomenological and existential state ... Our potential for material connection engenders pleasures and pains, values and dangers, and attractions and fears, which are entirely different from those which follow, for men, from the necessity of separation.[47]

Consequently, women value not autonomy, but relationships with others, and 'intimacy with the "other" comes naturally. Caring, nurturance, and an ethic of love and responsibility for life is second nature'.[48]

Robin West acknowledges that not all men are 'separate' and not all women 'connected'. Men do physically connect at times in their lives and can care, love and nurture, yet it is the male power to construct society in their image which ensures that women remain primarily carers.[49] Carol Gilligan identified the 'different voice' in her research upon women but emphasises that 'the care perspective in my rendition is neither biologically determined nor unique to women'.[50] She found in her research that most people reason both in terms of justice and care – everyone has, if only from childhood, experienced inequality (justice) and connection (care) with another upon whom as a child they were dependent – but that one tends to dominate.[51] Where the circumstances raise questions of care and responsibility, such as the relationship which a health care professional has with his child patient, might it not be the case that those circumstances influence which mode of reasoning

---

44  *Op cit*, fn 41, Gilligan, p 38.

45  *Ibid*, p 147.

46  West, R, 'Jurisprudence and Gender' (1988) 55 *University of Chicago Law Review* 1.

47  *Ibid*, p 14.

48  *Ibid*, p 18.

49  *Ibid*, p 71.

50  Gilligan, C, 'Reply by Carol Gilligan'; Kerber, LK *et al*, 'On *In a Different Voice*: an interdisciplinary forum' (1986) *Signs* 304, p 327.

51  Gilligan, C, in Dubois, EC, Dunlop, MC, Gilligan, CJ, MacKinnon, CA and Menkel-Meadow, CJ, 'Feminist discourse, moral values and the law – a conversation' (1985) 34 *Buffalo Law Review* 11, pp 47–48.

dominates in relation to a problem presented by that child patient? Could this not also be the case with the judiciary, who see the power of the law as being to effect a particular outcome in respect of that child?

# PARENTAL CONNECTIONS

It might be expected that of all the parties involved with decisions relating to the medical treatment of children, the parents would be motivated by considerations of care, obligation and appreciation of interdependence, rather than the application of abstract concepts of conflicting and competing rights. My own assumption was that the love which parents felt and their own needs to ensure the well-being (even survival) of their child would position them in support of health care professionals seeking legal approval for medical treatment. Only S's father took this stance, the parents of E, the mother of S and the father in *South Glamorgan* supported the refusal of their children to the proposed medical treatment. Of course, caring for another is far more complex than simply wanting the other to be kept alive, extending to respect for their values, empathy for their wishes and sensitivity to their needs whilst avoiding causing them pain and preventing them from harm and reconciling all this with their own very real needs as parents of an extremely ill child.

E's parents, themselves Jehovah's Witnesses, supported him in his decision to refuse consent to the usual treatment for leukaemia which necessitated blood products: 'The parents oppose this application with a quiet but powerful reliance upon their religious beliefs.'[52] Ward J rejected the position taken by the parents: 'Parents may be free to become martyrs themselves, but it does not follow that they are free in identical circumstances to make martyrs of their children.'[53] S's mother had turned to the faith of Jehovah's Witnesses and felt that S should decide for herself whether she wanted to receive blood. Johnson J referred to the reports which were before the court by way of comment upon the family situation of S:

> Dr J said that there had been occasions when he and his team had been concerned at what the mother had said in front of S; for example, that she did not want S to have transfusions and would rather that S died. He was asked by Mr Daniel if that had not been a tactless remark on the part of the mother. Dr J said that he thought it was rather more than tactless.[54]

In both these cases, the court fails to acknowledge the importance of the faith of the parents in fulfilling their obligation to care for their child. A parent who believes that the soul is contaminated by the blood of another would perceive

---

52   *Op cit*, fn 17, *Re E*, p 389.

53   *Ibid*, p 394, quoting *Prince v Massachusetts* 321 US 158 (1944).

54   *Op cit*, fn 21, *Re S*, p 1073.

a blood transfusion as causing tremendous harm to their child. Whilst they may receive the support of those sharing their faith, they expose themselves to criticism from other sections within society. Yet, their position balances the sacrifice of their own emotions of love and affection and need for a continuing relationship with their child against the tenets of their faith directly relating to his or her future quality of life. Religious beliefs were not at issue in the *South Glamorgan* case in which A was described as exercising damaging control over her family. Douglas Brown J noted her father's 'strong wish that she be not removed by force from the room'.[55] His Lordship noted that A 'does not want to go to this unit. Her father is of the same state of mind and it may be – I do not know – that there is a connection between those two circumstances'.[56] The suggestion is that A's father's support for his daughter's decision is due to her domination of him rather than a compassionate appreciation of the violence necessary and the harm which would be caused to her by removing her forcibly from where she felt secure and by his apparent collusion in this outcome. The conflict posed for those with close emotional relationships with the child is most clearly acknowledged in *Re W*. W was an orphan, who had been in foster care as her aunt 'as the testamentary guardian of the children [was], through no fault of hers ... unable to care for them'.[57] Lord Donaldson MR acknowledged that W's aunt was:

> ... faced with an appalling dilemma. Naturally she was deeply involved emotionally. She very much wanted to respect W's wishes, but feared that some of the other adolescents in the unit were not helping W. She was also worried about the effect which the publicity might have on W's younger brother as well as on W herself. However, she was adamant that W must not be allowed to die.[58]

There was some recognition of the impact of W's refusal upon her aunt and brother as people emotionally connected to her who were intimately understanding of her sad past and whilst sensitive to the importance of W's wishes, also admitted their own desires to see her live a happier life and the hurt which they would suffer should she die.

The positions taken clearly show the conflict between the parents' own needs and those of their children and the extent to which the conclusion ultimately reached by them can only be appreciated in the light of all the circumstances of their relationships, their values and their understanding of the consequences of the alternatives.

---

55  *Op cit*, fn 26, *South Glamorgan County Council v W and B*, p 581.
56  *Ibid*, p 585.
57  *Op cit*, fn 24, *Re W*, p 761.
58  *Ibid*, p 763.

# PROFESSIONAL CONNECTIONS

## Health care professionals – why resort to legal action?

The health authority in *E* and the local authorities in *S*, *W* and *South Glamorgan* may have approached the court, upon legal advice, for consent or reassurance that the refusal was a competent refusal which should be respected. Again this analysis turns upon uncertainty surrounding autonomy, this time in apprehension of legal action and, if accepted, may provide a further concluding point for our consideration. However, fear of legal action may prove to be a real but not a sufficient explanation.

Health care professionals clearly do not have a 'blood' relationship with many of the children they treat, they may have built up a relationship with the child during the period in which the treatment has been given, and they will certainly have a 'professional' relationship with their patient. Their profession is the diagnosis and treatment of diseases and infections, the monitoring, improvement and restoration of health and the provision of palliative care. Can the cases not be explained in terms of the desire of the health care professionals to fulfil their professional responsibility to care for their patient? A child who is refusing medical treatment considered in the clinical judgment of the health care professionals to be in her best interests poses for those professionals a conflict between their own desire to carry out the recommended treatment and the duty to sacrifice this to the wishes expressed by the child. Both courses of action present the possibility of causing harm. Providing treatment which is clinically indicated involves the harm of treatment provided against the wishes of the child, possibly necessitating force causing indignity and trauma. Respecting the wishes of the child may result in a deterioration in their health or even death. It further harms the professionals who may have to witness the worsening condition of a child whom they believe they can help.[59] Either course of action has wider consequences, providing treatment may discourage resort to health care, respecting the refusal courts the possibility of criticism for effectively letting a child die. The balance arrived at by the health care professions is demonstrated by legal action and given voice to in the judgments. Weighing the balance in favour of treatment, the court in *E* and *South Glamorgan* denied that forced treatment would have any real adverse effects. In the former, Ward J rejected the view that the trauma resulting from forced treatment

---

59   There is no direct acknowledgment in the cases considered here of the impact of refusal upon the medical professionals. The feelings engendered by treatment refusal have been noted elsewhere. In the context of the treatment of anorexia, Rebecca Dresser suggests that, confronted with refusal, health care professionals may experience anger or find their patience exhausted as well as being forced to acknowledge their own mortality and wrestle with a complex set of emotions surrounding food and cultural pressures relating to body size: Dresser, R, 'Article and commentary on anorexia nervosa: feeding the hunger artists: legal issues in treating anorexia nervosa' (1984) 2 Wis L Rev 297.

would have a detrimental effect upon E's progress, believed that he would respond to the judgment of the court and that, in the balance, 'any emotional trauma in the immediate course of treatment or in the longer term will not outweigh, in my judgment, the emotional trauma of the pain and the fear of dying in the hideous way he could die' as 'graphically' described by Dr T.[60] Douglas Brown J accepted the medical evidence that forcibly removing A to a psychiatric unit for assessment and treatment would not have any lasting adverse effects and further was outweighed by 'the desperate need' for her to be treated:

> ... [the evidence of Dr Ahmed Darwish] was that it was essential and urgent that A be assessed psychiatrically as an in-patient now ... The way he put it was that time was running out for A. She needed assessment and therapy vigorously and immediately.[61]

S was prepared to submit to a court order although Johnson J noted that she 'has said on previous occasions that if it was forced upon her it would be like rape and it would be those who had done it who would be the sinners'.[62] His Lordship referred to the extent to which S was fed up with having to cope, daily, with her condition countered by evidence that this was common amongst teenagers with long term illnesses but that after a few years their attitudes tended to change. Further, even if it was necessary to force treatment upon her, medical evidence suggested, as with 'anorexics and diabetics', that '[w]ith the passage of time they come to recognise that what ... has [been] done has been right for them'.[63]

## The judiciary – selecting arguments of best interests

Legal method, the objective application of legal principles as determined in precedent to the facts of the case in order to achieve justice through the prioritisation of conflicting rights in accordance with established rules, may ensure that, whilst parents and health care professionals are motivated by the ethic of care, the conclusion of the court is arrived at firmly in accordance with justice. There can be detected within the judgments references to the abstract principles of self-determination and bodily integrity: 'S's right to determine what happens to her body should not be overridden lightly'.[64] In E, Ward J noted that: '[t]he law must recognise that fundamental principle that adults of full capacity have freedom of choice',[65] explained the ethical principle of self-determination and submission of counsel that adults have an absolute right to

---

60  *Op cit*, fn 17, *Re E*, p 394.
61  *Op cit*, fn 26, *South Glamorgan County Council v W and B*, p 581.
62  *Op cit*, fn 21, *Re S*, p 1072.
63  *Ibid*, pp 1074–75.
64  *Ibid*, p 1074.
65  *Op cit*, fn 17, *Re E*, p 389.

refuse treatment, even if the result is death, before dismissing all as irrelevant because E was only 15 years of age. A finding of incompetence or that in the circumstances the autonomous decision of the individual should be overridden, shifts legal discourse from universal principles to a particularistic focus upon the child. As with parental consent to the treatment of young children, the question is what is in the best interests of the child. As Lord Donaldson MR said in *Re J*, this demands a focus upon the child whilst ignoring the interests of others.[66] Andrew Bainham has said of the best interests test, or welfare principle: 'The courts are much inclined to speak of the welfare principle as an absolute standard and an unproblematic concept which can act as a panacea for all ills affecting children. This is not altogether surprising since it is they who get to define its content in any given situation.'[67] Within the breadth of interests selected by the court in their conclusions as to the best interests of these children, we can locate the explanation for judicial rejection of the acceptance of these children as autonomous individuals and detect that the judiciary, as the parents and the health professionals, are motivated by a sense of obligation and responsibility with a view to the consequences and not simply an assessment of the just result. The child is not perceived as a physically and emotionally boundaried individual but the assessment of her interests situates her within the context of existing relationships, past experiences and possible futures. The judiciary are confronted with refusals by teenagers: S, fed up with years of on-going treatment; W, reacting to a catalogue of personal losses; E, responding to religious beliefs which would fade into perspective with time; A, abandoned by her mother and failed by professional support. Their own parents are either cold and cruel, unable to provide 'gestures of affection or words of affection',[68] prepared to martyr their child,[69] or ineffectual, having failed to secure adequate help for their child and now dominated by her.[70] The judiciary carefully selects the evidence, putting their own gloss upon it to support a conclusion which will prevent a child with a painful medical condition from choosing to die; after all, as Ward J said, 'life is precious'.[71] In the circumstances, facilitating the provision of treatment in the face of refusal is portrayed as very much the caring thing to do.

There is no clear conclusion to the resolution of a conflict between the self and others arising out of relationships of care, dependent as it is upon the context of that relationship. The relationships between parent and child, the nature of their interdependence and the context in which parents reach a

---

66   *Op cit*, fn 12, *Re J*.
67   Bainham, A, 'Handicapped girls and judicial parents' (1987) 103 LQR 334, p 339.
68   *Op cit*, fn 21, *Re S*, p 1074.
69   *Op cit*, fn 17, *Re E*, p 394.
70   *Op cit*, fn 26, *South Glamorgan County Council v W and B*.
71   *Op cit*, fn 17, *Re E*, p 393.

conclusion whether or not the refusal of their child to consent to medical treatment should be respected, is clearly different from those of the child with the caring professionals. Those in professional caring relationships could not stand by and let the child suffer harm by refusing treatment. Because they cared, the parents in these cases had formed a different view. What is clear is that reaching a conclusion on the basis of relationships, responsibility and the provision of care can result in a course of action which, as with medical treatment provided against the wishes of an older child, is experienced as hurtful, forceful and oppressive by the one cared for.

## BECAUSE WE CARE

Caring for a child imposes responsibility for her physical and mental health and well-being. Basic health care of children is undertaken under the supervision of parents, in the best interests of their child, as an everyday aspect of parental care. It is not, however, the case that as she develops, the child grows into a world of isolation. Parents continue to provide practical and emotional support for their children long past the age when the child is able to make decisions for herself. Caring for their physical and mental health and well-being brings children and parents into contact with health care professionals who inevitably become involved professionally and personally with the child. It is also inevitable that there will be disagreements amongst those involved in this web of relationships in the fulfilment of their responsibilities of caring.

Both Carol Gilligan and Robin West explain that connections are valued by those lacking power. This may undermine the argument that the legal solutions arrived at in these cases are reasoned from an ethic of care as the middle-class, male-dominated medical and legal professions may not seem to be paradigm examples of the powerless. Is it not the case that, confronted with the refusal of a competent patient to the treatment which they could be providing, they are experiencing at that moment powerlessness? That as individuals we both value separation and connection, and that cases such as these encourage resolution in terms of relationships, connections and care? Rather than attempt to articulate justice and provide explanations for forced treatment in terms of the rights of the abstract autonomous individual of liberal legal theory or the paternalistic overriding of those rights,[72] it would be instructive to listen to the parents of sick children, health care professionals

---

72  The ethic of care model may lead to the same result as a paternalistic decision but not necessarily. Importantly, the individual is located within a web of relationships rather than perceived as an isolated individual, decisions proceed from a focus upon care and the avoidance of harm to the self and other as opposed to an objective assessment of benefit to the other, and a wider conception of the harm which may be caused by different actions is employed.

and lawyers acting in partnership in order to secure the well-being of the child. If the 'different voice' can be heard in what they say, decisions relating to the medical treatment of children may be more convincingly explained in terms of the responsibility of caring than presently achieved with expressions of autonomy. What we hear may enable us to develop, out of the vague best interests test, an ethic of care model for health care decisions in relation to children which explains why, because we care, sometimes medical treatment may be imposed upon them despite their wishes to the contrary.

# CHAPTER SEVEN

# RESEARCH BODIES: FEMINIST PERSPECTIVES ON CLINICAL RESEARCH

*Marie Fox*[1]

## INTRODUCTION

My aim in this chapter is to demonstrate why the issue of clinical research is a particularly appropriate topic for feminist interrogation. I contend that women are doubly disadvantaged in medical research – there is bias against female researchers and females as research subjects.[2] In essence, I argue that research offers a microcosm of how women are represented in health care law. Thus, although women represent a slight majority of the population, and the bulk of health care consumers,[3] they are marginalised by clinical researchers, unless the research relates to reproduction.[4] In other contexts, diseases which are exclusive to women are inadequately funded, while research into diseases affecting both sexes is overwhelmingly conducted on men, ignoring gender differences in responses to treatment, such as differential rates of absorption and excretion.[5] Thus, just as law privileges the male – or at least the man of reason[6] – as its subject, so the male is the subject of medical research. Symbolically, the use of the male body as reference for clinical judgments necessarily renders female hormonal cycles, menstruation and pregnancy exceptional rather than ordinary events, as well as providing the rationale for much reproductive research. Concerns about the injustice of women's under-representation have spawned recent scholarship asserting the right of women to be included in clinical trials. In this essay I wish to sound a note of caution

---

1   Thanks to Margot Brazier, Jean McHale, Thérèse Murphy, Sally Sheldon, Bonnie Steinbock and Michael Thomson.

2   Keville, T, 'Gender bias in medical research and clinical testing' (1994) 16 *Women's Rights Law Reporter* 18. It should be noted that bias on the grounds of gender intersects with various factors, such as class, race, sexual orientation, disability, etc.

3   Foster, P, *Women and the Health Care Industry: An Unhealthy Relationship?*, 1995, Buckingham: Open University Press, p 2.

4   See Murphy, T, 'Bursting binary bubbles: law, literature and the sexed body', in Morison, J and Bell, C (eds), *Tall Stories? Reading Law and Literature*, 1996, Aldershot: Dartmouth.

5   Laurence, L and Weinhouse, B, *Outrageous Practices: How Gender Bias Threatens Women's Health*, 1994–97, New Brunswick: Rutgers University Press, though on the contested nature of evidence regarding these differential effects see Institute of Medicine, *Women and Health Research*, 1994, Washington DC: National Academy Press, Vol 1, p 6.

6   Naffine, N, *Law and the Sexes*, 1990, Sydney: Allen & Unwin.

regarding this somewhat uncritical acceptance of the benefits of clinical research. In particular, I argue that it may be ethically problematic for feminists to assert the right of women to participate as equals in trials, while ignoring the oppression of non-human animals in which much clinical research is grounded. Furthermore, in so doing they implicitly endorse traditional scientific models of medicine and the values inherent in such models, whereas I contend that women still have reason to be wary of the masculinist orientation of scientific ideology. One consequence of this orientation may be that, though the topic of clinical research requires feminist scrutiny, it may prove particularly resistant to such critique.

## THE DEFINITION OF CLINICAL RESEARCH

In standard medico-legal texts, research is traditionally classified in a number of ways. It is first distinguished from conventional treatment which uses approved methods and techniques for therapeutic purposes. It is then subdivided into two broad classes of research. The first consists of those which do not require any direct interference with the subject – for example, those involving use of personal medical records alone.[7] My focus is on the second category, which involves direct physical or psychological interference with the subject. Such research is generally further divided into two types:

(a) therapeutic research which is performed on a patient and uses new methods and techniques which carry prospects of direct benefit to that patient;

(b) non-therapeutic research which involves the use of new procedures or drugs for purely or mainly scientific purposes and is unlikely to benefit the individual participant, although it may offer some collective benefit.[8]

Although much of the literature has been devoted to the therapeutic/non-therapeutic dichotomy, recently it has come under attack. First, technological innovations may render it difficult to distinguish between research and innovative therapy. For instance, should a new surgical technique, such as keyhole surgery, be subject to special regulation?[9] Secondly, the lobbying of health advocacy groups, notably those representing AIDS patients, has forced recognition of the view that 'high quality clinical care and responsible research form a continuum'.[10] Certainly the polarisation of research and

---

7   See McHale, J and Fox, M with Murphy, J, *Health Care Law: Text and Materials*, 1997, London: Sweet & Maxwell, pp 593–95.

8   This distinction derives from the Declaration of Helsinki, see Montgomery, J, 'Law and Ethics in International Trials', in Williams, C (ed), *Introducing New Treatments for Cancer*, 1992, Chichester: Wiley.

9   *Ibid*, fn 7, McHale and Fox, p 568.

10  Whyte, R, 'Clinical trials, consent and the doctor-patient contract' (1994) 15 *Health Law in Canada* 49, p 50.

treatment is problematic, since the notion that research generates fuller duties to disclose risks depends upon acceptance of the beneficent motivations for treatment. Nevertheless, it may be worth retaining the research/therapy distinction, since advances attributed to medical research have been obtained at the cost of blighted lives, especially amongst oppressed populations, thus justifying a greater obligation to disclose risks in the research context.[11]

## MAINSTREAM BIOETHICAL CONCERNS PERTAINING TO RESEARCH

In this section I shall outline feminist concerns about research which substantively overlap with those of mainstream bioethicists, and demonstrate how they expand the boundaries of those traditional concerns. I shall then address issues of particular interest to feminists, which have been relatively neglected in mainstream bioethical and medico-legal texts.

### The question of consent

The issue which has attracted most attention from ethicists and lawyers has been consent to research, since, in the absence of statutory regulation, authority to carry out research on an adult human subject derives from that person's consent.[12] This focus may be a reflection of the individualist rights-based foundation of health care law, which imposes responsibility on the

---

11   Although Nazi and Japanese experiments during World War Two overshadow all subsequent abusive medical research, other infamous examples include the Tuskeegee experiments in 1932–72 which used approximately 400 black males to determine the natural course of syphilis, even though the treatment had existed for centuries (see Jones, J, *Bad Blood: The Tuskeegee Syphilis Experiment*, 1981, New York: The Free Press), and experiments to test radiation as a therapy carried out in the USA until the early 1970s (see McNeill, P, *The Ethics and Politics of Human Experimentation*, 1993, Cambridge: CUP, Chapter 1). Research carried out in New York in the 1960s, in which 22 chronically ill patients were injected with live cancer cells without their knowledge, demonstrated the vulnerability of the elderly to research abuse (see Golner, J, 'An overview of legal controls on human experimentation and the regulatory implications of taking Professor Katz seriously' (1993) 38 *Saint Louis University Law Journal* 63). Other examples have focused upon women. For example, in 1971 research on the side-effects of oral contraceptives involved experiments on 398 Chicano women in San Antonio, Texas. Of these women, 76 were given placebos instead of contraceptives. Ten became pregnant within months. Yet this work continued to be funded until 1974 (see Corea, G, *The Hidden Malpractice*, 1985, New York: Harper Colophon, pp 13–14). At the National Women's Hospital in Auckland, New Zealand, in the decade from 1966, women diagnosed with cervical cancer were left untreated to observe the natural history of their disease (see Coney, S, *The Unfortunate Experiment*, 1988, Auckland: Penguin). In AIDS research on prostitute women servicing US military stationed at Subic Bay naval base in the Philippines in 1989, one group of eight HIV-positive women was not told what their diagnosis meant, and observed to study the impact of positive thinking on disease (see *op cit*, fn 5, Laurence and Weinhouse, pp 23–24).

12   Brazier, M, *Medicine, Patients and the Law*, 2nd edn, 1992, Harmondsworth: Penguin, p 413.

individual research subject to protect herself from abuse through giving or withholding consent.[13] It has been amply demonstrated that notions of capacity and consent are gendered,[14] and all the usual difficulties of ensuring informed consent apply to clinical trials. Additionally, research poses particular problems, leading some commentators to query whether informed consent is truly possible in this context.[15] The ability of the intended experimental subject to consent to procedures where the results are uncertain or of dubious benefit is called into question.[16] In this regard, the Law Commission has suggested provisionally that 'a person should not be guilty of an offence if he [sic] causes injury to another, of whatever degree of seriousness, if such injury is caused during the course of properly approved medical research (ie approved by a Local Research Ethics Committee (LREC)) and with the consent of that other person'.[17] Crucially, such a recommendation assumes the efficacy of LRECs and the validity of consent, which McNeill argues deals inadequately with the consequences of human experimentation, since it fails to address fully the weighting of risks and benefits of experimentation for subject and society.[18] Although virtually all documented cases of abusive research have concerned failure to employ satisfactory informed consent procedures,[19] courts have tended to limit their role to ensuring that risks are explained.[20]

Of course, failure to obtain any consent at all will render the researcher liable to an action in trespass; and if the information given is inadequate this could lead to negligence proceedings. There are no decided English cases concerning the quantity or content of information that should be disclosed to a subject in a clinical trial, although it is generally accepted that the law as set out in *Sidaway* and subsequent cases does not apply in the context of clinical research.[21] Thus, someone who volunteers for research is entitled to a fuller explanation of the nature of the trial and of the risks than would be the case in relation to treatment. It is highly probable that English law would follow

---

13 Miller, C, 'Protection of human subjects of research in Canada' (1995) 4 *Health Law Review* 8.

14 See Wells and Foster, this volume.

15 Beecher, H (1970) *Research and the Individual: Human Studies* 5; Thornton, H, 'Clinical trials – a brave new partnership?' (1994) 20 *Journal of Medical Ethics* 19.

16 Bassiouni, M, Baffes, T and Evrard, J, 'An appraisal of human experimentation in international law and practice: the need for international regulation of human experimentation' (1981) 72 *The Journal of Criminal Law and Criminology* 1597, pp 1611–12.

17 Law Commission, *Consent in the Criminal Law*, Law Com No 139, 1995, London: HMSO, paras 8.38–8.52.

18 *Op cit*, fn 11, McNeill, pp 135–38.

19 Berg, J, 'Legal and ethical complexities of consent with cognitively impaired research subjects: proposed guidelines' (1996) 24 *Journal of Law, Medicine and Ethics* 18.

20 Brazier, M, 'Law, ethics and consent to randomised trials', in Social Science Research Unit, *Breast Cancer, Randomised Controlled Trials and Consent*, 1994, London: Institute of Education.

21 See Kennedy, I, 'The law and ethics of informed consent and randomized controlled trials',

Canadian law,[22] in adopting an objective test requiring a researcher to disclose all relevant facts which a reasonable subject would wish to know, and to provide the opportunity for questions, to which full and honest answers should be given.[23] However, as Morehouse points out, 'there are many ways of introducing a research project to a patient which fall short of pressurising the patients, but certainly do not conform to total objectivity'.[24] Particular problems arise in the context of consent to randomised controlled trials (RCTs) which compare treatments or approaches in two or more groups of subjects who are allocated randomly to those groups.[25] In recent years RCTs have been promoted as the most scientifically valid method of evaluating different procedures; yet, as Oakley argues, they pose particular problems for feminist researchers, pertaining not only to the vexed question of consent,[26] but whether chance allocation may be antithetical to feminist practice and to the epistemology, ownership and distribution of certainty.[27] In particular, she expresses concern at how 'the tension between the scientific requirements of research and the humane treatment of individuals ... is expressed in the very strategy of designing an experiment so as to restrict people's freedom to discuss with one another the commonality of the process in which they are engaged'.[28] In regulating the conduct of clinical research, therefore, law treads a fine line in balancing scientific advancement against individual inviolability.[29]

---

22  In 1965 the Saskatchewan Court of Appeal held that the subject should be informed of 'all the facts, probabilities and opinions which a reasonable man might be expected to consider before giving his consent', *Haluska v University of Saskatchewan* (1965) 53 DLR 2d 436, p 444 *per* Hall J. LREC guidelines state that the subject should be given an information sheet; Royal College of Physicians guidelines suggest that she should be told the purpose, procedures, risk (including distress), benefits (including to others), informed that she may decline to participate or withdraw at any time and given a statement about compensation for injury, Royal College of Physicians, *Guidelines on the Practice of Ethics Committees in Medical Research Involving Human Subjects*, 3rd edn, 1996, London: Royal College of Physicians.

23  See Montgomery, J, *Health Care Law*, 1997, Oxford: OUP, pp 343–45; *op cit*, fn 7, McHale and Fox, pp 574–75.

24  Morehouse, R, 'Dilemmas of the clinical researcher: a view from the inside' (1994) 15 *Health Law in Canada* 52.

25  See McHale, J, 'Guidelines for medical research – some ethical and legal problems' [1993] Med LR 160, p 167.

26  Kennedy suggests that in the context of randomised controlled trials, the materiality of risk should be defined according to what the particular patient would want to know, *op cit*, fn 21, Kennedy, p 221.

27  Oakley, A, 'Who's afraid of the randomized controlled trial', in Roberts, H (ed), *Women's Health Counts*, 1990, London: Routledge.

28  *Ibid*, p 188.

29  Katz, J, 'The Nuremberg consent principle: then and now', in Annas, G and Grodin, M (eds), *The Nazi Doctors and the Nuremberg Code: Human Rights in Human Experimentation*, 1992, New York: OUP, p 235.

## Difficulties in ensuring accountability

To a limited extent the introduction of guidelines and ethical review procedures (particularly since the 1975 revision of the Declaration of Helsinki) has shifted the focus from the issue of consent to that of ensuring compliance with codes of research practice. However, the emphasis on compliance in recent years may be attributable to a desire to safeguard the integrity of scientific research, rather than protection of individual patients. Cases of deception and fraud are becoming more common, since scarce funding leads to pressure to show results for money invested and to publish widely for career advancement.[30] Moreover, since reporting of clinical trials is not mandatory, unsuccessful trials are frequently abandoned or not written up.[31] Certainly, violations of ethical canons of research have been reported with increasing frequency in recent years and defining culpable research misconduct has proven controversial.[32] Although the Royal College of Physicians indicated the need for a body to investigate allegations of fraud in 1991, no action has yet been taken to establish one.[33] Ultimately, therefore, it is the threat of litigation that holds researchers accountable.

Since 1968 official NHS policy has been that LRECs should oversee clinical research within the NHS. LRECs are governed by Department of Health (DoH) guidelines, in which their function is defined as advising on whether a research proposal is ethically acceptable.[34] There is no requirement for trials undertaken outside the NHS to receive ethics committee approval, although some private organisations have established their own ethics committees. Indeed, a researcher contravenes no law in carrying out research without ethics committee approval, though failure to obtain such approval will lead to difficulties in publishing findings. Even where approval is sought, the practices and effectiveness of ethics committees are disputed. A particular concern is that monitoring of research is inadequate after the initial approval is granted.[35] Effective policing is crucial given that most committees approve over 90% of proposals, after asking the researchers to consider minor modifications.[36] This predisposition to approve may indicate that lay

---

30  O'Reilly, J, 'More gold and more fleece: improving the legal sanctions against medical research fraud' (1990) 42 *Administrative Law Review* 393.

31  *Op cit*, fn 5, Institute of Medicine, p 68.

32  Deer, B, 'Trust me I'm a doctor' (1997) *The Sunday Times Magazine*, 2 November; Slapper, G, 'Doctored research' (1997) *The Times*, 4 November; Mihill, C, 'Falsified research "threat to patients"' (1997) *The Guardian*, 6 November; Smith, R, 'Time to face up to research misconduct' (1996) 312 BMJ 789; Parrish, D, 'Falsification of credentials in the research setting; scientific misconduct?' (1996) 24 *Journal of Law, Medicine and Ethics* 260.

33  *Op cit*, fn 7, McHale and Fox, p 595.

34  Department of Health, *Guidelines to Local Research Ethics Committees*, 1991, London: HMSO, para 1.1.

35  *Op cit*, fn 11, McNeill, pp 3–6; Neuberger, J, *Ethics and Health Care: The Role of Research Ethics Committees in the United Kingdom*, 1992, London: King's Fund Institute.

36  *Op cit*, fn 13, Miller, p 9.

members on ethics committees are relatively disempowered. Certainly, they are generally under-represented and, lacking research expertise, dependent on researchers for information regarding research practices. Nor are those who are the subjects of research represented on the committee.[37] Additionally, one British study found that women and ethnic minority groups are poorly represented, although the DoH guidelines require that committees be composed of both sexes.[38] McNeill contends that ethics committees are typical of self-regulating groups in their failure to deal adequately with non-compliance, for which there is generally no sanction, especially if the researcher is not seeking overseas grants or publication in international journals.[39] In the USA similar criticisms[40] prompted President Clinton to establish the recently appointed National Bioethics Advisory Commission to frame recommendations on the appropriateness of certain government policies in bioethics, including principles for the ethical conduct of research.[41] There have been calls to establish such a commission in the UK.[42]

## The relationship between the investigator and research subject

Further concerns stem from the problematic relationship between the physician and research subject. It has been extensively documented how in the research context the physician's role changes – she becomes, in Katz's words, a 'physician-investigator'. Not only does this entail a potential conflict in loyalties to patients, employers and research aims, owing to her multiple priorities as teacher, researcher, physician and administrator,[43] it also follows that her subject is likely to regard her in a more ambivalent light. As Kennedy suggests, the physician's primary duty to care for her patient is inevitably compromised by her duty to carry out clinical trials with due scientific rigour,[44] yet the patient may not feel truly free to refuse to help her doctor. Indeed, the demands of scientific rigour leave the patient in an even more

---

37  *Op cit*, fn 11, McNeill, p 6.

38  *Op cit*, fn 34, Department of Health, para 2.5; *op cit*, fn 35, Neuberger, Chapter 2.

39  *Op cit*, fn 11, McNeill, p 110.

40  Katz, J, 'Human experimentation and human rights' (1993) 38 *Saint Louis University Law Journal* 7.

41  Protection of Human Research Subjects and Creation of NBAC, Exec Order No 12,975, 60 Fed Reg 52,063, 1995. See Mastroianni, A and Kahn, J, 'Remedies for human subjects of cold war research: recommendations of the advisory committee' (1996) 24 *Journal of Law, Medicine and Ethics* 118.

42  See, *op cit*, fn 25, McHale, pp 184–85.

43  *Op cit*, fn 24, Morehouse, pp 52–53.

44  *Op cit*, fn 21, Kennedy, p 218. It should also be noted that RCTs may adversely affect the trust upon which the doctor-patient relationship is ideally founded – see *op cit*, fn 27, Oakley; and Rawlings, G, 'Ethics and regulation in randomised controlled trials of therapy', in Grubb, A (ed), *Challenges in Medical Care*, 1992, Chichester: Wiley, pp 41–42.

vulnerable position than usual in her engagement with physicians, since the researcher must view her subject with dispassion and detachment:

> ... the commitment to objectivity invites the investigator's thought processes to become objectified and, in turn, to transform the human beings who are the subjects of research into data points to be plotted on a chart that will prove or disprove a research hypothesis.[45]

Given this, and the historical legacy of human experimentation as one of imbalance towards the interests of the researcher,[46] I would suggest that it is more accurate to designate the person on whom experimentation is performed as the research *object*. Certainly the recent practice of describing such persons as participants in the research is highly questionable. While Miller suggests that such terminology indicates a paradigm shift from protectionism to securing consultation and consensus,[47] it may be that adoption of this rhetoric simply masks inherent disparities of power in the relationship. As Monica Rudberg argues, 'there is not just a difference in degree between researcher and object, there is a difference in kind – a difference between knower and known'.[48] Such power imbalances are especially prevalent where the research object is differentiated from the investigator by factors such as gender, class, race, ethnicity, and, I shall argue, species.

## SPECIFICALLY FEMINIST CONCERNS IN RELATION TO RESEARCH

It will be apparent that while feminist criticisms of research practices are linked to traditional bioethical concerns, they also go beyond such concerns. The history outlined above has led to an emphasis on shielding women from participation in clinical trials. In this section my argument will be that as a consequence of this protectionist policy, the research object is explicitly and implicitly constructed as male and largely premised on the exclusion (or at least under-representation) of women.[49] It is only recently that exclusion has been identified as a bioethical issue, due to paradigm shifts in how enrolment

---

45  *Op cit*, fn 40, Katz, p 35.

46  *Op cit*, fn 11, McNeill, p 13.

47  *Op cit*, fn 13, Miller, p 11.

48  Rudberg, M, 'The researching body: the epistemophilic project', in Davis, K (ed), *Embodied Practices: Feminist Perspectives on the Body*, 1997, London: Sage, p 185.

49  The claim that women are under-represented has been used to signify both that the proportion of female (or male) participants is less than the proportion of females (or males) affected by the disease under study, and that the study design provides inadequate statistical power to detect gender differences, while the term 'exclusion' is generally understood to apply when women (or men) are explicitly barred from participation by the study protocol; see *op cit*, fn 5, Institute of Medicine, p 30.

in clinical trials has come to be viewed. Initially research on human subjects was seen as a necessary aspect of public health, then as a transgression of individual rights tantamount to torture, while of late it has come to be regarded as a form of access to better medical care.[50] The latter shift is largely due to the HIV/AIDS pandemic, which has politicised clinical research, resulted in clinical trials being reconstituted as treatment when there is no proven treatment for a medical condition, and led to articulation of the concept of just allocation of access to research.[51] Stimulated by this lead, patients with other diseases (notably breast cancer and Alzheimer's) and their families, have asserted rights to participate in trials of experimental drugs and treatments.[52] Moreover, the thalidomide and DES disasters highlighted how policies designed to protect pregnant women from research risks may conversely have exposed them to risks deriving from the absence of data about the impact of taking certain drugs while pregnant.[53] Thus being a research subject is no longer viewed as an unqualified sacrifice – rather it is a potentially risky opportunity. The result is that researchers, long sensitised to the need to protect research subjects, must now also focus on the need to *include* certain populations.

## The construction of the research subject

### *Explicit exclusions*

Various research protocols and guidelines have explicitly excluded certain groups of women, particularly pregnant women. The most significant legal measures in this regard were federal regulations in the United States, which expressly barred women who were pregnant or of child-bearing age from recruitment for clinical trials. Although such blatant exclusions never existed in the UK, DoH guidelines state that if it is intended to use women as research subjects, the possibility of their being or *becoming pregnant* should always be

---

50  Alto Charo, R, 'Protecting us to death: women, pregnancy and clinical research trials' (1993) 38 *Saint Louis University Law Journal* 135, p 152.

51  Ironically, even in the context of clinical trials on those affected with HIV/AIDS, women have been excluded. For instance, when the Food and Drug Administration approved the AIDS drug AZT in 1987, not one of the 63 federally sponsored studies had evaluated its effects on women. The result was that women were having toxic side-effects at the high doses deemed safe and efficacious in men, see, *op cit*, fn 5, Laurence and Weinhouse, p 5.

52  Elks, M, 'The right to participate in research studies' (1993) 122 *Journal of Laboratory and Clinical Medicine* 130, p 132.

53  Thalidomide was marketed in 1958 as an antidote for nausea in early pregnancy, and caused defects, particularly limb malformations, in approximately 8,000 children before it was withdrawn in 1962. DES was first prescribed in America in 1943, in an effort to avert miscarriages. Its efficacy was challenged as early as 1953, and by 1971 the FDA had banned its use during pregnancy after substantial evidence that it was associated with high rates of cervical cancer in the daughters of DES users.

considered, and the recruitment of women of child-bearing age justified.[54] Clinical research thus constitutes another field where the foetus is implicitly pitted against the pregnant woman, raising important questions concerning female autonomy and the relative value of women's health. HIV research affords stark examples of attitudes which prioritise foetal protection over benefit to the pregnant woman, since research protocols construct women as vectors of disease.[55] Thus, for example, women are denied the right to participate in trials of drugs designed to combat opportunistic infections, because of risk to the foetus.[56] Significantly, despite an increasing number of studies which demonstrate that exposure to chemicals and environmental toxins can affect sperm, there is no suggestion that men be excluded from research in order to protect their unborn children.[57] Understandably, therefore, recent feminist analyses of biomedical research have focused on the inequities of this situation.

Crucially, as the DoH guidelines demonstrate, the caution which researchers feel about using pregnant women extends to all fertile women. As Merton points out, this treats all women, regardless of their sexual orientation or attitudes towards child-bearing, as potentially mothers – as always pregnable.[58] This construction of women as reproducers and their consequent exclusion from participation in clinical trials, parallels how women of reproductive age have been excluded from 'inappropriate' employments. As Michael Thomson argues, in 19th-century and contemporary biomedical discourse, female reproductive capacity is constructed as inherently pathological and susceptible to damage, thus legitimising women's exclusion from certain activities.[59] Although the justifications for explicit exclusions are generally couched in the rhetoric of protecting women and their unborn children, the issue which looms largest for those sponsoring or conducting

---

54  *Op cit*, fn 34, Department of Health, para 4.5; Royal College of Physicians, *Guidelines on the Practice of Ethics Committees in Medical Research Involving Human Subjects*, 1996, London: Royal College of Physicians, categorise pregnant and nursing women as 'vulnerable participants' and indicate that some committees require that consent to research is not sought in the immediate period around childbirth unless that is unavoidable (para 8.8), although the Council for International Organisations of Medical Sciences and World Health Organisation, *International Ethical Guidelines for Biomedical Research Involving Human Subjects*, 1993, advise that no special problems arise in eliciting consent from these women.

55  Faden, R, Kass, N and McGraw, D, 'Women as vessels and vectors: lessons from the HIV epidemic', in Wolf, S, *Feminism and Bioethics: Beyond Reproduction*, 1996, New York: OUP.

56  Lowe, D, 'HIV study raises ethical concerns for the treatment of pregnant women' (1995) 10 *Berkeley Women's Law Journal* 176.

57  See *op cit*, fn 5, Laurence and Weinhouse, p 72; Merton, V, 'Ethical obstacles to the participation of women in biomedical research', in *ibid*, Wolf, pp 226–27.

58  Merton, V, 'The exclusion of pregnant, pregnable, and once-pregnable patients (aka women) from biomedical research' (1993) 12 *American Journal of Law and Medicine* 369.

59  Thomson, M, 'Employing the body: the reproductive body and employment exclusion' (1996) 5 SLS 243, p 253; Jacobus, M *et al*, *Body Politics: Women and the Discourses of Science*, 1990, London: Routledge.

trials is likely to be fear of liability for any teratogenic impact. Yet, Merton has convincingly argued that such fears are more apparent than real, since no successful claim has ever been brought and a proper warning of known and unknown risks, including the risk of chromosomal and/or teratogenic damage would probably extinguish claims of prenatal or preconceptual harm by subjects and their children.[60] Researchers have also invoked guidance excluding or cautioning against use of pregnant or pregnable women to justify their failure to recruit women for clinical trials. Again, feminist lawyers have challenged this rationale, arguing that there is potentially greater liability if unsafe products are marketed, since pharmaceutical companies do not bar women, including women of child-bearing capacity, from purchasing or being prescribed such drugs. As Merton points out, such regulations are not an insurmountable obstacle to the inclusion of women, and the failure to challenge them 'seems to demonstrate that the regulations are the product, not the cause, of a research tradition that has excluded women for quite other reasons'.[61]

## The implicit exclusion of women

Other reasons for the exclusion of women from clinical protocols may be less overt. First, in scientific literature there is a particularly marked tendency to define and perceive the male as generically human, and the female as a special sub-group.[62] This is related to a second factor, the dearth of female scientific researchers, which is largely glossed over in the bioethics literature. As Ruth Wallsgrove points out, girls learn at an early stage that science is not for them.[63] The absence of role models and skewed workplaces discourages women from entering the field, and makes it more likely that they will face hostility, such as biases in the tenure process, difficulty in getting first authorship on papers, and sexual harassment.[64] Although the women's movement has produced more female scientists, they encounter various exclusion mechanisms, which render it particularly difficult to develop a feminist practice in the discipline of science.[65] Moreover, a woman scientist experiences an identity conflict which intensifies the fragmented identity experienced by all physician/researchers. As Keller argues, 'any scientist who

---

60  Op cit, fn 58, Merton.

61  Op cit, fn 57, Merton, p 226. See also, op cit, fn 50, Alto Charo.

62  Dresser, R, 'Wanted: single, white male for medical research' (1992) 22 Hastings Center Report 24.

63  Wallsgrove, R, 'The masculine face of science', in Brighton Women and Science Group, Alice Through the Microscope: The Power of Science over Women's Lives, 1980, London: Virago.

64  Op cit, fn 5, Laurence and Weinhouse, pp 51–59.

65  Rose, H, Love, Power and Knowledge: Towards a Feminist Transformation of the Sciences, 1994, Bloomington: Indiana University Press, p 14.

is not a man walks a path bounded on one side by inauthenticity and on the other by subversion'.[66] One promising counter-trend is the growing number of (overwhelmingly female) nurse and midwife researchers which has resulted from the increased professionalisation of these disciplines. Although such research may be perceived as lower status, the involvement of more women researchers may, nonetheless, alter the dynamics of the researcher/object relationship.[67] A third crucial factor accounting for the exclusion of women relates to the gender identity of those funding medical research. In Britain most funding is provided by the pharmaceutical industry, while the remainder comes from the Medical Research Council, private charities and health departments.[68] Thus, the choice of problems for study in medical research is substantially determined by the same powerful group – of mainly white, middle-class men – who conduct the research.[69] Given this, inevitably the allocation of resources for biomedical research has been enormously skewed toward the health needs of this group. Consequently the health of women is largely ignored, or attention is focused on narrow aspects that are of interest to men.[70] An even more compelling reason for excluding women is that it is easier and more cost-effective to use men. Not only do women, as primary caregivers, have less mobility and time to attend to their own medical needs (thus requiring special efforts to target them for participation in clinical trials) but researchers claim that it is more difficult to study women. Since female hormonal profiles can vary (depending on whether they are pre-menstrual, pregnant, menopausal, taking oral contraceptives or hormone replacement), larger numbers of women are needed in order to obtain meaningful results, with the result that experiments become more expensive. Greater inclusion of women thus equals 'noise' in the data.[71]

## The impact on women of exclusion from clinical trials

The impact on women of their exclusion from clinical trials has been huge. It is surely not a coincidence that almost every recent health scandal – thalidomide, DES, the Dalkon Shield, breast implants and toxic shock syndrome – has involved women's health.[72] As one commentator argues, 'practically all drugs

---

66  Keller, EF, cited in Rose, *op cit*, fn 65.

67  On the tensions experienced by the nurse-researcher, see Thomson, L, 'Combining care with randomised research: questions for breast care nurses', in SSRU, *op cit*, fn 20. Generally, see Harding, S, 'The instability of the analytical categories of feminism', in Harding, S and O'Barr, J (eds), *Sex and Scientific Inquiry*, 1975, Chicago: University of Chicago Press, p 289.

68  Faulder, C, *Whose Body Is It Anyway?*, 1985, London: Virago, p 101.

69  Hubbard, R, 'Social effects of some contemporary myths about women', in Lowe, M and Hubbard, R (eds), *Rationalizations of Inequality*, 1993, New York: Pergamon Press.

70  *Op cit*, fn 2, Keville, p 19.

71  *Op cit*, fn 50, Alto Charo, p 141.

72  *Op cit*, fn 5, Laurence and Weinhouse, p 7.

on the market should have a warning label that says "This drug had never been studied in women, particularly women of child-bearing age". Women prescribed drugs now are essentially experimental subjects, without knowing it, agreeing to it, or wanting it'.[73] The relative neglect of women's health needs raises issues of justice,[74] as well as calling into question the scientifically dubious practice of marketing drugs and procedures which have been inadequately tested for their impact on women.[75] Since the choice and definition of problems for research is influenced by the under-representation of women at all stages of the research process, research on conditions specific to females receives low priority, funding and prestige. Even breast cancer is not a major research priority, despite being the most prevalent form of cancer.[76] Less politicised diseases, such as dysmenorrhoea or incontinence in older women, fare much worse in funding terms. Significantly, reproduction is the only context in which massive resources are devoted to issues that primarily affect women. Arguably, the result has been that a natural process controlled by women has been converted into a clinical process controlled by men, a development directly related to men's interest in controlling the production of children.[77] This depiction of women's bodies as simply research material for man's desire to control creation is most compellingly articulated in Robin Rowland's vision of women's bodies as *Living Laboratories*.[78] It is also worth noting the inadequacies of contraceptive research, which has overwhelmingly concentrated on women. Laurence and Weinhouse point out that oral contraceptives were first approved for marketing after less than five years of study.[79] Almost three decades later doubts linger about their safety, while even less is known about the effects of sex hormones in hormone replacement therapy.[80] Other contraceptive innovations have been equally troublesome, most notably the Dalkon Shield intra-uterine device.[81] Such case histories, combined with the abuses noted above, suggest that women cannot afford to be sanguine about the benefits of clinical research.

---

73  Alice Dan, Director, Center for Research on Women and Gender, University of Illinois, cited in Laurence and Weinhouse, *op cit*, fn 5, pp 74–75.

74  Sherwin, S, 'Women in clinical studies: a feminist view', in Institute of Medicine, *op cit*, fn 5, Vol 2.

75  *Op cit*, fn 5, Institute of Medicine, Chapters 2 and 3.

76  McPherson, K 'What do we know about breast cancer, and what do we need to know?', in SSRU, *op cit*, fn 20.

77  Rosser, S, 'Revisioning clinical research: gender and the ethics of experimental design', in Holmes, H and Purdy, L (eds), *Feminist Perspectives in Medical Ethics*, 1992, Bloomington: Indiana University Press, p 130.

78  Rowland, R, *Living Laboratories: Women and Reproductive Technology*, 1992, London: Cedar.

79  *Op cit*, fn 5, Laurence and Weinhouse, p 80.

80  Douglas, G, *Law, Fertility and Reproduction*, 1991, London: Sweet & Maxwell, pp 62–66; 'What every woman knows' (1995) *The Guardian*, 21 October.

81  Hicks, K, *Surviving the Dalkon Shield IUD: Women v The Pharmaceutical Industry*, 1994, New York: Teachers College Press.

Moreover, certain diseases which affect both sexes are wrongly labelled as male diseases. Thus, while common diseases, such as Alzheimer's, depression, osteoporosis, sexually transmitted diseases, immunologic diseases, diabetes, multiple sclerosis, and respiratory illnesses, disproportionately affect women, there is a paucity of research about the impact of existing treatments upon women. This is particularly true of heart disease, the primary killer of both women and men in the West. Very little heart disease research focuses upon high risk groups of women, like the elderly or poor black women who have had several children.[82] Given this, it is not surprising that women are more likely to experience adverse reactions to prescribed drugs, possibly because the dosage levels have been determined by testing in men.[83] Pregnant women are particularly disadvantaged by the paucity of knowledge about therapeutics for them.[84]

## Framing a feminist response: engendering science?

In view of the potential practical benefits of including women in clinical trials, combined with the symbolic harm of excluding them for their own protection, it is understandable that recent feminist writing has emphasised women's rights to participate in clinical research. Yet, against the historical backdrop of the abusive research documented above, such advocacy is premised on a rather uncritical acceptance of the medical model of research. By endorsing the inherent values of scientific method, such scholarship prioritises the research imperative, disregarding the costs to human and non-human research objects. It is strangely at odds with feminist critiques of scientific medicine, which caution wariness of a discipline that has viewed biology as destiny and appeared to offer prospects of domination rather than liberation. Feminist scientific scholarship has been facilitated by the publication, in the 1960s, of Thomas Kuhn's revolutionary thesis that scientific theories are rooted in paradigms which reflect the historical and social context in which they are conceived. The work of Kuhn and others has opened up understandings of scientific thought to considerations of social and political influences,[85] undermining scientists' dismissal of politically engaged arguments as antithetical to a scientific method which emphasises the value of detachment and the 'objective pursuit of truth'. Inspired by this work, feminist standpoint theorists have exposed how scientific data has been gathered and interpreted from a particular (male) perspective. Furthermore, such data is commonly

---

82  Bess, C, 'Gender bias in health care: a life or death issue for women with coronary heart disease' (1995) 6 *Hastings Women's Law Journal* 41.

83  *Op cit*, fn 5, Laurence and Weinhouse, p 383.

84  Kass, N, Taylor, H and King, P, 'Harms of excluding pregnant women from clinical research: the case of HIV-infected pregnant women' (1996) 24 *Journal of Law, Medicine and Ethics* 36.

85  See Keller, EF, 'Feminism and science' in *op cit*, fn 67, Harding and O'Barr, p 236.

presented in androcentric language which shapes the concepts and provides the frameworks through which ideas are expressed.[86] More radical feminist critiques locate bias within science itself, questioning the assumptions of rationality and objectivity which underpin the scientific enterprise.[87] They contend that construction of the subject/object dichotomy is a male way of relating to the world which excludes women. For instance, Susan Bordo reads the Cartesian objectivism upon which modern science is premised as an 'aggressive intellectual flight from the feminine'.[88] Furthermore, as Keller has argued, the ideological link between objectivity, autonomy and masculinity, is in turn linked to scientific goals of power and domination.[89] The Frankfurt School's contention that the very logic of science is a logic of domination thus assumes a gendered form, since science is perceived as conquering nature, visualised as female.[90]

At the very least, scientific method is adversarial, rooted in the perception that competition advances science. This is exemplified by the 'race' to discover DNA. Significantly, James Watson's version of the discovery of the helical form of DNA erases the major contribution of fellow crystallographer, Rosalind Franklin.[91] Watson's account constructs her as 'a threat not simply to men but to science itself'.[92] Rose has pointed to a comparable sense of international rivalry which underpins the Human Genome Project, highlighted by the use of imagery resonant with masculinity and chivalry, portraying it as a search for a modern grail.[93] Although such imagery is coupled with that of international co-operation, as Salbu contends:

> While co-operation is important to the rapid development of scientific theory, it should be subordinate to the dominant and driving force of competition. Competition is vital to scientific advancement because of the role it plays in industry, effort, innovation, investment, and creativity ... highly motivated scholars are driven to compete against one another for a sense of

---

86  See Holmes, H, 'Can clinical research be both ethical and scientific?', in *op cit*, fn 77, Holmes and Purdy.

87  *Op cit*, fn 66, Keller, p 236; *op cit*, fn 77, Rosser, p 133.

88  See Bordo, S, 'The Cartesian masculinization of thought', in *op cit*, fn 67, Harding and O'Barr, p 249.

89  *Op cit*, fn 66, Keller, pp 238–41.

90  Keller, EF, 'Making gender visible in the pursuit of nature's secrets', in De Laurentis, T (ed), *Feminist Studies/Critical Studies*, 1986, Bloomington: Indiana University Press, p 69; *op cit*, fn 48, Rudberg, pp 191–92: 'Nature itself is depicted as a woman, even a "resisting" woman whom the researcher tries to both "conquer" and penetrate.'

91  Watson, J, *The Double Helix: A Personal Account of the Discovery of the Structure of DNA*, 1968, New York: Atheneum.

92  Jacobus, M, 'Is there a woman in this text?', in *Reading Women*, 1986, London: Methuen. For a discussion of how the course of science might have been altered had Franklin discovered the structure first, see Keller, *ibid*, pp 71–73. Rose, *op cit*, fn 67, pp 15–16, notes other examples where the contribution of women is not credited, and points to continued gender biases in the accreditation system, although science is now more alert to this problem.

93  *Op cit*, fn 65, Rose, Chapter 8.

accomplishment, academic prestige and potentially lucrative consulting appointments.[94]

In this competitive atmosphere, not only may female contributions be erased, but the figure of the scientist is most definitely gendered – he is embodied as a romantic scientist hero, or in a more recent incarnation as the 'researching family father'.[95] Against this backdrop it is revealing that the most innovative feminist scholarship has emerged in the field of primatology, largely as a result of the pioneering work of Donna Haraway. Rose argues that it is not accidental that Haraway's fields of enquiry – primatology and the story of human origins – are more open to deconstruction than most branches of science, and speak with clarity to the feminist and anti-racist enquirer. Significantly, Haraway also calls into question the human-other boundary. However, Rose cautions that the excitement generated by path-breaking feminist scholarship in the observational sciences must not lead us to underestimate the greater difficulties in reframing experimental sciences (like medical research) which are premised on violence and more closely linked to biotechnology.[96] Such difficulties are compounded by the fact that the discipline of bioethics, which supposedly holds science to account, itself appears resistant to feminist critique, to the point where some writers question whether bioethics is a facilitator of biomedicine rather than a genuine critic.[97]

# ANIMALS AS EXPERIMENTAL OBJECTS

In addition to sanctioning a scientific ideology which has constructed women as reproducers and often proved antithetical to their interests, a further problem with an uncritical endorsement of the current research paradigm is that it disregards interests other than those of women. For instance, Bonnie Steinbock has accused some feminist writers of downplaying the moral issues raised when a pregnant women chooses to participate in a clinical trial, knowing it could damage a foetus which she proposes to carry to term.[98] Equally, I would argue that they fail to address the interests of non-human

---

94    Salbu, S, 'Should AIDS research be regulated? a Manhattan project for AIDS and other policy proposals' (1994) 69 *Indiana Law Journal* 425, p 445.

95    *Op cit*, fn 48, Rudberg, pp 185–89.

96    *Op cit*, fn 65, Rose, pp 85–86.

97    Purdy, L, *Reproducing Persons: Issues in Feminist Bioethics*, 1996, Ithaca: Cornell University Press, pp 1–5; *op cit*, fn 55, Wolf, pp 18–21.

98    Steinbock, B, 'Ethical issues related to the inclusion of pregnant women in clinical trials', in Institute of Medicine, *op cit*, fn 5, Vol 2. The special status of children as objects of research is beyond the scope of this essay, but the vulnerability of children in the paediatric research context is a significant issue, see Nicolson, R, *Medical Research with Children*, 1985, Oxford: OUP. Moreover, there may well be some commonalities between women and children as research objects, given how women are infantilised in the research context.

animals. Until recently, bioethical preoccupation with human experimentation has meant that little attention has been devoted to the controlled violence perpetrated on laboratory animals.[99] However, Tom Beauchamp has hypothesised that animal research could emerge as a significant bioethical concern, in much the same way as human research did. He contends, '[w]e are only beginning to witness the detailed examinations of these issues that are needed, just as they were desperately needed for research involving human subjects in the early 1970s'.[100] Similarly Tom Regan has contended that increasing recognition of the need to legislate justice for animals, reflects the changing place of animals in the moral weave of our culture.[101] Significantly, such concerns are absent from recent feminist writing on clinical research. Feminist scholarship thus replicates the disregard for animal life in conventional bioethical and medico-legal writing. For instance, Vanessa Merton contends that 'pharmacokinetic screens of all new drugs should be conducted in women and men, and animal studies should include female as well as male animals ... reproductive studies must be conducted in animals prior to clinical studies in human subjects'.[102] This marked tendency to treat only the final stages of a scientific study, when experimentation is performed on humans, as raising important ethical questions, is at odds with the usual feminist emphasis on contextualising issues. Such scholarship codifies the animal body as inferior and replicates the hierarchical ordering of masculinist science, which has arrogated to itself the power to name women and animals, defining them as other to the human male.[103] Indeed, as Birke has argued, women have been rendered other precisely by the strategy of comparing them to animals:

> ... anti-feminist arguments frequently seem to reduce us to the level of mindlessness ... the image invoked is of a bovine mindlessness, chewing the cud. In the middle of the 19th century, women's biology was held to be limited ... reducing us to the status of animals. Women's intelligence, like animals, has typically been compared to men's and found wanting.[104]

If, in the research context, the human's status as subject/object is contested, with the consequence that women have sometimes been treated as 'living laboratories', the redundancy of animal bodies is even more marked. Their legal status as property[105] enables scientific ideology to designate them as research tools. Feminist endorsement of the research imperative uncritically

---

99  *Op cit*, fn 65, Rose, p 88.

100  Beauchamp, T, 'The moral standing of animals in medical research' (1992) 20 *Law, Medicine and Health Care* 7, p 16.

101  Regan, T, 'Progress without pain: the argument for humane treatment of research animals' (1987) 31 *Saint Louis University Law Journal* 513.

102  *Op cit*, fn 57, Merton, p 235.

103  Birke, L, *Feminism, Animals and Science: The Naming of the Shrew*, 1994, Buckingham: Open University Press, p 7.

104  *Ibid*, p 104.

105  Francione, G, *Animals, Property and the Law*, 1995, Philadelphia: Temple University Press.

assumes both the efficacy of animal studies and the legitimacy of treating animals as disposable research fodder.[106] Moreover, it represents a departure from the strong links forged between feminist and anti-vivisection movements in the late 19th century.[107] In deconstructing boundaries which have been erected between women and men, feminists stand accused of leaving others intact. Thus, although it may have been an understandable initial response to women's intermediate positioning between men and animals for feminists to seek to distance themselves from animals, Carol Adams has argued that such a position 'assimilates the malestream culture's contempt for animals within feminist theory. The human/animal boundary is left secure while women are moved from one side of it to the other'. She contends that a more radical and ethical feminist response is to call the human/animal dualism into question.[108] She urges feminists to reject a hierarchical ordering and cultural construction of some bodies as so completely and solely matter that their bodies become immaterial.[109] It seems to me that adoption of such a position affords feminists an important opportunity to begin to reframe science. As Zuleyma Tang Halpin observes:

> Once the scientist begins to feel for her research animal, the self versus other duality begins to break down, and it becomes easier for the interrelatedness of subject and object to be acknowledged. Once this happens it becomes easier to question the paradigm which proclaims power, control and domination as the ultimate goal of science. Viewed from this perspective, the animal welfare issue poses a major threat to patriarchal science.[110]

## CONCLUSION

The issue of clinical research throws up massive dilemmas for feminist commentators. It is clear that feminists cannot simply opt out of involvement in clinical research, given the benefits it promises. For instance, Oakley has highlighted how randomised controlled evaluation of breast cancer has been responsible for producing persuasive evidence that 'conservative' treatments are superior to 'radical' treatments, and that short courses of treatment are as effective as longer courses.[111] Such successes make it difficult to resist the lure

---

106 For a critique of both positions see Fox, M, 'Animal rights and wrongs: medical ethics and the killing of non-human animals', in Lee, R and Morgan, D (eds), *Death Rites: Law and Ethics at the End of Life*, 1994, London: Routledge.

107 *Op cit*, fn 65, Rose, p 87.

108 Adams, C, *Neither Man Nor Beast: Feminism and the Defense of Animals*, 1994, New York: Continuum, pp 11–13.

109 *Ibid*, p 13.

110 Halpin, ZT, 'Scientific objectivity and the concept of the "Other"' (1983) 12 *Women's Studies International Forum* 191.

111 *Op cit*, fn 27, Oakley, p 192.

of science, and are also indicative of the changing face of science. Scientific research is rendered more palatable by legal developments, especially in the USA, which have removed many obstacles to women's participation in clinical trials. In time the 70-kilogram male may be replaced as the research standard, especially since the smaller female body represents more of the population and is thus a truer scientific standard. Nevertheless, other legal and scientific developments may be less progressive. For instance, the perceived need to guard against litigation and the vogue for evidence-based medicine mean that more and more unnecessary and futile tests are likely to be required on humans and non-humans. Harmonisation of European health law is likely to accelerate this process, given the inadequacy of the European Union's animal protection policies and its commitment to the use of animal experiments which are perceived as facilitating the economic success of the Union.[112] Thus, although the lack of diversity amongst clinical researchers and the limited participation of women in research trials is ethically problematic, it is symptomatic of a much larger problem with scientific medicine, which recruitment of more women will not solve.

Thus, an ethical feminist position recognises the need to frame a new science, rather than simply pressing for the admission of women. Rose has argued that the very fact that women are largely shut out of the productive system of scientific knowledge, with its ideological power to define what is and is not objective knowledge, paradoxically offers feminists an opportunity to frame a distinctively feminist science which eschews foundations in violence and competition.[113] A feminist science would entail less emphasis on the dispassionate approach which has left women, minorities and animals vulnerable to objectification and abuse. It would encompass a challenge to the biotechnology industry which consumes a disproportionate share of a research budget, which might be more equitably allocated.[114] It would espouse a research methodology which eschews the failed technology of animal experimentation and allows a greater role for alternative/complimentary medicine rooted in more intuitive, personalised forms of health care, while simultaneously taking the social and economic environment into account.[115] In this I would argue that feminists can draw inspiration from

---

112 See Council Directive (86/609) of 24 November 1986 on the approximation of laws, regulations and administrative provisions of the Member States regarding the protection of animals used for experimental and other scientific purposes (OJ L358/1, pp 1–13); Brooman, S and Legge, D, *Law Relating to Animals*, 1997, London: Cavendish Publishing, pp 121–24.

113 *Op cit*, fn 65, Rose, pp 22–23; see also, Dickersin, K and Schnaper, L, 'Reinventing medical research', in Moss, K (ed), *Man-Made Medicine: Women's Health, Public Policy and Reform*, 1996, Durham: Duke University Press.

114 See Whitty, this volume.

115 Doyal, L and Doyal, L, 'Western scientific medicine: a philosophical and political prognosis', in Birke, L and Silvertown, J (eds), *More than the Parts: Biology and Politics*, 1984, London: Pluto Press.

the women's health movement of the 1970s, which encouraged women to question medical authority, take responsibility for their own bodies and express new demands for clinical research and access to health care.[116] It seems to me more productive to draw on this strand of feminist thought rather than one which, in the name of equality, implicitly endorses the patriarchal structure of clinical medicine.

---

116 *Op cit*, fn 65, Rose, p 134.

# CHAPTER EIGHT

# 'IN A PERFECT WORLD': FEMINISM AND HEALTH CARE RESOURCE ALLOCATION

*Noel Whitty*

[I]n a perfect world any treatment which a patient, or a patient's family, sought would be provided if doctors were willing to give it, no matter how much it cost ...[1]

## THE (NEW) POLITICS OF HEALTH CARE

In the 1990s, the provision of health care appears to have gained a central political significance. Responding to the public perception of a crisis in the United States health care system, a central plank of the 1992 Clinton presidency was a health care task force committed to universal health care.[2] In spite of the combination of spiralling medical expenditure yet ever-decreasing population coverage, President Clinton unambiguously pledged to give every American 'health care that can never be taken away, health care that is always there'.[3] Despite the claims that the reform plan would make a grossly unfair health care system more equitable for all, it was decisively rejected by Congress and a coalition of vested interests.[4]

In the United Kingdom in recent years, the perception has grown that the National Health Service (NHS) may share some of the characteristics of the American health care system. One of the most notable features has been the ballooning in expenditure on private health insurance.[5] Yet, at the same time as this apparent public loss of faith in state provision, pledges to 'save the NHS' remain a central part of the political currency. All political parties

---

1   *R v Cambridge HA ex p B* [1995] 2 All ER 137, *per* Bingham MR.

2   See Gostin, L, 'Foreword: health care reform in the United States – the presidential task force' (1993) 19 *American Journal of Law and Medicine* 1; and Marmor, T, 'The national agenda for health care reform: what does it mean for poor Americans?' (1994) 60 *Brooklyn Law Review* 83–103.

3   'Transcript of President's address to congress on health care' (1993) *New York Times*, 23 September. US health care expenditure is around 15% of GNP; in contrast, UK expenditure is around 6%.

4   On the political and economic reasons for the defeat of the Clinton plan, see Daniels, N, Light, D and Caplan, R, *Benchmarks of Fairness for Health Care Reform*, 1996, New York: OUP. It is also worth noting how the Conservative Right equated feminism (through the persona of Hillary Rodham Clinton) with health care reform.

5   Average household expenditure on health insurance increased 190% between 1986 and 1996. However, 1997 figures indicate a finite consumer market as a result of the rising cost of premiums: see 'Private Health Falters' (1997) *The Guardian*, 24 September.

declare support for the principle that NHS treatment should be universally provided on the basis of 'clinical need' rather than the ability to pay.[6] Any explicit acknowledgment of the need for 'rationing' of health care has been carefully avoided within mainstream British political discourse.[7]

In reality, rationing of health care has always been a fact of life within the NHS.[8] Prior to 1990, 'health authorities tended to set priorities in accordance with pressures emanating from two directions: from above came funding and health targets set by the [Department of Health and Regional Health Authorities]; from below came the demands of clinicians seeking sufficient resources for their specialities'.[9] Cooper made this point as far back as 1975:

> Rationing in the NHS has never been explicitly organised but has hidden behind each doctor's clinical freedom to act solely in the interests of his individual patient. Any conflict of interest between patients competing for scarce resources has been implicitly resolved by doctors' judgments as to their relative needs for care and attention.[10]

In 1990, aspects of the NHS rationing process became transparent as a result of the National Health Service and Community Care Act; legislation introduced as part of the Conservative agenda to subject certain public service provision to 'contract government'.[11] Through the creation of an 'internal market' in the NHS, responsibility for health care provision was devolved by central government to the local level on the alleged grounds of promoting accountability and cost-effectiveness.[12] The internal market required 'purchasers' (health authorities, GP fundholders and social services departments) to contract with 'providers' (NHS trusts and independent organisations) for the range of health services deemed necessary in each local area.[13] A combination of medical and management personnel, therefore, was expected to decide on health care priorities and the best allocation of resources.

---

6   See the Department of Health website for policy documents at http://www.open.gov.uk.

7   The need to maintain the public perception that the Conservative Party is less 'trustworthy' in relation to NHS matters, and thus electorally vulnerable, has dominated Labour Party health policy: see Sopel, J, *Tony Blair: The Moderniser*, 1996, London: Michael Joseph, p 252.

8   'Rationing' mechanisms are classified in different ways: *deterrence* (imposing charges); *delay* (hospital waiting lists); *deflection* (GP primary care only); *dilution* ('clinical judgment' determines priority); and *denial* (exclusion of certain treatments). See Harrison, S and Hunter, D, *Rationing Health Care*, 1994, London: IPPR, pp 24–31.

9   Lenaghan, J, *Rationing and Rights in Health Care*, 1996, London: IPPR, p 9 (reference omitted).

10  Cooper, M, *Rationing Health Care*, 1975, London: Croom Helm, p 59.

11  See generally Morison, J and Livingstone, S, *Reshaping Public Power*, 1995, London: Sweet & Maxwell.

12  Both of these rationales are heavily disputed: see Cooper, L *et al*, *Voices Off: Tackling the Democratic Deficit in Health*, 1995, London: IPPR.

13  See generally Montgomery, J, *Health Care Law*, 1997, Oxford: OUP, pp 83–113; and McHale, J and Fox, M, *Health Care Law: Text and Materials*, 1997, London: Sweet & Maxwell, pp 32–47.

The effects of the operation of the NHS internal market have proven to be highly contentious. Management costs have soared and patients of GP fundholding practices have been admitted to hospital more quickly than patients of non-fundholding practices. More pertinently for the purposes of this chapter, there are claims of widespread variation in NHS provision throughout the country; certain medical treatments are now either excluded or subject to different conditions depending on geographical location.[14] Whatever the reasons for this variation, the inevitable logic of an internal market, the exercise of devolved powers by health authorities, or different conceptions of patients' 'clinical need', in the public mind, the criteria for NHS provision is now perceived as unfair and unprincipled.

Since May 1997, the Labour government has signalled further reforms in terms of the institutional structures and priorities of the NHS. In particular, the Secretary of State for Health, Frank Dobson, has confirmed the future abolition of the NHS internal market (but the retention of the purchaser/provider division); the creation of a NHS efficiency task force; and the introduction of pilot 'alternate primary care-led models of commissioning health care based on the principle of fairness and meeting local needs'.[15] Thus, from April 1998, 42 projects throughout England, consisting of health authority, GP fundholders and non-fundholders commissioning health care in partnership, will be piloted as a suitable replacement for the current competitive model. A new Advisory Committee on Resource Allocation will also advise the Health Secretary on:

(a) the distribution of resources across primary and secondary care, in support of the goal of *equitable access to health care for all*; and

(b) to develop and apply methods which are as objective and needs-based as available data and techniques permit.[16]

The White Paper, *The New NHS*, published in December 1997, provides no further illumination on the actual criteria that will determine future priority-setting. Eschewing any discussion of rationing, it argues that shifting responsibility for commissioning health care to local primary care groups will provide more efficient and fairer standards of treatment. The need for standard-setting is stressed, through the creation of a new Institute for Clinical Excellence, and the development of 'evidence-based National Service Frameworks' to ensure consistency in health care provision. However, one is

---

14  See House of Commons Select Committee on Health, 'Priority Setting in the NHS', *Purchasing*, 1995, London: HMSO, Vol 1.

15  Department of Health, '8th Wave of Fundholding Deferred', press release, 20 May 1997. See also 'NHS Savings Targeted by New Task Force', 11 June 1997; 'Fairness and Equity for Hospital Treatment', 16 July 1997; and 'New Partnerships for Improved Health Services', 30 September 1997, *op cit*, fn 6.

16  Department of Health, 'Cash Formula to Help Tackle Health Inequalities', 11 September 1997 (emphasis added), *op cit*, fn 6.

left no wiser as to how, and why, historic patterns of discrimination within NHS provision will change so as to meet 'people's needs, irrespective of geography, class, ethnicity, age or sex'.

The NHS, therefore, is currently in another state of transition. Government policy indicates a moving away from a market ethos determining the provision of health care, but with no clear indication of what a 'fairer NHS' will mean in practice, and a stated commitment to devolve priority-setting in health care to meet local-level needs, while, at the same time, increasing centralised oversight.

## THE DOMINANCE OF HEALTH ECONOMICS

Despite the political rhetoric of fairness and equality in relation to NHS provision, when attention is focused on devising resource allocation policies, the debate seems to be dominated by a specialised, impenetrable discourse of 'health economics'.[17] Economic models for assessing concepts such as 'demand', 'costs' and 'outcomes' in health care have generated a literature which claims to tell the story of the NHS by figures alone. Media coverage of access to NHS services largely accepts these basic economic 'fundamentals'. The language is one of financial crisis within the NHS: 69 out of 100 health authorities and 125 out of 425 NHS trusts in debt; hospital building repairs estimated at £10 billion; and projected total NHS expenditure reflecting a zero funding increase between 1998 and 2000.[18] The consequence of limited resources is an inevitable list of horrors: closure of hospital wards, reduced staffing levels, cancelled operations, longer waiting lists, patient charges, and the increased rationing of certain services and medication.

The existence of a 'crisis' in NHS funding and spending priorities, however, is nothing new. Battles over health resources have always existed, and will inevitably increase in a political climate so hostile to increasing state expenditure. What is now being articulated are the tensions created by the combination of NHS management changes, especially, the introduction of 'efficiency' strategies and, thus, the challenge to doctors' clinical freedom, expensive advances in medical technology, and much more vocal public demands for health care. It is these factors which have forced the criteria used to allocate health care into the public domain. In particular, public disquiet has been most strongly pronounced against the perceived limitation of doctors' traditional autonomy:

---

17  I am not suggesting here that there is no diversity of positions amongst health economists. For example, see Wordsworth, S, Donaldson, C and Scott, A, *Can We Afford the NHS?*, 1996, London: IPPR.

18  See (1997) *The Observer*, 15 June. The July 1997 Labour Budget increased NHS funding for 1998–99 by £1.2 billion. To avert a 'winter crisis' in NHS hospitals in 1997, an extra £250 million was promised: see (1997) *The Observer*, 12 October.

Doctors had the lion's share of power within the system and, therefore, it was said, clinical priorities prevailed and patients considered themselves to be in safe hands ... In the modern system, however, doctors are no longer pre-eminent because aspects of their authority are shared with health service managers and resources are not at their complete disposal.[19]

Rationing in the NHS, therefore, has become a lightning rod for a number of intersecting political, economic and medical forces battling for recognition and supremacy. Despite the camouflage, the allocation of NHS resources is much more than about the amounts of public funding available. The potential for inequality and unfairness in the distribution of health care, caused by a range of institutional and political factors other than inadequate resources, is slowly starting to be acknowledged.

## MEDICAL LAW: ONLY A QUESTION OF RESOURCES?

Law, whether statute or judge-made, appears to offer little guidance on resource allocation policy. The NHS Act 1977 goes no further than imposing a general obligation on the Secretary of State to promote 'a comprehensive health service'. *The Patient's Charter* suggests a 'citizen's right' to certain standards of health care, but this concept of citizenship is not legally enforceable.[20] At first glance, the role of the courts in relation to NHS rationing appears minimal and insignificant. Allocation of resources is unambiguously defined as involving policy questions unsuited to a judicial forum. The issue has arisen in two legal contexts: negligence actions for compensation and in public law actions.

In negligence contexts, the lack of sufficient resources has sometimes been put forward in defence of a particular standard of treatment. The question for the courts, therefore, is whether the *Bolam* standard of care should shift in recognition of the financial constraints under which the NHS operates.[21] The issue remains undecided. In *Knight v Home Office*[22] the extent of resources appears to be a relevant factor in determining the standard of care owed to a patient. However, in *Bull v Devon HA*,[23] it is implied that limited resources cannot justify lowering the standard of legal liability.

Increasingly, it is in the field of public law that the issue of resource allocation is discussed by the courts. Where the legality of decisions (usually

---

19 Newdick, C, *Who Shall We Treat?*, 1997, Oxford: OUP, pp xi–xii.

20 See generally Barron, A and Scott, C, 'The Citizen's Charter Programme' (1992) 55 MLR 524; and Cooper, D, 'The Citizen's Charter and Radical Democracy: Empowerment and Exclusion Within Citizenship Discourse' (1993) 2 SLS 149.

21 On *Bolam* generally, see Sheldon, this volume.

22 [1990] 3 All ER 237.

23 (1993) 4 Med LR 117 (CA).

by health authorities) to ration health care is challenged by judicial review, the position of the courts appears to be emphatic: resource allocation is a 'non-justiciable' subject. In a series of decisions, judges have stated that the courts cannot 'enhance the standards of the National Health Service';[24] have 'no role of general investigator of social policy and of allocation of resources';[25] and 'cannot arrange the lists in ... hospital'.[26] In justifying this position, judges have argued that 'in principle the allocation of resources between patients is a matter for the health authority and not for the courts';[27] is a matter 'for Parliament';[28] and 'questions to be raised, answered, and dealt with outside the court'.[29] One of the remarkable features of the case law after 1990 is the absence of any comment on the existence of an internal market within the NHS. The judgments give no hint that new factors may have entered the resource allocation debate, requiring a more principled elaboration of the reasons for traditional judicial deference.

The case of *Re B* provides a good illustration of these points, as it involved an attempt to broaden substantially the judicial role in the determination of health care allocation.[30] The father of a 10-year-old girl with leukaemia challenged the decision of Cambridge Health Authority not to fund further medical treatment of B as it was considered not in her best interests on medical grounds nor 'an effective use of resources'. In the High Court, Laws J (who has argued that the common law embodies fundamental human principles)[31] ruled that the threat to B's right to life required the health authority to justify its decision objectively. It had 'to do more than toll the bell of tight resources' and 'to explain the priorities that had led them to decline to fund the treatment'. The Court of Appeal quickly reversed the decision. Bingham MR ruled that the health authority had acted perfectly lawfully in its consideration of the medical advice on B, and that it was under no obligation to justify how it allocated its funds. Where 'difficult and agonising judgments have to be made as to how a limited budget is best allocated to the maximum advantage of the maximum number of patients', the courts had no role to play. Access to health care was to be determined by health service management (ministers, health authorities, hospitals and so on) in conjunction

---

24  *R v Secretary of State for Social Services ex p Hincks* (1980) 1 BMLR 93 (CA), *per* Bridge LJ.

25  *R v Central Birmingham HA ex p Collier*, 6 January 1988, unreported, *per* Gibson LJ.

26  *Ibid, per* Brown LJ.

27  *Airedale NHS Trust v Bland* [1992] 2 WLR 357, *per* Hoffman LJ.

28  *Wilsher v Essex AHA* [1986] 3 All ER 801, *per* Browne-Wilkinson VC.

29  *R v Central Birmingham HA ex p Walker* (1987) 3 BMLR 32, *per* MacPherson J.

30  *Op cit*, fn 1, *R v Cambridge HA ex p B.*

31  See Laws, J, 'Is the High Court the guardian of fundamental human rights?' [1993] *Public Law* 59; for general discussion see Hunt, M, *Using Human Rights Law in English Courts*, 1997, Oxford: Hart Publishing.

with the medical profession's clinical judgment as to the best interests of patients.[32]

Medical law textbooks have also ducked consideration of the politics of health care. The criteria for access to medical treatment is generally sidelined by discussion of the core topics of doctor-patient relationship and 'life and death' ethical issues. When rationing of health care is considered, the typical textbook approach emphasises the finite nature of NHS resources and characterises the primary allocation of funding as a 'political' question for 'Parliament'. As to how these funds should be expended, there is relatively uncritical deference to the concept of doctors' 'clinical judgment' of patient need, but with the caveat that scarce resources should be distributed 'justly' or 'fairly' or 'equally.' Discussions of theories of justice in this context (more often viewed as an issue for bioethics rather than law) tend to focus heavily on liberal egalitarian philosophers such as John Rawls and Ronald Dworkin.[33] As with other areas of medical law, little or no mention is made of the range of contemporary feminist scholarship questioning the gendered nature of law, philosophy, medicine, science and other aspects of society.

## SOME FEMINIST QUESTIONS ABOUT RESOURCE ALLOCATION

Resource allocation in health care has not featured in feminist scholarship to any great extent. While the issue raises some important concerns of feminist political theory, there is little guidance for assessing fairness or equality in NHS allocation policy. This is partly due to the fact that feminism's primary focus in medical law has been on challenging traditional medical practices and discourses in the 'reproduction ghetto of Medical Law Woman'.[34] Rather than appeals for more 'health care' resources and more medicalisation, the emphasis has been in the opposite direction: the need to spend less and in ways more responsive to women's needs. As Peggy Foster has highlighted, women consume nearly 65% of resources in an NHS that is often characterised by patriarchal, exploitative, harmful, expensive and unnecessary

---

32 The High Court decision in *R v North Derbyshire HA ex p Fisher*, 2 September 1997, unreported, appears to challenge this conclusion somewhat. In a detailed examination of the health authority's memoranda, Dyson J ruled that an absolute ban on the funding of a drug treatment for MS patients, contrary to an NHS Executive policy statement, was illegal on the ground of irrationality.

33 See Dworkin, R, 'Justice in the Distribution of Health Care' (1993) 38 *McGill Law Journal* 883.

34 See Murphy, T, 'Bursting binary bubbles: law, literature and the sexed body', in Morison, J and Bell, C (eds), *Tall Stories? Reading Law and Literature*, 1996, Aldershot: Dartmouth, p 70; and Murphy, T, 'Feminism on flesh' (1997) VIII *Law and Critique* 37.

medical care.[35] In the need to decentre medicine, and its ally, medical law, little space has been devoted to the broader question of just allocation within health care systems.

This chapter imagines some feminist questions and responses to the growing rhetoric on the need for 'fairness' in the allocation of health care. Many recurrent themes of feminist scholarship are brought into focus by this issue: the State and markets, concepts of justice and difference, decision-making in public administration, medical professionalism, appropriate political strategies and so on, which serve to highlight both the challenges, and complexities, of feminist engagements with medical law. My aim is to draw upon some of this writing in order to problematise the standard account of resource allocation in the NHS sketched out above. In particular, I attempt a partial feminist critique of the dominant judicial discourse on NHS resources. By exploring different usage of the public/private dichotomy, I hope to expose how resource allocation is insulated from critical scrutiny on a number of grounds such as gender, race, class and sexual orientation. In highlighting the politics of some aspects of health care provision, I want to unmask the inequities hidden within the current system and to broaden the debate to address different forms of state, economic and medical power.

There are three sections to my argument. In the first section, I examine the courts' continued promotion in health care contexts of an inadequate concept of state power and political institutions. This is, of course, only symptomatic of the wider failure in British constitutional theory at coping with the shifts in the locus of public power away from Parliament to undemocratic quangos and regulatory bodies in furtherance of the free market.[36] In contrast, contemporary feminist political theory has increasingly focused on the nature of state power and the need to democratise access to public institutions and services. My limited focus here is on the way that judicial disclaimers of responsibility for, or influence over, NHS allocation policy conceals its gendered features.

In the second section, I highlight how judges uncritically replicate the dominant terms of the health resources debate by their affirmation of the inevitability of a market paradigm in rationing decisions. Legal discourse in resource allocation cases typically mirrors the stereotypical 'health economics' approach; the fundamental question is 'limited resources'. The extent of public provision of services is uncritically viewed as primarily conditioned by market criteria. While such norms may appear as gender-neutral, the effects of a market model determining the extent of state-funded health care often disproportionately impact on women and other disadvantaged groups.

---

35  Foster, P, *Women and the Healthcare Industry: An Unhealthy Relationship?*, 1995, Buckingham: Open University Press, p 2. See also, Doyal, L, *What Makes Women Sick*, 1995, London: Macmillan; and Foster, this volume.

36  *Op cit*, fn 11, Morison and Livingstone.

In the third section, I examine the consequences of the judicial privileging of a construction of the doctor-patient relationship as essentially private and non-political. Medical legal discourse reinforces the belief that the allocation of health care on the basis of 'clinical judgment' is an inherently fair and value-neutral process. Instead of questioning whether medical practice replicates social hierarchies on grounds such as gender, race, class and sexual orientation, it is assumed that the doctor's determination of a patient's best interests is insulated from such forces. The debate over the equity of NHS rationing policies, therefore, proceeds on an idealised view of the doctor-patient relationship, one which submerges the question of any power imbalance or social prejudice existing between the two parties. In reducing the NHS rationing debate to an exclusive question of limited resources, legal discourse deflects critical attention away from the power and influence of the medical profession. I will suggest that a prerequisite for fairer NHS rationing policies is a feminist reconstruction of the doctor-patient relationship; one that rejects the concept of a generic medical relationship and takes account of the diversity of 'lived experiences'.

## Political = Parliament

In this section, I briefly problematise three related aspects of judicial discourse in health care contexts. First, I want to draw attention to the inadequacy of the court's construction of political power and the institutions of government. Secondly, I comment on the limited institutional role of the courts in regulating the exercise of public power in relation to health care. Thirdly, while arguing for increased public participation in the setting of priorities within the NHS, I question how inclusive and empowering current reform proposals are likely to be.

Courts constantly define and redefine the boundaries of law and politics, public and private. One of the main devices which judges use to justify their refusal to intervene in health resource questions is by classifying the issue as for 'Parliament' alone. This effectively discounts the role of other institutions, discourses and cultural practices in shaping social reality. As Fraser and Lacey have argued, equating 'the political' with the central branch of government remains:

> ... utterly inadequate for theorising the conditions of the modern social democratic state, in which a wide range of institutions ranging from the legislature through quangos, pressure groups, businesses, banks, unions, the family, the church and so on must all be acknowledged to wield what are properly seen as forms of political power.[37]

---

37  Fraser, E and Lacey, N, *The Politics of Community*, 1993, Toronto: University of Toronto Press, p 75.

The simplistic appeal to 'Parliament' as a mechanism for controlling government is especially inadequate in the context of health care allocation policy. Not only does it disregard the reality of the recent structural changes within the NHS which have devolved power *away* from central government, it ignores the history of government deference on this issue, precisely to avoid responsibility for rationing decisions, to the medical profession. Even if parliamentary oversight was not so limited, the fact remains that historically disadvantaged groups may have little or no influence at this level.[38] Legal discourse in this context, therefore, contributes to the maintenance of the status quo. No other hierarchies of power are acknowledged, let alone disrupted, when courts tailor their construction of what is 'political' in this way.

Secondly, the justifications put forward for the circumscribed nature of judicial intervention require challenge. The history of the expansion of judicial review has less to do with a concern that courts not make 'political' decisions, than the character of the decision in question. Judicial deference is stronger in some areas rather than others, and one of the dividing lines appears to be whether decisions will have major policy implications or can be limited to protecting individual interests. Judicial rhetoric on deference to Parliament, and the limited grounds of judicial review, is often just rhetoric. The question to be asked, therefore, is why the courts' perception of their role is so narrow in the health care context and what are the political consequences of judicial abstention. As James and Longley have argued:

> The courts have a part to play in structuring decision-making and ensuring that the policy choice made, even if reasonable, is explained and justified ... This is not an argument for judges interfering with decisions, but for refining the decision-making process, and consequently reducing any sense of unfairness and ultimately recourse to litigation.[39]

In asking these questions, I do not mean to suggest that litigation strategies are the best way forward in challenging discriminatory health care policies or medical power. Feminist scepticism of law and rights discourse in any health care context is well placed.[40] Courts are generally not effective in institutional terms as regulators.[41] The devising of a rationing policy requires processes more participatory and factually nuanced, less adversarial and conclusory, than the legal process can ever be. There are, however, a number of factors which point to the need for more feminist scholarship on this issue. Judicial

---

38  See Phillips, A, *Engendering Democracy*, 1991, Oxford: Polity Press; and Lovenduski, J and Norris, P (eds), *Women in Politics*, 1996, Oxford: OUP.

39  James, R and Longley, D, 'Judicial Review and Tragic Choices' [1995] *Public Law* 367. See generally, Teff, H, *Reasonable Care: Legal Perspectives on the Doctor-Patient Relationship*, 1994, Oxford: Clarendon Press, pp 46–51.

40  See generally Smart, C, *Feminism and the Power of Law*, 1989, London: Routledge.

41  See Ogus, A, *Regulation: Legal Form and Economic Theory*, 1994, Oxford: Clarendon Press, pp 115–17; and generally Galligan, D (ed), *A Reader on Administrative Law*, 1996, Oxford: OUP.

review challenges to health authority decisions will inevitably continue. The UK courts are appropriating a human rights-based jurisdiction and an equality jurisprudence will develop. At the European level, the case of *D v United Kingdom*,[42] where the proposed deportation of an AIDS patient to a country with inadequate medical facilities was ruled to be inhuman treatment, points to increasing usage of the discourse of health care rights.[43] More generally, such 'tragic cases' (for example, Diane Blood) are often the stage for legal, medical and media forces perpetuating traditional notions of femininity, masculinity and maternity and require a critique.

Thirdly, the need to politicise health care policy beyond current boundaries, ensuring greater accountability and public participation in decisions about resource allocation, is a welcome feature of reform proposals. Government policy states that NHS priority-setting is to be responsive to 'local needs'. Most famously, Oregon conducted 'grassroots' surveys on its health care policy[44] and, in 1996, the Institute for Public Policy Research (IPPR) experimented with 'citizens' juries'.[45] There is insufficient space to discuss these proposals in any depth but two points need to be made. The first is to question whether public participation actually entails empowerment. As Mansbridge notes:

> [T]he transformation of 'I' into 'we' brought about through political deliberation can easily mask subtle forms of control. Even the language people use as they reason together usually favors one way of seeing things and discourages others. Subordinate groups sometimes cannot find the right voice or words to express their thoughts, and when they do, they discover they are not heard.[46]

Secondly, even where new structures are set up to encourage public participation in health care decision-making, the fact remains that the greatest deference may be to the views of medical professionals. In the public mind, 'clinical judgment' remains the best determinant of rationing policy.

## The inevitability of the market paradigm

In this section, I want to highlight how legal discourse contributes to the dominant terms of the health care resources debate. Judicial language is peppered with references to scarce NHS resources, costs, accounts and

---

42 European Court of Human Rights, 2 May 1997. See ECHR website at http://www.dhcour. coe.fr/eng/D.JUD.html.

43 *Op cit*, fn 13, McHale and Fox, pp 7–10.

44 *Op cit*, fn 19, Newdick, pp 30–36.

45 *Op cit*, fn 9, Lenaghan, pp 71–95; and Cooper, L *et al*, *Voices Off: Tackling the Democratic Deficit in Health*, 1995, London: IPPR.

46 Mansbridge, J, 'Feminism and democracy' (1990) 1 *American Prospect* 127; and Murphy, this volume.

management dilemmas; the traditional discourse of the economist. In their affirmation of the inevitability of a market paradigm in rationing decisions, judges hinder the development of a wider political discourse on justice in the allocation of NHS resources. This failure, of course, is not confined to the health care context but is part of a wider failure within public law to respond to the political agenda of the New Right; as Harlow puts it, 'the effect of the ostrich posture has been to leave the field clear for economists ...'.[47] Most significantly for this chapter, the implications for women of market criteria determining the extent of public services such as health care is not addressed.

The case of *Re B* provides a particularly vivid example. In the leading judgment, Bingham MR uncritically adopted the neatness of economic calculus, 'how a limited budget is best allocated to the maximum advantage of the maximum number of patients', as the basis of resource allocation policy. This is not to suggest that economic criteria are irrelevant to resource allocation decisions; my point is the complete absence of any countervailing legal discourse to the dominance of market criteria in discussions of access to public health care.

Feminist theory, in contrast, does provide some of the analytical tools for unmasking the contemporary NHS resource allocation debate. I want to draw on some of this literature to suggest ways in which terms such as markets and efficiency in the health care context can be problematised. It should be highlighted, however, that this issue is a complex and politically contentious one, as feminist scholarship dealing with aspects of the free market is (obviously) not homogenous.

First, capitalism can be viewed as historically gendered through the division of market and private spheres, where the majority of women engage in both low-pay employment and unpaid work in the home.[48] Female-dominated occupations have also been described as 'overwhelmingly analogous to the tasks of mothers/wives/housewives, that is, to the type of work women have traditionally performed in the private sphere'.[49] Yet the norms of the market appear as gender-neutral; it is 'a depersonalised analysis dealing only with abstract suppliers and consumers of resources'.[50] For example, in the health care context, the use of terms such as 'efficiency' may appear unbiased. The move to make hospitals more efficient may lead to earlier discharge of patients, yet the consequences are left unacknowledged:

---

47  Harlow, C, 'Changing the mindset' (1994) 14 OJLS 433.

48  See Brown, W, *States of Injury: Power and Freedom in Late Modernity*, 1995, Princeton: Princeton University Press, pp 166–96.

49  Gatens, M, *Feminism and Philosophy: Perspectives on Difference and Equality*, 1991, Bloomington: Indiana University Press, p 135. See generally, Olsen, F, 'The Family and the Market' (1983) 96 *Harvard Law Review* 1497; and Pateman, C, *The Sexual Contract*, 1988, Oxford: Polity Press.

50  Elson, D, 'From survival strategies to transformation strategies: women's needs and structural adjustment', in Beneria, L and Feldman, S (eds), *Unequal Burden: Economic Crises, Persistent Poverty and Women's Work*, 1992, Boulder: Westview, p 34.

Someone at home must continue the care of these patients. Women are much more likely than men to put the needs of their families ahead of paid work, and they are paid less for the work they do outside of the home ... The economics of the family thus tend to dictate that the adult males' higher income not be jeopardised, and that the women, who have less pay to lose, stay at home with those in need of care. Yet staying at home only marginalises women further in the workforce, and so the cycle continues.[51]

Not only is there an assumption that a home exists for each patient, but it assumes that a carer is available and able to cope. Other economic strategies may appear gender-neutral on their face but, in reality, discriminate against women. For example, QALYs impact most heavily on the elderly which, on current rates of life expectancy, means a disproportionate impact on women. Similarly, the attachment of health care insurance to employment also assumes a standard employment pattern which does not exist for any number of reasons relating to gender, race, class, age and so on. As Barker argues, any 'criterion of economic well-being that excludes any consideration of unequal distributions of income, wealth, and political power rationalises the status quo and perpetuates these inequalities'.[52]

Secondly, not only does (public sector) market ideology conceal unequal gender relations, it shifts the focus away from the State by appearing to absolve it for the inadequacy of those services remaining within the public sector. The market becomes the determinant of what is possible in the public sector as 'government frequently is now expected to look like as well as perform in a manner consistent with private sector models'.[53] Feminism generally is somewhat wary of this language of 'rolling back the State', and the moving of economic relations (back) into the 'private' sphere; traditionally equated with the absence of government scrutiny and regulation.[54] As Thornton has pointed out, the 'contemporary imperative of governments [is] to privatise spheres of life in which a public focus is advantageous for women'.[55] When government withdraws completely from the provision of essential services (for example, water), not only is the concept of citizenship being redefined, there is also a disparate impact on gender, race and class grounds. In the context of health care, for the majority of people, there is no possibility of choice between market (private health care) and state (NHS provision); the latter is the only option available.

---

51  Lindemann Nelson, H, and Lindemann Nelson, J, 'Justice in the allocation of health care resources: a feminist account', in Wolf, S (ed), *Feminism and Bioethics: Beyond Reproduction*, 1996, Oxford: OUP, p 357; and see Biggs, this volume.

52  Barker, D, 'Economists, social reformers and prophets: a feminist critique of economic efficiency' (1995) 1 *Feminist Economics* 35.

53  Aman, A, 'Administrative Law for a New Century,' in Taggart, M (ed), *The Province of Administrative Law*, 1997, Oxford: Hart Publishing, p 105.

54  On the 'myth' of a non-regulated sphere of social life, see Rose, N, 'Beyond the public/private division: law, power and the family' (1987) 14 JLS 61.

55  Thornton, M (ed), *Public and Private: Feminist Legal Debates*, 1995, Oxford: OUP, p xvi.

Feminist challenge to NHS allocation policy, therefore, is a complex task, involving contextual rethinking of the concepts of public and private, State and market. Free-market ideology needs to be contested without discounting the gains women *may* make from participation in the market;[56] while ensuring equitable public provision of services such as health care (or welfare payments) without perpetuating the role of the State in the regulation and subordination of women.[57] This is no easy task as, in challenging the contemporary ideology of 'more of the market and less of the State',[58] the impression is given that traditional manifestations of state power are unproblematic. It needs also to be emphasised that the structure of the NHS presents novel obstacles. The NHS, in its reorganised form, is a hybrid combination of State/market and public/private. It remains in public ownership but is increasingly managed and regulated according to economic criteria.[59] The attempted redefinition of the citizen/patient as consumer is most clearly articulated in the ideology lying behind *The Patient's Charter*.[60]

A critical theory of both market and State is thus necessary in any feminist political project on health care reform.[61] The importance of a dual critique is further reinforced by the growing recognition that societies with the lowest income differences are the most healthy; thus, improving health care cannot be divorced from the goal of reducing economic inequality amongst groups.[62]

## Constructing the doctor-patient relationship

Reading the resource allocation cases might lead one to believe that it is only due to the scarcity of resources that every patient cannot receive NHS

---

56  I stress the word 'may' here. For different perspectives, see Flynn, L, 'The internal market and the European Union: some feminist notes', in Bottomley, A (ed), *Feminist Perspectives on the Foundational Subjects of Law*, 1996, London: Cavendish Publishing, pp 279–97; Mohanty, C, 'Women Workers and Capitalist Scripts: Ideologies of Domination, Common Interests and the Politics of Solidarity', in Alexander, J and Mohanty, C (eds), *Feminist Genealogies, Colonial Legacies, Democratic Futures*, 1997, London: Routledge, pp 3–29; and Hennessey, R, 'Queer Visibility in Commodity Culture', in Nicholson, L and Seidman, S (eds), *Social Postmodernism*, 1995, Cambridge: CUP, pp 142–83.

57  See generally, Connell, R, 'The State, Gender and Sexual Politics: Theory and Appraisal', in Lorraine Radtke, H and Stam, H (eds), *Power/Gender: Social Relations in Theory and Practice*, 1994, London: Sage, pp 136–73; and Goetz, AM, 'No More Heroes? Feminism and the State in Australia' (1994) *Social Politics* 341.

58  *Op cit*, fn 50, Elson, p 38.

59  See Hughes, D, 'The reorganisation of the NHS: the rhetoric and reality of the internal market' 54 MLR 88.

60  *Op cit*, fn 10, Cooper.

61  The absence of a sufficiently comprehensive account of state power in feminist critical theory has been addressed by a number of writers: see *op cit*, fn 48, Brown; and Cooper, D, *Power in Struggle: Feminism, Sexuality and the State*, 1995, New York: New York University Press.

62  See Freedman, L, 'Reflections on emerging frameworks of health and human rights' (1995) 1 *Health and Human Rights* 315.

treatment. According to Bingham MR in *Re B*, 'in a perfect world any treatment which a patient, or a patient's family, sought would be provided if doctors were willing to give it, no matter how much it cost ...'.[63] The British Medical Association, in its statement of medical ethics, acknowledges the need for NHS doctors 'to be aware of cost-effectiveness as well as clinical effectiveness in the care provided for the patient'.[64] But no further critical enquiry appears to be warranted. The traditional doctor-patient relationship appears unproblematic provided there is 'value for money'.

Opinion polls have consistently shown that doctors are the most trusted group to make decisions as to allocation of resources.[65] The basis for this trust is the concept of clinical judgment: doctors, drawing on their medical/ethical expertise, 'know' the best course of action in terms of health care.[66] Medical law's construction of the doctor-patient relationship solidifies this perception. The doctor and patient in this discourse are generic identities; no distinctions are drawn as to who the doctor is and who the patient is. No social hierarchies or prejudices appear to exist, except in terms of a benevolent medical paternalism on the part of the doctor.[67]

This section emphasises the need for a reconstruction of the doctor-patient relationship in medical ethics and law before a debate on the fairness of NHS rationing can proceed. I will argue that the current concept of clinical judgment needs to be discarded because it ignores the fact that medical practice replicates social hierarchies on grounds such as gender, sexual orientation, race and class. The doctor-patient relationship does not exist in a vacuum, but operates in tandem with other institutional practices and social/cultural traditions. I argue for a concept of the doctor-patient relationship that acknowledges its political nature across diverse terrains such as gender, race, class, sexuality, religion, age or disability. In place of the assumption that the doctor's office is immune from social prejudices, the doctor-patient interaction needs to be politicised and open to critical scrutiny.[68]

To substantiate this argument, I first highlight three characteristics of law's construction of the doctor-patient relationship as private and non-political. I then focus on two contexts where feminist critiques of doctor-patient interactions have clearly demonstrated the politicised nature of medical knowledge and practice. As these case studies show, instead of access to

---

63  *Op cit*, fn 1, *R v Cambridge HA ex p B*, p 137.

64  British Medical Association, *Medical Ethics Today*, 1993, London: BMA, p 300.

65  *Op cit*, fn 8, Harrison and Hunter, p 39.

66  See Sheldon, S, *Beyond Control: Medical Power and Abortion Law*, 1997, London: Pluto Press, pp 50–51.

67  See Thomson, this volume.

68  Such a step would also facilitate exposure of the institutional politics of the health care system in terms of the prioritisation of different branches of medicine, and the asymmetry between medical, nursing, public health and social work professions.

health care hinging on the availability of resources, a range of other social and political factors (that are ignored in resource allocation debates) often determine the issue.

First, there is a long history of judicial deference to doctors as members of an eminent profession, exercising their expertise for the best interests of the general public. This is most apparent from the dominance of the *Bolam* test in medical law, 'a potent symbol of judicial acquiescence in traditional mores'.[69] Instead of viewing a profession capable of wielding institutional power, medical law is based on a narrative of individual doctors (and individual patients).

Secondly, the 'clinical judgment' of doctors is generally depoliticised and perceived as off limits to any outside public scrutiny. Unlike the situation with other professions, doctors are rarely challenged on the logic or consistency of medical treatment.[70] In medical legal discourse, the combined effects of perceived scientific rationalism and medical professionalism renders clinical judgment value-neutral.[71] Consequently, where resources are said to be allocated on the grounds of clinical judgment, the common sense reaction is that such a decision is inevitably the best outcome and requires no further justification.

Thirdly, the discourse of medical *ethics* plays an important role in the legitimation of medical power. As Roberts points out, 'doctors make a distinction between the *private* sphere of doctor-patient interaction ruled by ethical principles and the *public* sphere of health law and policy from which they keep their distance'.[72] This concept of private ethics has, until now, facilitated doctors characterising resource allocation as 'political' and outside their concern. The reality of medical practice was always otherwise; clinical decisions inevitably involved choices as to resource allocation and different branches of medicine (particularly, 'cutting-edge' high-technology areas such as transplant surgery) battled for the larger proportion of funds. The effect of the NHS internal market has now made this stance untenable; clinical judgment is now explicitly subject to auditing (albeit to varying degrees), destroying any claim that the doctor-patient relationship is immune from scrutiny.

The first context which highlights the inadequacy of the traditional construction of clinical judgment is drawn from the work of Dorothy Roberts. Her focus is on how white feminist accounts of the medical profession 'often

---

69  *Op cit*, fn 39, Teff, p 51. The history of regulation of the medical profession, as with the legal profession, is largely based on self-regulation.

70  *Op cit*, fn 19, Newdick, p 94.

71  Harding, S, *The Science Question in Feminism*, 1986, Milton Keynes: Open University Press.

72  Roberts, D, 'Reconstructing the Patient: Starting with Women of Color', in *op cit*, fn 51, Wolf, p 121 (emphasis added).

assume that doctors treat all women the same or that medical practice is more fundamentally shaped by gender than it is by race and class'.[73] By adopting the perspective of women of colour, she explores how the grounds of race, gender and class intersect to produce disparate treatment of patients:

> Race, class, and gender structure doctors' knowledge of their patients and their interpretation of the ethical principles they apply to their interactions with their patients. [The] point is not only that physicians bring to their encounters with patients the same prejudices as exist in the rest of society. The relationship between doctor and patient is determined by political arrangements and not solely by the individual characteristics of the two actors.[74]

For example, one study of doctor-patient relations discovered that 'the darker a woman's skin and/or the lower her place on the economic scale, the poorer the care and efforts at explanation she got'.[75] The stereotyping of women as 'undesirable' mothers because of their racial and class identity has resulted in disproportionately higher rates of sterilisations, abortion and use of implantable contraceptives among black and white working-class women.[76] As Roberts argues, these consequences are not just the result of individual racial prejudice within the medical profession, they reflect society's historical devaluation and stigmatisation of black motherhood. Transforming the doctor-patient relationship, therefore, is not just about changing the norms of medical practice; it also requires 'a reconstruction of society's view of the patient'.[77]

The second context which challenges the apparent objectivity of medical knowledge, and the legal construction of NHS access as non-political, is especially interesting as it demonstrates how participation in the private health care market may benefit groups of patients who face prejudice in the public sector. The study is Davina Cooper's analysis of the regulation of lesbian access to donor insemination services in the early 1990s. This is a particularly useful focus as it demonstrates the multifaceted nature of the relationship between the State and NHS doctors, as well as the inaccuracy of conceptualising the medical profession as monolithic in its practices and attitudes.

When the Conservative government enacted s 13(5) of the Human Fertilisation and Embryology Act 1990 (HFEA), obliging clinics to take account of 'the need of [a] child for a father', it was able to rely on a dominant medical professional discourse for legitimacy. Yet, at the same time, the government saw the need for increased regulation of NHS doctors. The consequence was the subjecting of both clinics and women seeking assisted

---

73  *Op cit*, fn 72, Roberts, p 123.
74  *Ibid*, p 124.
75  Dundas Todd, A, *Intimate Adversaries: Cultural Conflict Between Doctors and Women Patients*, 1989, Philadelphia: University of Pennsylvania Press, p 77.
76  *Op cit*, fn 35, Foster, p 22.
77  *Ibid*, fn 72, Roberts, p 129.

reproduction services to heightened state scrutiny. Nevertheless, in another example of how the medical profession can mediate and diffuse state control over its practices, the HFE Authority (composed of medical and lay personnel) drafted a Code of Practice for clinics which lessened the effect of s 15(3). The practical impact of HFEA on clinics, therefore, was limited, as the majority which had previously refused lesbian clients only continued to do so. In contrast, the impact of HFEA on prospective lesbian mothers was more significant. Apart from the personal effects of the general reinforcement of traditional familial discourses, there was a changed perception of state provision of medical services:

> As long as clinics ... were regarded as part of the voluntary sector, many lesbians deemed them less intrusive than the NHS. For women, fearful that their sexual status might be monitored, assisted reproduction – with its attendant conditions of confidentiality and vulnerability – appeared safer outside state-run institutions. [M]ore trust [could] be placed in such clinics as a result of their non-state identity.[78]

This mirrors in some respects the experience of women seeking abortion. Due to a combination of factors such as delay, deprioritisation and medical hostility within the NHS, around 50% of all terminations were privately funded up until 1991. The decision to 'go private' in such situations is obviously dependent on a range of factors, including access to private income, and for some individuals may only have been voluntary in a limited sense. One result of this history of 'unofficial privatisation' was the further deprioritisation of abortion services within certain NHS areas. Since 1992, however, the impact of the internal market has forced a change of abortion policy: the percentage of NHS-funded terminations has increased from 57% to 71% in 1995. As Sheldon argues:

> The most likely explanation for this trend would seem to be the desire of both the providers and purchasers to keep resources within the NHS. In addition, it may be that providers tend to accept that there is a need for NHS abortion services; consultant gynaecologists who were formerly reluctant to terminate pregnancies have become more willing when such activity increases departmental income.[79]

Research on the actual decision-making processes of health authorities and general practitioners, however, reveals that informal means-testing and moral prejudice, rather than health needs, continues to influence the number and geographical location of abortions performed within the NHS.[80]

---

78 *Op cit*, fn 10, Cooper, pp 89–90. See also, Stevens, P, 'Lesbians and doctors: experiences of solidarity and domination in health care settings' (1996) 10 *Gender and Society* 24.

79 *Op cit*, fn 66, Sheldon, pp 56–57.

80 Abortion Law Reform Association, *A Report on NHS Abortion Services*, 1997, London: ALRA. The refusal of IVF treatment on the grounds of age, or allegedly unsuitable parenting credentials, could also be interpreted as rationing in line with ideas of appropriate femininity and maternity: see *R v Ethical Committee of St Mary's Hospital (Manchester) ex p Harriott* [1988] 1 FLR 512; and *R v Sheffield HA ex p Seale* [1996] MLR 326.

In conclusion, while it has been argued that the women's health movement has 'encouraged some doctors within mainstream medicine to become more open and less authoritarian within the doctor-patient relationship',[81] the examples discussed above highlight the continued institutional indifference and resistance to equitable, non-biased exchanges between doctor and patient. As long as medical practice contributes to, and replicates, wider societal prejudices and inequalities, NHS resource allocation policies cannot be other than discriminatory.

## A SHORT CONCLUSION: FEMINIST ENGAGEMENT WITH HEALTH CARE NARRATIVES

The absence of grand theories is, undoubtedly, a good thing. In their place, feminism prefers to privilege the particular and local. Given the complex array of forces and actors involved within the NHS, it is highly unlikely that any overarching theory of justice in the distribution of health care is possible or desirable. However, the need for some feminist 'benchmarks' in health care allocation is indisputable; even more so, in contemporary political climates, as the State reinvents its obligations towards the citizen in the swell of the market. I have sought to show that one-dimensional accounts of the State, the market and the doctor-patient relationship conceal the complexities of the NHS rationing debate. Despite the rhetoric of equity and fairness, resource allocation policies may mask deep inequalities in access to health care. Reform of health care systems is on the political agenda for the foreseeable future but, to date, feminist attention within medical law has been directed elsewhere. Feminism now has 'an opportunity to do more than defend the threatened interests of women. It may transform our very notions of what health care is, and for that matter, of what justice is, as well'.[82]

---

81  *Op cit*, fn 35, Foster, p 190.
82  *Op cit*, fn 51, Lindemann Nelson and Lindemann Nelson, p 367.

# CHAPTER NINE

# HEALTH CONFIDENTIALITY
# IN THE AGE OF TALK

*Thérèse Murphy*

## LISTEN UP

In this chapter, I mobilise an 'erotics of talk'. I appropriate this expression, and a good deal of the underlying analysis, from Carla Kaplan.[1] She uses it to challenge feminist literary criticism to revisit cherished texts, unpacking the cosy consensus which represents finding voice as the *sine qua non* of liberation, and forcing new readings of resistance, silence and conversation in women's writing: I use it to map out a health care schema that is less preoccupied with the politics of voice and more open to the possibility of meaningful communication. More generally, I use it to revive inquiry into the intimate, and to maximise the dialogic potential of Habermasian theories of communicative ethics.[2]

To make my case for an erotics of talk, I proceed as follows. I begin with a sketch of the cultural turn to 'talk'. I outline what I see as its two key components: first, the Habermasian-inspired vogue for 'communicative ethics', in particular the theorisation of dialogue itself as a superior form of democratic action to prevailing interest-based, and ultimately consumer-oriented, democratic politics; and second, the near-global embrace of the 'politics of voice', in particular the transformative power of breaking silence and finding 'voice'. I think this turn to talk is a good thing for three reasons. First, it offers welcome respite from tired anxieties about women's propensity for talk, particularly our passion for chitchat and gossip.[3] Second, talk forces debate: it reminds us that there are many things that must be argued out, and that often 'there is no final end, no final proof of what is right or wrong, only the possibility of continuing debate about it'.[4] And finally, talk is, at the same time, 'the necessary condition for changing the terms of the debate, for effecting change in individual and intimate as well as public life'.[5]

---

1    Kaplan, C, *The Erotics of Talk: Women's Writing and Feminist Paradigms*, 1996, New York: OUP.

2    For a brief sketch of theories of communicative ethics, see below, pp 159–60.

3    *Ibid*, Kaplan, p 4.

4    Weeks, J, *Invented Moralities: Sexual Values in an Age of Uncertainty*, 1995, Oxford: Polity Press, p 153.

5    *Ibid*.

But I am not sanguine about talk. In the second section of this chapter, I argue that, in many, too many, instances, talk eludes us. Mostly, this happens because voice, or one of its proliferating synonyms: 'visibility', 'talking back', 'speaking up' (or 'out'), has come to be seen as sufficient for talk, thereby allowing monologue, or worse, self-talk, to masquerade as dialogue. Monologue and self-talk may be speech acts, but their communicative capacity is low-grade when compared with dialogue: monologue is cited as a signifier of speaker-power, but its reception is frequently tinged with boredom, resentment and frustration; and self-talk has an even more negative image, fuelled by associations with madness and childishness.

Let me be clear here: I am not against voice *per se*. It is, after all, a component of talk. Moreover, as I will explain below, it is also not without independent merit. My point is that there is more to talk than voice. There is, most crucially, the need for a listener, one 'capable of hearing that voice and responding appropriately to it'.[6] Without such a listener (whom I'll call the ideal listener), there is no possibility of dialogue. Instead, a speaker will founder, either because all voices are rendered inaudible in a din of destructive noise, or because s/he speaks with the voice of a particular group that has been consigned to self-talk by inhospitable styles of listening and exclusionary norms of speech competence.

These latter points about inhospitable listening and exclusionary speech norms lead me to a second problem with the contemporary celebration of coming to voice: exuberance about voice obscures the speaker-bias inherent in the prevailing etiquette of discursive interaction. As Nancy Fraser reminds us, 'capacities for consent and speech, the ability to participate on a par with others in dialogue ... are capacities connected with masculinity in male-dominated classical capitalism'.[7] Consider, for example, why it is that, after formal impediments to participation have been removed, many speakers continue to remark on the embarrassment, discomfort and frustration which accompany the task of communication. Why is it that 'in formal situations of discussion and debate ... many people feel they must apologize for their halting and circuitous speech'?[8] Speakers tend to blame themselves for failing to measure up to norms of speaking style and decorum: I will suggest that we should be thinking about blaming the norms.

My third problem with the contemporary privileging of voice is that it heightens the already-stagnant aura of the intimate sphere. I believe that 'the personal is political', but I also desire the freedom and openness that the private makes possible. And I believe that excessive attention to voice (I'm

---

6   *Op cit*, fn 1, Kaplan, p 15.

7   Fraser, N, *Justice Interruptus: Critical Reflections on the 'Postsocialist' Condition*, 1997, New York: Routledge, p 126.

8   Young, IM, *Intersecting Voices: Dilemmas of Gender, Political Philosophy, and Policy*, 1997, Princeton, NJ: Princeton University Press, p 164.

thinking here particularly of its manifestation as a desire for visibility or recognition) is speeding up the popular dash towards the public sphere. But, as Jeffrey Weeks explains, the consequent abandonment of the intimate has produced unfortunate side-effects.[9] Two of these are of particular concern here: first, this abandonment may impede the development of less familiar forms of intimacy, ie, forms which reach beyond the sexual or the familial and which also acknowledge the age of technology. Second, this abandonment of the private sphere blunts 'the promise of democracy' which, according to Anthony Giddens, inheres in intimacy's 'imperative of free and open communication'.[10] I would like to reverse this abandonment of the intimate. In particular, I would like to see intimacy claw back a place in theoretical inquiry and become a respectable facet of individual well-being, rather than a tool of oppression and abuse.[11]

In calling for inquiry into these things, appropriate listening, participatory parity, and intimacy, I am centring that which is often devalued, occluded, or unfulfilled, yet almost always desired. In Kaplan's words, I am centring the 'erotic'.

But what has this to do with health confidentiality? In this chapter, I use health care as a case study in the creation of true talk. Situating the doctrine of consent and the growth of talk therapy as health care's politics of voice, I pursue confidentiality as a possible source of this politics' essential complement, ie, an erotics of talk. In particular, I argue that the contemporary privileging of consent and talk therapy has failed to generate dialogue in health care. Paralleling the problems with voice outlined above, health care has ended up privileging monological rather than dialogical modes of talk. It has individualised rather than empowered.[12] It has infected itself with an often ugly and contestatory politics. Finally, its chosen strategies have obscured both the need for competent listening and the impact of power differentials which impede effective speech for particular patients.

The problem runs deep. Consent and therapeutic talk are over-exposed; yet, our expectations of them continue to build. In this chapter, I nominate confidentiality as a possible locus of more productive dialogue in health care. I argue that it has the capacity to blunt the excesses of a politics of voice that has over-invested in consent and therapeutic talk. Confidentiality's potential lies in the fact that it frames the listener, not just the speaker, and thereby

---

9    *Op cit*, fn 4, Weeks, pp 124–54.

10   Giddens, A, *The Transformation of Intimacy: Sexuality, Love & Eroticism in Modern Societies*, 1992, Stanford, CA: Stanford University Press, pp 188, 194: 'A symmetry exists between the democratising of personal life and democratic possibilities in the global political order at the most extensive level ... The advancement of self-autonomy in the context of pure relationships is rich with implications for democratic practice in the larger community.'

11   Here I am echoing one of the dominant themes of Jeffrey Weeks' recent work, *Invented Moralities, op cit*, fn 4.

12   I take these distinctions from Iris Marion Young who uses them to differentiate forms of talk-based therapy: see, *op cit*, fn 8, Young, pp 75–94.

recentres talk. A second attraction of confidentiality is that its long-standing, if incomplete, support for the values of trust, faithfulness, and loyalty, might serve to foreground intimacy, thereby enhancing the democratisation of health care interactions. Finally, I will argue that confidentiality's legal appendages (like the public interest defence for confidence breakers), although in need of massive restructuring, present ready-made tools for minimising the over-identification and misplaced quest for empathy which characterise many contemporary situations of dialogue, as well as some versions of Habermasian talk theory.[13]

# SPEAKEASY

Of late there has been an all-round turn to voice and talk. 'Speaking up', 'speaking out', 'voice', and 'visibility' feature prominently in modernist manifestos: meanwhile, starring as their postmodern counterparts, one generally finds 'discourse', 'semiotics' and 'performance'. Talk theory, or communicative ethics, is also very much in vogue. As I see it, all this leads inexorably to the following question: might talk have what it takes to captivate all of us, sating the modern yearning for recognition and identity, as well as accommodating the postmodern dalliance with mimesis, contingency, and repetition?

Voice and talk certainly have a tremendous following, both in terms of numbers and diversity. Let's begin with some examples which depict the grip of the former. First, searching for voice is a respected pursuit of contemporary literary criticism, particularly feminist literary criticism. Here one is urged to read different texts, and to read the same texts differently.[14] The skill is to 'read between the lines, from the margins'.[15] The aim is to rescue what has been silenced, neglected or disregarded. Voice is, in fact, an organising force not just of feminist literary criticism, but of feminism more generally. And it performs to similar effect in a multitude of other social movements, suggesting that getting a voice is now 'a *sine qua non* of any liberatory politics',[16] or, as bell hooks says, that 'moving from silence into speech is for the oppressed, the colonized, the exploited, and those who stand and struggle side by side a gesture of defiance that heals, that makes new life and new growth possible'.[17]

---

13   I base this aversion to inappropriate empathy on Young's challenge to dominant versions of communicative ethics: see, *op cit*, fn 8, Young.

14   See Heilbrun, C and Resnik, J, 'Convergences: law, literature, and feminism' (1990) 99 Yale LJ 1913, p 1942.

15   Munt, S, 'Introduction', in *New Lesbian Criticism: Literary and Cultural Readings*, 1992, pp ii–xv, xiii, New York: Columbia University Press.

16   *Op cit*, fn 1, Kaplan, p 147.

17   hooks, b, *Talking Back: thinking feminism, thinking black*, 1989, Boston: South End Press, p 9.

Looking more closely at the example of feminism, Kaplan asks us to consider whether there is a word more evocative of, or more resonant with, contemporary feminism than voice:

> Book titles announce *'another voice', 'a different voice'*, or resurrect the *'lost voices'* of women poets and pioneers; fictional figures ancient and modern, actual women famous and obscure, are honored [*sic*] for speaking up and speaking out ... for the collectively and personally silenced the term has become a trope of identity and power: as Luce Irigaray suggests, to find a voice (*voix*) is to find a way (*voie*).[18]

On this account, the speech act is much, much more than words: it is 'the expression of ... movement from object to subject – the liberated voice'.[19] It is, in short, the antidote to cultural silencing. Feminism is not alone in believing this: others too have found voice and, with it, a way. As Henry Louis Gates makes clear, 'black people had to represent themselves as "speaking subjects" before they could even begin to destroy their status as objects'.[20] Gay and lesbian comings out and, more controversially, 'outing' are also bound up with voice; as is the current buzz around the queering of history, nation and planet. As Rosemary Hennessy makes clear, queering's 'distinctly postmodern rescripting of identity, politics, and cultural critique' finds voice in a visibility that incorporates, *inter alia*, 'community policing' by the Pink Panthers; Queer Nights Out; Kiss-Ins; and (shopping) Mall Zaps, as well as savvy slogans like 'We're here, we're queer, get used to it'.[21]

As noted above, talk theory has also been the subject of recent popular surges. Its most famous manifestation is probably Jurgen Habermas' 'communicative ethics',[22] a proposal for truly participatory democracy where norms, policies and practices are challenged and adjudicated upon by everybody from the 'ideal speech situation', ie, 'a situation of dialogue free of external pressures and internal distortions, in which participants ... respond to the force of the better argument alone'.[23] For Habermasians, '[c]ommunication is not a merely procedural or ancillary element in ethics or in social structures. Instead ... human speech is considered as a form of action and ethical values are grounded by discourse'.[24] Alongside Habermas' 'communicative ethics',

---

18  Lanser, S, *Fictions of Authority: Women Writers and Narrative Voice*, 1992, Ithaca, NY: Cornell University Press, p 3 (quoted in *op cit*, fn 1, Kaplan).

19  *Op cit*, fn 17, hooks.

20  Gates, HL Jr, *The Signifying Monkey: A Theory of African-American Literary Criticism*, 1988, New York: Oxford University Press, p 129.

21  Hennessy, R, 'Queer visibility in commodity culture', in Nicholson, L and Seidman, S (eds), *Social Postmodernism*, 1995, Cambridge: CUP, p 145.

22  See, *inter alia*, Habermas, J, *The Theory of Communicative Action*, Vol I: *Reason and the Rationalisation of Society*; Vol II: *Lifeworld and System: A Critique of Functionalist Reason*, trans McCarthy, T, 1981, 1987, Boston: Beacon Press.

23  *Ibid*.

24  Farrell Smith, J, 'Communicative ethics in medicine: the physician-patient relationship' in Wolf, SM (ed), *Feminism and Bioethics: Beyond Reproduction*, 1996, New York: OUP, p 184.

other high points in contemporary talk theory have been provided by Richard Rorty's cavalier 'liberal ironist',[25] and Luce Irigaray's magical eulogy on conversation, 'When Two Lips Speak Together'.[26] None of this is easy reading material. Take the example of Rorty's ironist. He can seem a disconcerting character: a hardened sceptic, who maintains that there is no ideal speech situation, insists that even our most basic commitments are contingent, and luxuriates in the disturbing-sounding 'cacophony and disorder'.[27] Yet he has one overweening need: he needs to talk, 'needs this with the same urgency as people need to make love'.[28] This is because 'only conversation enables him to handle ... doubts, to keep himself together, to keep his web of beliefs and desires coherent enough to enable him to act'.[29] Thus, the ironist's passion renders him not just human, but reassuringly familiar.

Let's recap. In this section, I have endorsed voice and talk theory, placing particular emphasis on the former's phenomenal allure. Yet, the doubts raised in the introduction still linger: is getting a 'voice' enough? As you know, I suspect that it is not enough. Voice does not imply cultural reframing; it doesn't even guarantee cultural conversation. The same can often (although not always) be said about theorising about talk. In the next section, I spell out my objections by asking what has all this talk (and theory about talk) amounted to?

## TOWARDS AN 'EROTICS OF TALK'

Although enthralled by the emancipatory potential of voice, and excited by the deliberative model of democracy that communicative ethics promises, I am increasingly unsure that progress is actually being made towards these ideals. There are two reasons behind this uncertainty. First, amidst the hoopla over voice, I sense little dialogue and conversation, only monologue, self-talk, and non-productive 'cacophony and disorder', and I wonder why it is that we have forgotten about the importance of good listening? (Here I find Kaplan's epigraph a timely, if disturbing, provocation: she quotes Jean-François Lyotard's claim that in 'a language game of the just ... one speaks only inasmuch as one listens, that is, one speaks as a listener'.)[30] Second, I am

---

25  See Rorty, R, *Contingency, Irony, and Solidarity*, 1987, Cambridge, Mass: Harvard University Press.

26  See Irigaray, L, *This Sex Which Is Not One*, trans Porter, C, 1985, Ithaca, NY: Cornell University Press, pp 205–18.

27  *Ibid*, Rorty.

28  *Ibid*, p 186.

29  *Ibid*.

30  Lyotard, J-F, *Just Gaming*, trans Godzich, W, 1985, Minneapolis: University of Minnesota Press (quoted in *op cit*, fn 1, Kaplan, p 2).

disturbed by portrayals of dialogue itself. These depict an anodine and unattainable state of discursive interaction, one which overemphasises identification with others and obscures informal impediments to participatory parity. Against this background, I use this section to probe voice and talk a little more closely. I begin with four general problems of engagement associated with voice and talk as currently practised. Thereafter, I move to a closer analysis of their particular manifestation in the health care context.

The first disturbing feature of contemporary practices of voice and talk is explained by Foucault. In *History of Sexuality*,[31] Foucault cautions against the confessional impulse that often motivates voice. He transports us to the Middle Ages, reminding us that, historically, torture was the 'dark twin' of confession, 'accompan[ying] it like a shadow, and support[ing] it when it could go no further'.[32] Pushing on with this paring away of confession's guile, Foucault reveals 'a ritual that unfolds within a power relationship' wherein the 'agency of domination' resides not 'in the one who speaks ... but in the one who listens and says nothing; not in the one who knows and answers, but in the one who questions and is supposed not to know'.[33]

Foucault's account, if one accepts it, complicates the pleasure one is encouraged to take from the act of speaking out. It also forces a questioning of the fitness of one's audience(s) and trounces the egalitarian ambitions of dialogue. A further setback to these ambitions is generated by the accounts of narrators' *modus operandi* which dominate contemporary narrative theory. As Kaplan explains, these accounts posit desire as narration's driving force, but their description of this desire takes a very particular form, one in which the narrator 'seeks to seduce and to subjugate the listener, to implicate him in the thrust of a desire that can never quite speak its name – never quite come to the point, but that insists on speaking over and over again its movement toward that name'.[34] A similar representation of desire emerges in an account of narrative progress as a 'sexual act ... the fundamental orgiastic rhythm of tumescence and detumescence, of tension and resolution, of intensification to the point of climax and consummation'.[35] The problem with these accounts is that they evoke a disturbingly narrow participatory norm: in Kaplan's words, it is one in which narrative exchange shapes up as 'a battle or a contest', and assumes a 'fundamentally male and heterosexual' orientation.[36]

31  Foucault, M, *The History of Sexuality, An Introduction*, 1980, New York: Vintage, Vol 1.

32  *Ibid*, p 59.

33  *Ibid*, pp 61–62.

34  Brooks, P, *Reading for the Plot: Design and Intention in Narrative*, 1985, New York: Vintage, p 61 (quoted in *op cit*, fn 1, Kaplan, p 16).

35  Scholes, R, *Fabulation and Metafiction*, 1979, Urbana: University of Illinois Press, p 26 (quoted in *op cit*, fn 1, Kaplan).

36  *Op cit*, fn 1, Kaplan, p 17.

The exclusionary proclivities that skew narrative theory are also apparent in the third feature of contemporary practices of voice and talk that I want to discuss. This is the tendency of (some) Habermasians to compromise otherwise alluring accounts of communication by prescribing dialogic conditions which obscure the distorting impact of speech norms and over-emphasise commonality. These tendencies have been well documented by Nancy Fraser and Iris Marion Young. Fraser focuses on Habermas' recuperation of the public sphere, particularly the way in which his well-intentioned bracketing of social inequality may actually end up compromising the ideal of participatory parity in deliberation. Fraser reminds us of the myriad ways in which inequality infects even formally inclusive deliberative bodies, citing an example familiar to many readers, ie, faculty meetings and other mixed-sex bodies where:

> ... men tend to interrupt women more than women interrupt men; men also tend to speak more than women, taking more turns and longer turns; and women's interventions are more often ignored or not responded to than men's.[37]

Fraser confronts us with the inequality which taints speech norms and calls for a more inclusive etiquette of speaking form and style. On her account, conventionally prized speech is rendered suspect, and our allegiance to norms of assertiveness, combativeness, orderliness, and 'literal' language (ie, as opposed to figurative language, like metaphor or hyperbole, or body language, like gesticulation or tears) receives a substantial jolt.[38] In short, Fraser unmasks power by reintroducing social conditions, like gendering and ethnicity, which train voices to speak (and not to speak) in many different ways, ways often discounted by the norms of prized speech.

I also want to incorporate Iris Marion Young's critique of communicative ethics in my reconstruction of talk. Young's concerns are generally similar to Fraser's, but here I want to concentrate on her criticisms of Seyla Benhabib's feminist elaboration and revision of Habermas.[39] Young supports Benhabib's project of injecting greater attention to the specific differences among people into Habermas' account of moral respect and reciprocity in dialogue, but she is worried by Benhabib's method. Benhabib promotes attention to symmetry and reversibility of perspective amongst dialogic participants, ie, being able and willing to take another's standpoint, as the way forward. Young argues that this is both impossible and politically fraught. She cautions that 'when people [particularly privileged people] obey the injunction to put themselves in the position of others, they too often put *themselves*, with their own particular experiences and privileges, in the positions they see the others'.[40]

---

37 *Op cit*, fn 7, Fraser, p 78.
38 See also, *op cit*, fn 8, Young, pp 64–65.
39 See, *inter alia*, Benhabib, S, *Situating the Self*, 1991, New York: Routledge.
40 *Op cit*, fn 8, Young, p 48.

Their action carries several risks: first, closure of 'the creative exchange' that differences might produce; second, unknowing misrepresentation of others' situations; and third, undeserved praise for the seeming magnanimity of the privileged.[41] Finally, 'the idea of reversing perspectives assumes that the perspectives brought to a situation are equally legitimate. [But,] [w]here structured social injustice exists, this may not be true'.[42]

The final disturbing feature of voice and talk I want to raise concerns the elusiveness of productive 'cacophony and disorder'. A good example of this is the 'crisis' which played out after a surfacing of voices dented feminism's assumed univocalism. I have no doubts about the value of this surfacing; yet, I was very unnerved by the fact that (at least initially) the ensuing 'cacophony and disorder' was both mean-spirited and an engine of temporary stasis. More importantly, it also allowed space for sceptics yet again to consign feminists to the shameful realm of self-talk, a space typically occupied by the mad and the childlike. On this occasion, feminism's madness and childishness was confirmed by the fact that we had trapped ourselves in 'a hen party of supposed meaninglessness',[43] guilty of addressing others so like ourselves that we had no true interlocutors, even in our own self-defined community.[44]

Let's turn now to health care. It is yet another field that is in the grip of the politics of voice. The once 'silent world'[45] of doctor and patient is said to have been transformed. It is no longer populated by the generic, all-knowing doctor and the generic, always-silent patient. Diseased bodies have become individuated, speaking beings; they are patients with voice, visibility and rights. The emphasis on informed consent has been central to the rise of voice in health care and a further key element, particularly in the United States, has been provided by the popularisation of talk therapy. Yet, in my view, neither of these developments forges dialogue or enhances the democratisation of health care interactions. In the following paragraphs, I delineate four reasons in support of this view.

First, let's consider health care's consistent privileging of consent. We know that to consent to something is to agree to it; and that to be asked to consent, is a mark of respect. Yet isn't there 'a subterranean specter of inequality in the language of consent',[46] arousing the suspicion that the consenting party has given in? The lengthy ladder of disrespect for patient refusals inhibits cocksure denials of this.[47] It suggests that consent has layers of meaning; some masking power, others revealing it. Wendy Brown is

---

41  *Op cit*, fn 8, Young, pp 44–49.
42  *Ibid*, p 48.
43  *Op cit*, fn 1, Kaplan, p 13.
44  *Ibid*.
45  See Katz, J, *The Silent World of Doctor and Patient*, 1984, New York: Free Press.
46  Brown, W, *States of Injury*, 1995, Princeton, NJ: Princeton University Press, p 163.
47  See Foster, Fegan and Fennell, Fox, de Gama, Wells, this volume.

forthright about her own suspicions on this issue: 'consent is profoundly at odds with radical democratic forms of equality and autonomy ... [it] marks relations of subordination.'[48] Ultimately, Brown leaves us hanging as to the way forward; however she does taunt us with a concluding question: 'why is consent the only language we have for mutual agreement that is not contract, and what is revealed by the failure of language here?'[49] Of course, it might be objected that health care emphasises not just consent, but *informed* consent. But I am not satisfied by this amendment. On this model, 'communication consists of a delivery mechanism',[50] and dialogue drops out of the picture, ousted by a timed, uni-structured transfer of information from one source to another. Moreover, the pressures on both 'sources' (ie, patient and professional), generated by differences in power and authority, disappear from view, hidden by the assumed baldness of medical facts.[51]

My second specific grumble about the privileging of voice in health care is somewhat evocative of the crisis generated by 'cacophony and disorder' in feminism. It concerns the proclivity of patient voice (singular) towards slithering dangerously into voices (plural). Consider the patient who wishes to terminate a pregnancy. Her voice has recently been joined by, amongst others, that of the foetus; of a teenager's parent(s); and of litigious 'expectant' fathers. As I see it, this proliferation of voices has produced little meaningful dialogue: coercion and pressure are its hallmarks, rather than respect and recognition. Here, voice is adversarial and argumentative, and sometimes it is hands-on violent (as in the firebombing of US health care facilities which provide abortion services and the harassment of personnel). Moreover, although the cultural conversation about abortion may appear increasingly cacophonous, it is, at least from certain speaking positions, less and less inclusive. Take the example of the woman who has terminated one or more pregnancies. Her voice is infrequently heard. It is also prey to vulgar mishearings. Moreover, when heard, this voice is suspiciously uniform: it is tentative and, in my view, unnecessarily tortured, and the substance of its speech seems to have been censored. Today, in giving voice to the decision to abort, one *must* declare oneself saddened by the 'choice'.[52]

Thirdly, amidst all the hoopla over patient voice, it is easy to miss the grim truth that within health care there is a strong residual preoccupation with containing speech in certain circumstances. Consider the US case of *Rust v Sullivan*,[53] wherein the Supreme Court approved a ban on abortion information in government-aided family-planning facilities. The ban was later

---

48   *Op cit*, fn 46, Brown.

49   *Ibid*.

50   *Op cit*, fn 24, Farrell Smith, p 187.

51   *Ibid*.

52   Hartouni, V, *Cultural Conceptions: On Reproductive Technologies and the Remaking of Life*, 1997, Minneapolis: University of Minnesota Press, pp 5–6, 51–67.

53   500 US 173 (1991).

lifted by the Clinton administration but its short history provides 'an important lesson about the political determination of doctors' ethical principles'.[54] The *Rust* court didn't simply compromise the notion of truth-telling in health care; rather, it implicitly approved a hierarchical account of this core ethical duty, ie, 'truth-telling for those patients with resources [who can avoid government-funded facilities] and deception for those without'.[55] *Rust* is thus a valuable reminder of how censorship can retain its unpredictable, aggressive vibrancy amidst a cultural conversation that proclaims a fascination with voice.

Finally, let's examine health care's favourite mode of talk: therapy. Therapy purports to centre talk, '[c]onfessional therapeutic talk needs other people: the therapist and sometimes fellow confessors. Their function is to encourage the confession, bear witness, and absolve'[56] – but, as Iris Marion Young argues, it generates only minimal dialogic resonance. Instead, therapeutic talk bolsters Foucault's cynicism about the empowering possibility of confession:

> Confessional talk ... is monological: even though it requires the presence of others, it remains one individual reciting her individual story ... [and it] tends to be depoliticizing and individualizing ... [its] self-reflective exercise diverts her from locating her life in the context of wider social institutions and problems and also discourages her from forming dialogic bonds with others in relations of solidarity and resistance. The solution to ... problems lies solely or primarily in herself ...[57]

Young confronts the assumption that dialogue is a goal of therapeutic treatments, documenting US therapeutic treatment programmes (especially those for pregnant addicts) which compel a contrary account. She spotlights four unnerving features of such programmes: first, the retelling of clients' stories by expert knowledges; second, the centrality of client surveillance; third, an emphasis on client normalisation, often sedimenting structural social inequalities; and finally, a kowtowing to notions of individual blame and self-refashioning capacity. I found Young's account to be utterly compelling: but, it is also extremely bitter medicine at a time when therapeutic treatments purport to offer the humane alternative to punishment and retribution.

So, what's to be done about all these contemporary problems with voice and talk? My proposal, following Fraser, Kaplan and Young, is that we 're-member' talk. Re-membering talk doesn't mean jettisoning voice, but it does mandate acknowledging that 'discourse requires not only the right and wherewithal to speak, but in addition, the possibility that speech will be

---

54  Roberts, D, 'Reconstructing the patient: starting with women of color', in *op cit*, fn 24, Wolf, p 132.
55  *Ibid*.
56  *Op cit*, fn 8, Young, p 91.
57  *Ibid*.

listened to and heard in the fullest sense possible'.[58] The key question is: how is this re-membering of talk to come about? One way might be to represent voice as as much a trope of intimacy as of power.[59] This is what Kaplan does. She centres the desire for dialogue, pairing those who are speaking up and out, arguing, or counter-narrating, with listeners. And, in an inspired move, she gives this desire a delightful name: an 'erotics of the talk'.

What is Kaplan up to here? Why an erotics of talk? Is it pure effect (or even affectation)? Or, is her choice of words as descriptive as it is captivating? I think so. Kaplan, in explaining her choice, invokes Audre Lorde, Anthony Giddens and an array of feminist takes on Habermas. Summarising, 'erotics' seems to serve at least three key (and probably interdependent) purposes. First, invoking the erotic transports us to the intimate sphere, and thereby generates democratic opportunities because of intimacy's profound capacity for interimbricating reciprocity, equality and recognition. Intimacy, however, is neither always, nor inevitably, coterminous with positive values and outcomes. It also carries connotations of abuse, and of cloying sameness and over-identification. To counteract these problems, Kaplan brings a second and third possible meaning of 'erotics' into play. First, 'erotics' evokes the ideal, the possibility of utopia: 'As Audre Lorde has argued, the erotic is a kind of ethical geiger counter which we can use to determine "which of our various life endeavors brings us closest to that fullness ...".'[60] Thus, an 'erotics of talk' does not imply that a Habermasian-type 'ideal speech situation' will automatically fall into place once voice and listener are paired, or, more generally, that only intimacy's positive aspects will flourish; but, crucially, it does foreground our longing and need for these things. Secondly, because a satisfactory 'erotics' has to allow for diverse desires, it may reduce the risk of cloying sameness, or over-identification, that inheres in some versions of intimacy. In other words, because the erotic mandates respect for difference, or particularity, as part of its quest for 'satisfaction', tendencies towards false identification (as noted by Fraser and Young in some versions of Habermasian communicative ethics) are more likely to be quelled.

In summary, then, I think one can say that Kaplan is right: the 'erotic' is eminently suitable. '[It] is itself a communicative medium, empowered to both revitalize social interaction and mark our social "failure" to provide an "open forum" and ... therefore it is only logical to talk about an erotics of talk.'[61]

---

58  Meehan, J, 'Introduction', in *Feminists Read Habermas: Gendering the Subject of Discourse*, 1995, New York: Routledge, p 12.

59  *Op cit*, fn 18, Lanser, p 186 (quoted in *op cit*, fn 1, Kaplan, p 92).

60  Lorde, A, *Sister Outsider*, 1984, Freedom, CA: Crossing Press, p 55 (quoted in *op cit*, fn 1, Kaplan, p 15).

61  *Op cit*, fn 1, Kaplan, p 16.

Rachel Mackay

Save tR

27/11

# TRUST, POWER AND KNOWLEDGE IN HEALTH CONFIDENTIALITY

What, then, does all this abstraction mean when it's applied to health care? I shall argue that it implies the need to foreground the search for an ideal listener. And, if we're lucky, doing this might also ignite a new discourse about how best to capture the democratising promise of intimate relationships. In this section, I nominate confidentiality as a possible vehicle for implementing Kaplan's notion of an erotics of talk in health care. The basic idea is to generate a partnership (although not necessarily a harmonious one) with consent (which in my schema represents voice as power), and thereby boost the possibilities of meaningful talk.

I appreciate that confidentiality must seem a surprising, if not ridiculous, vehicular choice for generating dialogue in health care. Where commentators agree on confidentiality, they generally highlight negative, not positive, features.[62] Two complaints have received particular prominence. First, the complaint that health confidentiality lacks clarity. Particular sticking points include the muddled overlap of its legal and ethical foundations, as well as the increasingly dishevelled appearance of legally sanctioned exceptions to the basic requirement of confidence. Its malleable frontiers also make it a tool of illegitimate concealment. The second prominent complaint about health confidentiality is that it is startlingly moribund in the face of the proliferating challenges posed, *inter alia*, by the faceless intimacies of modern care; and by communications technology that fuels health managers' definitions of the 'need to know', as well as research teams' cravings for data that might generate a competitive edge; and finally, by the frequent calls for reduced confidentiality protection for those with communicable diseases, especially HIV/AIDS, and for revelation of genetic information 'in the public interest'.

I have no quibble with this checklist of complaints about the current state of health confidentiality. However, the issues they raise with respect to the pressing need for a sound health information infrastructure are not my immediate concern here;[63] instead, I want to tap into the core of confidentiality in an effort to counteract the excesses of health care's politics of voice and unleash the potential of dialogue. Basically, I want to play on confidentiality's capacity to foreground listening and intimacy, whilst still preserving difference. I shall use the concluding paragraphs of this section to outline two crucial elements of this project.

---

62  A good account of health confidentiality is offered by, *inter alia*, McHale J, and Fox, M, with Murphy, J, *Health Care Law: Text and Materials*, 1997, London: Sweet & Maxwell, pp 439–506.

63  For a good account of the challenges involved in developing a sound health information infrastructure from current legal and ethical bases, see Gostin, L, 'Health information privacy' (1995) 80 *Cornell Law Review* 451.

As I see it, the key attraction of confidentiality is its link (albeit largely unexplored) with the concept of trust. Trust foregrounds core virtues like intimacy, commitment and risk. (Risk qualifies as a virtue because it compels alertness to context, warning us away from 'promiscuous trustworthiness' and 'undiscriminating distrust'.)[64] Unfortunately, in health care, as elsewhere, sustained inquiry into the virtues of trust has been choked by the icy appeal of notions like contract and consent. The latter feed our fascination with the morality of cool relationships between equals,[65] but they tend either to sidestep trust completely or import 'a limitation of trust to minimal and secured trust'.[66] In addition, their associations with formal channels of accountability, and also with autonomy, can obscure vulnerability and undermine dialogue.

However, the hegemony of contract and consent is not absolute. Health care still needs our goodwill towards trust. Increasingly, for example, it exploits the tradition of 'doctor knows best' and the unusual pleasure that attaches to successful trusting, in order to sugar-coat its reliance on a modern 'network' trust, what Anthony Giddens calls 'system trust', in the impersonal, faceless commitments of experts who may rarely, if ever, be encountered in person. Deep down, health care knows that 'whatever happens to human beings, trust is the atmosphere in which it thrives'.[67] Unfortunately, it has yet to face up to the task of theorising trust's virtues, a project that might place limits on trust's current exploitability.

I need to pause here: theorising trust may be a lamentably undersubscribed activity, but in commending it to you, I do not wish to catapult us into the sickly empathy or over-identification that cling to certain versions of intimate trust, and that are sometimes mistakenly assumed to be the key to effective dialogue.[68] Moreover, 'trust is a notoriously vulnerable good, easily wounded and not at all easily healed. [It is also] not always a good, to be preserved'.[69] Once again, health confidentiality may offer a route forward: exceptions like 'in the public interest' and 'need to know' have the capacity to function as safety valves, maintaining difference and reminding us that dialogue rather than identification, or complete agreement, is the ultimate goal. As Annette Baier reminds us, 'there are immoral as well as moral trust relationships, and trust-busting can be a morally proper goal'.[70] Unfortunately, my abstract enthusiasm for these defences withers very rapidly upon examination of their current operation. In practice, these

64   Baier, A, *Moral Prejudices: Essays on Ethics*, 1995, Cambridge, Mass: Harvard University Press, p 16.

65   *Ibid*, p 116.

66   *Ibid*, p 119.

67   Bok, S, *Lying*, 1978, New York: Pantheon Books, p 31.

68   Above, pp 162–63.

69   *Ibid*, Baier, p 130.

70   *Ibid*, p 95.

exceptions do not generate democratic disruptions of trust; rather, they make the search for an ideal listener (and, often, the search for voice) more protracted for *certain groups* of patients. To conclude, I will make three points about the current operation of the 'public interest' exception to the obligation of confidentiality, followed by one brief comment on the 'need to know'.

First, truth-telling, for patients and professionals alike, is lauded, but what 'truths' get heard when patients speak up in doctors' offices? Or when they are seen in surgery waiting rooms by neighbours, friends or colleagues? Moreover, what happens to 'truths' that are subsequently disclosed and disseminated 'in the public interest'? An appropriate backdrop for these inquiries is provided by the Anita Hill-Clarence Thomas story.[71] This is a story that 'dramatized, if not theatricalized ... the limits on a woman's ability to tell the truth about sex and power'.[72] I think that it has parallels in health care. Ask yourself: are the mandates of health confidentiality not just case-specific, but also gender, sexual orientation and race-specific? Recently, the 'public interest' exception seems to have been gripped by plague narratives about HIV-positive playboys, pregnant addicts and 'kids having kids'.[73] Take the experience of confidentiality of Jennifer Clarise Johnson, a 23-year-old black woman, who, in 1989, became the first woman in the United States to be convicted of exposing her child to drugs while pregnant. In the following quotation, Dorothy Roberts tells Johnson's story, showing how 'race and class, along with gender, help to define the principle of confidentiality':

> The government learned of Johnson's crack addiction only because she confided in her obstetricians who delivered her babies at a public hospital. Her admission prompted the hospital to test her and her babies for drugs. The hospital then reported her to government authorities. Second, the most damaging testimony at her trial came from Johnson's own obstetricians. They testified about Johnson's confidential confession that she used crack shortly before labour.[74]

The second feature of current 'in the public interest' discourse which disturbs me is the increasing characterisation of both of the competing interests in confidentiality cases as public, ie, the interest in confidentiality and the interest in disclosure. The basic question here is: where does the essence of the obligation of confidence lie? Is it in the private interests of the individual who imparts the confidential information, or in the public interest in ensuring that

---

71  Morrison, T, *Race-ing Class, Engender-ing Power: Essays on Anita Hill, Clarence Thomas, and the Construction of Social Reality*, 1992, New York: Pantheon Books.

72  Gilmore, L, *Autobiographics: A Feminist Theory of Women's Self-Representation*, 1994, Ithaca, NY: Cornell University Press, p 224, note 1.

73  For elaboration of the argument that 'public concern over crack babies contains all the characteristics of a response to a plague' see Daniels, CR, 'Between fathers and fetuses: the social construction of male reproduction and the politics of fetal harm' (1997) 22 *Signs* 579, p 586.

74  *Op cit*, fn 54, Roberts, p 127.

confidentiality is maintained? An observation in *W v Egdell* suggests a judicial drift towards to the latter:

> ... it is important to insist on the public interest in preserving W's right to confidence ... W of course had a strong personal interest ... in restricting the report's circulation. But these private considerations should not be allowed to obscure the public interest in maintaining professional confidences.[75]

But Bob Lee takes issue with this characterisation. He argues that defining the obligation of confidence as a public-interest matter makes it easier for judges to reach the conclusion that it is outweighed by other factors. The judges themselves suggest that it makes little difference, but I prefer Lee's version, mainly because it fits with my emphasis on the need to delineate the private, or intimate, sphere.[76] As I see it, defining the obligation of confidence as a public-interest matter jeopardises the privacy of certain groups of patients. It risks generating a tiered guarantee of confidence, a version of what Jeffrey Weeks calls 'regulated privacy'.[77] This is because a public interest in protecting patient privacy is easy prey for a competing public interest in disclosure where a particular patient's behaviour is not already sanctioned by law, accepted custom or dominant lifestyles. Confidence may thereby become dependent on the 'fortunate coincidence' that one's behaviour happens to fit with the mores of the 'contingently reigning majority', or on an ability to reshape the public agenda.[78]

The final aspect of 'in the public interest' I want to discuss is the case of Dr Phillip Bennett.[79] Bennett is the doctor from Queen Charlotte's Hospital in West London who, in a 1996 interview with the *Sunday Express* about ethics in practice, raised the example of one of his then patients. The patient was reported to be pregnant with twins and considering termination of one twin. She was described as single and in straitened circumstances. It was reported that she already had one child and that she felt that she could not support two more. Initially, the patient proved surprisingly media-genic: she was defended as a tragic victim of circumstance, pushed to make an impossible decision. But then, in a later story, the *Daily Express* reported that it was now able to reveal the 'true' story of Dr Bennett's patient: she was a working woman, about to take maternity leave from a well-paid job, married to a company director, and she described herself as 'certainly not impoverished – far from it'.[80] Finally, a short time later, in the wake of a legal skirmish by the

---

75  [1990] 1 All ER 835, pp 847–48.

76  Lee, R, 'Deathly silence', in Lee, R and Morgan, D (eds), *Death Rites: Law and Ethics at the End of Life*, 1994, London: Routledge, pp 279–302.

77  *Op cit*, fn 4, Weeks, p 141.

78  *Ibid*.

79  Details about this case are taken from Sheldon, S, 'Multiple pregnancy and re(pro)ductive choice: *R v Queen Charlotte Hospital, Professor Phillip Bennett, North Thames RHA and Social Services of Brentford and Hounslow LBC, ex parte SPUC, ex parte Philys Bowman*' [1997] 5 FLS 99.

80  (1996) *The Times*, 16 August.

Society for the Protection of the Unborn Child, it emerged that Dr Bennett's patient had had the termination prior to publication of the first *Express* story.

Bennett, faced with media criticism, maintained that patient details were altered in the original report in order to protect confidentiality. The thing which most interests me about this account is: why these specific alterations? Why offer an account of a single mother of limited means who already had one child? Is it because such a mother is one of those appropriately selfless women who can be permitted the 'choice' of abortion, without risk of harm to the image of wholesome maternity?[81] If so, I view the Bennett story as a disturbing emblem of 'the degree to which pro-life discourse has so saturated public debate as to now set its terms and seem part of the fabric of fact'.[82] I read traces of the same phenomenon in a *Guardian* letter, published a short time after the story broke, which reaches out for a more nuanced approach than was generally evidenced:

> I am concerned by the barbarity of a culture which has let me know about the situation of the woman in question. By what right is her agony made public? The public may not know her name at the moment, but her privacy is invaded by our ill-informed discussion of her private life.[83]

I find it hard to unpack my response to this letter. I want to echo the letter-writer's sentiments but also, paradoxically, feel a need to declaim them. The letter-writer asks: 'By what right is her agony made public?'; I want to ask: why assume 'agony'? Making this assumption of agony may be a parallel act to Dr Bennett's 'good intentions', but both run similar risks of exacerbating the diminishing vocabulary around abortion. And that, in my view, is not in the public interest.

Finally, I want, briefly, to raise another increasingly irresistible, imminently imperative limit to the intimacy which might be generated by health confidentiality, ie, the need to know. This is fast reaching the health managers' all-time favourites list. But, do they really need to know? Or, have they too succumbed to knowledge, amidst our cultural conversation that so obsessively equates silence with death?

## CONCLUSION: 'I'M TELLING YOU STORIES. TRUST ME'[84]

In this chapter, I have told a story about the cultural turn to talk. I did my best to be fair to this development, but ultimately I condemned it as partial, incomplete and distorted because of its singular emphasis on a politics of

---

81  Sheldon, S, *Beyond Control: Medical Power and Abortion Law*, 1997, London: Pluto Press.

82  *Op cit*, fn 52, Hartouni, p 6.

83  *Op cit*, fn 79, Sheldon, p 106.

84  Winterson, J, *The Passion*, 1989, New York: Vintage, p 13 (quoted in *op cit*, fn 72, Gilmore, p 224).

voice. The solution I proposed is provocative and immodest. It calls for the generation of voice's essential complement, ie, an erotics of talk which will foreground appropriate listening, participatory parity and intimacy. Finally, as an opening ploy in the erotics of talk, I probed health confidentiality as a possible vehicle for maximising dialogue in health care. I seem to have thrown up more questions than answers. But, then, this has been my story. Trust me?

# CHAPTER TEN

# REWRITING THE DOCTOR: MEDICAL LAW, LITERATURE AND FEMINIST STRATEGY

*Michael Thomson*[1]

## INTRODUCTION

Feminist theorists have successfully problematised the disciplines of law and medicine.[2] More pertinently, the interaction of these disciplines has been recognised as an important axis for feminist strategic engagement.[3] In this chapter I intend to build upon this work. I shall argue that consideration of the female subject constructed at the axis of law and medicine has potentially profound implications that reach beyond these disciplines. Before moving on to provide an outline of the theoretical basis for the project argued for within this chapter, there is value in providing a more general introduction.

Contrary to initial reactions, the legal academy has discovered that it is not immune to the seductive force of postmodern theory. Whilst law's claim to a universal truth may have been, for some, the most lamented casualty of postmodern legal theory, the revelation of the contingency of the (legal) subject has been equally fundamental. Yet it has not all been loss. Inherent in this theoretical position are strategic possibilities. Most notable is the issue of resistance. Briefly, if the (legal) subject is a product of discourse and practice then it becomes possible to challenge the dominant discourse and tell a different story, to open up new possibilities.

---

1   The author would like to thank Sally Sheldon, Thérèse Murphy and Katherine O'Donovan for their helpful comments and suggestions on earlier drafts of this chapter.

2   See, for example, O'Donovan, K, *Sexual Divisions in Law*, 1985, London: Weidenfeld and Nicolson; Smart, C, *Feminism and the Power of Law*, 1989, London: Routledge; Foster, P, *Women and the Health Care Industry: An Unhealthy Relationship?*, 1995, Buckingham: Open University Press; Ehrenreich, B and English, D, *For Her Own Good: 150 Years of the Experts' Advice to Women*, 1979, London: Pluto Press.

3   Smart, C, 'Disruptive bodies and unruly sex: the regulation of reproduction and sexuality in the nineteenth century', in Smart, C (ed), *Regulating Womanhood: Historical Essays on Marriage, Motherhood and Sexuality*, 1992a, London: Routledge and Kegan Paul, pp 7–32; Smart, C, 'Penetrating women's bodies: the problem of law and medical terminology', in Abbott, P and Wallace, C (eds), *Gender, Power and Sexuality*, 1991, Hampshire: Macmillan, p 157; Smart, C, 'The woman of legal discourse' (1992b) 1 SLS 29; Thomson, M, 'Employing the body: the reproductive body and employment exclusion' (1996) 5 SLS 243; Murphy, T, 'Bursting binary bubbles: law, literature, and the sexed body', in Morison, J and Bell, C (eds), *Tall Stories? Reading Law and Literature*, 1996, Aldershot: Dartmouth, p 57; Fegan, E, '"Fathers", foetuses and abortion decision making: the reproduction of maternal ideology in Canadian judicial discourse' (1996) 5 SLS 75; Thomson, M, 'Legislating for the monstrous: access to reproductive services and the monstrous feminine' (1997) 6 SLS 401.

Whilst this may be the case, we must recognise that some stories are more open to retelling than others. With this in mind it is worth noting the intense investment in the Woman[4] of law. She is constructed from enduring narratives and discourses. It is arguable that these narratives are so socially engrained as to make direct resistance (in isolation) a questionable strategy. Yet recognising that the legal Woman is very often the 'medical' Woman, and, more importantly, that law quite clearly employs medical knowledges and the figure of the doctor to a significant degree in the construction of this (medico-) legal Woman, it becomes possible to offer an alternative, or rather complementary, strategy for change.[5]

To explain this a little further, whilst trying not to place myself in advance of my argument: gender – which may be conceptualised as a social relation, a structural code – is a made, not a given. 'Like sexuality ... gender is not a property of bodies ... but the set of effects produced in bodies, behaviours, and social relations ... by the deployment of a complex political technology'.[6] Given that this social relation is predicated on the 'conceptual and rigid structural opposition of the two biological sexes',[7] then the construction of sexual difference may be understood as a *technology of gender*, that is, as central to the construction of gender and gender inequality. As such, and as Rosalyn Diprose has noted:

> [T]he central issue in redressing women's social subordination within patriarchal social relations is not so much male control of women's bodies as the way in which women's bodies are socially constituted in relation to men ... [T]he limitations on freedom are primarily due to ways in which women's bodies are constituted and valued in relation to men and in circulating discourses about sexual difference.[8]

Recognising scientific and medical knowledges as privileged sites at which the sexed body is constructed and affirmed, therefore, locates these knowledges within the discourses which construct and maintain gender and gender inequalities:

---

4    Written in this way, Woman denotes a recognition of the 'distinction between Woman and women. This is familiar to feminists who have for some centuries argued that the *idea* of Woman (sometimes the *ideal* of Woman) is far removed from real woman', *op cit*, fn 3, Smart (1992b), p 35. It is worth adding Smart's qualification that the concept of 'real woman' is itself problematic: 'the claim to an absolute reality located in the body of women against which the excesses of patriarchy can be measured has become less tenable.'

5    Reference within this chapter to the 'Woman of law', 'legal Woman', etc, is not meant to suggest that the law constructs a coherent and unified female subject. Rather, it is merely meant to highlight the commonalities that exist within the female subject positions figured within legal discourse. More specifically it is meant to highlight the degree to which the legal Woman is determined by her body – albeit with, at times, quite different results.

6    de Lauretis, T, *Technologies of Gender: Essays on Theory, Film and Fiction*, 1987, London: Macmillan, p 3 (quotations omitted).

7    *Ibid*, p 5.

8    Diprose, R, *The Bodies of Women: Ethics, Embodiment and Sexual Difference*, 1994, London: Routledge, pp 119–24.

[B]iomedicine is ... one of the discourses which make up the world in which we ordinarily dwell. Biomedicine is a field of knowledge and ... there is no field of knowledge that does not presuppose and constitute at the same time power relations. Further biomedicine is not just one among many fields of knowledge which regulate bodies in the so-called common good: it holds a privileged place in disseminating knowledge about what a body is, how it functions and the nature of its capabilities. And in this, biomedical knowledge does its own social dichotomising in delineating the normal body from the abnormal. So it is possible not only that biomedical science is involved in the restoration and expansion of bodies upon which it practices, but that as a field of knowledge it may play a part in the constitution of those bodies prior to any alienation.[9]

Whilst being cognisant of the broader productive relationship between biomedicine, sexed bodies and gender noted above, in this chapter I intend to focus on one aspect of this relationship. It is the figuring of the doctor, and the doctor/(female) patient relationship that this allows, which I want to argue has strategic possibilities. Recognising the complex relationship between law, the doctor, and the (medico-)legal Woman we can start to formulate a new strategy of resistance. Whilst the (medico-)legal Woman has a problematic permanence and appears securely anchored in a complex and shifting network of discourses and practices, it becomes possible to consider a rewriting of the doctor whose story, whilst socially entrenched, seems more open to movement.[10] Importantly, rewriting the doctor has the potential to realign the relationship between women/Woman, biomedicine and the law and perhaps to open up the legal Woman to more direct strategies of resistance.

Whilst advocating this strategy, a degree of caution is appropriate. Rewriting the idea of the doctor is in itself insufficient. What is being encouraged here is one strategy within a plurality which are needed in this area. The relationship between women and biology/biomedicine, and the relationships between different members of the health care team are two non-exhaustive examples of other possible sites of resistance. Another note of caution arises if it is recognised that at times women benefit from their alliance with doctors. The privileging of medical autonomy/clinical judgment has at times been clearly advantageous for women. Making access to abortion and reproductive services a matter of clinical discretion has proved more beneficial for some women than a centrally determined system would have been. Similarly such privileging of medical decision making has acted in women's favour when partners have challenged decisions to terminate.[11]

---

9    *Op cit*, fn 8, Diprose, p 124.

10   Whilst I refer to 'the doctor', I do not wish to argue that this figure, or medicine itself, is uniform or monolithic. Rather, I wish merely to suggest that there are recurring narrative themes that persist in the discourses that construct the doctor. That is to say, that whilst the general practitioner, surgeon, psychiatrist, oncologist and so on may be figured quite differently, they share common features.

11   See, Sheldon, S, '"Subject only to the attitude of the surgeon concerned": the judicial protection of medical discretion' (1996) 5 SLS 95.

From these examples it is clear that whilst we may embark upon rewriting the doctor we must also consider how decision making would take place within any new structure.

Interrogating both postmodern and feminist theory, this paper aims to provide a justification for this strategy. In the process I want to rely to some extent on narratives from literature and popular culture. My aim in doing this is simple. Employing such narratives works at a superficial level to highlight the 'story-telling' nature of law as a social narrative. In conceiving of law in this way we highlight both its contingency and the possibility of producing new stories.

## FEMINISM, POSTMODERNISM AND THE LEGAL SUBJECT

Having just outlined the project with which I wish to engage, I want in this section to provide a brief outline of my theoretical framework. As the introduction notes, the feminist strategy I wish to facilitate is premised on a postmodern conception of the subject. Postmodernism may be understood as 'typically centr[ing] on a critique of the modern ideas of reason and the rational subject'. As such it is argued that:

> It is above all 'the project of the Enlightenment' that has to be deconstructed, the autonomous epistemological and moral subject that has to be decentered; the nostalgia for unity, totality, and foundations that has to be overcome; and the tyranny of ... universal truth that has to be defeated.[12]

The collapsing of the universal narrative under the postmodern gaze has focused attention, as suggested above, on the Enlightenment narrative of the universal moral subject. Within this project the subject is read as 'a construction of texts, discourses, and institutions',[13] and as a 'variable and complex function'[14] of these discourses and practices:

> The individual subject is rendered inextricable from discourse, a post through which various kinds of messages pass, which leaves her a mere 'nodal point' for the ever-shifting play of dissonant language games. With the postmodern rejection of all projects claiming to be universal, the unity of the subject is deconstructed and revealed as plural, fragmentary, and contingent.[15]

---

12  Baynes, K *et al* (eds), *After Philosophy: End or Transformation*, 1987, Cambridge, MA: MIT Press, p 68.

13  Schlag, P, 'Normative and nowhere to go' (1990) 43 *Stanford Law Review* 167, p 173.

14  Foucault, M, 'What is an author?', in Rabinow, P (ed), *The Foucault Reader*, 1986, Penguin: London, p 118.

15  Stychin, C, 'Identities, sexualities, and the postmodern subject: an analysis of artistic funding by the national endowment for the arts' (1994) 12 *Cardozo Arts and Entertainment Journal* 79, pp 89–90 (quotations omitted). Importantly, this does not necessarily mean a collapsing of the self, a complete dissolution of agency:

> [T]he postmodern deconstruction of subjecthood has revealed the subject not only as socially constructed but also as a product of discourse. This discovery, however, need not ...

This postmodern collapsing of the universal subject has had important implications for feminist thought. At one level, feminists have unpacked the essential peripheral or marginal position of women within the Enlightenment search for the universal subject. As Nancy Hartsock explains, within this logic: 'the philosophical and historical creation of the devalued "Other" was the necessary precondition for the creation of the transcendental rational subject outside of time and space, the subject who is the speaker in Enlightenment philosophy.'[16] Hartsock explains further, citing de Beauvoir: 'Evil is necessary to Good, Matter to Idea, and Darkness to Light.'[17]

More interesting for the purposes of this chapter has been the general deconstruction of the legal subject. Feminist legal engagement with law's subject has been a profitable, if not a constant, enterprise.[18] Feminist theory has assumed many positions both within postmodernism and outwith. For example, it has recognised, with differing levels of sophistication, the legal subject as both (universally) male[19] and as dependent for its subjectivity upon its place within the legal landscape. That is to say, whilst some feminists have argued that the legal subject is, at very least, predictable, others have contended that law constructs the figure it wishes to regulate.[20]

If we are persuaded by this latter argument, law's subject becomes a more complex character as legal subjectivity may differ with each regulatory instrument. Yet, as the following section illustrates, whilst we may recognise such potential complexity, when we occasionally see the female subject of law's imagination, she holds few surprises.

---

15 [cont]
> mean that the status of the subject is reduced to nothing more than the intersection of various language games ... Subjects are constructed by discourse, and as subjects we actively and creatively participate in our self definition through discourse. This realisation demands that our understanding of subjecthood transcend the binary between liberal, universal conceptions and the poststructuralist dissolution of all notions of a grounded subjectivity. Rather, we must recognize individual activity in 'self' definition and interpretation. (*Ibid*, p 93.)

16 Hartsock, N, 'Foucault on power: a theory for women?', in Nicholson LJ (ed), *Feminism/ Postmodernism*, 1990, London: Routledge, pp 157–60.

17 *Ibid*. See also *op cit*, fn 8, Diprose, 'the constitution of sexual difference is such that the "established myths" about masculinity and femininity constitute women as other to man and man is maintained as the norm as a consequence', p 123.

18 Other theorists have, of course, addressed this issue. Queer theorists, for example, have interrogated the construction of the gay legal subject. See Stychin, C, 'Unmanly diversions: the construction of the homosexual body (politic) in English law' (1994) 32 *Osgoode Hall Law Journal* 503.

19 MacKinnon, C, *Feminism Unmodified*, 1987, London: Harvard University Press; Naffine, N, *Law and the Sexes*, 1990, London: Unwin Hyman; Duncan, S, 'The mirror tells the tale: constructions of gender in criminal law', in Bottomley, A (ed), *Feminist Perspectives on the Foundational Subjects of Law*, 1996, London: Cavendish Publishing, pp 173–89.

20 See, for example, Sheldon, S, '"Who is the mother to make the judgment?": the construction of woman in English abortion law' (1993) 1 FLS 3, p 4. For a quite different perspective on female legal subjectivity see, Duncan, S, '"Disrupting the surface of order and innocence": towards a theory of sexuality and the law' (1994) 2 FLS 3.

# THE (MEDICO-)LEGAL WOMAN

Whilst it may be asserted that Woman is a gendered subject position which legal (and other) discourses brings into being,[21] feminist scholarship has not ignored the degree to which biomedical discourse shapes, and perhaps even allows, these constitutive discourses. This, as Carol Smart has argued, has its origins in the end of the 18th century which marked an important moment in the history of gender:

> What was witnessed was a polarization of genders in which differences became increasingly fixed and rigid, and at the same time naturalized. Scientific [including medical] discourses were central to this process, giving new vigour to traditional religious and philosophical beliefs about the inferiority of women. Women became more and more closely associated with their bodies, and their bodies became both overdetermined and pathological. *It becomes possible to argue that scientific, medical and later psychoanalytical discourses operated to create the very gender differences we have come to take for granted as natural.*[22]

It is this association with the body, the biologically overdetermined, which very often characterises the Woman of law. Whilst it cannot be argued that this Woman is a homogenous or unified subject, there is a continuity in the way she is repeatedly defined by her body.[23] She exists with differing degrees of visibility in law's discourses. There are, of course, areas where the (medico-)legal Woman is most visible. The legal regulation of abortion or access to reproductive services, for example, is clearly constituted in part upon, and in turn becomes part of the network of discourses which constitutes, this (medico-)legal Woman.[24] Elsewhere in legal discourse, however, it is also possible to unpack law's biomedical association between women and their bodies. Here, as in the more obvious areas of legal regulation noted above, the discourses of law and medicine commingle to produce a subject constantly in need of surveillance and regulation.[25] This may be seen, for example, in areas of employment law[26] and family law.[27]

---

21  *Op cit*, fn 3, Smart, 1992b, p 34.

22  *Op cit*, fn 3, Smart, 1992b, p 36 (my emphasis).

23  For example, white women and women of colour may both at times be constructed in a way which privileges the biological, yet with quite different results in terms of the legal subject position which emerges. See, for example, Roberts, DE, 'Punishing drug addicts who have babies: women of colour, equality, and the right to privacy' (1991) 104 *Harvard Law Review* 1419.

24  Thomson, M, *Reproducing Narrative: Reproduction, Gender and Law*, 1998, Aldershot: Dartmouth.

25  *Op cit*, fn 3, Smart, 1992a, p 7.

26  See, *op cit*, fn 3, Thomson, 1996.

27  See generally O'Donovan, K, *Family Law Matters*, 1993, London: Pluto Press.

So far I have argued that postmodern theory has dissolved the idea of the universal subject and that this has facilitated the deconstruction of the legal subject. I have also noted how feminist scholars have engaged with this project. More precisely I have highlighted how feminists have responded to the legal Woman. The focus that has been placed on medico-legal discourses has also been detailed. In the next section I want to provide something which is perhaps more adventurous. I want to move on to focus on the doctor. Whilst the role of biomedical/sociobiological discourses is well documented, I want here to address what may be characterised as a particular technology of gender. I want to consider the construction of the doctor and how this is figured within law. Why focus on the doctor? My interest in the doctor is threefold. First, the doctor is imagined in law as the point at which women interface with scientific, medical and health technologies. Secondly, and following from this, how the doctor is figured in legal and other discourses informs the dominant ideal doctor/(female) patient relationship. Finally, and as a corollary to the above, as a subjective presence constructed within legal and other discourses he exists as a focus for resistance. Whilst I recognise that medicine is neither monolithic nor exclusively male, I want to emphasis that the doctor that is referred to here is very much an ideal type. That it to say, I refer to a model of the doctor which is privileged, arguably valorised, within the discourses of law, popular culture and elsewhere. Hence my referral to the doctor exclusively as 'he'.

To achieve the objectives detailed above I want to take a slightly unusual route. I want to embark upon this project by first looking at the film *Now Voyager*. This film presents a very vivid and useful example of the dominant model of the doctor which I want to argue exists as an important technology of gender. It also illustrates the doctor/(female) patient relationship which follows from this model and acts as a further technology of gender. Turning then to law, I want to consider the degree to which the relationship outlined in consideration of *Now Voyager* inhabits the legal imagination.

## TWO STORIES

### The film

The 1942 film *Now Voyager*[28] exists as one of Hollywood's first forays into the now recognised media-genic world of the doctor. The film has been the subject of much criticism. Whilst critics such as E Ann Kaplan have

---

28  For a discussion of this film see Jacobs, L, '*Now Voyager*: some problems in enunciation and sexual difference' (1981) 7 *Camera Obscura* 89; Plaza, M, 'The mother/the same: the hatred of the mother in psychoanalysis' (1981) 2 *Feminist Issues* 75; Kaplan, EA, *Motherhood and Representation: The Mother in Popular Culture and Melodrama*, 1992, Routledge: London, p 107.

approached the film for what it tells us of popular culture's representation of motherhood, I want here to assess the role of Dr Jaquith.

Kaplan summarises the film as '[g]enerically a "woman's melodrama"', and notes that the 'text asks the spectator to identify with, and to appreciate, the daughter's, Charlotte Vale's, development to maturity and autonomy – her triumphing over her oppressive mother'.[29] Kaplan, rather than addressing herself to the figure of Dr Jaquith, contends that his psychoanalysis is used merely 'as a narrative discourse, as a means for producing character change and explaining mother-daughter interaction'.[30] Providing a different focus, I want here to concentrate not on the analysis but the analyst.[31] I want to argue that *Now Voyager* contains a powerful and enduring narrative which figures the doctor as a normalising moral presence; he is, as Foucault states, 'Father and Judge, Family and Law'.[32]

Dr Jaquith enters the cold and matriarchal Vale house on the request of Charlotte's sister-in-law. He is quick to offer Charlotte (Bette Davis) the promise of a cure to her mental illness and equally quick to blame Mrs Vale for her daughter's ill-health. The doctor appears as the only male figure within the house before Charlotte 'recovers'. There is little reference to Mr Vale and Jaquith is clearly placed in the role of the Father, reasserting patriarchy in the family. This is seen, not only at the level of his very presence and his interaction with Mrs Vale, but also in Charlotte's transformation. When the film begins, Charlotte is dressed very much as a child. Her hair is severe, her dress simple, she is desexualised. Once removed from the sphere of her mother, brought within the sphere of the Father, Charlotte is transformed. Charlotte becomes sexualised, grows up. The doctor as Father, or at least as a masculine presence, allows Charlotte to become a woman and this, of course, is only possible by reference to the masculine.[33] This is addressed in psychoanalytical terms by Kaplan:

---

29  *Op cit*, fn 28, Kaplan, p 110.

30  *Op cit*, fn 28, Kaplan.

31  Whilst it is significant that Jaquith is a psychoanalyst, this does not negate his usefulness as an example of 'the doctor'. As I noted above, whilst it should be recognised that different health professionals will be figured differently, there are strong recurring narrative themes which connect these subject positions. It is these themes that need to be highlighted if the doctor and the doctor/(female) patient relationship is to be understood and rewritten.

32  Foucault, M, *Madness and Civilisation: A History of Insanity in the Age of Reason*, 1989, London: Tavistock, p 272.

33  Whilst this argument may be made in a number of ways, it is worth noting the work of Luce Irigaray. Considering 'How she became not he', Irigaray argues that this is evident in language: 'Thus, instead of remaining a different gender, the feminine has become, in our languages, the non-masculine, that is to say an abstract non-existent reality. Just as an actual woman is often confined to the sexual domain in the strict sense of the term, so the feminine grammatical gender itself is made to disappear as subjective expression, and vocabulary associated with women often consists of slightly denigrating, if not insulting, terms which define her as an object in relation to the male subject.' Irigaray, L, *je, tu, nous: Towards a Culture of Difference*, 1993, London: Routledge, p 20.

... for a short space during the opening sequence, the film touches on deeper psychoanalytic (even Lacanian) levels, showing Mrs Vale as a mother who tries to keep her daughter down with her in the imaginary – who refuses to release her child into the patriarchal Symbolic. In the first scene, Charlotte, although technically adult, barely has access to language, especially when in the presence of her overpowering mother. The psychiatrist's role is to represent the Third Term (the Father, the Law) that has to come between mother and daughter. This achieved, Charlotte is able to separate and to form an adult sexual relationship of her own.[34]

Once Charlotte is removed, once she becomes a sexual actor, Mrs Vale correspondingly diminishes in power. She becomes bedridden, feeble, to an extent comic, and ultimately she dies. Interestingly, men, other than Dr Jaquith, only enter the house once Mrs Vale is bedridden and only when Charlotte emerges as a mature sexual actor. Patriarchy has been restored.

The normalising patriarchal role of the doctor is prevalent throughout the film, although perhaps not so dramatically as in the initial cleaving of Charlotte from the sphere of her mother. Once Charlotte has been brought under the influence of 'the Father, the Law', Jaquith's presence and influence remains apparent. This is perhaps most clearly seen in the manner in which Jaquith regulates Charlotte's first sexual relationship.

It is clear from the start that Jerry, the object of Charlotte's affections, is married, albeit unhappily. We learn of his home life, his manipulative wife and his two daughters. Inevitably, after a period of great happiness, the relationship between Charlotte and Jerry finishes. Charlotte flees Boston for the countryside 'retreat' of Dr Jaquith. Exhausted, perhaps on the verge of another breakdown, Charlotte finds solace and strength not in the (direct) ministerings of Jaquith but in Tina, Jerry's daughter who also happens to be a patient of the doctor. Charlotte gains strength first as Tina's nurse but then also as her *surrogate* mother. Charlotte and Jerry's relationship becomes mediated through Tina. Yet the propriety of this (three-way) relationship is maintained by the doctor. Charlotte's involvement with Tina's case and therefore with Jerry is conditional on the doctor's consent; as he reminds Charlotte 'What the Lord giveth, the Lord taketh away'. Tina becomes the relationship's bond. She becomes their child – so long as the relationship remains sexless.

Dr Jaquith therefore normalises Charlotte and the relationships that Charlotte has. He standardises Charlotte's relationship with her mother, and then with the other members of her family. More generally, he reasserts patriarchy in the Vale household, principally by allowing Charlotte a sexual identity. Having given Charlotte a sexual identity, the doctor ensures that it is confined within 'proper' limits. Not only is it heterosexual, but it is also confined to the marital/familial. Charlotte is placed in a pseudo-marital

---

34 *Op cit*, fn 33, Irigaray, p 114.

relationship and given a *surrogate* child. Yet the relationship is premised on abstinence. Sex would destroy not only the fragile bond between Charlotte, Tina and Jerry, but it would also threaten the *real (de jure)* relationship between Jerry and his wife and children. Charlotte has been given sex but it has also been taken away – 'What the Lord giveth, the Lord taketh away'.

The analysis presented above suggests a particular model constructed for the doctor in the regulation of gender. *Now Voyager* may be located within a complex network of discourses and practices which constructs the doctor in a normalising and prescriptive role. He prescribes appropriate gender, defining the normal and abnormal, mediating between society (or at least collective/majority expectation) and the individual. In the following section I want to move on to consider the degree to which this model can be read within legal discourse.

## The written word

To what extent does the figure of Dr Jaquith inhabit law's imagination? This question has been considered on a few occasions. I have discussed elsewhere, for example, the role of the doctor in asserting appropriate sexual/gender behaviour in the provision of treatment services under the Human Fertilisation and Embryology Act 1990.[35] Sally Sheldon has similarly assessed the role of the doctor as a 'parallel judge' in the Abortion Act 1967.[36] Consideration of the parliamentary discourses and the provisions of these statutes reveals a familiar image and role ascribed to the doctor. To give a little more detail: the debates around the Abortion Act 1967 sees the doctor cast as an honourable, expert and chivalrous man.[37] Typically, doctors were referred to as 'professional men',[38] 'professional medical gentlemen',[39] men who belonged to a 'high and proud profession'.[40] Being a member of such a profession he practised with 'skill, judgment and knowledge'.[41] '[H]ighly skilled and dedicated',[42] he operated within the profession's 'own ethical and

---

35  *Op cit*, fn 3, Thomson (1997). In terms of the broader intent of the legislation and the broader context it may be located within, see Herman, D and Cooper, D, 'Getting "the family right": legislating heterosexuality in Britain, 1986–1991' (1991) 10 *Canadian Journal of Family Law* 40.

36  Sheldon, S, *Beyond Control: Medical Power and Abortion Law*, 1997, London: Pluto Press; also, *op cit*, fn 24, Thomson, 1998.

37  It was not until the final stages of the debate that David Steel alluded to a 'body of professional men and women'. This was the only time within these debates that the possibility that the doctor may be a woman was explicitly recognised. Hansard, *HC Deb*, Vol 750, col 1346, 1967 (13 July).

38  Jenkins, Hansard, *HC Deb*, Vol 749, col 967, 1967 (29 June).

39  Hobson, Hansard, *HC Deb*, Vol 747, col 531, 1967 (2 June).

40  Lyons, Hansard, *HC Deb*, Vol 732, col 1090, 1966 (22 July).

41  Hobson, Hansard, *HC Deb*, Vol 747, col 531, 1967 (2 June).

42  Mahon, Hansard, *HC Deb*, Vol 750, col 1352, 1967 (13 July).

medical standards'.[43] He is constructed throughout the debates as upstanding, respectable and altruistic.[44] He is very much our dashing Dr Jaquith. This clearly facilitates the role to which he is appointed.

As I have noted, in *Now Voyager* Dr Jaquith delimits and ensures an appropriate gender and sexuality for Charlotte. He constructs her sexual identity and then 'manages' that identity. Within the enacting discourse of the Abortion Act the doctor is given the same defining role. To illustrate we can look to the 'case study' David Steel presented to the House of Commons in defence of his Bill. Steel talks of a request for a termination which a doctor had received from a young woman:

> He talked to the girl and put her in touch with people who could help her, her pregnancy is now going through in the normal way. It does not follow that because women desire terminations it will automatically be carried out. If we can manage to get a girl such as that into the hands of the medical profession, the Bill has succeeded in its objective.[45]

The doctor's role is clearly to encourage gender appropriate behaviour.[46] This role was also clearly seen in the passage of the Human Fertilisation and Embryology Act 1990. At one point Lord MacKay warned against an outright prohibition on single women receiving treatment services, arguing that such women would merely go elsewhere:

> On the other hand, if the law recognises that in a very small number of cases single women will come forward for treatment, it may be better to encourage them to seek advice. With the child and welfare amendments we have just discussed there is a likelihood that through counselling and discussion with those responsible for licensed treatment they may be discouraged from having children once they have fully considered the implications of the environment into which their children would be born or its future welfare.[47]

This mediating and normalising role is not just confined to legislative construction. This image of the doctor inhabits broader legal discourses. In *Whitehouse v Jordan*,[48] which is considered in more detail in Sally Sheldon's contribution to this volume, an action was bought on behalf of Stuart Whitehouse, a severely brain damaged boy of 10, against Mr Jordan who, it was claimed, had caused Stuart Whitehouse's injuries as a result of professional negligence in the management of his birth. At the time of the birth Mr Jordan was a senior registrar working for the West Midlands

---

43 Steel, Hansard, *HC Deb*, Vol 747, col 464, 1967 (2 June).

44 See *op cit*, fn 20, Sheldon.

45 Steel, Hansard, *HC Deb*, Vol 750, col 1349, 1967 (13 July). Steel makes a similar argument during the Parliamentary consideration of the Human Fertilisation and Embryology Bill. He asserts that the 1967 legislation had created a legal climate where doctors may see women before they abort and persuade them otherwise: Steel, Hansard, *HC Deb*, Vol 171, col 210, 1990 (24 April).

46 *Op cit*, fn 20, Sheldon.

47 MacKay, Hansard, *HL Deb*, Vol 516, col 1098, 1990 (6 March).

48 [1981] 1 All ER 267.

Regional Health Authority. The action against Mr Jordan focused on the use of forceps in the delivery. Whilst the case may be subject to a number of critical readings, of relevance here is the way in which the court responded to Mr Jordan and Mrs Whitehouse, Stuart's mother.

Within the judgment Mr Jordan is cast very much as the diligent, gifted and respectable clinician. He is described as: 'a senior registrar, of near consultant status, esteemed by his professional colleagues',[49] and as 'a member of the obstetrical unit ... which had a high reputation'.[50] Mrs Whitehouse, on the other hand, is described as: 'a difficult, nervous and at times aggressive patient',[51] as 'anxious and distressed',[52] and as 'intensely ... tense'.[53] It was noted that: '[s]he was unable, or refused, to agree to vaginal examination during her pregnancy, or to have a lateral X-ray, though urged to do so',[54] and that '[s]he was identified clearly as likely to be a difficult case'.[55]

Whilst judicial responses to the parties are telling,[56] perhaps more important than this is the way in which the interaction of Mrs Whitehouse and Mr Jordan is played out in the court. This is seen very clearly in the response to the evidence given by the parties, more particularly in the privileging of the evidence given by Mr Jordan. Mrs Whitehouse asserted before the court that the force with which the trial labour by forceps was attempted was so severe as to lift her hips up off the bed; as she testified, when the forceps were applied: 'it felt like a deadened electric shock that lifted my hips off the table, up off the bed.'[57] This was denied by Mr Jordan. What is interesting is the extent to which Mrs Whitehouse's evidence was dismissed without real consideration. It was found to be 'more than inexact "in *clinical* detail".'[58] Mr Jordan's denial was privileged and accepted. This was the case even though the court was to go on to state that direct experience was to be prioritised over other forms of knowledge. However, this seems only to be the direct experience of the doctor not the patient. His subjectivity is clearly given priority over hers. As Lord Wilberforce stated, 'for myself, I would regard Mr Jordan's first-hand account of the matter as of cardinal importance'.[59]

The court unambiguously constructs Mr Jordan as the rational, competent decision maker. This is clearly the image required for the doctor to assume a

---

49   [1981] 1 All ER 267, p 271.
50   *Ibid.*
51   *Ibid.*
52   *Ibid.*
53   *Ibid,* p 273.
54   *Ibid,* p 271.
55   *Ibid.*
56   See Sheldon, this volume.
57   *Ibid,* p 273.
58   *Ibid* (my emphasis).
59   *Ibid.*

prescriptive and normalising role. Mr Jordan, like Dr Jaquith, is clearly seen as 'Father and Judge, Family and Law'. His word is Truth, accepted as Law.[60] Mrs Whitehouse, on the other hand, is given the similarly necessary role of the irrational, aggressive and difficult woman. The status of Mrs Whitehouse and Mr Jordan is further illustrated in a brief consideration of the court's response to the expert evidence. Whilst Mrs Whitehouse's testimony is summarily dismissed, the consideration of the standard of care maintained during the trial labour by forceps proceeded on the basis of a report written by Professor McLaren. What makes this noteworthy is the fact that Professor McLaren, Mr Jordan's senior, had prepared the report for the hospital. It had also been made after discussion with Mr Jordan, with the suggestion that if it should be unfavourable it could be altered.[61] The report had used the word 'disimpacted', which it was said could suggest that the head of Stuart Whitehouse had become 'impacted', or stuck, due to excessive traction by Mr Jordan. The lengthy consideration of the meaning of 'disimpacted' – and by implication the conduct of Mr Jordan – therefore had little to do with Mrs Whitehouse's testimony but was the result of 'friendly fire'. Thus, a careless word by a supporting colleague (and prior joint defendant) is given greater credibility and consideration by the court than the claims of the plaintiff.

*Whitehouse* illustrates how the construction of the doctor detailed in *Now Voyager* may be read within broader legal discourses. It illustrates how women's experience of law may be coloured by this. Whilst Mr Jordan is not constructed in a directly prescriptive and normalising role, the response of the court to the parties comes from within this model. Sheldon, in her consideration of the case, further highlights this in noting that it was repeatedly suggested in court that Mrs Whitehouse's labour was complicated by her failure to accept the authority of the doctors.[62] Having argued that the doctor may be understood as an important axis at which gender is constructed and regulated I want now to move on and address the possibilities for challenging this.

## REWRITING THE DOCTOR

If we accept the privileging of the discursive, the role of discourse in the construction of the subject, then we need to assess the role of active participation:

---

60 This statement may clearly be tied to Sally Sheldon's critique in this volume of the law regarding medical negligence. Sheldon highlights how the standard of care, that is the legal standard, is set by the medical profession. The law is clearly descriptive of medical practice rather than prescriptive, or, as Sheldon forcefully argues, it follows what is accepted practice rather than what is acceptable practice.

61 [1981] 1 All ER 267, p 283.

62 See Sheldon, this volume, p 22.

the result of the forces that create subjectivity is not a seamless whole. There are gaps and ambiguities within the interstices of language that prevent a uniform determination of subjectivity ... Subjects are constituted by multiple and sometimes contradictory discourses. Individual subjects resist, mutate, and revise these discourses from within them.[63]

As this suggests, recognising the lack of a fixed narrative structure allows strategies of resistance:

Because discourses, no matter how authoritative, by their very nature lack fixity, they invite ... undermining ... [C]hanges, even major transformations, may be generated by the rhetorical practices of social agents who penetrate, dissimulate, and reorder the structures of discursive space in their ... quests to construe the world in a manner that conforms to their perceived interests.[64]

The privileged social discourse of law, with its claim to a universal and authoritative narrative, has been the focus for many resistant discourses, experiencing what Peter Dews has referred to as a 'burgeoning plurality of the languages of rebellion'.[65] Very much part of these 'languages of rebellion' have been feminist challenges to law. Yet whilst feminism has made real gains – for example in undermining law's claim to universal truth[66] – the association between women and their bodies remains an obstacle. As feminists have challenged overtly discriminatory practices, the methods of discrimination have become more difficult to read. Aspects of the emergence and regulation of the New Reproductive Technologies,[67] employment exclusion policies premised on foetal welfare[68] and the growth of 'foetal rights' more generally are examples of the way in which medical-scientific discourses reinterpret the female body, maintaining a body requiring surveillance and control. Therefore, the degree to which women remain tied to their bodies – or more importantly tied to particular organs, processes, or readings of them – makes (direct) resistance, other than in the most incremental way, a necessary but limited strategy.

Beyond this there is also the limits of the imagination. The possibility of figuring new possibilities, new relationships and realities, is limited to an extent by the degree to which our imaginations are tied to the present and the past. Those who have called for new 'stories' have had to look back to myth

---

63 Hekman, S, 'Reconstituting the subject: feminism, modernism, and postmodernism' (1991) *Hypatia* 44, p 59.

64 Coombe, RC, 'Room for manoeuvre: towards a theory of practice in critical legal studies' (1989) 14 *Law and Social Inquiry* 69, pp 97–98.

65 Dews, P, 'The *nouvelle philosophie* and Foucault' (1979) 8 *Economy and Society* 147, p 149.

66 O'Donovan, K, 'Law's knowledge: the judge, the expert, the battered woman, and her syndrome' (1993) 20 JLS 427.

67 Smart, C, '"There is of course the distinction dictated by nature": law and the problem of paternity', in Stanworth, M (ed), *Reproductive Technologies: Gender, Motherhood and Medicine*, 1987, London: Polity Press, p 98.

68 *Op cit*, fn 3, Thomson (1996).

and pre-history. Luce Irigaray, for example, has called for the embracing and reinvigorating, or reassessment, of pre-history.[69] Marina Warner makes a similar argument in relation to myth.[70] Peter Goodrich's eloquent writings regarding the intriguing Courts of Love may be understood as one such project.[71] Yet with this historical-cultural distance it is hard to be optimistic about such a strategy unless it is coupled with a plurality of other resistant practices. One such strategy must be to rewrite the doctor and hence the doctor-patient relationship that the dominant model facilitates.

Whilst we have to search pre-history and myth for stories to retell regarding women, if we choose to rewrite the doctor our task is considerably easier. The history of the modern medical profession is a relatively contemporary and accessible story. It is a lively and intriguing story of competition, money and status, of class struggle, international power dynamics and women's bodies – a bestseller and a blockbuster! A history within our knowledge, it appears a much more feasible project to reassess this history. We can retell medicine's story, focusing on aspects of its occupational project, its desire for social status and fiscal reward, its use of women's bodies.[72] Coupled with this, we can look at health care provision before the emergence of the current model. The past is also not so distant that we cannot imagine a different developmental trajectory.

Whilst we can retell medicine's largely ignored history, we also need to ask: what stories do we need if we are to suggest a different future? It is clear that we need to move beyond a system where the doctor contributes to a discourse which defines and constructs a female body which demands surveillance and control. The doctor needs to be located in a position where he does not exist as a primary axis for the construction of sexual difference which is used as the basis for gender inequality. We need to rewrite the doctor to facilitate a role which allows greater female autonomy. Some of Luce

---

69 Irigaray interestingly challenges the perception of pre-history as fairytale or legend. Such a reduction she claims is 'concomitant to repressing and destroying certain cultural dimensions that relate to the economy between the sexes. Such an approach also leads to a partial, reductive, and fruitless conception of History'. Op cit, fn 33, Irigaray, p 24.

70 'A myth is a kind of story told in public, which people tell one another; they wear an air of ancient wisdom, but that is part of their seductive charm. Not all antiques are better than a modern design – especially if they're needed in ordinary, daily use. But myth's own secret cunning means that it pretends to present the matter as it is and always must be ... But, contrary to this understanding, myths aren't writ in stone, they're not fixed, but often, telling the story of the same figures ... change dramatically both in content and meaning. Myths offer a lens which can be used to see human identity in its social and cultural context – they can lock us up in stock reactions, bigotry and fear, but they're not immutable, and by unpicking them, the stories can lead to others. Myths convey values and expectations, which are always evolving, in the process of being formed, but – this is fortunate – never set so hard they cannot be changed again, and newly told stories can be more helpful than repeating old ones.' Warner, M, *Managing Monsters: Six Myths of Our Time*, 1994, London: Vintage, pp 13–14.

71 Goodrich, P, *The Courts of Love and Other Minor Jurisprudences*, 1996, London: Routledge.

72 See *op cit*, fn 24, Thomson; also *op cit*, fn 2, Foster.

Irigaray's work has moved in this direction. One project that she has embarked upon is to reassess the nature of pregnancy and particularly the role of the placenta.[73] Whilst Irigaray's focus is biomedical science, it is suggestive of the broader project of rewriting that needs to be embarked upon. Irigaray argues that the placenta performs a complex mediating role which allows two organisms to co-exist peacefully, 'strangely organized and respectful of the life of both'.[74] Taken at its most mundane level, this reimagining of pregnancy moves us beyond the dominant model of pregnancy as conflict and pathology which facilitates a high level of intervention and management.[75] Concomitantly, it allows a more constructive image of pregnancy to emerge.[76]

At a day-to-day level we also need to refigure the doctor so that he does not exist as a point through which the state's interest in the female body is played out. One area we may want to address in order to achieve this would be the reassessment of the doctors who inhabit the Abortion Act 1967 and the Human Fertilisation and Embryology Act 1990. As an element of feminist strategy, it is clear that we need to recognise that the Doctor of law, like the Woman of law, is not a unified and homogenous subject. He is going to have to be addressed at the various points he appears in legal (and other) discourse, as is the specific nature of the relationship he has with the Woman of law.

On a slightly frivolous note to end, perhaps we can look briefly to George Eliot's *Middlemarch* and the figure of Tertius Lydgate. In Eliot's useful social history we find the following exchange regarding the newly arrived doctor, an exchange which suggests a different doctor and a different doctor/(female) patient relationship:

Mrs Cadwallader:  He is a gentleman. I heard him talking to Humphrey. He talks well.

Lady Chettam:  Yes, Mr Brooke says he is one of the Lydgates of Northumberland, really well connected. One does not expect it in a practitioner ... For my part I like a medical man more on a footing with the servants; they are often all the cleverer.

---

73  Although this project is an attempt to challenge the Darwinian and Pavlovian models of social (dis)organisation it can be used in the *rewriting* exercise I propose.

74  *Op cit*, fn 35, Irigaray, p 38.

75  'The relative autonomy of the placenta, its regulatory functions ensuring the growth of the one in the body of the other, cannot be reduced either to a mechanism of fusion (an ineffable mixture of the bodies or blood of mother and foetus), or, conversely, to one of aggression (the foetus as foreign body devouring from the inside, a vampire in the maternal body). These descriptions are of imaginary reality and appear quite poor indeed – and obviously extremely culturally determined ...'. *Ibid*.

76  *Ibid*, pp 37–44.

# CHAPTER ELEVEN

# FRAMEWORKS OF ANALYSIS FOR FEMINISMS' ACCOUNTS OF REPRODUCTIVE TECHNOLOGY[1]

*Derek Morgan*

A few preliminaries. I am, amongst the contributors to this collection of essays, perhaps uniquely ill-qualified to address feminisms' responses to reproduction. I cannot and do not speak from personal experience, nor do I have any handy experiences to share; although I realise that that begs a number of *methodological* questions. I am not a feminist, although I realise that that begs a number of *definitional* or *conceptual* questions which I address elsewhere. I am a white, heterosexual, middle-aged, male academic and thus, by definition, not systematically oppressed, other than by things of my own making. I do not have the presumption, then, to be able to identify with what it is 'like' to be oppressed, any more than I have the presumption to believe I can have a concept of possession which would be meaningful in any way. In this sense, then, I do not have any direct *knowledge* on which I could plausibly base a claim to *say* anything.

It is true that I once co-authored a book which addresses some aspects of the regulation and reception of some so-called reproductive technologies, but that ill qualifies anybody to do anything, except trade in academic reputation; and I realise that that begs a number of *representational* questions too. All this discloses a number of personal, or as used to be said, *political* questions. Perhaps they are now more frequently viewed as *theoretical* questions; the personal is theoretical.[2]

I have for the past 10 years been, perhaps, more interested in ethical or philosophical aspects of health care and medical practice than in legal ones. My colleagues and students will tell you that this constantly shows; philosophers and ethicists will say that it does not. Of course, this raises a number of *epistemological* questions and affects the way in which this essay is shaped, let alone coloured. I have in that time been interested in thinking

---

1   In writing of 'feminisms' I do so in the sense implied by Davies, M, *Asking the Law Question*, 1994, Sydney: the Law Book Company, p 172 *et seq*. Throughout this essay I have followed my customary practice of referring to and citing from only materials which I have to hand in my study when I write. Each reference in support of a proposition should, then, be regarded only as representative or emblematic of literature which could have been cited. Glaring omissions from my citations might charitably be understood in this light; more likely, in fact, they are based on ignorance. The usual suspects have not read this essay; therefore the usual caveat is omitted.

2   I have a colleague who holds that we academics are all like scientists; our best work is necessarily done, to be arbitrary, under the age of 30. I'm 43.

about what we might call 'uses of the body', particularly in its reproductive and affective aspects. The body has now been recognised as an immensely more complex index of social attitudes and ambivalences, cultural expressions and expectations and public representations and regulation.[3] There have been changes in or challenges to what we might call:

(a) *'The body of knowledge.'* We are living in a state of epistemological turbulence: 'it is as though Durkheim's motto has been reversed. Rather than studying social phenomena as if they were natural phenomena, scientists now study natural phenomena as if they were social phenomena.'[4] There are suggestions that the very basis of ethical inquiry and the knowledge available to us have changed radically,[5] and these suggestions have been roundly denounced as evidencing 'despairing rationalism without reason'.[6]

(b) *'Knowledge of the body.'* Radical scientific changes in what can be achieved, whether through cloning or genetic testing, recovery, storage and use (sometimes posthumously), of gametes, have seen what I call the reconstitution of the body. Science has acquired the power 'to define situations beyond what it knows about them'.[7] The expansion of the capacity to act 'has not been accompanied by a comparable expansion of the capacity to predict, and as a result the prediction of the consequences of scientific action are necessarily less than the action itself'.[8] Whether this comes about as a result of a conspiracy of the scientific and medical professions against the laity,[9] or more specifically – with reproductive medicine – against women,[10] to push professional dominance into domains traditionally outside medicine's province, or whether we are witnessing the destabilisation of the boundaries of lay and professional

---

3    Considered, for example, in collected volumes such as Komesaroff, PA (ed), *Troubled Bodies: Critical Perspectives on Postmodernism, Medical Ethics and the Body*, 1995, Melbourne: Melbourne University Press.

4    de Sousa Santos, B, *Toward a New Common Sense: Law, Science and Politics in the Paradigmatic Transition*, 1995, London: Routledge, p 34.

5    Gilligan, C, *In a Different Voice: Psychological Theory and Women's Development*, 1982, Cambridge, Mass: Harvard University Press (comprehensively criticised by O'Neill, O (with commentary by Nussbaum, M), 'Justice, gender and international boundaries', in Nussbaum, M and Sen, A (eds), *The Quality of Life*, 1993, Oxford: Clarendon Press, pp 303–35; Lyotard, J-F, *The Post-modern Condition: A Report on Knowledge*, 1979, Manchester: Manchester University Press, 1992.

6    Rose, G, *Mourning Becomes the Law: Philosophy and Representation*, 1996, Cambridge: CUP, p 7.

7    *Ibid*, de Sousa Santos, p 47. And see the important work of Beck, U, *Risk Society: Towards a New Modernity* (trans Ritter, M), 1992, London: Sage.

8    *Ibid*, de Sousa Santos, p 9.

9    As suggested for medicine generally by Illich, I, *Limits to Medicine. Medical Nemesis: The Expropriation of Health*, 1977, Harmondsworth: Penguin.

10   Suggested, *inter alia*, by Dworkin, A, *Right-Wing Women: The Politics of Domesticated Females*, 1983, London: The Women's Press; Spallone, P, *Beyond Conception: The New Politics of Reproduction*, 1989, Basingstoke: Macmillan.

competence in an age of democracy, as Roy Porter has recently argued, with medical and nursing professionals driven to break out from the iron cages which professional strategies have built for them,[11] falls to be discussed elsewhere.

This has resulted in two senses in what we might call 'the individuation of the body'. First, it has led to arguments as to whether I 'own' 'my' body;[12] and whether in consequence or otherwise I might do what I want with 'my' body, whether by way of sale or other use of tissue,[13] surrogacy,[14] bodily alteration and so on. This individuation of the body with its emphasis on individual autonomy and the market, suggests that 'the West has evolved a culture preoccupied with the self, with the individual and his or her identity, and this quest has come to be equated with (or reduced to) the individual body and the embodied personality ...'.[15] This in turn has resulted in changes of views on 'autonomy' and legal control with respect to medical care which have been sanctioned or permitted by the courts; thus, we have seen changes in only the last 10 years through cases such as *Re MB*,[16] *Bland*,[17] *Re C*[18] and *Re T*,[19] *Gillick*,[20] and *Bolitho*.[21]

Finally, although not uncontroversially, the nature of the patient has changed. I do not mean this in the usual fashion which attends that assertion, that people have become more rights-oriented, more consumerist about health care and the deliverers of health care, although I believe that thesis could be defended.[22] What I mean, additionally, is that the patient has disappeared, if

---

11 Porter, R, *The Greatest Benefit to Mankind: A Medical History of Humanity from Antiquity to the Present*, 1997, London: HarperCollins, p 702.

12 Locke, J, 'An essay concerning the true original extent and end of civil government', 2nd Treatise (1960) para 27, in Laslett, P (ed), *Two Treatises on Government*, 1960, Cambridge: CUP, p 287; Kass, L, 'Is there a right to die?' (1993) 23(1) *Hastings Center Report* 34–43, showing the context in which Locke's famous remark on 'body ownership' occurs, and Hyde, A, *Bodies of Law*, 1997, Princeton, NJ: Princeton University Press, pp 54–57, discussing the misunderstanding of Locke's 'unsophisticated pun' which has given rise to the confusing claim that I might 'own' my own body.

13 See, Radin, MJ, *Contested Commodities: The Trouble with Trade in Sex, Children, Body Parts, and Other Things*, 1996, Cambridge, Mass: Harvard University Press and Posner, R, *Sex and Reason*, 1992, Cambridge, Mass: Harvard University Press, for two opposing views.

14 For opposing arguments see, for example, *ibid*, Radin, and Shalev, C, *Birth Power: The Case for Surrogacy*, 1989, New Haven: Yale University Press.

15 *Ibid*, Porter, p 7.

16 [1997] 2 FLR 426.

17 *Airedale NHS Trust v Bland* [1993] 1 All ER 821.

18 *Re C* [1994] 1 All ER 819.

19 *Re T* [1992] 4 All ER 649.

20 *Gillick v West Norfolk & Wisbech AHA* [1986] 1 AC 112.

21 *Bolitho v City and Hackney HA* [1997] 4 All ER 771.

22 Perhaps the modern *locus classicus* in this vein is Kennedy, I, *Treat Me Right: Essays in Medical Law and Ethics*, 1988, Oxford: OUP. For an essay specifically focusing on the possible contribution of human rights to women's health see Cook, RJ, *Women's Health and Human Rights*, 1994, Philadelphia: Philadelphia and Pennsylvania Press.

by 'the patient' we are understood to mean some generic, stand-all representative. In place we have patients who have gender, class, race, ethnicity, age and identity; we have a theatre teeming with peoples all of different constitutions and complexions.

## THE CONCERNS OF REPRODUCTION

Reflecting on what I had been asked to address in this essay, I realised the enormity of the field that had been suggested to me. Reproduction might cover prevention (contraception, sterilisation), negotiation, or what Hilary Homans has identified as a 'contraceptive career'[23] (which might include family 'planning'), assistance (reproductive technologies, surrogacy), alternatives (childlessness, chosen or otherwise, adoption), consequences (termination of pregnancy,[24] foetal therapies, maternal management, parenthood, parenting, suitability, child rearing, child support), images and ideologies (of motherhood, fatherhood and parenthood), responsibility, regulation, and so on. Each of these has drawn forward feminisms' analyses, critiques, evaluations, constructions. I decided to look, albeit cursorily, at different sorts of responses that feminisms' jurisprudences have offered to reproductive technologies, although, in fact, I shall say little about *specific* technologies. My concern in this chapter has been to read a number of signposts which feminisms' scholars have left[25] and to offer a translation of what I read on those posts.[26]

I decided to look at reproductive technologies for four reasons. First, perhaps better than any other area of reproduction, technological assistance in conception is the most emblematic of *different* feminisms' approaches to

---

23  Homans, H, 'The medical construction of a contraceptive career', in Homans, H (ed), *The Sexual Politics of Reproduction*, 1985, Aldershot: Gower, pp 45–63.

24  Equal access to abortion across Europe as being guaranteed under the European Convention on Human Rights was voted on by the Parliamentary Assembly of the Council of Europe 74 to 56 (see (1993) 341 *The Lancet* 1271–72) but failed to secure the necessary two-thirds majority for acceptance requiring individual Member States to consider new legislation. Catherine Lalumière had hoped by this measure not only to increase women's rights but also to *reduce* abortion tourism.

25  Any number of books or articles detail particular aspects of reproductive technology; for a valuable bibliographical source see McHale, J and Fox, M, with Murphy, J, *Health Care Law: Text and Materials*, 1997, London: Sweet & Maxwell, pp 695, 751 and 812; and for an accessible, introductory review of a 'feminist approach to ethics', see pp 119–28.

26  This notion of translation bears a specific meaning, and is far from uncontroversial. I mean by 'translation' the process of augmenting and modifying the original which involves neither objectification and appropriation nor annihilation of the texts in question: 'I will have to change the text as I am reading it, but this does not mean that I am destroying it to further my own interests ... It is not a compromise, but a reconciliation, a closing of the distance between the translator and the other's text, between one language and another. And, as Jacques Derrida suggests, a translation considered in this way ensures the survival of a text, enabling it to live on and grow after its publication.' *Op cit*, fn 1, Davies, p 178 (references omitted).

reproduction (notice that I do not here say differences between). The development of assisted reproduction programmes and the medicalisation of infertility '... raise some of the most difficult questions for feminist theory and practice'.[27] The techniques and trappings of assisted conception — AI, IVF, GIFT, cryopreservation of gametes, eggs and embryos, gamete and embryo donation, and surrogacy, also challenge traditional views of procreation and parenthood, a challenge which has legal as well as ethical implications. According to Lene Koch, 'one of the most difficult problems that has confronted feminist critics of in vitro fertilization (IVF) and the other new reproductive technologies, is the great enthusiasm for IVF among involuntarily childless women'.[28] Carol Smart has even doubted that there can be a satisfactory feminist response to reproductive technology; to argue that they contribute to and reinforce (male) dominant ideologies of motherhood and womanhood is to deny individual women's experiences and announced intentions, may be to suggest that individual women are not able – autonomously – to choose for themselves, to weigh and balance the consequences of infertility treatments and the possible opportunity costs of the treatments and the very real costs of disappointment and 'failure' in conception. On the other hand, to argue that they contribute to and liberate women from the burdens of unlooked-for consequences of infertility in them or their presently chosen partner is to suggest an uncomfortably determinist approach to mental and physical well-being and notions of personhood.[29]

The second reason why I wanted to focus on reproductive technology is that concern with and demand for reproductive medicine has become a global matter. The existence of a few specialist clinics has revealed a global market for assisted conception services. And with the facilitation of travel and the phenomenon of speed, the ability to avail oneself of the services available at the reproductive tourist office make the franking of the stamp on the ethical envelope more interesting. Where technological development results in the blurring of national boundaries, the increasingly difficult task of one country insulating itself from events elsewhere in the world has given rise to the possibility of what has been called 'procreative tourism' and 'ethical dumping'.[30]

One small example will suffice. Following the birth of twins to a 59-year-old English woman in an Italian clinic because of doubts about the desirability of any UK clinic offering treatment to a post-menopausal woman, then Health

---

27  Anleu, SR, 'Reproductive autonomy: infertility, deviance and conceptive technology', in Peterson, K (ed), *Law and Medicine*, 1994, Melbourne: La Trobe University Press, p 36.

28  Koch, L, 'IVF – an irrational choice?' (1990) 3(3) *Issues in Reproductive and Genetic Engineering* 235.

29  *Feminism and the Power of Law*, 1990, London: Routledge, pp 223–24.

30  For a critical analysis of one particular 'case' of globalisation and the effect of that on a national regulatory scheme see Morgan, D and Lee, RG, 'In the name of the father? *ex parte Blood*: dealing with novelty and anomaly' (1997) 60 MLR 840.

Secretary Virginia Bottomley lamented that '[w]e cannot stop people going to any country in the world for treatment but maybe we'll renew our efforts to have discussions with other countries as to the examples we set and how they can establish ethical controls over some of the dramatic achievements in modern medicine'.[31] Almost immediately following this, the French junior health minister Phillipe Douste-Blazy announced its government's intention to introduce legislation to prohibit in vitro fertilisation of post-menopausal women[32] and the Italian health minister Mariapia Garavaglia was quoted as saying that 'desires are not rights, and babies are not consumer goods' and announced the imminent establishment of a commission to establish 'controls over the treatment of sterile and post-menopausal women'.[33]

The third reason for focusing on reproductive technologies is their complexity. Anne Maclean has suggested of surrogacy that it is complex and difficult because it raises not one issue but a cluster of issues, and issues of different sorts at that. 'It is easy to confuse considerations relevant to one of these issues with considerations relevant to another, or to misunderstand the character of a particular claim or a particular objection.'[34]

There is no single moral issue called surrogacy, and in much the same way, this is true of reproductive technologies generally. People's (moral) worries about surrogacy arrangements will vary greatly depending on the type of surrogacy in question, the relationships of the parties involved to one another, whether it is a commercial transaction and in what circumstances, and so on. And this moral concern will engage a variety of wider concerns too; not just about the family and parenthood, but about one's whole attitude to what life brings. It seems to me that this is also an important observation about reproductive technologies more generally. The sorts of worries, or objections, the 'issues of different sorts' as Maclean puts it, will carry different force in different circumstances. Thus, worries about resource implications (which can of course involve ethical concern), are very different sorts of worries from those deep, inarticulate (speech of the heart) worries about the basic legitimacy of an action or of a general attitude exemplified in an action.

Concerns with surrogacy, then, like reproductive technologies more generally, cluster around commerce, commodity, consumerism and

---

31  See (1993) *The Independent*, 28 December; (1993) *The Guardian* 28 December, reporting an interview on the BBC *Today* programme, 27 December 1993.

32  (1994) *The Guardian*, 5 January, although this was followed immediately by protests from various parts of the political spectrum and different interest groups.

33  (1994) *The Guardian*, 6 January. For a careful consideration of some of the possible consequences of treating reproduction and issue as if they *were* items of the consumer market see *op cit*, fn 13, Radin.

34  Maclean, A, *The Elimination of Morality*, 1993, London: Routledge, p 202.

community. In the late 20th century, the belief is rife if not reasonable (and perhaps not so novel) that anything can be bought; that money can buy not only love (or at least its counterfeit) but also anything else (or at least its counterfeit). But, as Margaret Radin points out, the double bind is that 'both commodification and non-commodification may be harmful'[35] and 'it should be clear that there are coherent feminist arguments on both sides of the general issue of baby-selling (commissioned adoption)' as on reproductive technologies more generally.[36]

Finally, reproductive technologies, in their recent manifestations of the past 30 years at least,[37] and the legal accommodations and responses to them, allow us to witness the architectural and engineering dimensions of the *constitutive* aspect of law, rather than, which is often the case, its archaeological and anthropological sitings. The importance of this interpretative dimension is that it proposes that law (like other social institutions), shapes how individuals conceive of themselves and their relations with others. 'The underlying assumption is that social institutions are actualized through a set of assumptions, categories, concepts, values and vocabularies that we have internalized so that we are not consciously aware of how they have affected our ideas and behavior.'[38]

Set against these backgrounds, feminisms' analyses of reproductive technology, laws and regulation, have drawn from feminisms' analysis of law and feminisms' analysis of reproductive technology. As Anne Bottomley has suggested, '... authors do not hold in common an agreed formula for what feminism is about other than a shared commitment to the exploration of gender relations'.[39] Feminisms have enjoyed a number of central themes, which Bottomley summates as '... narratives of the feminine, as constitutive of law-in-modernity by exclusion, by difference and by denial ...'.[40] Reproductive technologies have, I think, brought forward a variant on that analysis, one in which the narrative has been characterised not so much by exclusion, difference and denial, but by the possibilities and problems of *place* and *priority*. It is important to recall that infertility – like fertility – will affect different women and different men in different ways, and in ways that will differ dramatically according to culture, age, class, status and wealth. 'The handicap imposed by reproductive impairment will be at its most severe for

---

35  *Op cit*, fn 13, Radin, p 127.

36  *Op cit*, fn 13, Radin, p 149.

37  Duelli Klein, R, 'What's new about the "New" Reproductive Technologies?', in Corea, G *et al*, *Man-Made Women: How New Reproductive Technologies Affect Women*, 1985, London: Hutchinson, pp 64–73.

38  Sarat, A and Felstiner, W, *Divorce Lawyers and their Clients: Power and Meaning in the Legal Process*, 1995, New York and Oxford: OUP, p 13. I am grateful to Katherine O'Donovan for originally drawing this to my attention.

39  Bottomley, A, *Feminist Perspectives on the Foundational Subjects of Law*, 1996, London: Cavendish Publishing, p vi.

40  *Ibid*, p 1.

an uneducated woman living in a small community where few options other than motherhood are culturally sanctioned.'[41]

Legal responses to reproductive technologies may not, of course, prioritise feminisms' concerns, they may instead exhibit, acquiesce in or constitute societal, theological, patriarchal, technological concerns, some or all of which may be antithetical to those of some or all women, and some or all of which may at least be taken into account if not prioritised. And it is here that one of the sites for feminisms' analyses and critiques of reproductive technologies has been at its most active. In prioritising these other concerns or sites, real damage may be done to the interests of all and to individual women. Cautioning against the tyranny of classifications, Margaret Davies reviews some standard 'categories of feminism', recalling that the tyranny is especially critical unless the temporality and provisional nature of the classifications is carefully attended to. The identity of groups is not fixed or constant, and assigning membership to a group is often an act of domination in itself: 'the fixing of such identities by a dominant ideology has always been one of the ways in which oppression is institutionalised.'[42] Reviewing arguments from liberal feminism, radical feminism, intersectionist jurisprudence,[43] feminism and postmodernism, Davies illustrates how a supposed complementarity of interests and concerns can be radically reordered through metamorphoses of method and representation.

What links many of feminisms' responses to reproductive technologies, as feminisms' responses to law's regulation of them, Davies argues, is a commitment to a project not only directed at substantive 'women's issues', such as rape, abortion, discrimination, and pornography, but one which '... poses a challenge to the fundamental structure of law itself.'[44] It is a challenge to the substantive law, to the ordering concepts of law,[45] to law's (liberal) ideology and to its conceptual self-image, much as to the image of knowledge itself.[46] Feminisms constitute transformative theories as well as transformative politics; the *aim* of feminisms is always transformation, and as a process, feminisms are always in transition as a dynamic. It is in identifying and achieving that transformation that there are different emphases within feminisms, and these are reflected both in the analyses of law and its

---

41  Doyal, L, *What Makes Women Sick: Gender and the Political Economy of Health*, 1995, New Brunswick, New Jersey: Rutgers University Press, p 147.

42  *Op cit*, fn 1, Davies, p 175.

43  'One of the assumptions made by some writers is that taking women as a group is a sufficient basis for feminist thought, without being sensitive to other systems of oppression which are not co-extensive with, but do "intersect" with gender oppression', *op cit*, fn 1, Davies, p 202.

44  *Op cit*, fn 1, Davies, p 172.

45  For an example of a recharacterisation of such a project see Stang Dahl, T, *Women's Law: An Introduction to Feminist Jurisprudence* (trans Craig, RL), 1987, Oslo: Norwegian University Press.

46  *Op cit*, fn 1, Davies, pp 172–79.

limitations or possibilities, as well in the specific site of reproductive technologies.

## FEMINISMS' RESPONSES TO REPRODUCTION AND REGULATION

I think it is possible to identify three main sorts of analysis of reproductive technologies, which I shall call the 'critical', the 'contextual' and the 'choice' models. Neither form is meant to suggest an exclusive boundary, each displays some unifying themes, and each serves to expose 'perhaps the greatest philosophical achievement of feminism over the past 20 years ...' which is in revealing that '... in the practice of moral and political philosophy ... the long absence of women's generic interests from the agenda of these subjects could not be innocently explained'.[47] Each shares a number of organising themes and is clustered around an identifiable core of concerns; these are, principally, concerns with procreation, parenthood, the nature of the family and personal identity. Of course, there are the wider concerns of feminisms, such as patriarchy, as the backdrop against which these particular concerns are framed.

Feminisms' responses to reproductive technologies share a number of salient characteristics. First, there is a general scepticism or rejection of the biomedical model of medicine. Secondly, and possibly but not necessarily flowing from this, is a belief that whether reproductive technologies are the wrong sets of responses to the wrong sets of problems, or whether at best they promise a limited set of successful outcomes for a very limited set of questions for a limited set of people, there is nonetheless something to be understood about the appeal that they have. Third, there is a belief in most perspectives of feminism, that where reproductive technologies do properly have a place in late-20th-century westernised societies' responses to the consequences of infertility, they should be free from explicit manipulation by the State to secure other, underlying policy goals which exist for the benefit of the State rather than for the benefit of the individual users of reproductive technologies. Let me address first the scepticism with the biomedical model of medicine before turning to review the main tenets of what, crudely, I have called the 'critical', the 'contextual' and 'choice' analyses of reproductive technologies.

---

47 Frazer, K, Hornsby, J and Lovibond, S, *Ethics: A Feminist Reader*, 1994, Oxford: Blackwell, p 4.

## The biomedical model

Based on the notion of Cartesian dualism,[48] this model holds that health and disease can be explained through an engineering metaphor in which the body comprises a series of separate but interdependent systems. Ill-health is the mechanical failure of some part of one or more of the components of this engine, and the medical task is to repair the damage. The mind is separated from the body and the individual is separated from the social and cultural contexts of their lives. 'Illness' is an objective, positivistic fact, a descriptive, not an evaluative term. Such a model has, in fact, as many feminist scholars acknowledge, led to enormous successes in understanding different types of disease and exploring treatment, and it is mistaken to reject the powerful investigative force which the medical model suggests. However, what has followed from this as well has been a neglect of prevention, now thought to be a major factor in the incidence of infertility, and an over-reliance on a curative model in explaining the causes of disease and the different ways in which illness might be experienced.[49] Medical and legal concern with issues of reproductive technology have generally strayed little beyond this biomedical model. And it is in the concentration of reproductive technologies with physical aspects of women's health that the biomedical model has had its greatest and potentially most harmful impacts. The Foucaudian identification of a new kind of power relationship, in which 'authorities who understand our bodies have gained the right to make and enforce rules about morality',[50] flows directly from this model. The most thoroughgoing critics of the biomedical model are also those most critical of the whole project of reproductive technologies.

---

48 Descartes, R, 'Meditations on the first philosophy in which the existence of god and the distinction between mind and body are demonstrated', in Haldane, E and Ross, G (eds and trans), *The Philosophical Works of Descartes*, 1967, Cambridge: CUP, pp 144–99. Descartes argued that the physical body, in line with emergent anatomical science, should be understood as a machine, but that there were other parts of the person which could not be accommodated within this vehicle. The expression 'mind' he used to identify aspects of human consciousness, which in almost all respects differed from the opposite characteristics possessed and exhibited by the body.

49 The best short introduction to this subject of which I am aware remains Doyal, L and Doyal, L, 'Western scientific medicine: a philosophical and political prognosis', in Birke, L and Silvertown, J, *More than the Parts: Biology and Politics*, 1984, London: Pluto Press, pp 82–109. Other accessible accounts are in Kennedy, I, 'The rhetoric of medicine', in *The Unmasking of Medicine*, 1981, London: Allen & Unwin, pp 1–25. The importance of the *philosophical* enterprise on which Kennedy has engaged himself – the exposure of a philosophical misconception at the centre of modern medicine – and the problems which may be encountered in the ethical enterprise are carefully and cogently explored in *op cit*, fn 34, Maclean, pp 187–201; especially important in the present context is her elaboration of how all contemporary medical education and practice *'dehumanises* and *diminishes* the people with whose health and well being they are charged', see p 199.

50 Foucault, M, *The History of Sexuality* (trans Hurley, R), 1978, Harmondsworth: Penguin, p 146.

## The critics

Four central points of criticism have emerged from the early life-cycle of reproductive technologies, and they have remained unanswered as far as those opposed to any use of such technologies are concerned. First, originally developed to address one specific cause of infertility in women, blocked fallopian tubes, IVF moved rapidly from the experimental to the clinical. It is in this step that those who see some advantages to the development of treatment services to address the consequences of infertility are prepared to tolerate the availability of choice for individual women while remaining critical of the overall project of medically assisted conception. More explicitly, the critics charge that reproductive technologies generally and IVF specifically are techniques which augment medical control over procreation generally and over women's choices and preferences in procreation specifically. Social screening and medical assessment have become part of a new ability to licence parenthood to those deemed by the medical profession fit for the burdens and responsibilities. Compared with embryonic matter, such as gametes and embryos, women's physical health has been neglected. Rita Arditti and Gena Corea in the United States, and Renate Duelli Klein and Patricia Spallone in Australia and the United Kingdom focused at an early stage on what was being overlooked or left out of the context of reproductive technology. Thus in her interview programme with women who had left an IVF programme without a child, Duelli Klein recounts recurrent sentiments of abuse, misinformation, and malpractice, resulting in their lives being 'wrecked by the trauma of being living laboratories'.[51] Seeing IVF as a 'cure' for infertility ignores the iatrogenic causes of women's fertility problems, such as the IUD and excessive abdominal surgery, and the compromises to which reproductive health is subjected by poor health care, nutrition and other environmental factors.

Secondly, the critics allege that IVF was also seen as an example of manipulating the female body to serve patriarchal needs. Whether in facilitating the surgical removal of ova from healthy women to help in overcoming the consequences of a partner's low sperm count or motility, or in encouraging infertile women to go to extraordinary lengths to satisfy a partner's desire for a child, 'IVF was viewed as another example of putting all the risk and responsibility for reproductive failure on the shoulders of the woman'.[52]

---

51 Duelli Klein, R, *The Exploitation of Desire: Women's Experiences with In Vitro Fertilisation*, 1989, Victoria: Deakin University Press, p 7; Corea, G and Ince, S, 'Report of a survey of IVF clinics in the USA', in Spallone, P and Steinberg, DL (eds), *Made to Order: The Myth of Reproductive and Genetic Progress*, 1987, London: Pergamon.

52 Alto Charo, R, 'The interaction between family planning and the introduction of new reproductive technologies', in *op cit*, fn 27, Peterson, pp 65–66, on which this paragraph draws.

Thirdly, the fiscal and emotional costs of IVF, compared with the likelihood of failure to conceive and deliver a child, would not be seen as a reasonable choice in a world in which childbearing was regarded as only one option in complex lifestyles. The existence of the demand for reproductive technologies evidences western society's attachment to perceiving women as unfulfilled without children. The belief in chosen childlessness is disvalued or dismissed, or characterised as the choice of the sexual or relational deviant. Doubts have been expressed by many commentators, such as Christine Crowe, arguing that IVF does not, in any event, represent a proper choice, since other options like chosen childlessness or adoption are not open or available to all women.[53]

Fourthly, IVF has revealed a profound attachment to genetic lineage which cannot be shared equally between the sexes. Women gestate and deliver, men could only stand by and admire their own physical characteristics as reflected in their children. Attachment to genetic lineage, especially by and for men, has had a distorting effect on women's stated desires to circumvent the consequences of infertility.

## The contextualists: '... no daughters to comfort her and no sons to support her'[54]

It might be thought that for any contextual account of reproductive technologies to be given this *necessarily* implies a commitment to a liberal, contingent, in parts rights-based model. I want here to show why I believe that that would be mistaken, although it is undoubtedly *one* of the contexts which is available.

> To view infertility as a medical construction and the desire to have a biologically related child as a social product does not deny the consequences of such definitions. While it is essential to critique the process of medicalisation and to be continually wary of the development of technologies and interventions that aim to alleviate infertility, these 'treatments' do not determine totally the capacity of individuals to make choices. That the available options are limited, restrictive and may involve medical intervention does not deny some scope for negotiation, bargaining and resistance.[55]

Without good health, a person's ability to act upon at least some of the choices they make or would wish to make is curtailed. Providing the means by which citizens may preserve and restore or secure their health may be thought to be

---

53　Crowe, C, 'Women want it: IVF and women's motivations for participation', in *op cit*, fn 51, Spallone and Steinberg, and 'Mind over whose matter? Women, in vitro fertilisation and the development of scientific knowledge', in McNeil, M, Varcoe, I and Yearley, S (eds), *The New Reproductive Technologies*, 1990, Basingstoke: Macmillan, pp 27–57.

54　*Op cit*, fn 41, Doyal, p 147.

55　*Op cit*, fn 27, Anleu, p 36.

a fundamental task of any modern State. So, when we come to speak of health, we are of necessity required to address at least a package of *conceptual* questions,[56] *political* questions — the role and responsibility of the State in securing, promoting or damaging the health of its citizens and those whom it affects directly and indirectly, intentionally and accidentally, through the extraterritorial effects of its behaviour,[57] and those of *gender*. As Lesley Doyal has recently reminded us, many women's lives are severely constrained because they are denied the opportunity to make real choices about procreation. This inability to influence one of the most fundamental aspects of biological functioning can have profound effects on both physical and mental health.[58]

This has two aspects; first is the prevention of unwanted pregnancy and responding sympathetically and appropriately to the consequences of contraceptive failure. The second is the circumvention of unlooked-for childlessness and responding sympathetically and appropriately to the sequelae which may ensue. This does not necessarily entail that the functional equivalent of access to services for the termination of pregnancy must be mirrored in the provision of reproductive technology programmes. The equivalent of access to abortion services does not necessarily mean that there must be a corresponding 'right' to access to infertility treatment services, much less that there must be or is a 'right' to have a child. Both are connected, however, to the basic notion of reproductive self-determination: 'infertility can be a major disability and its treatment should be seen as a basic element in reproductive self-determination, along with abortion, contraception and maternity care.'[59]

I do not want to be thought to imply that each or any of these different types of question – the conceptual question, the political question and the gendered question – can or does stand independently of any one other or of all. There are cross-cutting intersections and intermixtures of all of them, and the points of intersection and interlayering will often be complex but interesting and important. Feminisms' accounts of reproductive technologies

---

56 Boorse, C, 'On the distinction between health and disease' (1975) *Philosophy & Public Affairs*, p 5; *op cit*, fn 41, Doyal; Oakley, A, *Essays on Women, Medicine and Health*, 1993, Edinburgh: Edinburgh University Press; Nordenfelt, A, 'On the relevance and importance of the notion of disease' (1993) 14 *Theoretical Medicine* 15.

57 Townsend, P and Davidson, N (ed), *Inequalities in Health* (The Black Report), 1982, Harmondsworth: Penguin; Williams, B, 'The Idea of Equality', in Laslett, P and Runciman, WG (eds), *Philosophy, Politics and Society*, 1962, Oxford: Blackwell, pp 110–31; Nozick, R, *Anarchy, State and Utopia*, 1974, Oxford: Blackwell, p 233.

58 *Op cit*, fn 41, Doyal, p 93. Are there two problems with this: (1) the effects of environment and diet in men's reproductive health, and (2) recent (contested) changes in the legal regulation of the consequences of failing to control one's fertility?

59 *Op cit*, fn 41, Doyal, p 147.

are part of feminisms' accounts of science and the reason, logic and technological certainty and neutrality which it celebrates.[60]

Lene Koch has centrally captured the difficulties which reproductive technologies cause for many critical feminist commentators: 'there is no doubt that IVF is a powerful transformer of women's reproductive consciousness and an irresistible technology that few women can refuse.'[61] The role of the family, and conceptions of personal identity and human nature, are underlined in many ways by programmes of assisted conception, especially in the way in which rational women will use and pursue infertility programmes even when they know that the success rates are low. Koch, in interviews with a sample of women entering and participating in an IVF programme in Copenhagen, observed that although in a number of cases women felt deprived of accurate or realistic information, this did not seem to matter: 'it did not seem to have influenced these women's decisions, neither to start IVF in the first place, nor to continue after one or more failed attempts.' She argues that to want a child and to try to have it '... is an exercise of the reproductive freedom that the feminist movement has argued for since its very beginning'.[62] This wish to have a child – this authentic wish of the women concerned – 'does not become less strong because it is socially constructed. Given the information which is available about the success rates of IVF programmes, why do these 'infertile' women appear to persist with irrational hopes and beliefs in the outcome of their project? Her conclusion is an important one: ' ... as each new reproductive technology enters the market, the definition of infertility changes.' Infertile women are only allowed access to their infertility – it can only become an established fact – once they have followed *all* the acceptable rites of passage, including the latest treatment service, no matter how experimental. If these are seen only as a choice for a child, then they may indeed be regarded as irrational, given the paucity of the established rates at which women leave IVF programmes with a child. However, if it is acknowledged that 'human identity is closely affected by parental status and *childlessness is an identity which is hard to obtain* and must be fought for in a pronatalist society, since no doubt must exist as to the certainty of the condition',[63] a rational understanding of reproductive technologies is revealed.

What Koch here describes is what might be called the problem of *access to infertility*; whereas infertility used to be considered to be a matter of fate: 'it is nowadays turning into a deliberate decision, at least in a certain sense. Those who give up without having tried the very latest methods (an endless series)

---

60  A good introduction to feminisms' accounts of science is Rosser, S, *Teaching Science and Health from a Feminist Perspective*, 1986, New York: Pergamon Press; especially useful in the immediate contexts are pp 3–22, 38–61 and 77–89.

61  *Op cit*, fn 28, Koch, p 236.

62  *Ibid*.

63  *Ibid*.

have to take the blame. After all, they could have kept trying.'[64] The social role of fertility will always in some sense be seen as chosen,[65] part of the '... noiseless social and cultural revolution ...' in which the exponential development of science and technology, while supposedly serving health, has in fact '... created entirely new situations, has changed the relationship of humankind to itself, to disease, illness and death, indeed, it has changed the world'.[66]

Thus, judged only against the likelihood of producing a baby, a woman's initial introduction to and continued participation in an IVF programme might to outsiders lack rationality; it is transformed, however, when it is seen as 'a new element in the procedure by which the woman establishes her future identity'. The decision or the desire to try IVF becomes independent of the efficiency of the technology, because it is '... judged by the yardstick of another rationality'.[67] Koch is no proponent of IVF programmes, far from it indeed; IVF is a dangerous and expensive technology, which changes motherhood in detrimental ways and it is a high-risk, low-efficiency technology whose costs foreclose the development and application of preventive, cheap low-technology solutions that every woman can afford to choose. IVF programmes deleteriously affect the priorities of the health services, but that does not mean that they are not pursued by rational women.

Lesley Doyal offers a similar analysis of the contexts of reproductive technology, in which some of the millions of infertile women are drawn by their desire for a child into the 'epicentre of high-technology gynaecology and obstetrics'.[68] She is more concerned with the cultural contexts of fertility, in which the status of mother is still a 'central' one for many women and for whom '... an inability to become a biological parent may have a profound effect on women's sense of themselves and their well-being', in which they may suffer a major life crisis, may indeed be 'disabled'.[69] Reproductive technology may, then, be seen not just as a response to infertility but more profoundly as a (bio)technological response to a total life and social crisis *to the person as a whole*. In other words, infertility treatments might, on this view, be recontextualised as something other than a 'medical model' response to particular cellular dysfunction in the reproductive system; rather it is a response to a life-threatening position. The cruel irony, then, is that while reproductive technologies '... have recently been hailed as the miracle solution for all those who cannot conceive within their own bodies', the reality is that

---

64  Beck, U and Gernsheim Beck, E, *The Normal Chaos of Love*, 1995, Oxford: Polity Press, p 126, and see especially pp 102–39.

65  Katz Rothman, B, *The Tentative Pregnancy: Prenatal Diagnosis and the Future of Motherhood*, 1986, New York: Viking, p 29.

66  *Ibid*, Beck, p 204.

67  *Op cit*, fn 28, Koch, p 241.

68  *Op cit*, fn 41, Doyal, p 145.

69  *Op cit*, fn 41, Doyal, p 146.

'they are suitable for only a small percentage of infertile women and only a few of these can afford them'.[70] In an arresting phrase which recalls the culturally differentiated experiences of women, to which feminisms particularly have become more attentive, Doyal examines the severe handicaps of a woman unable to have children and who may have '... no daughters to comfort her and no sons to support her'.[71]

## Reproductive 'choice'

Rosalind Petchesky has observed that the critical issue for feminists is not so much the content of women's choices, or even the 'right to choose', as the social and material conditions under which choices are made. 'The fact that individuals themselves do not determine the social framework in which they act does not nullify their choices nor their moral capacity to make them.'[72] The most visible complaint is that where access to reproductive technologies is permitted, the State should not discriminate against certain individual women because of their sexual orientation, status preference, their race or social status. And yet, almost universally, where legislation has addressed these questions, judgments about 'fitness to parent' are explicitly or implicitly made by the State on grounds which characterise some women as unfit to mother or to parent.

Reproductive technologies have provided some people who are 'infertile' with the hope and chance of having a child and have opened up the possibility of new and exciting opportunities for the formation of families with the separation of genetic, gestational and social parenthood in ways that previously belonged to the realm of science fiction.[73] Even those enthusiastic about their advent remain conscious of the challenge to '... respect the reproductive rights of infertile people to have access to reproductive technology, while critically evaluating and seeking to transcend the narrow confines of the definition of 'family' within which reproductive technology operates'.[74] And yet it remains the case that, for most women, infertility is a life sentence; new technologies are characterised by their exclusivity, for the relatively more wealthy, 'suitable couple', who are eternal optimists – Koch's new rationalists as we might call them. And the problem, with their high cost and low 'success' rates and abysmal side-effects, is that the very existence of technological solutions to circumventing infertility may be diverting resources

---

70   *Op cit*, fn 41, Doyal, p 145.

71   *Op cit*, fn 41, Doyal, p 147.

72   'Reproductive freedom: beyond "a woman's right to choose"' (1980) *Signs* 674, p 675.

73   Bennett, B, 'Gamete donation, reproductive technology and the law', in *op cit*, fn 27, Peterson, p 41.

74   *Ibid*.

away from broader strategies for responding to and preventing 'reproductive impairment'.[75]

## METAMORPHOSES: ETHICS, HEALTH AND FAMILY

Reproductive technologies understood in their widest sense have arrived at a time of what Boaventura de Sousa Santos describes as a 'state of epistemological turbulence'.[76] He suggests that after the 19th-century scientific euphoria and the concomitant aversion to philosophical speculation, epitomised by positivism, we have, at the end of the 20th century, been seized by the near-desperate desire to complement our knowledge of things with our knowledge of our knowledge of things – in other words, with knowledge of ourselves, *independent of any surrounding moral values.*[77] The emergence of the concern with women's interests and health has occurred at a time of other changes which have taken deep root in the practice of ethical and legal thought, some of which are reflected in feminisms' works, some of which have occurred as a *direct or indirect result* of the placing of women as the central concern in enquiry. Within that is the imperative of recognising and acting upon the realisation that while they share a gender identity and a common biology, '... women are differentiated by factors such as age, sexual preference, race, class and, very importantly, geopolitical status – the wealth or poverty of the country in which they live'.[78] This caution is particularly necessary in the era of emergent globalisation: social, economic and cultural circumstances shape reproductive experiences in such a way that it is as inappropriate to speak then of 'the infertile' as it has become to speak of 'women'. Thus, for some women, 'infertility can be a major disability and its treatment should be seen as a basic element in reproductive self-determination, along with abortion, contraception and maternity care'.[79]

In dialogues and constructions of health care law and ethics, Susan Wolf has identified what she has called the rise of a 'new pragmatism' that challenges old paradigms in bioethics, especially those of the so-called principle-based approaches. The goal of this new, emergent, pragmatic paradigm is to change the nature of ethical colloquy about access – in this case – to health care. Feminist and race-sensitive scholarship, in particular, has rendered suspect any bioethical approach geared to the generic 'patient'.[80]

---

75  *Op cit*, fn 41, Doyal, p 149.

76  *Op cit*, fn 4, de Sousa Santos, p 34.

77  *Op cit*, fn 4, de Sousa Santos, p 20; emphasis added. A remarkably similar point is being made in Foucault's *History of Sexuality, op cit*, fn 50, especially pp 135–45.

78  *Op cit*, fn 41, Doyal, p 2.

79  *Op cit*, fn 41, Doyal, p 147.

80  Wolf, S, 'The rise of the new pragmatism' (1994) 20(4) *American Journal of Law & Medicine* 395–45, p 415, and see Gillon, R and Lloyd, A (eds), *Principles of Health Care Ethics*, 1994, Chichester: Wiley.

The hegemony of western modes of thought, which have much dominated western political, social and moral philosophy for the last 200 years or so, has been under new assail. Feminisms' and post modernisms' accounts of ethical practices propose a shift towards the understanding of morality as a socially embedded practice, a shift which identifies moral decision-making in medicine (as in other professional and public organisational settings) as increasingly subject to formalised procedures and constraints. Across a broad range in the landscape of contemporary medicine '... ethical choice and agency are now embedded as never before in a network of explicit rules and formal procedures and processes for making decisions'.[81]

The shift thus identified is part of a rethinking of the very nature of ethical theory itself; its relationship to the human subjectivity and the cultural context that produces it, the kind of knowledge it can be expected to provide and the force and authority of its claims and its relationship to practice are part of the reconstruction under way. This kind of postmodern philosophical orientation of moral philosophy fundamentally affects our grasp of the relationship between theory and practice. It purports to expose the extent to which classical ethical theories '... rest on assumptions about the transcendental character of reason and a "philosophy of the subject" ... that are no longer tenable'.[82] In other words, it is being claimed that ethical conclusions are being produced and constructed, rather than found from contemplation. The older questions are being displaced by a postmodern approach which aims to examine the ways in which meanings and legitimacy of moral notions are established, reinterpreted and transformed over time.

Or, so at first it might appear. Critics of this approach come from at least two directions. First, there is a strand of feminisms which reject a so called 'justice of multiplicities',[83] claiming that it ignores common interests which emerge from grand theoretical narratives. One potential consequence is that 'by refusing to lump women's interests together, modern feminist writing may appear to be abdicating itself from the legal arena'.[84] In another area, Patricia Williams has indicated the problem of rights discourse which could be implied here: 'the problem with rights discourse is not that the discourse is itself constricting but that it exists in a constricted referential universe.'[85] The conferring of rights on the 'historically disempowered' is 'symbolic' of part of the human condition which has been left out: 'rights imply a respect that

---

81  Jennings, B, 'Possibilities of consensus: towards democratic moral discourse' (1991) 16 *The Journal of Medicine and Philosophy* 447.

82  *Ibid*, p 448.

83  Fraser, L and Nicholson, A, 'Social criticism without philosophy: an encounter between feminism and postmodernism', in Ross, A (ed), *Universal Abandon? The Politics of Postmodernism*, 1988, Minneapolis: University of Minnesota Press.

84  Jackson, E, 'Contradictions and coherence in feminist responses to law' (1993) 20 JLS 398, p 399.

85  *The Alchemy of Race and Rights*, 1991, Cambridge, Mass: Harvard University Press, p 159.

places one in the referential range of self and others, that elevates one's status from human being to social being.'[86] Far from classical ethical theories resting on assumptions about the transcendental character of reason and an untenable philosophy of the subject, this approach suggests that rights-based approaches are one example of beginning to take some of those excluded claims seriously.

The second type of critical reception which has been offered despairs the apparent impasse of postmodernism and the incoherence of the 'new ethics' which it appears to suggest. A brilliantly succinct example of this argument is made by Gillian Rose in her final book *Mourning Becomes the Law: Philosophy and Representation*.[87] Deploring the 'despairing rationalism without reason',[88] she castigates libertarian extensions of the rights of individuals as amounting to an extension, not an attenuation, of coercion, and claims that communitarian empowerment of ethnic and gender pluralities presupposes and fixes a 'given distribution of "identities" in a radically dynamic society'.[89]

There is, I think, a sense, properly understood within postmodernism itself,[90] that what is needed here, what is happening, is not in fact the discovery of new philosophical approaches to knowledge and understanding, but more importantly, the *rediscovery*, certainly within the practice of modern medicine, dominated by the 'medical model' or the 'biomedical approach', of something which has been lost; *the person as a whole*.

What is entailed here is not the metaphysical entity of modern bioethics in speaking of the person, not the generic 'patient' which Wolf has sought to banish, what is envisaged is the recovery of the person in the ordinary sense – the individual human being, together with the environment, physical and social, of which she or he is a part. As Maclean explores and explains, the major loss engendered by the medical model of illness and health is medicine itself and those it subjects to its treatments. This is a major sickness of modern medicine, which will be resolved ('the healing of medicine itself') only when there has been a recovery of what overly science-dependent medicine has lost – human beings. In place of the patient we need to recover the person.

---

86  *Op cit*, fn 85, Williams, p 153.

87  *Op cit*, fn 6, Rose.

88  *Op cit*, fn 6, Rose, p 7.

89  *Op cit*, fn 6, Rose, p 5.

90  In the sense suggested by *op cit*, fn 5, Lyotard, p 28: 'Postmodernism thus understood is not modernism at its end but in the nascent state, and this state is constant.' The relationship between postmodernism and feminism has been a problematic one, but to that extent no different to other sites of challenge; for an introduction see Nicholson, LJ (ed), *Feminism/Postmodernism*, 1990, London: Routledge, especially in the present context the essays by Benhabib, Haraway and Butler. The projects identified by Wolf, Jennings and Maclean are, it seems to me, examples of the postmodern move away from large theoretical explanations in favour of a localised discourse but, as Rose demands, *with attention to wide, or grand strategy and not as a substitute for them.*

The point that must now be made is this:

> ... the recovery of the human being is the recovery, at the same time, of the values which form the framework of his life as a moral being, or a member of a moral community ... structural features of our everyday moral life ... not principles of which one could be *ignorant* unless one were ignorant of moral considerations as such.[91]

What Maclean believes is needed is the equivalent of Wolf's broad path teeming with people, accommodating 'multiple proposals and critiques as to method, full with attention to feminist, race-attentive and other contributions'. While the precise contours and geography of this space will need careful mapping and landscaping, it is the functional equivalent of de Sousa Santos's plea for a move away from our 'near desperate desire' to be filled with '... knowledge of ourselves ... independent of any surrounding moral values',[92] to supplement a 'culture preoccupied with self'[93] with one sensitive to and sensitised by principles of moral community.

There is a third change which needs to be remarked, and that is in the nature of the form which family has come to take in the latter decades of the 20th century. Even without the advent of reproductive technologies, family forms in the late 20th century have become more varied than in the 18th century, 19th century and even early to mid 20th century. Where it exists, parenthood is certainly no longer, if it ever was, a straightforward matter; it can now be broken into three distinguishable elements: biological parenthood, legal parenthood and the holding of parental responsibility, in such a way that 'the resulting structure of parenthood in English law is one in which a medieval land lawyer would have taken pride'.[94] The consequences of this we have hardly begun to hazard at. Marilyn Strathern has suggested that the new reproductive technologies and the legislative and other actions to which they have given rise seek to assist natural process on the one hand and the social definition of kinship on the other. But:

> ... this double assistance creates new uncertainties. For the present cultural explicitness is revolutionising former combinations of ideas and concepts. The more we give legal certainty to social parenthood, the more we cut from under our feet assumptions about the intrinsic nature of relationships themselves. The more facilitation is given to the biological reproduction of human persons, the harder it is to think of a domain of natural facts independent of social intervention. Whether or not all this is a good thing is uncertain. What is

---

91  *Op cit*, fn 34, Maclean, p 199.

92  *Op cit*, fn 4, de Sousa Santos, p 20.

93  *Op cit*, fn 11, Porter, p 7.

94  Eekelaar, J, 'Parenthood, social engineering and rights', in Morgan, D and Douglas, G (eds), *Constituting Families: A Study in Governance*, 1994, Stuttgart: Franz Steiner Verlag, p 87, citing the Children Act 1989 for the introduction of the third component, parental responsibility.

certain is that it will not be without consequence for the way people think about one another.[95]

The deployment of reproductive technologies is affecting assumptions which we bring to understandings, not only of family life, but to the very understanding of family itself and cultural practice:[96] '... the way in which the choices that assisted conception affords are formulated, will affect thinking about kinship. And the way people think about kinship will affect other ideas about relatedness between human beings.'[97] And, I would add, the way in which we think about relatedness between human beings will affect the way in which we think about the relationship between individuals, groups and the State.

Writing of reproductive technologies becomes part of an exercise in exploring the intellectual history – in which, here, we can only be concerned or competent to chart the origins of that history – of technology, rationality and society. Reproductive technology may have brought us to the customs house of human history, where we have to declare what we are taking with us, decide which of the imposts we will pay, and what we will abandon. We are crossing a Rubicon for which there is no return ticket, in which, indeed, there is no duty-free zone. Legal responses to and regulation of technology illustrate the way in which we might examine the challenges raised by reproduction itself. Feminisms' analyses propose a challenge to the fundamental structure of law itself,[98] and how an understanding of reproductive technologies may challenge the fundamental structures of identity and knowledge themselves. Surveying some frameworks for feminisms' analyses of reproductive technologies, reviewing responses to the 'noiseless social and cultural revolution' which Ulrich Beck suggests they represent,[99] and establishing their intellectual history[100] is an important part of the project to ensure that they do not come to be thought of as having occurred in what Christopher Hill has ironically observed, of the other English revolution, as a 'fit of absence of mind'.[101]

---

95 Strathern, M, 'The meaning of assisted kinship', in Stacey, M (ed), *Changing Human Reproduction*, 1992, London: Sage, pp 167–68. This essay is a succinct introduction to cultural and linguistic concepts deployed in arguments about the family, demonstrating, in her use of examples, the way in which what are taken as natural facts are themselves social and cultural constructs.

96 Strathern, M, *Reproducing the Future: Anthropology, Kinship and the New Reproductive Technologies*, 1993, Manchester: Manchester University Press.

97 *Ibid*, p 149.

98 *Op cit*, fn 1, Davies, p 172.

99 *Op cit*, fn 64, Beck, p 204.

100 For a template within which this might be forged see *op cit*, fn 4, de Sousa Santos, pp 1 and 40 *et seq*.

101 Hill, C, *The Intellectual Origins of the English Revolution*, 1965, Oxford: Clarendon Press, p 1.

# CHAPTER TWELVE

# BODY TALK: RETHINKING AUTONOMY, COMMODIFICATION AND THE EMBODIED LEGAL SELF

*Carl F Stychin*

## INTRODUCTION

Within the dominant paradigm of property law, the question of body ownership is dealt with in a straightforward fashion. Although individuals may hold certain, limited rights in their bodies, justifiable in terms of the principles of liberal autonomy, there is no general, recognised right of ownership of the body. In this chapter, I argue that although this conclusion may be doctrinally 'correct' in English law, the reasoning obscures how body ownership is an important location of legal controversy which demands a more nuanced analysis; one which is grounded in the centrality of gender both to the body and claims to its ownership. Specifically, I want to argue that legal reasoning around body ownership must begin from specific experiences of embodiment; rather than from a position of abstract and 'universal' reason, from which the body becomes an object of (legal) knowledge. This approach demands a reappraisal of the liberal concept of autonomy as the basis for rights in the body, in favour of a more relational understanding of autonomy grounded in the connectivity and interdependence of bodies. Thus, my aim here is to provide a more enriched discourse of bodies.

I begin with an attempt to consider the body as property, drawing on a rich 'corpus' of work which arises out of feminist and other theories. Following on from the more general discussion, I deploy three examples in order to illuminate this theoretical standpoint:

(a) abortion and foetal rights;

(b) surrogacy; and

(c) 'female genital mutilation'.

In each case, I will show how a feminist standpoint which begins from the experience of embodiment, rather than the abstraction of mind over body, can provide a compelling analysis of these controversial areas. However, before reviewing the feminist reappraisal of autonomy and body ownership, it may prove useful to consider the dominant paradigm of how the body is 'read' in terms of rights of ownership. I begin, then, with a brief encapsulation of the 'traditional' response of the law to these questions.

## BODIES BEFORE THE LAW

Legal theorists have spent considerable energy of late exploring the body so as to answer the question 'who owns it?'. Much of this work has relied upon property law. This approach to the body is hardly surprising. Medical technology has forced lawyers to confront body ownership on a variety of fronts; reproduction, organ transplantation, cloning, and other forms of genetic engineering all are scientific 'advances' which appear to call out for a legal framework. Scholars frequently turn to the 'traditional' paradigms in which they have worked, in order to find answers to these novel problems.

For example, Harris concludes that the rhetoric of property is unnecessary and generally unproductive in the context of bodies.[1] While we may recognise the importance of the freedom to use (and refuse) our bodies as we please (which Harris calls the 'bodily use freedom principle'), the language of body ownership 'potentially proves too much', because we do not possess the bundle of rights which are assumed to flow from proprietary claims over an object.[2] Property consists of a set of trespassory rules and a spectrum of ownership rights, and that paradigm does little to help us understand the body in law.

Munzer reaches a similar conclusion. He reasons that 'people do not own, but rather have some limited property rights in their bodies'.[3] The concept of ownership is inapplicable to the body because the law recognises restrictions, for example, on the ability to transfer parts of the body. Nor is there a recognised liberty to consume or destroy our bodies.[4] Munzer also argues, however, that there are some body rights which can properly be characterised as proprietary, with the criterion being whether the law protects the choice to transfer the right.[5] He further divides these property rights into strong and weak versions. A 'weak property right' is the recognition of a choice to transfer the body part or product gratuitously; a 'strong property right', by contrast, is a right to transfer for 'value'.[6] Examples of strong property rights would include, in some jurisdictions, the right to sell bodily fluids, or the 'publicity right' recognised in American law; that is, the right to exploit commercially interests in one's body (for example, the right of Elvis Presley's estate to market 'Elvis').[7] Munzer concludes that, while people do not 'own' their bodies, in the traditional property law sense of a bundle of rights to

---

1     Harris, JW, 'Who owns my body' (1996) 16 OJLS 55.

2     *Ibid*, p 65.

3     Munzer, SR, *A Theory of Property*, 1990, Cambridge: CUP, p 37.

4     *Ibid*, p 43.

5     *Ibid*, pp 48–49.

6     *Ibid*, p 49.

7     *Ibid*, p 52.

control, transfer and destroy, they do have some limited, legally recognised rights to the body.

It is not my intention to criticise either Harris or Munzer on their formulation of legal doctrine. Indeed, their analyses of property law in relation to bodies seems highly plausible. Rather, my interest is in how these theorists (like many others) exemplify the way in which the body can be turned into an object of knowledge capable of being studied as an abstract, universal 'thing', separate from, and subject to, the processes of human reason. As a consequence, an analysis of body ownership provides no space for the recognition that questions of ownership resonate differently depending upon the body in issue. That is, legal theory in this (as in so many other) areas fails to appreciate that bodies have been objects of knowledge in our cultural and legal tradition and, as such, they have been culturally 'produced' by discourses such as law in different ways. In other words, bodies are the 'products of the way that culture organises, regulates and remakes itself'.[8] In particular, bodies which have been produced in opposition to the 'universal' white, male body which 'naturally' disciplines itself to legal reason, have long served as objects of study for legal, medical, and other knowledges in the west. Such knowledges have claimed rights of ownership over these bodies. Bodies of knowledge can then regulate the bodies which they own (and which they own because they are produced by these same discourses). Thus, my argument is that to conclude unproblematically that 'we' do not own our bodies obscures many of the central issues which ownership of the body raises. For example, feminist claims to body ownership often have been grounded in the desire for 'control over the interpretations placed upon the body and the *meanings* attached to bodily functions'.[9] In this regard, it has been argued that body ownership is a helpful concept because it captures women's urgent 'need to seize control of the imagery of self that is presented to them by society'.[10]

My focus in this chapter is the production of the sexed body in opposition to a 'universal' male subjectivity. Yet, I also recognise that bodies cannot be reduced to their construction as sexed alone. While bodies are produced as sexed, they are simultaneously produced as raced, and these (and other) productions interact. This point will become particularly apparent in my discussion of 'female genital mutilation'. My specific interest is in relocating the body, informed by a feminist theory which recognises the cultural construction of the body as an object of knowledge. Hopefully, this argument

---

8    Gatens, M, 'Towards a feminist philosophy of the body', in Caine, B, Grosz, EA and de Lepervanche, M (eds), *Crossing Boundaries: Feminisms and the Critique of Knowledges*, 1988, Sydney: Allen & Unwin, p 62.

9    Farsides, C, 'Body Ownership', in McVeigh, S and Wheeler, S (eds), *Law, Health and Medical Regulation*, 1992, Aldershot: Dartmouth, p 38.

10   *Ibid*, p 40. See also Wald, A, 'What's rightfully ours: toward a property theory of rape' (1997) 30 *Columbia Journal of Law and Social Problems* 459.

might provide an alternative to the 'traditional' legal theoretical standpoint, which too readily produces the body as its own object for study and regulation.

# BEGINNING WITH THE BODY

In this section, I propose to take up the challenge offered by Grbich, that the task of feminist legal theory must be to inquire 'into the ways in which legal reasoning transforms the embodied imaginings from male lives into the "objective" form of doctrine which passes for the normative'.[11] For example, knowledges of the body arise out of (some) male experiences of the(ir) bodies, but those knowledges become constructed as objectivity itself. Feminist theory and practice long have confronted this reality of bodily production, and one of the starting points has been an interrogation of the mind/body dualism, which is particularly associated in western philosophy with Descartes.

Central to Cartesian philosophy is the notion that 'the body exists as an idea, and as such, can be an object of knowledge'.[12] For traditional jurisprudence, this mind/body dualism has been implicit and central to the formulation of legal theory. Law 'has always been predicated as a function of the mind and therefore in a hierarchical opposition to materiality which law serves to order and govern'.[13] Bodies must be regulated by law, just as our bodies must be regulated by our minds.

Furthermore, feminist theory has recognised that the construction of the mind/body dualism and its application in legal theory have deeply gendered implications. In fact, the mind/body dualism is *central* to the social construction of gender:

> ... the mind/body polarisation has historically functioned hand-in-hand with the ways in which the relations between the sexes are conceived and, particularly, with the social, cultural and legal homogenisation of women's specificities into models produced by and functioning in the interests of a universalism that disguises its affinity with patriarchy.[14]

How has this relationship between the Cartesian mind/body dualism and gender oppression been achieved? The answer can be found in the ways in which both women and the body have been constructed as the inverse to those 'culturally valued terms, such as reason, civilisation and progress'.[15]

---

11 Grbich, JE, 'The body in legal theory', in Fineman, MA and Thomadsen, NS (eds), *At the Boundaries of Law*, 1991, New York: Routledge, p 69.

12 Vasseleu, C, 'Patent pending: laws of invention, animal life forms and bodies as ideas', in Cheah, P, Fraser, D and Grbich, J (eds), *Thinking Through the Body of the Law*, 1996, Sydney: Allen & Unwin, p 107.

13 Cheah, P and Grosz, E, 'The body of the law: notes toward a theory of corporeal justice', in *ibid*, Cheah, Fraser and Grbich, p 3.

14 *Ibid*, p 4.

15 *Op cit*, fn 8, Gatens, p 60.

That is, 'woman' has been constructed as synonymous with the body – woman becomes embodiment – and, by extension, she is constructed as irrational by (her) 'nature' (as opposed to reason and culture). While culture demands of woman her reproductive capacity, in order to reproduce the culture, she is constructed as outside of that same culture. Finally, these mind/body, culture/nature dualisms are apparent in the construction of the public and private spheres, through the delineation of the 'family' (private life; the domain of women) and public, political life (the world of men).

Given the centrality of the mind/body dualism to legal analysis, and its historical role in the subjugation of women, my argument is that an analysis of the question 'who owns the body' demands a new approach. Specifically, body ownership needs to be analysed in such a way that it resists the construction of the body as an object of (man's) knowledge. A feminist inspired analysis of property in the body requires that we theorise beginning from the body and from specific experiences of embodiment; rather than from a standpoint of 'universal' reason which historically has constructed woman as Other.

We must also recognise that the way in which law relates to bodies needs to be rethought. If we seek to resist the mind/body dualism in theory, then we need to begin by reconceptualising law's relationship to bodies. The logic of the mind/body dualism is that reason (which comes to be equated with the law) is the means for the 'rational' management of the body (which, by definition, is in need of such mind control). A more critically inspired jurisprudence would argue from the position that law regulates the body in a controlling and oppressive way; in the service of dominant, ruling interests. So too, feminist theory sometimes has regarded the body 'as passive and reproductive but largely unproductive'.[16] All these theoretical approaches share an underlying allegiance to the Cartesian dualism. An alternative would be to start by situating law as productive; law is 'exercised in a positive way to produce bodies as the instruments of rational subjects or agents'.[17] It is the law which produces bodies in order that they then may be differentiated from the reason 'embodied' in the law: 'law helps to constitute and organise our very sense of the nature and activities of the body. It shapes our understanding of the body, obliging us to think of bodies in certain ways, and not in others.'[18] Legal reason can then govern the bodies it produces. The body thus can be given rights, can be recognised as subject to contractual exchange, and can be analysed as the object of proprietary interests. After all, 'in order for the law to function at all it must first and foremost have a hold over bodies'.[19]

---

16   Grosz, E, *Volatile Bodies*, 1994, Bloomington: Indiana University Press, p 9.

17   *Op cit*, fn 13, Cheah and Grosz, p 16.

18   Naffine, N, 'The body bag', in Naffine, N and Owen, RJ (eds), *Sexing the Subject of Law*, 1997, Sydney: Law Book Company, p 84.

19   Cheah, P, Fraser, D and Grbich, J, 'Introduction: the body of the law', in *op cit*, fn 12, Cheah, Fraser and Grbich, p xv.

Once produced, the body can then be invested with legal characteristics. How we understand those characteristics brings us squarely back to the issues I began with: ownership, property, and autonomy. It also leads to the question of how useful is it, in terms of a feminist politics, to invest the body with these characteristics? Recall that I started this chapter with a classic statement of law, namely, that we lack the full bundle of rights in our bodies for them to qualify as an object of our ownership interest *per se*. For example, we have no right to sell or to destroy ourselves. This description, however, depends upon a particular reading of property whereby the individual possesses absolute 'dominion' over an object. That is the classic, liberal legal conception of property which became dominant in the 18th century. But, as Gordon has argued, there are in fact 'very few plausible instances of absolute dominion rights'.[20] Rather, property interests are routinely fragmented and split, yet the belief in absolute dominion persists as a central element of legal liberalism. As Ryan observes, 'the usual experience of owning something is not that of being sovereign over something we may abandon at a moment's notice, but of being tied to its fate by a network of social and often legal ties'.[21] Consequently, we should approach blanket statements about ownership of the body with some caution, for 'it is impossible to generate consistent results from such an abstraction as property, so that exceptions and refinements will inevitably creep in that soon allow any result to be reached in any case'.[22] That is, claims that we do not 'own' our bodies rely upon a very specific and particular conception of ownership, absolute dominion, which is something of a legal fiction, and always subject to exceptions. Indeed, 'property itself is now subject to regulation to such an extent that it cannot serve symbolically or substantively as the boundary between individual rights and governmental power'.[23] Thus, Hyde convincingly argues that courts will sometimes find a property interest in the body, and sometimes not; but those results are reached on the basis of ethical and political considerations, and not legal doctrine.[24]

A more interesting inquiry than 'do we own our bodies?' might well be a consideration of which conception of property is most fruitfully adopted in relation to the body, or whether the discourse of property is useful at all in terms of political strategy. For example, Hyde suggests that the very fact that we may '"experience" our bodies as independent and self-controlled', as something over which we have absolute dominion, is itself a product of, and

---

20   Gordon, RW, 'Paradoxical property', in Brewer, J and Staves, S (eds), *Early Modern Conceptions of Property*, 1995, London: Routledge, p 96.

21   Ryan, A, 'Self-ownership, autonomy and property rights' (1994) 11 *Social Philosophy and Policy* 241, p 247.

22   Hyde, A, *Bodies of Law*, 1997, Princeton: Princeton University Press, p 75.

23   Nedelsky, J, 'Reconceiving autonomy: sources, thoughts and possibilities' (1989) 1 *Yale Journal of Law and Feminism* 7, p 20.

24   *Ibid*, Hyde, p 75.

helps serve the needs of, the liberal order.[25] After all, we must be prepared to sell our body's labour as a product in the market-place. Thus, whether or not we 'own' our bodies in law would seem beside the point. For liberalism, 'what is important is that everyone be able to imagine a world in which our relations to our bodies is one of ownership and sale'.[26] In this way, an inalienable property right is rhetorically and legally transformed into a right which is fully transferable for consideration.[27]

Many legal scholars have sought to resist this construction. For example, returning to Munzer, he recognises that although we do not own our bodies, this conclusion does not answer the question whether we have property rights in parts of our bodies.[28] In the end, he argues 'uneasily' against the appropriateness of the language of property in that context. Generally, arguments of this type turn on the issue of 'commodification', and centre broadly upon the implications of turning 'all human attributes' into 'possessions bearing a value characterizable in money terms, and by implying that all these possessions can and should be separable from persons to be exchanged through the free market'.[29] That is, the claim is made that the recognition of property rights in parts of the body will necessarily lead to their commodification, and human beings will be reduced (literally) to the sum of their parts. For much feminist theory, this assumed connection between property and a market for the sale of that which is deemed to be property is an unattractive prospect, particularly since, as Radin argues, 'concerns about commodification are mixed up with concerns about the effects of poverty, sexism, and racism on the would-be sellers, as well as concerns about harm to innocent third parties'.[30]

Munzer elaborates upon this argument, deploying a Kantian conception of human dignity. His assumption is that property talk will inevitably slip into the language of the market, leading to the sale of body parts.[31] Such a market, he concludes, is an offence to human dignity and is morally objectionable, first, if there is

> ... selling for a reason that is insufficiently strong relative to the characteristics of the parts sold. It is also morally objectionable for others, such as buyers and brokers, to participate in a market for body parts if by doing so they offend the

---

25 *Op cit*, fn 22, Hyde, p 52.

26 *Ibid*, p 76.

27 See Gold, ER, *Body Parts: Property Rights and the Ownership of Human Biological Materials*, 1996, Washington, DC: Georgetown University Press, p 175.

28 Munzer, SR, 'An uneasy case against property rights in body parts' (1994) 11 *Social Philosophy and Policy* 259.

29 Radin, MJ, *Contested Commodities*, 1996, Cambridge, MA: Harvard University Press, p 6.

30 *Ibid*, p 8.

31 *Ibid*, Munzer, p 279. See also *ibid*, Gold, p 21, arguing that 'in awarding property rights, we value goods exclusively in accordance with economic modes of valuation'; the assumption being that 'all non-economic values can be translated into a market price'.

dignity of sellers or themselves ... Finally, it is morally objectionable for a market in body parts to exist if its operation offends the dignity of enough participants in the market.[32]

Although Munzer's argument is intuitively appealing, there is a questionable rhetorical move implicit in the reasoning, one which can be illustrated by reference to another theorist: Petchesky. She offers an explicitly feminist defence of the language of property in relation to the body.[33] Although equally opposed to the commodification of the body and its reduction to an object in the market, she also recognises the historical malleability of the concept of property. She suggests that property language in relation to the body has considerable potential for reinvention and reimagination. Property talk might be deployed in such a way that it can be freed of the 'prevailing economism'[34] in its assumed relationship to the market, and also shorn of the liberal notion of absolute dominion. Petchesky notes the power of the language of property 'as a rhetorical strategy for political mobilization and defining identities',[35] and her view is that the task is to draw out new meanings which compete with, and challenge, 'an absolute, individual, and explicitly masculine model of property ownership'.[36] This might entail, for example, redefining 'all essential health care and services ... as common property to which all people are entitled access'.[37] Property thus potentially becomes 'a fundamental condition for women's development and strength as a social group and thus for their full participation as citizens'.[38]

Petchesky's analysis underscores how the language of property is not inherently connected to an economistic, market-driven model. Ryan makes a similar point, arguing that the language of self-ownership might be read as a duty of 'self-cultivation': 'we ought indeed to think, if not of ourselves, at any rate of our aptitudes and characters, as possessions – not in order to emphasize the right to do as we please with them, but in order to emphasize a duty to learn how to do with them what is pleasing to others.'[39] Thus, we have come full circle as the language of property now becomes the basis for altruism and a duty to others, taking us completely out of the market model.

The obvious criticism of both Petchesky and Ryan is their utopianism. That is, although property as absolute dominion, and as tied to the market, may be historically and culturally specific, it is specific to our historical and

---

32  *Op cit*, fn 28, Munzer, p 285.

33  See Petchesky, RP, 'The body as property: a feminist re-vision', in Ginsburg, FD and Rapp, R (eds), *Conceiving the New World Order*, 1995, Berkeley: University of California Press, p 387.

34  *Ibid*, p 388.

35  *Ibid*, p 387.

36  *Ibid*, p 393.

37  *Ibid*, p 403.

38  *Ibid*.

39  *Op cit*, fn 21, Ryan, p 257.

cultural circumstances. And although absolute dominion may be a legal fiction, fictions can have great rhetorical and political power. How likely, it might be asked, is it that 'we' can dislodge that meaning of property and avoid the fears of commodification of the body?

This is precisely the point which has been made by Nedelsky.[40] Focusing specifically on property rights in 'potential life' (the materials of human reproduction employed in the new reproductive technologies), Nedelsky comes out against the idea of thinking about these materials through the category of property. In developing an explicitly feminist framework, she responds to the counterargument that:

> ... it might seem that women's autonomy, power, and control vis à vis the medical establishment, might be enhanced not only by the general claim that a woman's body is her property, but by the position that all stages of potential life issuing from her body are her property – and remain so even when they are no longer within her body. Similarly, this position might be seen to aid women in struggles over power and oppression with their male sexual partners – both in regard to struggles specifically around reproduction and more generally.[41]

By contrast, Nedelsky argues that the language of property is more likely to foster commodification, control by others of women's bodies, and the alienation of women from their bodies' reproductive processes.[42] She draws this conclusion based on her reading of deep connections between property rhetoric and a 'particular vision of autonomy'[43] centred on commodification, exploitation, and individualism. At this point, then, we move from a consideration of bodies, property, and ownership, to the closely related issue of autonomy. Like property, there is no essential feature of human autonomy; rather, 'there are different visions of what autonomy consists in and what will promote it'.[44] Historically, the market has been seen as 'the vehicle for the exercise of autonomy', and Nedelsky argues that this is unlikely to be altered if we recognise property rights in the raw materials of the new reproductive technologies.[45]

In earlier work, Nedelsky developed an alternative conception of autonomy, one not dependent upon a market-driven, individualistic, proprietary conception.[46] Within liberal legal theory, autonomy serves the

---

40  See Nedelsky, J, 'Property in potential life: a relational approach to choosing legal categories' (1993) 6 *Canadian Journal of Law and Jurisprudence* 343.

41  *Ibid*, p 347.

42  *Ibid*. See also *op cit*, fn 27, Gold, pp 164–65.

43  *Ibid*, Nedelsky, p 350.

44  *Ibid*, p 356.

45  *Ibid*. In the United Kingdom, the requirements of consent, rather than the ownership of reproductive materials, have served as the primary basis of legal regulation; see O'Donovan, K, 'Whose genes are they anyway? Reproductive difficulties in the ownership debate', in Stern, K and Walsh, P (eds), *Property Rights in the Human Body*, 1997, London: King's College London, p 20.

46  *Op cit*, fn 23, Nedelsky.

project of constituting bodies as separate, individuated, and subject to the market. Autonomy has been central in law to managing our relationship to 'our' bodies, as well as our relationships to those of 'others'. It produces the body as separate, as our 'own', and is closely tied to the construction of the atomistic individual. The individual is constituted as self-determining and self-making, and autonomy is the exercise of that capacity of the self. Most simply, autonomy demands 'that people be treated as persons, as morally important individuals with their own decisions to make and lives to lead'.[47] In this model, exploitation is a denial of autonomy, and it is experienced when one has 'been coerced in some way into becoming instruments' for the life projects of others.[48] Nedelsky has argued that the paradigm of autonomy historically has been the isolated individual; the holder of rights against the world. The collective is constructed as the perpetual and singular threat to autonomy.[49] As a consequence, it becomes 'natural' that property is 'the central symbol for this vision of autonomy'.[50] After all, our conception of property and rights of ownership is founded on boundaries, and an isolated, definable 'thing' over which the individual holds the bundle of proprietary rights. Questions about 'who owns the body?' – however they may be answered – by and large are firmly grounded within that theoretical framework of the autonomous individual who holds rights against the world. What is obscured is the fact that property not only entails the exclusion of all others from the holdings of the isolated individual. It also demands of the state that it protect the enjoyment of those rights, and, in that sense, property just as easily could be identified as an area of public rather than private law.

Nedelsky, like many other feminist writers, calls for a reconception of autonomy which is not modelled on the isolated individual, but on a more integrated notion of the self. Such an understanding of autonomy would recognise our 'embeddedness in relations', and that what enables the individual to experience autonomy is not isolation, but relationships with others.[51] In that sense, the collectivity becomes both a source and a threat to autonomy, for 'autonomy is a capacity that exists only in the context of social relations that support it and only in conjunction with the internal sense of being autonomous'.[52] Thus, a 'social component' must be incorporated into the very meaning of autonomy, in order to move away from the isolated

---

47  Harris, J, *Wonderwoman and Superman: The Ethics of Human Biotechnology*, 1992, Oxford: OUP, p 124.

48  *Ibid.*

49  *Op cit*, fn 23, Nedelsky, p 12.

50  *Ibid.*

51  *Ibid*, p 10.

52  *Ibid*, p 25.

individual and the metaphor of property, towards an alternative conception.[53] For Nedelsky, a better metaphor is provided by the experience of child-raising, which she argues captures this experience of autonomy through connectivity.[54] The self is experienced through a relationship with another and we realise ourselves as autonomous only through social relations. The classic liberal conception of autonomy, by contrast, is an alienating vision: 'when we think of ourselves as determinate subjects or bodies possessing rights before the law, we cut ourselves off from the ongoing relations which constitute us in the first place'.[55]

In her analysis of the new reproductive technologies, Nedelsky makes a key point about a common confusion between ownership and control. Although we may want to recognise a legal interest in the individuals who are the source of reproductive material to make decisions about its use (or destruction), that does not necessarily make it property. Rather, the concern should be with 'fostering people's capacities to form relationships of intimacy, trust and responsibility. These issues involve allocation of control and decision-making authority, but they are not about ownership'.[56] The important point here is that there is no essential reason why the rhetoric of property must be invoked in relation to the body and its products. By the same token, there is no essential reason why it need not. In regard to reproductive material, Nedelsky's argument is that the dangers of alienation, commodification, and control outweigh any benefits.[57]

In the end, although Nedelsky and Petchesky may disagree on the merits of deploying the language of property in relation to the body, both ground their work in an explicitly feminist framework, and they both seek to broaden and challenge the prevailing notions of property, ownership, and autonomy, in favour of a more relational, connective model. Legal discourse inhabits this

---

53   *Op cit*, fn 23, Nedelsky, p 36. Thus, for example, O'Donovan, *op cit*, fn 45, p 25, argues that in the regulation of reproductive material, 'concepts of property law are inadequate, although language such as trust and gift, which has deep cultural roots outside law, may be appropriate'. *Op cit*, fn 27, Gold, p 173, goes further, arguing that 'the understanding generated by valuing the body as a resource to be mined and as an opportunity for profit may very well lead to the development of defective health care policies'.

54   *Op cit*, fn 23, Nedelsky, p 12.

55   *Op cit*, fn 13, Cheah and Grosz, p 24. See also *op cit*, fn 27, Gold, p 172: 'to analyze the world in terms of property discourse is not to see the world in terms of relationships, in terms of personal development, or any other way of valuing goods.'

56   *Op cit*, fn 40, Nedelsky, p 363.

57   The Warnock Committee similarly made the distinction between ownership and control when making recommendations concerning the status of frozen embryos; see *Report of the Committee of Inquiry into Human Fertilisation and Embryology*, 1984, London: HMSO, paras 10–11. Subsequently, Baroness Warnock referred to this distinction as 'rather a feeble evasion'; Warnock, M, 'Whose consent to what?' (1997) *The Times Literary Supplement*, 14 March, p 4. Kennedy also rejects the distinction; see Kennedy, I, *Treat Me Right: Essays in Medical Law and Ethics*, 1988, Oxford: Clarendon Press, p 119. Nedelsky, however, describes Kennedy's view as 'nonsense'; see Nedelsky, *op cit*, fn 40, p 362.

tension because, in order to serve the liberal project, it 'must produce images both of individual autonomy and of social cohesion'.[58] Liberalism needs both, but what writers such as Nedelsky, Petchesky, Ryan, and Hyde have sought to do is shift the balance, uncovering (and deconstructing) the paradoxes of property in the process. They thereby help us to confront more directly the inevitable social tensions between separateness and connection that law must answer every day.

As a starting point in confronting these tensions, what may be demanded is a recognition of the need to proceed from specific experiences of embodiment in developing theories of bodies; as well as the importance of appreciating, at the same time, that there is no single 'truth' of the body. Instead, 'it is a process and its meaning and capacities will vary according to its context'.[59] Thus, we can begin by noting the 'cultural and historical specificity of bodies'[60] and, in so doing, we start to theorise in resistance to the mind/body dualism and its gendered implications. Furthermore, when we reason from specific corporeal experiences, reason itself becomes explicitly 'embodied'; rather than constructed as separate from, and ruling over, the body.[61] In this way, feminist theory potentially can disrupt and deeply problematise a theoretical model of the body and the body politic.

For example, while some feminist theory draws upon the maternal body as a way to think through the meaning of autonomy, it is that same body which traditionally has been constructed as a constraint upon the exercise of (men's) capacity for autonomy. In this regard, Gatens has explored the male fantasy of the creation of a man-made social body.[62] Such a body (politic) is immortal and autonomous because it is no longer dependent upon the bodies of women. It is the absence of the mother figure (to be not born of woman) which is associated with true freedom, immortality, and power. Male autonomy thus is based upon freedom from women's bodies; which Gatens has termed the 'fantasy of masculine auto-reproduction'.[63] In this way, autonomy historically has been constructed as freedom from the body (of woman). As Naffine argues, 'bodily autonomy, in the Western sense, has involved the abstraction of men into universal, not sex-specific subjects'.[64] There continues to be a need for feminist inspired interventions on the body in a political and cultural climate in which this fantasy of masculine auto-reproduction is still produced. The experience of autonomy through the body, specifically through the maternal body, seems increasingly to be constructed

---

58 *Op cit*, fn 22, Hyde, p 78.

59 *Op cit*, fn 8, Gatens, p 68.

60 *Ibid*, p 69.

61 See Nedelsky, J, 'Embodied diversity and the challenges to law' (1997) 42 *McGill Law Journal* 91, pp 106–09.

62 *Op cit*, fn 8, Gatens, pp 63–66.

63 *Ibid*, p 64.

64 *Op cit*, fn 18, Naffine, p 93.

as Other both to reason, and to the desire for an autonomy experienced as freedom from women's bodies.

I want now to explore the implications of these theoretical claims through three specific examples, each of which raises separate (but related) questions about the meaning of autonomy, the body, and ownership. These issues are:

(a) abortion and the construction of 'foetal rights';

(b) surrogacy; and

(c) 'female genital mutilation' and other forms of body modification.

Ultimately, I believe that a feminist analysis of body ownership can shed light on a range of other issues, from organ donation to cloning. But, for my purposes, I hope that the analysis of these three issues will provide a starting point from which to begin thinking about a range of bodily experiences.

## Abortion and 'foetal rights'

In articulating a feminist perspective on body ownership, an obvious starting point is the law's regulation of abortion. Historically, feminist demands for abortion rights often have deployed the language of body ownership; namely, a woman's right to control her body and her destiny. Although this discourse continues to resonate strongly, advances in biomedical technology have rendered the rhetoric of body ownership problematic. Reproduction increasingly is not relegated to the 'private' realm. Instead, the maternal, reproductive body has become intensified as an object of knowledge, regulation, and control by legal and medical discourses.[65] As Hartouni argues, these discourses have 'recast the uterus as public space, embryos as public entities, and pregnancy as a state of endangered captivity' (for the foetus).[66] Moreover, liberal autonomy has never been articulated as the official justification for abortion law in the United Kingdom; rather, medical control has been the predominant rationale.[67]

In fact, autonomy-based arguments are being deployed, through the use of medical knowledges, not to bolster women's rights of control and ownership of the body, but instead, so as to facilitate the construction of the foetus as a separate, rights-holding 'being'. Thus, the foetus is being discursively abstracted from the woman's body (it becomes 'free floating'), and the doctor

---

65 See generally Thomson, M, 'Employing the body: the reproductive body and employment exclusion' (1996) 5 SLS 243.

66 Hartouni, V, *Cultural Conceptions: On Reproductive Technologies and the Remaking of Life*, 1997, Minneapolis: University of Minnesota Press, p 18.

67 See generally Sheldon, S, 'The law of abortion and the politics of medicalisation', in Bridgeman, J and Millns, S (eds), *Law and Body Politics: Regulating the Female Body*, 1995, Aldershot: Dartmouth, p 105; Sheldon, S, *Beyond Control: Medical Power and Abortion Law*, 1997, London: Pluto Press.

is constituted as best placed to protect its autonomy interest. The foetus becomes a patient, 'an entity requiring a separate physician and often a separate legal advocate'.[68] This construction, which has been facilitated by advances in medicine, exemplifies a point which I have already discussed; the male fantasy of autonomy as the transcendence of the maternal body. As the foetus is made into an autonomous being, the female body is erased from the picture.[69] It becomes simply the container holding the rights-bearing foetus.[70] The necessary connectivity between woman and foetus is rendered adversarial, as autonomy in this context continues to be defined in terms of a separate self, in need of protection from the (m)Other, now constructed as both a potential threat to the innocent and a perversion of the natural.[71]

One consequence of the application of liberal autonomy in relation to the foetus is that the female body becomes intensified as an object which must be controlled and regulated to protect the autonomy of the foetus (who cannot defend himself). But such a move is profoundly problematic from the perspective of women's autonomy. As an alternative to the construction of woman and foetus as bearing competing autonomy interests, Karpin suggests that autonomy in this context is better understood in terms of connections between woman and foetus, rather than as separation; which she describes as a 'nexus-of-relations perspective'.[72] In this perspective, the foetus is not understood through the language of isolated autonomy, in which it, in some sense, 'owns' its own 'body'. Rather, the necessary connectivity between woman and foetus implies that one cannot separate issues of foetal well-being from those of women's health.[73] Pregnancy as an embodied experience here defies the conception of autonomy grounded in the simple splitting of mind and body: 'the ambiguous determination of a pregnant woman's body/matter as both hers and an other's defies the transcendental idealised subjectivity of legal invention.'[74] Thus, the maternal body becomes a paradigm of connectivity, wherein autonomy must be understood not through individuation, but relationally: 'it makes obsolete a notion of subjectivity that

---

68  *Op cit*, fn 66, Hartouni, p 37.

69  See *op cit*, fn 65, Thomson, pp 259–60, and references therein.

70  This is particularly the case with respect to 'posthumous pregnancies' where, as Hartouni argues, motherhood 'can be sustained by mechanical means and a continuous infusion of chemicals even if there is no subject, no agent, to sustain it'; *op cit*, fn 66, Hartouni, pp 30–31. See also de Gama, this volume.

71  Wells and Morgan have argued that while the law has been deployed to protect the foetus from the pregnant woman, no attention has been paid by the law to 'a woman's interest in foetal well-being'; Wells, C and Morgan, D, 'Whose foetus is it?' (1991) 18 JLS 431, p 432.

72  Karpin, I, 'Reimagining maternal selfhood: transgressing body boundaries and the law' (1994) 2 *Australian Feminist Law Journal* 36, p 46.

73  Karpin, I, 'Legislating the female body: reproductive technology and the reconstructed woman' (1992) 3 *Columbia Journal of Gender & Law* 325, p 338.

74  *Op cit*, fn 12, Vasseleu, p 119.

is dependent for its subject status on distinction, separation and defensive opposition to others.'[75]

Mackenzie, however, suggests an even more complex relationship between foetus and woman, in which both connection and differentiation are enacted:

> Firstly, from the perspective of the woman, the foetus becomes more and more physically differentiated from her as her own body boundaries alter. Secondly, this gradual physical differentiation ... is paralleled by and gives rise to a gradual psychic differentiation, in the experience of the woman, between herself and the foetus ... Thirdly, physical and psychic differentiation are usually accompanied by an increasing emotional attachment of the woman to the foetus, an attachment which is based both in her physical connection with the foetus and in anticipation of her future relationship with a separate being who is also intimately related to her.[76]

Mackenzie demonstrates how pregnancy encompasses both the experience of relationality and connection, *as well as* separateness and individuation. It is that combination which renders pregnancy a unique experience of embodiment, one which is inadequately captured by the liberal rhetoric of autonomy, which fails to recognise how embodiment actually serves as a microcosm for broader social tensions between connectivity and a bounded, individuated self.[77]

The fact that the experience of pregnant embodiment defies the precepts of liberal autonomy is not meant to suggest, however, that women should not articulate political demands for abortion law reform (or the preservation of the status quo in the face of attempts at reactionary change) in the language of individual rights. Instead, my point is that medical discourses surrounding foetal health and *rights*, and the language of foetal viability, are profoundly problematic because they appropriate the language of liberal autonomy and apply it to the foetal 'body'. This has the inevitable effect of erasing the subjectivities of women. In that sense, the emergence of foetal rights discourse exemplifies the fantasy of masculine auto-reproduction, because woman's body increasingly is taken out of the reproduction equation; an object of control rather than an autonomous self. It is the doctor-foetus relationship, in

---

75  *Op cit*, fn 72, Karpin, p 46. See also *op cit*, fn 66, Hartouni, p 67; Williams, P, *The Alchemy of Race and Rights*, 1991, Cambridge, MA: Harvard University Press, p 185.

76  Mackenzie, C, 'Abortion and embodiment' (1992) 70 *Australasian Journal of Philosophy* 136, pp 148–49. See also Young's characterisation of the foetus as 'both a helpless dependent, and a voracious vampiric parasite'; Young, A, 'Decapitation or feticide: the fetal laws of the universal subject' (1993) 4 *Women: A Cultural Review* 288, p 293.

77  On this point, Irigaray argues that the placenta provides 'the mediating space between mother and fetus, which means that there's never a fusion of maternal and embryonic tissues. On the other hand, it constitutes a system regulating exchanges between the two organisms'; Irigaray, L, 'On the maternal order', in *je, tu, nous: Towards a Culture of Difference*, 1993, New York: Routledge, p 39. On the inadequacy of the language of liberal autonomy in the context of 'forced Caesareans', see Wells, this volume.

which the doctor ('father figure') is best placed to protect the rights of the foetus, which becomes increasingly dominant.[78]

Foetal rights discourse thus underscores the political indeterminacy of the language of autonomy in relation to the maternal body. The construction of an autonomy interest for the foetus could lead both to restrictions on women's right to abortion, and to legal surveillance of pregnant women;[79] and it represents a 'symbolic assault on a woman's sense of self precisely because it thwarts her projection of bodily integration and places the woman's body in the hands and imaginings of others'.[80] Cornell's description of the violation to women inherent in restrictions on abortion seems to resonate in the language of liberal autonomy, and brings us back to the metaphor of body ownership. In this regard, Cornell acknowledges that the idea of ownership of the body is a fantasy, but her point is that there needs to be recognised a vital right of 'bodily integrity' in the reproductive context; which entails 'the woman's right to be insulated from state imposition of the views of others on her own imaginary'.[81] Bodily integrity is an imaginary projection, but it is one which may be necessary for a coherent sense of self, in contrast to the fragmentation and dissolution of the pregnant body which flows out of a discourse of foetal rights.

I read Cornell's invocation of individuation as consistent with a reconception of liberal autonomy, for she is not advocating the straightforward application of liberal autonomy and the further reification of the mind/body dualism. Instead, Cornell seeks to challenge that universalistic paradigm by focusing on the specificities of embodiment. Similarly, Mackenzie deploys the language of autonomy in defence of abortion rights, but she argues that liberal notions of body ownership provide too weak a defence. The language of property 'justifies the demand for abortion in terms

---

78  On the doctor as 'father figure', see Thomson, this volume; Thomson, M, 'Legislating for the monstrous: new reproductive technologies and the monstrous feminine!' (1997) 6 SLS 401. Interestingly, some reproductive technologies such as alternative insemination and, perhaps someday, human cloning, are frequently constructed as a scientific nightmare which tampers with 'nature'. I suspect this at least partly can be explained by the way in which men potentially are distanced from the reproductive process by these and other new reproductive technologies. Female self-reproduction thus becomes a male nightmare, in no small measure because it forces men to justify why their presence in the reproduction equation is important. But, at the same time, as op cit, fn 66, Hartouni, p 48, argues, new reproductive technologies are sometimes constructed as a means to reinscribe traditional gendered meanings of reproduction, with medical advances serving to 'help women realize their maternal nature'.

79  That surveillance appears not to extend to men, who are absolved of responsibility for foetal well being; see Daniels, CR, 'Between fathers and fetuses: the social construction of male reproduction and the politics of fetal harm' (1997) 22 Signs 579. Daniels rightly notes that foetal health discourse is also 'deeply racialized', p 580.

80  Cornell, D, 'Bodily integrity and the right to abortion', in Sarat, A and Kearns, TR (eds), Identities, Politics, and Rights, 1995, Ann Arbor: University of Michigan Press, p 27.

81  Ibid, p 43.

of a right to an evacuated uterus, rather than a right to autonomy with respect to one's own life'.[82] 'The future of the foetus'[83] must be intrinsic to the abortion decision, a point which abortion rights rhetoric grounded in body ownership completely misses, and which may be of increasing importance in the face of medical advances. The combination of separateness and connection in pregnant embodiment means that bodily autonomy includes the right to terminate a pregnancy on the basis, not simply of self-ownership and bodily integrity, but of self-determination: 'it is a question of being able to shape for oneself an integrated bodily perspective, a perspective by means of which a woman can respond to the bodily processes which she experiences in a way with which she identifies, and which is consistent with the decision she makes concerning her future moral relationship with the foetus.'[84] Feminist theorists, such as Cornell and Mackenzie, seek to reappropriate that experience of the body and to reimagine it as a right. In an era of rapid advances in biomedical technology, such feminist work seems crucial as a means to develop an alternative language in the articulation of women's experiences of reproduction.

## The surrogate body

I now turn to a second arena of controversy which might usefully illustrate how we might reconceive the question of body ownership: surrogacy. In the United Kingdom, surrogacy has served as a site of political contestation in recent years. The Surrogacy Arrangement Act 1985 was enacted in order to outlaw private agencies offering surrogacy services, and it also outlaws surrogacy contracts and the sale of donor eggs. The question I want to consider in this section is how we might understand the issues raised by surrogacy in light of the reworking of autonomy and body ownership that feminist theory has undertaken.

The contradictions of liberal autonomy are particularly stark in a discussion of surrogacy. In this regard, the idea of the body as property depends centrally upon what Harris calls 'the bodily-use freedom principle'; our ability to do what we want with our 'own' bodies (providing, of course, we do not cause 'harm', however that may be defined).[85] As a consequence, the state no longer allows slavery, for individuals cannot be 'objects of property', to use Williams's famous phrase.[86] Slavery underscored how 'the body may be property in order to explain or justify human domination'.[87] But

---

82   *Op cit*, fn 76, Mackenzie, p 150.
83   *Ibid*, p 151.
84   *Ibid*.
85   *Op cit*, fn 1, Harris, p 62.
86   *Op cit*, fn 75, Williams, p 216.
87   *Op cit*, fn 22, Hyde, p 54.

we still assume that the products of the labour of the body are amenable to exchange relations, and the law will uphold those exchanges provided that the requirements of procedural and substantive fairness, and consent, are met. As Diprose points out, however, the premise of social exchange constitutively negates individual freedom and autonomy.[88] That is, we limit our freedom through entering into contractual exchanges. Gordon describes this as the paradox of property: 'the freedom to do anything one likes with property implies the freedom to create restraints on it, and thus to bind one's hands or the hands of one's transferees.'[89] Thus, 'the power to alienate, as it expresses autonomy, becomes the instrument for the subversion of autonomy'.[90] But such limitations are constructed as autonomy's fulfilment. In terms of body ownership, the interesting question for the law to determine is when, and under what conditions, the body can be the basis of exchange.

Diprose has outlined two competing models for considering this question. First, the contractual model, which, it might be argued, preserves liberal autonomy provided what is conceived as the subject of exchange is the body's labour product, rather than corporeality itself.[91] On a straightforward application of the Lockean labour theory of property, such transactions should be upheld. But, if such a model is so unproblematic, Diprose asks why the exchange of sexed body property has become so controversial. Specifically, what are the objections to surrogacy contracts – where the use of the womb is the subject of exchange for monetary value?[92]

Traditionally, there have been two objections to surrogacy contracts. First, the argument has been made that they extend male control over the female body, both because the surrogate's body is contractually made subject to control by another, and because the recognition of claims to the offspring pursuant to the contract amounts to an extension of paternity rights.[93] Second, it is sometimes questioned whether a woman's decision to become a surrogate can ever be 'really' autonomous.[94] The argument here is that there is great danger of coercion, especially of an economic nature, which will inevitably turn the bodies of poor women especially into 'baby machines'.

The problem with both arguments, as Diprose explains, is that these objections hold equally true for other types of service contracts that women routinely enter,[95] which further underscores the contradictions of liberal

---

88  Diprose, R, 'The gift, sexed body property and the law', in *op cit*, fn 12, Cheah, Fraser and Grbich, p 124.

89  *Op cit*, fn 20, Gordon, p 102.

90  *Ibid*, p 103.

91  *Ibid*, Diprose, p 122.

92  *Ibid*. This observation, I would argue, provides support for Hyde's point, *op cit*, fn 22, p 57, that the body of exchange relations always depends upon the existence of an alternative construction of a non-commodified 'sacred body' as its necessary supplement.

93  *Ibid*, Diprose, p 123.

94  *Ibid*.

95  *Ibid*, p 124.

autonomy. While the law ostensibly exists to protect autonomy, social exchange is premised on its negation. Furthermore, the body of market exchange is sometimes constructed as the body beyond the market. I want to suggest, however, that a reworked conception of autonomy grounded in connection and relationality, as well as individuation and separation, can help resolve these contradictions, and aid us in an analysis of surrogacy. If the self is understood as originating within social relations, rather than preceding them, then the pitfalls of surrogacy contracts are not dissimilar to feminist concerns regarding the construction of 'foetal rights'. Both potentially serve to erase the subjectivities of women.

For example, if surrogacy contracts are upheld by law, such a finding reinforces the male body as the rightful owner of 'procreative property', with the woman/surrogate reduced to a container or 'host'.[96] But, alternatively, if the law refuses to enforce the surrogacy contract, then women's bodies are constructed as Other to the world of social exchange,[97] which 'rebiologizes motherhood' in the process.[98] That is, 'gestation is regarded as precisely what activates or brings fully into play women's essential maternal core'.[99] Such a result reinforces the construction of women as Other to the social, in line with the mind/body dualism, and places them in the domain of 'nature', removed from the world of the bargain (and simultaneously non-autonomous).

How might this conundrum be resolved? Diprose's alternative to the contractual model is to understand the surrogacy arrangement as an example of the exchange of a gift, which is the second model she outlines.[100] But such gifts should not be conceived as isolated exchanges between strangers, for although we can give to those with whom we are not in pre-existing relationships (organ donation being a prime example), Gerrand persuasively argues that those relationships (and her focus is specifically on organ donation) are better analogised to acts of charity.[101] By contrast, in the surrogacy case, the gift might be a more productive description, if it is understood as integral to the creation (or continuation) of a relationship between the giver (surrogate) and the recipient (the ultimate care givers).[102] Such a gift would act as 'an enduring social bond which obligates the recipient to the donor'.[103] The act of surrogacy would embody the idea of social connectivity, as opposed to commodification, which 'stresses separateness both between ourselves and our things and between ourselves and other

---

96   *Op cit*, fn 88, Diprose, p 128.
97   *Ibid*.
98   *Op cit*, fn 66, Hartouni, p 81.
99   *Ibid*.
100  *Op cit*, fn 88, Diprose, p 132.
101  Gerrand, N, 'The notion of gift-giving and organ donation' (1994) 8 *Bioethics* 127.
102  See *op cit*, fn 29, Radin, p 93.
103  *Op cit*, fn 88, Diprose, p 132.

people'.[104] The choice to give of oneself by being a surrogate exemplifies, not a discrete contractual bargain or an isolated act of charity, but a more relational notion of mutual connection.[105]

This analysis might suggest that we should be critical of law's attempts to control surrogacy arrangements, for such legislative manoeuvres uphold the authority of law to restrict the 'imaginary domain' of women's sexuality. But what this analysis also implies is that the law should recognise that a woman's autonomy interest in this context demands recognition of the right of the surrogate to change her mind, and be released from the expectation that she will make the gift of the baby.[106] If we understand the parties to the surrogacy agreement in a relational context, then we should not think of that agreement as a discrete transaction involving the exchange of property for consideration. Rather, in a more relational model, it would be contrary to the idea of autonomy to expect a surrogate to make a fully informed decision to exchange somebody, her connection to (and differentiation from) which shifts in the course of the pregnancy. To demand by law such a giving is implicitly to reinforce the mind/body dualism. That is, the assumption is that the body (and its product) can be subjugated to the 'universal' reason of contractual exchange. Changing your mind therefore represents the defeat of reason and becomes constructed instead as a product of unbridled emotion, which, of course, long has been associated with women (who are unable to exercise self-control). The recognition of the surrogate's right to change her mind would be an acknowledgment that an informed (and rational) decision ultimately can only arise out of the particular embodied experience; in this case, the necessarily both connected and individuated experience of pregnancy and childbirth. A decision cannot properly be labelled autonomous until it is made in the light of that experience of embodiment, instead of demanding a decision which is prior to and that seeks to transcend the actual experience of the body.

---

104 *Op cit*, fn 29, Radin, p 94. Of course, within a discourse of commodification, the gift is understood as a disguised bargain, for which there is inevitably a *quid pro quo; ibid*, Radin, p 93.

105 As Titmuss argues in the context of blood donation, 'no such gift is or can be utterly detached, disinterested or impersonal. Each carries messages and motives in its own language'; see Titmuss, RM, *The Gift Relationship*, 1970, London: Allen & Unwin, p 210.

106 Whether there is a genetic 'connection' between surrogate and foetus strikes me as irrelevant to this argument.

## Female genital mutilation[107]

My third 'problem' of body ownership concerns a broad range of practices of body modification and excision sometimes referred to, and constructed, in the West as 'female genital mutilation' ('fgm'). The phrase actually refers to a wide range of practices currently performed in some African and Middle Eastern societies; but which equally might be applied (but rarely is) to a number of procedures frequently undertaken in the west: from obstetrical intervention to cosmetic surgery.[108] As a term, 'fgm' subsumes a plethora of very different practices performed in a diversity of societies on women of different ages (from childhood to adult), and it represents 'a complex culturally embedded critical act which signifies continuity and meaning, and expresses fundamental values'.[109]

'Fgm' has been raised to public consciousness in the West, in part through resistant voices of some women from those cultures where the practices occur. It has also been taken up as an issue in some western feminist struggles.[110] Moreover, 'fgm' has entered public discourse as a direct result of the conditions of globalisation. That is, 'concerns' in the West have been raised that women in diasporic communities 'here' are performing practices of body modification which have been exported from over 'there', that is, from the ubiquitous 'Third World'.[111] In the United Kingdom, these claims have led to legislative intervention, in the form of the Prohibition of Female Circumcision

---

107 Denoting the range of practices of body modification which form the basis of this discussion as 'female genital mutilation' is highly problematic, both because of the way in which 'mutilation' is a loaded term and because it imposes a false unity on a wide range of culturally and historically diverse practices. However, my intention in this discussion in part is to demonstrate how 'female genital mutilation' is a Western construct and I use the term for that reason. However, I place the term in inverted commas, following Fraser, so as to reinforce its constructedness and the false unity of the practices it signifies. I am particularly indebted in this section to the powerful analysis which has been advanced by David Fraser; see Fraser, D, 'The first cut is (not) the deepest: deconstructing "female genital mutilation" and the criminalization of the other' (1995) 18 *Dalhousie Law Journal* 310.

108 See *ibid*, p 317:

The practices grouped under the title of 'female genital mutilation' are generally of four types:

(1) 'circumcision' or sunna which involves the excision of the clitoral prepuce.

(2) Excision which involves not only the prepuce but usually the entire clitoris and sometimes part of the labia minora.

(3) Infibulation or Pharaonic 'circumcision' which involves the removal of the mons veneris as well as the entire labia and usually involves the closure of the vaginal orifice.

(4) Introcision involving the cutting of the vagina or splitting of the perineum with the fingers or a sharp instrument.

109 Obiora, LA, 'The little foxes that spoil the vine: revisiting the feminist critique of female circumcision' (1997) 9 *Canadian Journal of Women and the Law* 46, p 48.

110 See, eg, Daly, M, *GYN/ECOLOGY: The Metaethics of Radical Feminism*, 1978, London: Women's Press.

111 I also place the term 'Third World' in inverted commas to signify that, like 'fgm', 'it is a creation of the metropolitan, imperialist and colonizing discourses'; *ibid*, Fraser, p 312, note 6.

Act 1985, which outlaws the practices; and in the US, similar legislation has been enacted.

Debates around 'fgm' generally have been formulated around a central dichotomy. On the one hand, the practices have been articulated to a discourse of universal human rights, which condemns 'fgm' (but not western forms of body modification, such as cosmetic surgery) as a denial of the rights of women. Arguments within this discourse centre on the coercion which is attributable to 'fgm', especially the fact that it sometimes involves procedures performed on young girls. It is also constructed, especially within some feminist discourses, as a form of female subjugation, designed to deny women sexual pleasure from their bodies and, in that sense, it represents a fundamental denial of the bodily autonomy of women.[112]

On the other hand, cultural relativism acts as the opposite side of this binary.[113] Within this discourse, attempts to outlaw practices of 'fgm' are themselves an example of cultural imperialism by the West (and by Western, white feminists). Such arguments focus on the cultural specificity of the way bodies are experienced, and how sexual pleasure is a culturally specific social construct. Arguments about women's autonomy are met with claims that women themselves perform these acts of modification and that consent is present. Alternatively, the very ideas of consent and autonomy might be read as highly culturally specific concepts.[114] Finally, it is sometimes argued that the Western focus on 'fgm' serves (conveniently) to mask more pressing economic issues facing many developing nations, especially in an era of global capital and demands for economic 'restructuring'.[115] Human rights discourse does not extend to this arena. Instead, it provides a means to attack 'traditional' practices in an attempt to entrench further a Eurocentric cultural globalisation.[116]

It is not my goal here to resolve this debate by condemning or defending the varied practices of 'fgm'. To do either would be deeply problematic because, first and foremost, 'fgm' represents a diversity of practices which are no doubt experienced in a plethora of different ways depending on cultural and historical context.[117] Second, these practices occur in a range of social settings, and cannot be characterised as occurring in a single 'Third World'

---

112 See, eg, Walker, A and Parmar, P, *Warrior Marks: Female Genital Mutilation and the Sexual Blinding of Women*, 1993, New York: Harcourt Brace. For a critique of Walker and Parmar, see Obiora, *op cit*, fn 109, pp 54–64.

113 See, eg, Atoki, M, 'Should female circumcision continue to be banned?' (1995) 3 FLS 223.

114 Bibbings, LS, 'Female circumcision: mutilation or modification?', in *op cit*, fn 67, Bridgeman and Millns, p 164.

115 *Ibid*, p 159.

116 *Op cit*, fn 107, Fraser, p 325.

117 *Ibid*, Bibbings, p 151.

culture. To erase the diversity in 'fgm' practices is itself a form of neo-colonial thinking, where a singular 'Third World' 'them' is constructed as engaging in a unitary, 'readable' practice which can either be condemned or defended. As Fraser has argued, the problem with both the human rights and cultural relativist positions is that they share a view of 'culture' as static; when, in fact, the formation of culture is an ongoing, dynamic process.[118] Cultures are not 'autonomous' (in the classic liberal sense), but rather, as many have argued, the cultures of the coloniser and colonised are connected in a process of ongoing negotiation, where each shapes and is shaped by the other. Consequently, some writers have suggested that a useful point of departure for an analysis of 'fgm' would be the recognition of practices of body modification in the West as themselves forms of 'fgm', for all such practices represent the 'inscription of the female body with a complex set of social meanings'.[119] Such a redefinition of 'fgm' challenges its construction as a unitary 'Third World' practice of an 'alien' culture.

Reactions in the West to 'fgm' have been significantly shaped by medical and legal discourse, and for the most part have been grounded in claims of liberal autonomy for women; specifically, in control over the body. Autonomy becomes invoked most readily in the context of body modification performed on young girls who, it is argued, cannot freely 'choose' to be 'mutilated' given their dependence on adults and the social pressures placed upon them.[120] This view also serves to universalise what the cultural relativists would claim is a historically specific, Western construction of both childhood and autonomy.[121] But what has been the impact in the West of these medical and legal constructions of 'fgm'? Have these discourses served to 'protect' the liberal autonomy interests of women, ensuring rights of ownership of their bodies?

My argument is that, once again, classic liberal autonomy does not serve as a particularly useful paradigm in which to frame this controversy. The impact of the medicalisation and legalisation of 'fgm' in the West instead has reinforced the nature/culture; mind/body dualisms. It has done so through the construction of the category 'woman' as the embodied and the natural (and therefore in need of control and regulation). But, in addition, these discourses operate through what might be called a colonial lens. That is, the body of the racialised Other, here operating in tandem with the construction of a gendered Other, is firmly entrenched as an object of medical, legal, and even anthropological study.[122] This further serves to separate 'fgm' 'there'

---

118 *Op cit*, fn 107, Faser, p 330.

119 *Ibid*, p 343.

120 As in the case of surrogacy agreements, women are constructed as unable to consent to these practices.

121 See *op cit*, fn 114, Bibbings, p 164.

122 *Op cit*, fn 107, Fraser, p 336.

from body modification 'here', as fgm 'became a text treated in the professional discourses of the metropolitan center as doctors and lawyers began to define and limit the phenomenon to the boundaries imposed by their professional discourses'.[123]

'Third World' woman here is constructed through a mixture of gender and racial/colonial constructs. Not only is she outside the realm of social relations (pure nature), but it is a primitive nature in that she engages in practices which must be regulated by a civilised society. She must be made to recognise western medical and legal reason. In this way, the body of the 'Third World' woman is placed metaphorically outside of the body politic. She is not a subject who can speak to the issue of 'fgm' from her many different experiences, but is now firmly constituted as an object of knowledge, which 'reinstates the very silencing and stigmatization of women'.[124] For example, in the United Kingdom, Somali women have reported being subject to high levels of surveillance from the social work profession, keen to investigate whether they are practising 'fgm' in contravention of the law.[125] The criminalisation of 'fgm' thus serves as a means whereby the 'Other can be surveilled, harassed and otherwise disciplined'.[126] In that sense, bodily integrity and, by extension, individual autonomy, are severely undermined. The body becomes an object of knowledge and, *in the name of* a discourse of liberal autonomy, 'Third World' woman comes to be discursively owned by the West. She is the embodiment of a barbarity which must be civilised, tamed, or else excluded from the body politic. Such discourses serve to further 'reify Africa as the morally bankrupt antithesis of the West'.[127]

Within these dominant discourses, little attempt is ever made to locate 'fgm' in the 'broader geo-political context' of postcolonialism,[128] or to recognise the heterogeneity and diversity of the 'Third World'. As Obiora argues, 'the various forms of circumcision and their gradations of harm are conflated as "mutilation"; the entire continent of Africa, despite its complex heterogeneity, is reduced to a single research site. Further, the emphasis is on children, as if they were the sole subjects of the practice when, in reality, the ages of the circumcised vary from place to place'.[129] By being turned into an object of knowledge, there is little space left in which 'Third World' women can 'situate the practice in a broader developmental context', including

---

123 *Op cit*, fn 107, Fraser, p 368.
124 *Op cit*, fn 109, Obiora, p 49.
125 *Op cit*, fn 107, Fraser, p 372.
126 *Ibid*, p 368. Yet no case has ever been prosecuted in the United Kingdom.
127 *Op cit*, fn 109, Obiora, p 56.
128 *Op cit*, fn 107, Fraser, p 376.
129 *Op cit*, fn 109, Obiora, p 53.

'allocation of resources to women's education, economic participation, health care, etc'.[130]

What might the foregoing analysis suggest about how we conceive of bodies, ownership, and autonomy? For one thing, it demands a recognition of the way in which the ownership of women's bodies has been seized by Western medical and legal discourse. This appropriation is a continuation of practices of colonialism, in which the bodies of the colonised served as objects which had to be understood, analysed, classified; in order that they then could be regulated. While a reinvigorated conception of autonomy in this context will not lead to any 'answers' as to whether modification of the body (either 'here' or 'there') is a 'good' thing, it might force us to approach the issues differently. The prime question will not be whether the choices involved in body alteration are 'truly' voluntary in terms of liberal autonomy, as opposed to being coerced by community and familial pressure, or even 'false consciousness'. What autonomy demands is that we recognise that individuals are not isolated in frozen cultures with boundaries which serve to delineate them, like real property. Rather, the West is thoroughly implicated in the cultural conditions of the Other through the conditions of postcolonialism. The task is to break through that constructed isolation of culture and to create spaces to let the subjects of 'fgm' intervene within the discourse; allowing them to exercise rights of 'ownership' over the meanings of 'fgm' on their bodies. Such voices increasingly speak 'of the real ideological and material conditions of the Other' in a heterogeneous 'Third World' and diaspora.[131] Western support for (but not appropriation of) grassroots social movements in those places where 'fgm' is practised might be the most productive strategy, 'giving centrality to local initiatives'.[132] As Obiora observes, 'in organizing for change, effectiveness is better guaranteed if the change is actually perceived as necessary by the people at the grass roots level'.[133]

At the same time, as we break down the boundaries which liberal autonomy has constructed between self and other, we can listen to the voices of Western women (and men) who have engaged in practices of body modification. 'We' need to recognise that we too are the products of a cultural history of 'fgm', practices which grew directly out of the mind/body dualism. Women's sexuality was seen as in need of control by medical knowledge. That history must be reclaimed.[134]

---

130 *Op cit*, fn 109, Obiora, p 70.

131 *Op cit*, fn 107, Fraser, p 375.

132 *Op cit*, fn 109, Obiora, p 48. See also Smith, J, *Visions and Discussions on Genital Mutilation of Girls: An International Survey*, 1995, Amsterdam: Defence for Children International.

133 *Op cit*, fn 109, Obiora, p 69.

134 See Fegan and Fennell, this volume; Thomson, this volume.

Undoubtedly, the experiences of body modification in the West are widely diverse.[135] In some circumstances, modification may be internalised as an exercise in regaining a sense of ownership in the body; of seizing control of the body's imaginary domain. In others, modification may be emblematic of a process of fragmentation of the self, wherein the body comes to be disciplined by the practices of Western medicine and the demands of a globalised advertising industry that defines beauty in such a way that it coerces female body modification (and in that sense denies autonomy understood as choice).[136] Such narratives, however diverse, would arise directly out of experiences of embodiment, and can serve as a means to reclaim 'ownership' rights of the body; not in the sense of isolated autonomy, but through the connection that the sharing of experiences of embodiment might provide. A feminist theory of autonomy must work towards creating such discursive spaces, while maintaining a critical distance from those legal, medical, and other discourses which justify themselves in the language of autonomy, while seeking to regulate bodies.

# CONCLUSIONS

In this chapter, I have highlighted some of the inadequacies of our dominant understandings of body ownership in legal discourse. I have suggested that such views are grounded in a theory of liberal autonomy which is increasingly inadequate. Drawing on the work of feminist theorists, I have sought to work through an alternative conception of autonomy which arises out of the lived experiences of embodiment. Such an approach challenges the mind/body dualism which has been so central to Western, analytical jurisprudence. I elaborated upon these theoretical claims through three examples, drawn from separate arenas which currently serve as sites of contestation frequently articulated to a discourse of autonomy and body ownership. I attempted to interrogate each 'problem' of legal regulation of the body in order to underscore how a reinvigorated notion of autonomy, one which is located in a feminist theory of the body, can provide, if not answers, at least a better set of questions concerning bodies and their 'owners'.

---

135 See, *op cit*, fn 114, Bibbings.

136 On 'sexual surgery' in the West see, eg, Wolf, N, *The Beauty Myth*, 1990, London: Vintage, pp 241–49.

# CHAPTER THIRTEEN

# ON THE OUTSIDE LOOKING IN: PERSPECTIVES ON ENFORCED CAESAREANS[1]

*Celia Wells*

It would seem that it is never lawful for a doctor to force a competent person to have treatment against her wishes. If a Jehovah's Witness refuses a blood transfusion, knowing that she will most likely die, that wish will be respected.[2] If a terminally ill patient refuses treatment which would prolong her life, that wish will be respected. A person who could save the life of another by donating bone marrow cannot be forced to do so, even if it is necessary to save the life of her own child. A competent patient can refuse treatment irrespective of whether it jeopardises her own or another's life. The vast majority of legal commentators not only agree with the law's protection of patient autonomy, but would also extend this liberty to a pregnant woman in respect of treatment which would save the life of her foetus.[3] But courts have not always been so sure. Beginning with *Re S* in 1992,[4] judges have, on a number of occasions, acceded to doctors' requests to declare lawful decisions to carry out Caesarean sections on women who have refused consent. These decisions have attracted almost universal dissent in the legal and medical press,[5] and the Court of Appeal stemmed this tide in March 1997, pronouncing in *Re MB* that a woman cannot be compelled to undergo a Caesarean against her will if she is competent to take that decision, even if the likely result is her own death or that of her baby.[6] This may prove a victory of

---

1   I thank Alison Fryer-Jones for her research assistance and Cardiff Law School for paying her for it; I am also grateful to Sally and Michael for letting me write it. I claim ownership of all mistakes.

2   *Re T* [1992] 4 All ER 649.

3   Morgan, D, 'Whatever happened to consent?' (1992) 142 NLJ 1448; Stern, K, 'Court-ordered Caesarean sections: in whose interests?' (1993) 56 MLR 238; de Gama, K, 'A brave new world? rights discourse and the politics of reproductive autonomy' (1993) 20 JLS 114; Thomson, M, 'After *Re S*' (1994) Med L Rev 127.

4   [1992] 4 All ER 671.

5   Many articles in medical journals on a subject such as this will be written by lawyers. The case attracted less comment in the medical and midwifery journals than might have been expected: Crafter, H, 'Forcible Caesarean: a new direction in British maternity care? Thoughts on the case of Mrs S' (1994) 1 *Nursing Ethics* 53; Kargar, I, 'The right of refusal of treatment' (1992) 88(48) *Nursing Times* 23. For a medical defence of forced Caesareans, see Chervanak, F, McCullough, L and Skupski, D, 'An ethical justification for emergency, coerced Caesarean delivery' (1993) 82 *Obs and Gyn* 1029. See generally Annas, GJ, 'Protecting the liberty of pregnant patients' (1987) 316 *New England Journal of Medicine* 1213.

6   *Re MB* [1997] 2 FLR 426. Her refusal related to the anaesthetic rather than the operation, below, text accompanying fn 42.

Pyrrhic proportion, since incompetence has been established in all cases since *Re S*,[7] including in *Re MB* itself.

It takes a brave or foolish person to sing a different tune against the chorus of libertarian, autonomy-respecting voices, which disapproved *Re S* and now welcomes *Re MB*, but I find myself troubled by the near unanimity and certainty of the responses. That is not to say that I cannot see the force of its critics: how appalling to subject a person to a surgical procedure to which they have not consented. How inconsistent to allow people to refuse life-saving blood transfusions, or amputations,[8] but not allow a woman to refuse a Caesarean. Have the debates about the medicalisation of pregnancy and childbirth, brilliantly exposed in Ann Oakley's observational research, achieved nothing?[9] The following exchange demonstrates patient disempowerment to perfection:

Doctor [reading case notes]: Ah, I see you've got a boy and a girl.

Patient: No, two girls.

Doctor: Really, are you sure? I thought it said ... [checks in case notes] oh no, you're quite right, two girls.[10]

However, I am worried more by the assumption that the death of a woman in childbirth or of a full-term foetus through refusal of treatment raises a relatively simple question of autonomy versus paternalism than by my own ambivalence.

To begin with, there is a problem of comparing like with unlike; on what scales can the consequences of failing to act to save the lives of the foetus or the woman be weighed against the harm of ignoring the latter's expression of autonomy? There are problems with the slogans of rights and autonomy. There is a problem with how to conceptualise the interests of the foetus. When Blake Morrison wrote of the murder of James Bulger by two 10-year-olds, he expressed something of the ethereal shadows pervading the Caesarean debate:

Some deaths are emblematic, tipping the scales, and little James's death – green fruit shaken from the bough, an ear of grain sown back in the earth – seemed like the murder of hope: the unthinkable thought of, the undoable done.[11]

Here, I explore some of these doubts and questions by attempting to place the debate about 'enforced' Caesareans in a number of contexts. First, the feminist background, in which I include something of my own experiences with foetuses (these have bodily and cerebral dimensions). Secondly, I discuss *Re S*

---

7    These are discussed in detail below, pp 243–45.

8    As in *Re C (Adult: Refusal of Treatment)* [1994] 1 WLR 290.

9    Oakley, A, *Women Confined*, 1980, Oxford: Martin Robinson; Oakley, *The Captured Womb*, 1984, Oxford: Blackwells; Oakley, *From Here to Maternity*, 1986, Harmondsworth: Penguin.

10   *Ibid*, Oakley, *Women Confined*, p 41.

11   Morrison, B, *As If* , 1997, London: Granta Books, p 21.

and subsequent cases; and finally, I explore three underlying themes which help to shape my analysis of these cases. In Risks and Regrets, the nature of the decisions which women are asked to take and the appropriateness of the term 'enforced Caesarean' are considered. The extent to which it is sensible to talk about foetuses having or not having rights is then taken up in Foetal Protections; and briefly, in Medical Juridification, the nature and significance of the 'judicialisation' of medical decision-making is noted.

## HAVING BABIES AND WRITING OF FOETUSES

This section owes as much to the original 'personal is political' feminist slogan as to the force of more recent feminist theorising with its emphasis on difference, on gendering, on unevenness, and on complexity. While it has moved away from reliance on the ideas that 'law is sexist', or the later version, 'law is male', towards an approach based on gendered law,[12] feminist analysis inevitably remains rooted in subjective experiences.[13]

It is not because of the subject matter that I want to start with a personal account, although it is certainly worth reminding ourselves that pregnancy is neither a universal expectation (men do not share it) nor a universal experience (not all women want to or can become pregnant). Experience (in the broadest sense) contributes to the ways in which we make sense of and negotiate our way in the world.[14] This is one meaning of culture. What we write is a product of a complex of personal, historical and social factors. It might be neither sensible nor feasible to preface every piece of work with an autobiographical account, but never to reflect on the possible influences on our core values would be shortsighted. Thus, my rather uneventful obstetric history is given a small part in the drama, both because it is one of the significant factors in how I define myself and because, without it, my audience might wonder whether there is some significant personal explanation of the views I express here to which they are not privy. But there is a wider point and one which I seek to reflect throughout the essay. I adopt the strategy proposed by Marie Ashe to overcome the limitations both of an essentialist approach, with its assumption that all women have the same experiences, and an equal rights approach, which fails to deal with the significance of

---

12  Smart, C, 'The woman of legal discourse' (1992) 1 SLS 29; Naffine, N, *Law and the Sexes*, 1990, Sydney: Allen & Unwin, 1990.

13  Fegan, E, 'Fathers, foetuses and abortion decision-making: the reproduction of maternal ideology in Canadian judicial discourse' (1996) 5 SLS 75.

14  See, for example, Graycar, R, 'The gender of judgments', in Thornton, M (ed), *Public and Private – Feminist Legal Debates*, 1995, Melbourne: OUP, Chapter 12.

exclusively female experiences such as pregnancy, of infusing the '"inner discourse" of mothers into the law-language of maternity'.[15]

## A tale of maternity ...

I have three children. Each was delivered vaginally and each in a different hospital.[16] I was exposed during each pregnancy and labour to the temporal and geographical vagaries of obstetric fashion. All three overshot the 'normal' gestation of 40 weeks. The first was induced at 40 weeks plus 10 days for no other reason than lateness; the second was only seven days 'late' but, by presenting face-up, led to an interventionist labour. It is the only time I recall in my life wishing I could die. The anaesthetist's patient attempt to explain epidural pain relief was well-intentioned but quite unnecessary. Consent was not an issue, relieving the pain was. Ten years after the first, a very long time in obstetric fashions, I found myself, 12 days 'late' with my third, pleading for an induction from an incredulous registrar (I went into labour shortly after, thus saving him from having to blot his 'natural birth' copybook).

## ... and writing

Perhaps a more useful biographical dimension than that of having babies, an experience which is hardly unusual, is that I have written about foetuses or about enforced Caesareans more than once. I began to explore some of the issues around the maternal-foetal relationship in 1991 in an article arguing for a greater recognition of a woman's interest in protecting her foetus from third-party attack.[17] The catalyst was the Court of Appeal's decision in *Tait*[18] that a threat to kill a foetus did not amount to an offence, thus continuing the trivialisation of violence to women from spouses or partners, the level of which often increases when they are pregnant.[19] Then shortly after *Re S* was decided, I was invited to speak at a half-day conference entitled *Body Politics: Control Versus Freedom*,[20] on the topic 'Maternal versus Foetal Rights'.[21] I explain this for two reasons. The first, that my commitment and interest in this

---

15 Ashe, M, 'Law-language of maternity: discourse holding nature in contempt' (1988) 22 *New England Law Review* 521, p 527.

16 UCH, London; Princess Mary Maternity Hospital, Newcastle upon Tyne; and University of Wales Hospital, Cardiff.

17 Wells, C and Morgan, D, 'Whose foetus is it?' (1991) 14 JLS 431.

18 *R v Tait* [1990] 1 QB 290.

19 Middlesex Centre for Criminology (1997) *The Guardian*, 5 June.

20 March 1993, organised by the Feminist Legal Research Unit at the University of Liverpool.

21 Wells, C, 'Maternal fetal conflict', in Bridgeman, J (ed), *Body Politics: Control versus Freedom: The Role of Feminism in Women's Personal Autonomy*, 1993, pp 17–30, Liverpool: University of Liverpool; Wells, C, 'Patients, consent and criminal law' (1994) JSWFL 68.

area is, if not peripheral, then at least partly subliminal. Foetuses keep appearing in my work plans but I don't seem to have had complete control in putting them there. This is quite a useful description of pregnancy. The second reason is that Beverley Brown's contribution to that same conference provided the answer to my inchoate scepticism about the notion of maternal versus foetal rights and 'control versus freedom' as the organising theme. In her essay, Brown eloquently describes the 'psychic' dimension to discussions of women, law and medicine.[22] She points to the limitations of the control versus freedom (or autonomy) framework which on the one hand 'denies, displaces and invalidates much of women's relationship to their bodies' and on the other assumes a rationality, and an acceptance of liberalism which much feminist work has questioned. Thus, while personal accounts may be regarded as gratuitous, tedious or irrelevant (or all three), for me they affirm feminist critiques of the public/private divide and legal neutrality (for both mask social and political realities).[23] Classic individualism ignores women as a social group; individualism is 'classic middle-class territory' and, further, it invites rights-talk with the accompanying counterclaims such as 'right to choose', 'father's rights', and 'foetal rights'.[24]

It is not surprising that childbirth should have become a site of struggle for contemporary feminist politics.[25] Abortion and contraception were the key issues in the 1970s, replaced in the 1980s with campaigns such as that by the Women's Reproductive Rights Information Centre for the right to reproduce as well as the negative right not to.[26] Developing techniques and the desirability of screening for some well-established forms of assisted reproduction, such as donor insemination, meant that reproduction remained largely in male, or medical, hands.[27] A similar development took place over childbirth. On the one hand the natural childbirth movement gained strength while the potential for medical technology to 'control' undesirable outcomes, mainly in maintaining survival rates of low birth-weight babies, increased enormously. A notable irony is that, while hospitals were keeping ever more compromised neonates alive,[28] the medicalisation of 'early baby care' led to practices which were positively harmful such as the advice that babies should sleep on their fronts, the reversal of which led to a dramatic reduction in the

---

22  Brown, B, 'Bodily oppositions/controlling fantasies', in *op cit*, fn 21, Bridgeman.

23  See Thornton, M, 'The cartography of public and private', in *op cit*, fn 14, Thornton, Chapter 1.

24  *Ibid*, Brown, p 54; and see *op cit*, fn 17, Wells and Morgan.

25  See Harpwood, V, *Legal Issues in Obstetrics*, 1996, Aldershot: Dartmouth, Chapter 2.

26  Lovenduski, J and Randall, V, *Contemporary Feminist Politics* 1993, Oxford: OUP, p 225.

27  *Ibid*, p 232.

28  Wells C, '"Otherwise kill me", marginal children and ethics at the edges of existence', in Lee, R and Morgan, D (eds), *Birthrights*, 1989, London: Routledge, p 195.

number of SIDS (cot-deaths).[29] There can be no doubt that the meaning of pregnancy and birth has been constructed by medicine.[30] Any shifts in the cultural knowledge and understanding of maternity are negotiated against that particular model.

## COURT-ORDERED CAESAREANS – *RE S* AND BEYOND

To read any case is to read a construction of events prepared by and for lawyers.[31] Available media accounts, including interviews with the women themselves, have to be regarded as a further constructive interpretation. The language in which we receive the cases reflects the discourses of the legal and medical professions, and the judgments are built on a foundation comprising numerous assumptions about women, childbirth and mothering whose imprint on our cultural wallpaper(s), informs our opinions and responses to events. Carol Smart uses the 'Bad Mother' category to exemplify her thesis that 'Woman is a gendered subject position which legal discourse brings into being'.[32] One question to bear in mind as we think about them is whether these Caesarean cases represent the modern morality play whose earlier scripts included the 1623 Infanticide Act's imposition of a presumption of guilt on women when their illegitimate infants died; or the later concealment of birth offences, or the incarceration of unmarried mothers under the Mental Defective Act 1913.[33] Another is to recognise two characteristics of the medical model of pregnancy. First, the medical model emphasises the separateness of, and even adversarial relationship between, the pregnant woman and the developing foetus, and secondly, pregnancy is regarded as a series of discontinuous stages into which medicine can intervene, for example in reproductive technologies (egg harvesting, in vitro fertilisation), in foetal medicine (screening, monitoring, surgery), and so on to the birth process itself.[34]

Mrs S's third baby died during an emergency delivery by Caesarean section to which she had acquiesced in the face of a High Court declaration that it would be lawful to perform the operation despite her refusal to give consent. The foetus was full-term and, because of its position in transverse lie, without a Caesarean could not possibly be born alive. Medical evidence

---

29  The front-sleeping advice was particularly strong when my first baby was born. I was puzzled then, but understand now, why older women rushed up to me in the street, alarmed because the baby was on his front.

30  *Op cit*, fn 15, Ashe, p 537.

31  *Op cit*, fn 14, Graycar; Scheppele, K, 'Foreword: telling stories' (1989) 87 *Michigan Law Review* 2071; and *op cit*, fn 12, Smart.

32  *Op cit*, fn 12, Smart, p 34.

33  *Op cit*, fn 12, Smart, pp 37–39.

34  *Op cit*, fn 15, Ashe, p 540.

suggested that the life of Mrs S was also in grave danger without the operation (alive or dead, the foetus would still be there).[35]

The High Court has sanctioned Caesareans in at least seven cases since *Re S*,[36] but all have proceeded on grounds of incompetence to refuse or via treatment for mental disorder. None has relied on foetal or maternal welfare, a ground now removed following *Re MB*, and although I want to concentrate on the arguments in relation to competent, mentally ordered women, it is appropriate first to say something about incompetence and about mental health powers.

## Incompetence

Incompetence, or incapacity, is often regarded as giving the lie to courts' espousal of the right to refuse treatment.[37] *Re T*[38] may be understood in this way. Although Lord Donaldson stated clearly that 'an adult patient who ... suffers from no mental capacity has an absolute right to choose whether to consent to medical treatment, to refuse it or to choose one rather than another of the treatments being offered',[39] the Court of Appeal overrode T's refusal of a blood transfusion on two grounds: that she was unduly influenced by her Jehovah's Witness mother and that she had not had the opportunity to address the particular emergency which now made the transfusion vital. Similarly, in *Norfolk and Norwich v W*, a psychiatrist who had decided that the woman was not suffering mental disorder, nonetheless thought that she was unable to balance information in order to make a choice. As a result the judge authorised the use of 'reasonable force' to perform a forceps delivery and a Caesarean section if necessary.[40] An even starker deployment of the 'if you are refusing, you must be incompetent' line of reasoning is evident in *Rochdale v C*, where a woman who said she would rather die than repeat her previous experience of a Caesarean under epidural anaesthetic, was found by the judge to be unable 'to make any valid decision about anything of even the most trivial kind' because of the emotional stress and pain of labour.[41] And finally,

---

35  Transverse lie is an absolute indication for a Caesarean, Savage, W, 'The rise in Caesarean section – anxiety or science?', in Chard, T and Richards, M (eds), *Obstetrics in the 1990s: Current Controversies*, 1992, London: MacKeith Press, p 167.

36  Including *Norfolk and Norwich (NHS) Trust v W* [1996] 2 FLR 613; *Rochdale Healthcare (NHS) Trust v C* [1997] 1 FCR 274; and *Tameside and Glossop Acute Services Trust v CH* [1996] 1 Fam LR 762. See Widdett, C and Thomson, M, 'Justifying Treatment and other Stories' [1997] 5 FLS 77.

37  Harrington, J, ' Privileging the medical norm: liberalism, self-determination and refusal of treatment' (1996) 16 LS 348.

38  [1992] 4 All ER 649.

39  [1992] 4 All ER 652.

40  *Ibid, Norfolk and Norwich v W*.

41  Although C then consented, she complained afterwards that she did so under duress and, like S2, was granted legal aid to challenge the decision, see (1996) *The Guardian*, 17 December and 19 December. See p 245 below.

for all the talk in *Re MB* of a woman's right to refuse treatment, the Court of Appeal upheld the declaration that she lacked the capacity to refuse the anaesthetic injection without which the operation could not be carried out.[42] Her needle-phobia did not prevent her consenting to the operation itself. Butler-Sloss LJ reconciled any apparent contradiction between finding her competent to consent to one thing but incompetent to refuse another by asserting the principle that the test for capacity should be commensurate with the gravity of the decision to be taken – the graver the decision, the higher the threshold for rebutting competence. This all lends support to Harrington's view that courts find it easier to discount a patient's refusal than to find there has been a non-informed consent.[43]

## Mental Health Act 1983

Mental Health Act powers have been rendered considerably more attractive to doctors following the decision in *Tameside and Glossop Acute Services Trust v CH*[44] which controversially invoked s 63 powers allowing treatment for mental disorder to authorise a Caesarean without consent. CH, who suffered from paranoid schizophrenia, was found to be pregnant when detained under s 3 of the Act. Her doctors thought that if an induced labour or a Caesarean section were indicated she might be unco-operative and/or refuse consent. In anticipation, they applied for a declaration that it would be lawful to carry out a Caesarean section, with restraint if necessary, should she refuse to co-operate at the appropriate time. Granting the declaration on two grounds, lack of capacity to consent or, in the alternative, s 63 treatment 'for the mental disorder', the court held that an ancillary purpose of any necessary obstetric intervention was to prevent a deterioration in her mental health if a stillbirth occurred. Section 63 had not previously been interpreted to authorise treatment for a physical condition unrelated to the disorder and the mere fact of disorder should not overcome the need to establish competence.[45]

A Caesarean could be justified under restricted earlier interpretations of s 63 if the pregnancy were regarded as a threat to her mental health (the evidence was that she could not receive anti-psychotic drugs while pregnant). We might expect that the threat would need to be immediate and severe given that pregnancy is a condition which comes to a natural end. The court also justified the order on the ground that the consequence of failing to deliver a

---

42  *Op cit*, fn 6, *Re MB*.

43  *Op cit*, fn 37, Harrington, p 358: 'The reasonable patient, it seems, is less likely to be satisfied with a certain level of disclosure or to give sufficiently free consent when making a prior refusal of treatment than when alleging lack of informed consent in a negligence action.'

44  *Op cit*, fn 36.

45  See Grubb, A, 'Commentary on *Tameside and Glossop*' [1996] Med L Rev 193, p 195.

live baby would be a threat to her mental health. This required a double risk assessment – how likely was a stillbirth without the intervention, followed by how likely was the deterioration in her mental health, this latter of course having to be balanced against any possible deterioration brought about by the forced treatment.

Even had these grounds not been made out, the court was prepared to find her incompetent to refuse intervention. CH's detention under the Mental Health Act was unrelated to her pregnancy but, in 1997, 29-year-old S (referred to here as S2) was made subject to a s 2 order precisely because she refused to consider treatment for pre-eclampsia. Accepting that the original court was misled into believing that S2 was already in labour, the Court of Appeal has given her leave to seek judicial review of the declaration granted by the Family Division that her refusals be overridden.[46]

Few people would argue that a decision to refuse treatment in itself should ever justify Mental Health Act powers. The use of those powers aside, S2 apparently raised the same core question as the original *Re S*: should a doctor ever force treatment on a competent, mentally ordered woman in order to save her foetus's life (which in many cases coincidentally means saving hers)? Of course, the Court of Appeal's decision in *Re MB* has shifted the legal ground, applications such as that in *Re S* will now only be entertained on the basis of incompetence. I want now to concentrate on the question of principle raised by the *Re S* paradigm: was *Re S* wrong?

## The *Re S* paradigm

*Re MB* has firmly closed the door on the foetal interest argument left open by Lord Donaldson in *Re T* when he said that 'the only possible qualification [to a patient's absolute right to refuse treatment] is a case in which the choice may lead to the death of a viable foetus'.[47] The judgment itself in *Re S* yields very little about the real basis of the decision – whether it was foetal or maternal interests or both (assuming that it can make any sense to separate them in this way – on which see further below).[48] A declaration was granted in the following terms:

> Declaration that a Caesarian section and any necessary consequential treatment which the hospital and its staff proposed to perform on the patient was in the vital interests of the patient and her unborn child and could be lawfully performed despite the patient's refusal to give her consent.[49]

---

46  *R v Collins and others ex p S* (1997) *The Guardian*, 4 July.

47  *Re T (Adult: Refusal of Treatment)* [1992] 4 All ER 649, p 653.

48  Although Sir Stephen Brown has spoken about it in a public lecture: 'Matters of life and death: the law and medicine' (1994) 62 *Medico-Legal Journal* 52. Lord Donaldson wrote to him after the case saying: 'There will be all sorts of academic problems, but I agree with you.' See p 61.

49  *Re T (Adult: Refusal of Treatment)* [1992] 4 All ER 649, p 672.

There was a mis-statement of the American case of *Re AC*[50] but, that aside, the case has to stand or fall on the terms of the declaration itself, without assistance from any reasoning.

Many of the comments on this landmark case take issue with procedural shortcomings – that the hearing took only 18 minutes, and that no alternative medical opinion was sought.[51] Similarly, the speed and method of the decision-making in *Re L*, concerning a needle-phobic, has been criticised. Mr Justice Kirkwood formed the opinion, from telephone conversations with her doctors and with the Trust's barrister, that her phobia had put her own health and that of her unborn child at risk.[52] Some of these criticisms seem misplaced.[53] Understanding the cases as emergencies is needed in order to understand the nature of the issues they raise. They cannot be de-emergencied by the magic means of suspension of reality (or suspension of labour). The judge heard the evidence of S's consultant, that it was a 'life and death' situation which would deteriorate in 'minutes rather than hours'. The length of the proceedings has to be judged against that context, with the consequences of making the decision in favour of the declaration (albeit that it might later be regarded as wrong) weighed against those of a decision not to grant it (two deaths). A related procedural criticism is that Mrs S was unrepresented (although the Official Solicitor was represented in the role of *amicus curiae*). If it had been practicable to find representation for Mrs S, then of course it should have been arranged.[54] It may be possible to draw an inference from the fact that labour commenced on a Friday, and that a weekend elapsed before the decision to seek the declaration. While consultants and judges work at the weekends if necessary, both medical and legal institutions respect a Monday to Friday timetable for non-emergency work. This may have prolonged the period in labour before the decision to seek a judicial order was made and exacerbated the crisis.[55] One commentator suggests that discontinuity of care may have contributed to the apparently late-in-the-day discovery that Mrs S was implacably opposed to the operation on religious grounds.[56] However, there is evidence that something similar had occurred in the course of labour with her second child. The consultant wrote afterwards to Sir Stephen Brown to say that 'almost the same thing had

---

50  (1990) 573 A 2d 1235, DC Ct of Apps (en banc).

51  *Op cit*, fn 3, Thomson, p 135, note 59.

52  *Re L* [1997] 1 FCR 609.

53  Procedural safeguards such as representation and use of the Official Solicitor are set out in *op cit*, fn 6, *Re MB*.

54  *Ibid*.

55  The course of events was apparently this – the obstetrician had contacted the Coroner on the Monday morning to seek advice as he was certain that he would have two deaths on his hands by the end of the day. The coroner asked whether he had thought of seeking a court declaration, see *op cit*, fn 22, Brown, p 60.

56  *Op cit*, fn 5, Crafter, p 54.

happened with her second pregnancy'.[57] An early declaration of opposition to medical intervention may in any case, as we have seen, carry the risk of detention under the Mental Health Act.

These procedural objections sometimes mask the main issue, that of whether a woman's refusal of treatment be respected even when the outcome means that the foetus will die. As I suggested at the beginning of this essay, an uncritical focus on autonomy is unhelpful. The legal challenge mounted by S2 to have her detention declared unlawful acted as the touch-paper for a debate about non-consensual treatment in *The Independent*.[58] Among the considerable correspondence from readers was a woman who wrote of her mother's regret that fear of an operation led her to refuse a Caesarean which would have avoided the writer's cerebral palsy. Unsurprisingly, the woman herself also shared this regret. Another contribution, from a barrister, argued that the question was one for Parliament to decide, while a GP thought that doctors should always respect their patients' wishes. One letter (from a medical school address, profession unstated) suggested that the viable foetus should be saved so long as this does not endanger the mother's life; and lastly, one writer (no profession stated) argued that, since S had not decided to terminate the pregnancy lawfully, by allowing her pregnancy to progress to viability, she had responsibilities towards its safety. These letters encapsulate the underlying arguments, characterised as Risks and Regrets, Foetal Protections and Medical Juridification, which I now want to explore.

## RISKS AND REGRETS

The contexts in which decisions about Caesareans are being negotiated include a complex of medical, particularly, obstetric practices; risk assessment and understanding; medical screening; technology; social and cultural expectations; and individual determinants such as social situation and religious beliefs. Taken in its broadest sense to include not only formal rules, procedures and adjudications but also practices, discourses and ideologies, law can be regarded as a mediating institution to this matrix.[59]

Changing obstetric practices have resulted in a rise in the rates of Caesarean sections (CS), both in the UK (from 4.9% in 1970 to 11.8% in 1989) and, more dramatically, in the USA (5.5% to 24.7% over the same period).[60]

---

57  See, *op cit*, fn 22, Brown, p 61.

58  Between 21 and 28 February 1997.

59  In addition to the more common meaning of the word 'matrix' of 'a medium in which something is produced', the *Shorter Oxford English Dictionary* lists first the obsolete, but here appropriate, 'womb, occasionally ovary', 3rd edn, 1970, Oxford: Clarendon Press.

60  *Op cit*, fn 35, Savage, p 176. *Op cit*, fn 3, Thomson, citing (1988) *The Guardian*, 7 September, reports a British rate of 14%. See Audit Commission Report, *First Class Delivery*, 1997, reporting rates varying between 11% and 18%.

The World Health Organisation, noting that countries with some of the lowest perinatal mortality rates in the world have CS rates of less than 10%, concludes that there is no justification for any region to have a rate higher than 10–15%.[61] Undoubtedly defensive medicine has something to do with the rise.[62] For all those women resisting or regretting Caesarean intervention there are others left wondering whether such a procedure might have prevented their baby's birth-induced brain damage. Caesareans do carry some risk: of 78 maternal deaths after CS in the UK between 1985 and 1987, 14 are attributable to surgically related causes.[63] However, that does not mean that all Caesareans are undertaken for defensive reasons. It is important to distinguish between absolute and relative indicators for Caesareans. Only in relation to the latter is the debate about CS rates conducted.[64] The transverse lie of Mrs S's baby is recognised by Wendy Savage, well known as a non-interventionist obstetrician, as an absolute indicator for a Caesarean.[65]

In terms of risk, S1's baby could not be born alive without a section, and her own life was also at risk. When it comes to S2 or to CH, the risk indications are different. At the point at which S2 was sectioned, she had symptoms of pre-eclampsia. If those went untreated, her life, and that of her foetus, would be at risk. A Caesarean would not be the only treatment option,[66] but (as appears from the reports) S2's desire for a 'natural' pregnancy and labour led her to reject the possibility of any treatment. CH, also, concerned a pre-emptive declaration to authorise a Caesarean or other treatment in the light of her anticipated refusal.

It is helpful, then, in analysing the enforced Caesarean issue, to separate the possible risks to which the women's various refusals were directed. With some, such as S1, it seems clear that the relevant risk was that of death of the foetus and probably that of the woman herself. In some other cases, the objection taken to the procedure was based on an assessment of the possibility of death (to foetus, woman or both) measured against the harm (as perceived by the woman) of accepting medical treatment. Suppose the argument of S2 were not 'I wish I had died', but 'I wish I had not been sectioned, or subjected to a Caesarean', because she believes that her baby would have been delivered safely without that intervention. We cannot know, nor of course can she, whether her belief would have been proved correct. What we can know is that

---

61   Savage, citing 'Appropriate technology for birth' (1985) 2 *The Lancet* 436–37.

62   *Op cit*, fn 9, Oakley, p 209, comments that the rise must be due in part to the 'social structure of the medical profession: it cannot simply be a response to the medical needs of the individual woman'.

63   *Op cit*, fn 35, Savage, 247Table 12.VIII, p 181.

64   Oakley points to the medical-speak of the term 'elective' as 'chosen' but notes that it represents the 'dominance of the obstetrical empire since an elective delivery is one chosen by obstetricians and not by pregnant women': *op cit*, fn 9, Oakley, p 187.

65   See *op cit*, fn 46, *R v Collins*.

66   *Op cit*, fn 35, Savage, p 167.

pregnancy and childbirth have been subjected to increasing medicalisation, that obstetric fashions are highly volatile, and that challenges to the social control vision of pregnancy and labour have played a key role in achieving the retreat from some of the more interventionist orthodoxies, such as induction of labour.[67] How are these risks to be weighed and by whom?

The 'scientific' approach to risk assessment often despairs of 'the public's' inability to relate to statistical probabilities, and proceeds in the belief that, if only people understood the science of risk-talk, they would make objectively more sensible decisions. Increasingly, this is being challenged by social, cultural and psychology theorists as a fundamental misunderstanding of the conditioned and constructed subjectivities involved in risk-based decision-making.[68] Giddens' notion of the 'privatization of risks' provides insight to the relationship between modern technology and individual responses to risk.[69] Risk assessment is translated by experts (here doctors) into information accessible to 'lay' people (here patients), encouraging lifestyle or other decisions to be taken. But this process 'privatises' risks with the result that 'collectively produced dangers are "dumped" into the privatised worlds of individual victims and translated as realities one confronts individually and struggles with through individual efforts'.[70]

There has been an assumption in obstetric and midwifery practice that normal pregnant women will submit to monitoring and screening during their pregnancy. This has nothing to do with the chimera of high technology which (mis)informs so much public and other debate about 'medical dilemmas'. As Oakley has shown, long before the advent of high-technology reproductive options, many of the claims for the benefits of this particular version of medico-social control had been overstated.[71] On the other hand, patients have been seduced into a belief in the magic of screening, despite doubts increasingly voiced about the ethics, effectiveness and resource efficiency of genetic and other screening programmes.[72] In the process of reordering the world into one of prediction, design and control, where the normal is pathologised, the abnormal and the life-threatening become lost to view. The illusion of control over the risks and hazards in life leads not only to a culture of blame, where unlooked for deaths have to be accounted for, it also leaves individuals with confused expectations of medical and technological

---

67　It is interesting to speculate (another term with an obstetrical association – a 'speculum' is used for vaginal examination) whether high technology has merely shifted to earlier stages in the form of the assisted reproduction industry (cf 'labour').

68　See Pidgeon, N, 'Technocracy, democracy, secrecy and error', in Hood, C and Jones, D (eds), *Accident and Design*, 1996, London: UCL Press, p 164.

69　Giddens, A, *Modernity and Self-Identity*, 1991, Cambridge: Polity Press.

70　Baumann, Z, *Postmodern Ethics*, 1993, Oxford: Blackwells, p 202.

71　*Op cit*, fn 9, Oakley, Chapter 1. The Audit Commission, above concluded that £10 million was wasted annually on unnecessary ante-natal checks.

72　Green, J *et al*, 'Screening for fetal abnormalities: attitudes and experiences', in *op cit*, fn 35, Chard and Richards, p 65; and Foster, this volume.

practices. Individuals are allowed little say about the contents of the menu but are then expected to make appropriate choices from it.

It would be a mistake, therefore, to see risk in general, or the risks specific to obstetric practices, as a simple or merely scientific or rational phenomenon. A further dimension to this discussion of risk assessment and its relationship with 'autonomy' is that of regret. Suppose that S1 had written afterwards to Sir Stephen Brown, thanking him for authorising the doctor's decision to operate? Suppose that her religious beliefs led her to see the court's intervention as an expression of the divine will?[73] There is evidence that many patients who initially refuse treatment, acquiesce in the face of a court order. Chervenak *et al* report that, after a refusal is overridden, patients sometimes exhibit co-operative behaviour by, for example, 'coming to the hospital and physically resisting neither the placement of a venous line nor subsequent abdominal surgery'.[74] The patient in the *Rochdale* case apparently changed her mind and consented to the operation before word of the court's decision that she was incompetent to refuse/give consent reached the hospital.[75] A woman whose phobia about needles led to her refusal thanked doctors for obtaining a declaration authorising them to go ahead.[76] It is clear also that MB had no difficulty about consenting to the Caesarean, it was the anaesthesia which caused the problem.

Had doctors in these cases followed *Re MB* and their own professional ethical guidelines, these women might not have survived to voice their gratitude, or might be mourning the loss of their baby. In a blinding demonstration of medical hegemony, the guidelines issued by the Royal College of Obstetricians and Gynaecologists ignored *Re T* and *Re S* so effectively that the Court of Appeal in *Re MB* regarded them as a correct statement of the law: 'The law does not limit a woman's freedom because she is pregnant. Her bodily integrity cannot be invaded on behalf of her foetus without her consent.'[77] Although the guidelines go a long way towards recognising the professional obligations of doctors towards the woman and her foetus,[78] and the moral responsibilities of a pregnant woman to her foetus,[79] they conclude that 'it is inappropriate, and unlikely to be helpful or

---

73  See *op cit*, fn 22, Brown, and reports of a similar occurrence with her second pregnancy but somehow the Lord 'had provided' and that gave her 'strength ... and purpose to go on on this occasion', p 61.

74  *Op cit*, fn 5, Chervanak, McCullough and Skupski, p 1031.

75  *Rochdale Healthcare (NHS) Trust v C* [1997] 1 FCR 274.

76  *Re L* [1997] 1 FCR 609.

77  RCOG, 'A consideration of the law and ethics in relation to court-authorised obstetric intervention', *RCOG Guidelines Ethics*, No 1, April 1994, Appendix A, para 3.10.2. In stating that 'There is no legal justification for overriding a competent patient's wishes purportedly in her best interests' (para 3.8.7), the Guidelines anticipated the decision in *Re MB*, above.

78  *Ibid*, para 4.3.2.

79  *Ibid*, para 4.2.3.

necessary, to invoke judicial intervention to overrule an informed and competent woman's refusal of a proposed medical treatment, even though her refusal might place her life and that of her foetus at risk'.[80] Whether courts are the appropriate forum and the effect of their increasing involvement is discussed further below, but for the moment it is worth commenting that neither *Re S* nor *Re MB* yields a simple practical answer, how is a doctor or a court, or anyone, to determine whether a refusal is compromised or qualified by religion, phobia or ambivalence or whether a woman is competent to make such a decision. While it might be thought that acquiescence in the face of a court order is hardly best characterised as a valid change of mind, there is sufficient evidence of regret, and in some cases of the need to defer to a higher authority before feeling able as a matter of conscience to ignore religious dogma, at least to raise a doubt about the wisdom of this respect of 'autonomy'. Ishbel Kargar, secretary of the Association of Radical Midwives, commented after *Re S* that 'it appears that the rights of the unborn baby took precedence over the right of the mother to make decisions concerning her own body'. She went on to make this revealing slip:

> Whatever the personal beliefs which dictated the couple's refusal of surgery, and their apparent acceptance of a fatal outcome for both mother and baby, one wonders at the scene, as the mother was unwillingly anesthetized and operated on.[81]

In transforming the woman's right to refuse into that of 'the couple', the writer highlights the layered hierarchies at work here – are the institutions of law and medicine any worse or better at helping S1 negotiate her way through the complex social, cultural and economic structures which help determine her decision-making?

The pervasive ambivalence underlying many of these cases is sufficient to cast doubt on any simplistic portrayal of autonomy versus control. As one nursing commentator notes:

> No doubt the public are generally in favour of the decision, and my own findings are that midwives and student midwives are almost unanimous in their support of the judgment, but with major concerns as to its ethical implications.[82]

The framework of debate has to be extended to accommodate a complex of ethical, political, and ideological factors and, above all, to recognise that these cannot hope to yield an easy answer.

---

80  *Op cit*, fn 77, RCOG, para 5.12.

81  *Op cit*, fn 5, Kargar, p 23.

82  *Op cit*, fn 5, Crafter, p 53.

## FOETAL PROTECTIONS

It is sometimes assumed that, because foetuses do not have legal personality, they do not have rights or interests which are recognised by law. This is a serious mis-statement of their position in English law. Foetal interests are protected in many ways whether from injury by the woman carrying them or from third parties. Neither the foetus nor the putative father has any status to challenge a woman's decision to have a lawful abortion,[83] and a foetus cannot be the subject of a wardship order,[84] but that does not mean that foetuses are in some kind of legal void. Talking of rights is not particularly helpful, as Bix explains:

> It is compatible to say both 'I do not think it makes sense to speak of foetuses having rights' and 'I believe that abortion is wrong and immoral because it involves harming foetuses, harm which should not be condoned except in the most extreme circumstances'. Similarly it is compatible to believe both that foetuses are capable of having rights and that abortion should be allowed in most circumstances (because foetuses in fact do not have rights relevant to this situation, or whatever rights they have are overridden by the conflicting rights of the mother).[85]

In other words, statements that foetuses do or do not have rights do not assist in deciding the extent of or conflict between their rights or interests and those of others, in particular of the pregnant woman.

Criminal laws regulate women who are pregnant in order to provide foetuses with some protection from conception to birth. There are two overlapping offences, attempt to procure a miscarriage and child destruction, both subject to qualifications of the Abortion Act 1967. The attempt to procure a miscarriage offences under the Offences Against the Person Act 1861 make it an offence either for a pregnant woman or for any other person unlawfully to administer drugs or use an instrument with intent to procure a miscarriage.[86] To deal with the twilight period between pregnancy and the emergence of the foetus as a legal 'person' (that is, when it has an independent existence of its mother) the Infant Life Preservation Act 1929 created the woefully misnamed offence of child destruction. This offence is committed whenever a person with intent causes to die a 'child capable of being born alive' before it has an independent existence. Thus, once a foetus is viable,[87] procuring a miscarriage could amount to both offences. The miscarriage and child destruction offences

---

83 *Paton v BPAS* [1979] 1 QB 276.

84 *Re F (In Utero)* [1988] 2 All ER 193.

85 Bix, B, *Jurisprudence: Theory and Context*, 1996, London: Sweet & Maxwell, p 106.

86 Section 58. The offence is punishable with a maximum of life imprisonment.

87 That is, capable of breathing and living independent of its mother: *Rance v Mid-Downs HA* [1991] 1 QB 587.

are modified by the Abortion Act 1967[88] which allows qualified medical practitioners to carry out abortions in specified circumstances. A pregnancy may be terminated on four grounds.[89] The first ground, which applies only up to the 24th week, is that continuation of the pregnancy presents a risk (greater than if the pregnancy were terminated) of injury to the mental or physical health of the woman or of existing children. The other three grounds may apply at any stage of gestation and allow a termination where it is necessary to prevent grave permanent injury to the *physical or mental health* of the woman, or where the continuance of the pregnancy involves a risk to her life, or there is a substantial risk that the child would suffer from serious physical or mental handicap.[90] Provided that one of these grounds is satisfied, an abortion will not amount to either the miscarriage or child destruction offences.[91]

The relationship between the foetus and homicide offences should also be mentioned. The victim of homicide must be a human being, a person who has breathed independently of its mother. The Court of Appeal in 1990 rejected an argument that a threat to kill a foetus was a threat to kill a person.[92] More recently, however, the House of Lords has held that a pre-natal injury leading to post-natal death could amount to manslaughter.[93] There is no requirement in homicide that the person who dies needs to be a person in being at the time when the death-causing injury is inflicted. However, the House of Lords was not prepared to go as far as the Court of Appeal and to hold that any intention for murder directed at the pregnant woman could be 'transferred' to the foetus. Lord Mustill strongly dissented from the argument that, while *in utero*, the foetus was analogous to any other part of the woman's body – her arms, her leg: 'Not only were they physically separate but they were each unique human beings ... S and her mother were closely related but ... they were not, had not been, and in the future never would be "the same".'

Civil liability towards the foetus was restricted in 1976 with respect to injuries inflicted on it before its birth by the negligence of the defendant. The Congenital Disabilities (Civil Liability) Act allows proceedings only if the defendant would be liable in tort to the mother; the child can bring no action against its mother for ante-natal injuries, unless her negligent act was committed while driving. These criminal and civil provisions clearly demonstrate that, while the foetus has a different legal status from that of a baby, child or adult, it is nonetheless the subject of extensive protection from

---

88  As amended by the Human Fertilisation and Embryology Authority Act 1990, s 37.

89  Abortion Act 1967, s 1.

90  *Ibid*, s 1(b)–(d).

91  Section 5(1) and 5(2), dealing with the 1929 Act and the miscarriage offences respectively.

92  Under the Offences Against the Person Act 1861, s 16: *R v Tait* [1990] 1 QB 290.

93  *Attorney General's Reference (No 3 of 1994)* [1997] 3 All ER 936; [1996] 2 All ER 10; (1997) 147 NLJ 1185.

injuries by the woman in whose body it gestates and by third parties. The Abortion Act may be characterised as giving precedence to the health of the mother over that of the unborn child,[94] but that is the beginning, not the end, of any debate.

John Eekelaar argues that any duties a woman owes to her foetus should proceed from a social morality of mother and others towards the unborn, rather than from a notion of foetal rights, and that the closest analogy is that of parent to child who is born. 'Here, social morality, and the law, expect parents to make decisions which will frequently relegate their own interests beneath those of their children.'[95] While the moral obligations themselves might not vary between foetus-hood and baby- and childhood, Eekelaar points to differences between the maternal-foetal and the parental-child relationship which significantly affect the obligations a woman might owe to her foetus. She cannot divest responsibility in the way that parents can; the pregnancy itself carries risk to the woman; and the disapproval of abortion prescribes social and physical activity on the woman.[96] Neither parents nor pregnant women are expected to place themselves in life-threatening situations or at serious risk of psychological disturbance for the sake of their children or foetuses. Eekelaar concludes that legal enforcement of a reasonable expectation that she bring the pregnancy to term, at this late stage of pregnancy, is realistic and not unduly oppressive.[97]

The simple reason why enforced Caesareans cause a frantic challenge to our moral antennae is that the separation of the foetal and the maternal interest is at one and the same time a physiological, metaphysical, metaphorical and moral paradox. There is no simple line between being at full-term in a pregnancy and being the mother of a new-born baby. The gulf is nothing. The gulf is everything. To state that '... the issue at stake is parental obligation. A parent stands in an intimate moral relationship with his or her child ... ' is to state everything and answer nothing.[98]

## JURIDIFICATION OF MEDICAL DECISIONS

Space prohibits more than a sketch here. Decisions that doctors have been used to making in the privacy of their consulting rooms are increasingly transferred to the High Court where they are often treated as though the

---

94  *Re MB* [1997] 2 FLR 426, *per* Butler-Sloss LJ.

95  Eekelaar, J, 'Does a mother have legal duties to her unborn child?', in Byrne P (ed), *Medical Law and Ethics*, 1988, Oxford: King's Fund Press and OUP.

96  *Ibid.*

97  See also Bennett, B, 'Pregnant women and the duty to rescue: a feminist response to the fetal rights debate' (1991) 9 *Law in Context* 70, especially pp 83–85.

98  Chervenak, F *et al*, 'In reply' (1994) 83 *Obs and Gyn* 639.

dilemmas they present are novel, not merely novel in the courtroom. Speculation on the reasons for this developing judicialisation is of less importance here than the juridifying effect that the process brings.[99] The polarisation of autonomy and paternalism is one such effect. Autonomy is a problematic principle to guide moral decision-making for the simple reason that people aren't autonomous. To paint a picture of the world in which the decisions and processes leading up to the medical treatment have all involved a series of autonomous steps – becoming pregnant, whether to have an abortion, which ante-natal tests to undergo, where to have the baby – is a serious misrepresentation and the assumption that individuals are not subject to multiple influences in their beliefs or that p/maternalism is unwanted is unproven. Another effect is to bring the medical model or 'metaphor' of the woman as a machine into 'law-language'.[100] I am not suggesting that juridification leads to any particular outcome. Indeed, during the time I have been writing this essay, courts in this country have undergone an apparent change of heart on this question – from Re T's tentative and Re S's actual endorsement of the dual interests in the viably pregnant woman to Re MB's reassertion of the singular interest. Yet none of those cases has moved the debate beyond a simple ethical or medical model.[101] None has noted that the female body is for women 'the locus of nature, the site of powerful, undifferentiated or contradictory forces which underlie culture'.[102] The pregnant woman does not experience her foetus as a separate identity but as 'a total bodily indwelling'.[103] Neither law nor medicine has listened to women's account of pregnancy, childbirth and the early maternal bond. If they did, the answers would be no easier, but the debate would acquire the integrity it currently lacks.

# CONCLUSION

The development of foetal rights has been criticised for over-emphasising separateness, yet the use of autonomy as a guiding principle has the same effect.[104] Connectedness, rather than rights, is a more useful theme. The challenge of pregnant women is that neither foetal rights or best interests, nor

---

99   *Op cit*, fn 97, Bennett, points out that the use of law for previously private problems individualises issues, and obscures social difference and inequalities, p 86.

100  *Op cit*, fn 15, Ashe, p 527.

101  Nor, it might be noted, has any case yet been decided which has actually led to a refusal to grant the declaration sought – it is only the competent woman who can refuse, and her freedom to do so, it seems, has thus far only been asserted in cases in which she is found incompetent.

102  *Op cit*, fn 15, Ashe, p 544.

103  *Op cit*, fn 15, Ashe, p 549.

104  See Stychin, this volume.

autonomy arguments, provide any kind of satisfactory answer. The inscription of motherhood is not the issue. Pregnancy is a special state for which no parallel is easily, if at all, found. Acknowledging the specialness of that state can only lay the foundations for, rather than resolve, the profound dilemma which refusal of consent to a Caesarean section or other life-saving obstetric treatment raises. None of these arguments can escape the grip of social, political and historical manipulation by dominant groups.

This chapter began with a single cell of an argument – should courts ever override a woman's refusal of treatment in order to save the life of her foetus – which has multiplied and divided into a layered consideration of the contexts in which that question can be pursued.[105] I have rejected a simple reliance on autonomy, on the right to choose, the right to refuse or the right to bodily integrity, in favour of a considerably less certain and often flaky view. It can hardly be said often enough that neither doctors nor judges necessarily know best. Who does? But to found moral, legal or ethical argument on a notion of individual, atomised decision-making is not very appealing either. Perhaps it is right that doctors, lawyers and judges, who in Western societies number amongst the better-rewarded professionals in terms of both status and pay, should have to take the hard decisions, one of which may be to say to Mrs S, and her children, 'OK, if you don't want the treatment, we cannot make you'. None of us would want to have to take that decision – in any case part of my theme has been to argue that trying to isolate 'the decision' from the surrounding life layers is part of the problem. It is only with trepidation that any parallel at all can be drawn between the murder of a child, and the death of a foetus through abortion or other maternal decision. But our relationship with our children is emotional, emotive and everlasting. Blake Morrison, concluding a long passage in which he voices his fears for the safety of his child, fears which resonate strongly for me and confirm his guess that these are common parental terrors, writes:

> And all this supposes that we are kind to our son – haven't beaten him overmuch about the head ... And supposes we've let him be born in the first place, not plucked him out, or sucked him out, untimely ripped from the womb. Many of us have a death like this on our conscience: the children that might have been, the embryos. A murdered foetus: not to be equated with a murdered child. And yet, and yet. There are no weighing-scales for the guilty heart.[106]

The High Court, following *Bland*,[107] has declared on a number of occasions, that it is in the best interests of a person in PVS, or sub-PVS to die. Although the patient in those cases is not competent to refuse treatment, is it not odd

---

105 To take the metaphor further, the arguments have moved, like my two younger children, into the adolescent phase, succumbing to reason when and if they so choose.

106 *Op cit*, fn 11, Morrison, pp 55–56.

107 *Airedale NHS Trust v Bland* [1993] 1 All ER 821.

that they apparently give us less trouble than decisions that it may be in the best interests of a pregnant woman to give birth to a live baby or to survive the process of labour?

# CHAPTER FOURTEEN

# POSTHUMOUS PREGNANCIES: SOME THOUGHTS ON 'LIFE' AND DEATH

*Katherine de Gama*

## INTRODUCTION

This chapter examines the uses to which women's and men's bodies may be put, and the meanings inscribed upon them, in death and dying. Its starting point is the observation that the appropriation of the bodies of deeply comatose, persistently vegetative and brain stem dead pregnant women as foetal incubators is ethically problematic and, politically, to be fiercely resisted.[1] Law's acquiescence in this essentially futile, necrophiliac pursuit of potential 'life' stands out in sharp relief to the protection it accords to the reproductive products of a dead male provider. In the UK, the response of the Human Fertilisation and Embryology Authority to Diane Blood's relatively innocuous request to be inseminated with her husband's illegally stored sperm unleashed a macabre campaign of reproductive absolutism in which the spectral, disembodied form of the late Stephen Blood acquired an almost corporeal presence. Systematically effacing her own desires and her own agency in their pursuit, I will argue that, Blood's victory does nothing to realign gender relations. Instead, it represents a sentimental attempt to reconstruct the biological nuclear family in which, ironically, it is the woman who is rendered invisible. Tellingly, in popular discourse, though not in this paper, the term 'posthumous pregnancy' evokes a curious image of reproductive capacity which survives not the death of a woman, but a man.

Laura Purdy, commenting on the elaboration of foetal rights in medical, legal and bureaucratic discourses, claims Americans 'have more say over what happens to their bodies after death than many women do ... while they are still alive'.[2] Given the urgency of resisting the rising tide of non-consensual interventions upon the live pregnant body it is not surprising that Purdy's interest in the tragic scenarios which lie at the intersection of *Roe v*

---

1   Physically, brain death differs little from PVS. In brain death the higher and lower functions of the brain have ceased. PVS describes a number of conditions where irreversible damage has occurred to part of the higher brain but activity remains in the brain stem. The patient can breathe, circulate blood, digest food, filter waste, maintain body temperature and create new tissue but permanently lacks cognitive function.

2   Purdy, L, 'Are pregnant women fetal containers?' (1990) 4 *Bioethics* 289.

*Wade* and *Re Quinlan*[3] is confined only to brief comment on the widespread use of pregnancy exclusion clauses in 'natural death' or living will statutes. A pregnant woman now may have very little say over what happens to her body in dying and after death. Her status suspends even the obligations and prohibitions which otherwise the living regard themselves as owing to the dead. Nearly two centuries after the publication of Mary Shelley's *Frankenstein*, the Promethean travesty of maternal procreativity finds expression not in the fictional researches of the charnel houses, but in the routine but covert practices of high-tech medicine.[4]

## FRANKENSTEIN'S BABIES

In common with other non-consensual interventions on the pregnant body, few cases have found their way into the law reports and not one case on any issue surrounding the prolonged ventilation of a brain-dead pregnant woman has yet been argued on appeal in any jurisdiction. Media accounts and medical literature, however, reveal both a disturbing number of cases of bodies appropriated as foetal containers and a dearth of comment, criticism or attempt at justification. The phenomenon of the brain-dead pregnant woman emerged in the USA as a consequence of the Uniform Determination of Death Act 1981 which, specifically in order to facilitate the harvesting of quality organs for transplantation, stated the irreversible loss of brain stem function to be a necessary and sufficient definition of death.[5] However, pregnancy suspends this presumption of death: there is a legislative paternalism which finds explicit expression in the insertion of pregnancy exclusion clauses in the majority of US natural death statutes.

In the first reported case in New York in 1981, a foetus was salvaged at twenty-five weeks gestation from the body of an unamed woman who had been diagnosed as dead according to brain stem criteria seven days previously.[6] Professional opinion in these early days of experimentation on

---

3    410 US 113 (1973); (1976) 70 NJ 10; 355 A 2d 647.

4    Shelley, M, *Frankenstein, or the Modern Prometheus*, 1985, London: Penguin.

5    An individual who has sustained either (1) irreversible cessation of circulatory and respiratory functions, or (2) irreversible cessation of all functions of the entire brain stem is dead. A determination of death must be made in accordance with accepted medical standards.

6    Dillon, W, Lee, R and Tronolone, M, 'Life support and maternal death during pregnancy' (1982) 248 *Journal of the American Medical Association* 1089. Sampson, M and Peterson, L, 'Post-traumatic coma during pregnancy' (1980) 53 *Obs and Gyn* 2s–3s, had reported the case of a PVS patient, who was given hydration and nutrition via a gastro-nasic tube for seven months, who delivered at 33 weeks. The medical consensus was then that surgery could not be justified until 28 weeks. Dillon *et al*, however, reported it to be 24 weeks. At the same time the team unsuccessfully attempted ventilation of a woman at 18 weeks' gestation. Dillon *et al* reported a 1977 PVS case in which there was a live birth after 34 weeks. The woman was unconscious from the sixth week of pregnancy.

the bodies of brain-dead pregnant women was that heart failure could be delayed by ventilation for a maximum of two to three weeks, and that only by 'vigorous management and foetal monitoring'.[7] However, just two years later there were live deliveries 61 days, in San Francisco, and 84 days, in Virginia, after maternal death.[8] In 1986 in Santa Clara, California, a baby was delivered 53 days after her mother died of a brain tumour.[9] In 1988 the body of Marie Henderson was artificially sustained for 107 days.[10] In 1989 in San Bernardino, California a baby was delivered at 27 weeks, after 60 days of ventilation. In 1993 in Oakland, California, the bodily functions of Trisha Marshall were sustained for 105 days after she was shot dead after brandishing a meat cleaver at a disabled man in the course of a burglary.[11]

In Europe, in all but one reported case, posthumous pregnancy has so far been attempted only where the foetus has been potentially viable at the time of maternal death. Cases have been reported in the medical literature in 1984 in Finland, in 1986 in Britain and in 1995 in Spain.[12] The one British case suggests that many women described as merely comatose may, in fact, be brain stem dead. Deborah Bell, who suffered a brain haemorrhage at 24 weeks' gestation, was ventilated for five weeks and her child delivered alive.[13] This, the only case to come before the UK courts, did so in the curious context of an intellectual property dispute over the legal ownership of the dead woman's wedding photographs.[14] After several national newspapers obtained copies of the pictures, Deborah's husband entered into an agreement with the Daily Mail in which he granted exclusive rights to publication. The paper then obtained an injunction restraining the Daily Express from using the pictures. The defendant newspaper argued that Mr Bell could not grant an exclusive right as copyright was vested in either Mrs Bell or in the couple jointly. In the absence of a statutory definition of death, the court was required to ponder the problem of defining life and death. Millet J, giving judgment,

---

7    *Op cit*, fn 6, Dillon *et al*, cited in Lamb, D, *Death: Brain Death and Ethics*, 1985, Beckenham: Croom Helm, p 100.

8    Field, D, Gates, A, Creasy, R, Jonsen, A and Laros, R, 'Maternal brain death during pregnancy' (1988) 260 *Journal of the American Medical Association* 816; Nelson, H, 'The architect and the bee: some reflections on postmortem pregnancy' (1994) 8 *Bioethics* 247.

9    *Ibid*, Nelson, p 248.

10   *Ibid*, Nelson.

11   Hartouni, V, *Cultural Conceptions*, 1997, Minneapolis: University of Minnesota.

12   Vives, A, Carmona, F, Zabala, E, Fernandez, C, Cararach, V and Iglesias, X, 'Maternal brain death during pregnancy' (1996) 52 *International Journal of Gynaecology and Obstetrics* 67. In the specific case reported the dead woman's injuries were such that artificial support could be sustained for only 36 hours. A child was delivered at 27 weeks.

13   (1992) *The Independent*, 1 November. More recently, babies were delivered by Caesarean section to deeply comatose or PVS patients: Karen Battenberg, Audrey Montgomery and an unnamed Bristol woman; (1995) *The Guardian*, 4 May; (1997) *TV Quick*, July; Brown, S, 'Matters of life and death: the law and medicine' (1994) 62 *Medico-Legal Journal* 63.

14   *Mail Newspapers plc v Express Newspapers plc* [1987] 1 FSR 90 (ChD).

stated the evidence was that she was *probably* clinically and legally dead.[15] However, what is interesting is that clinical tests were never formally administered to establish the fact of death, as 'a diagnosis of brain death would have required a death certificate'.[16]

The dearth of cases in the literature betrays the many unpublished cases where 'life' support and foetal survival prove impossible.[17] Given the nature of news values it is not surprising that only two unsuccessful post mortem pregnancies have been widely reported. In 1986 in Georgia a child, three months premature and weighing only 17 ounces, was delivered stillborn. In 1992 in Erlangen, Germany, the case of 18-year-old Marion Ploch was pathbreaking because for the first time it attracted vociferous political controversy. Declared brain-dead after a road traffic accident at only three months gestation, her body was artificially sustained for 42 days, at an estimated cost of £40,000, until the pregnancy ended in miscarriage.[18] A public opinion survey in a mass circulation daily newspaper suggested that those in favour of ventilation were outnumbered by a factor of four to one. Hannah Wolf, spokesperson on women's affairs in the lower house of the Federal Parliament, was one of the few feminist voices: 'What is happening in this clinic is a scandal and inhumane. The mother is degraded to a nutrient fluid, disposable after use.'[19] Alice Schwarz, editor of *Emma*, added, 'The Pope will like it – women as incubators. I think it's perverse'.[20] Elsewhere, public opinion found expression in a zealous outcry against human experimentation which drew sustenance from the horrific endeavours of both Dr Frankenstein and Dr Mengele.

Shelley's tale of uncontrolled reason and critique of birth in the absence of woman rightly places the attempt at autoreproduction or ectogenesis firmly within the paradigm of transgression. Evelyn Fox Keller offers a reading of Shelley's work in a way which underscores my concerns about the appropriation of the undead womb:

It is the story of the mad scientist (or alchemist) pursuing secrets of life – not in the broad light of day ... but in the dark recesses of a secret laboratory ... often producing vile-smelling vapours in the process, until finally, he succeeds – not

---

15  In England there is no statutory definition of death, and a veiled assumption exists that life and death are matters best left to clinical discretion. Criminal law first addressed the issue obliquely, focusing on causation, in the absence of any determination as to whether the victim of assault was dead or not at the point at which ventilation was discontinued (*R v Malcherek; R v Steel* [1981] 2 All ER 422, pp 428–29, *per* Lord Lane LCJ). In *Re A* [1992] 3 Med LR 303 the parents of a child certified as brain-dead sought continued ventilation. Johnson J declared that for all medical and legal purposes the child was dead. This definition of legal death was confirmed by the House of Lords in *Airedale NHS Trust v Bland* [1993] 1 All ER 821.

16  (1992) *The Independent*, 1 November.

17  *Op cit*, fn 12, Vives *et al*.

18  (1992) *The Independent*, 1 November.

19  Cited in *Bild Zeitung*, 17 October 1992.

20  Cited in Singer, P, *Rethinking Life and Death*, 1995, Oxford: Clarendon, p 13.

merely in finding the secret of life, but in using that secret to produce life itself.[21]

Pitiless and fanatical in the narrow pursuit of scientific knowledge, the monster clearly is the doctor.

Anyone who has read *Airedale National Health Service Trust v Bland* or *Re Quinlan*[22] for their facts, rather than their legal points, will know that the comforting 'sleeping beauty' image of the persistently vegetative or permanently comatose patient is painfully inappropriate. Prolonged ventilation necessarily involves intrusions and indignities such as the surgical implantation of gastronasal tubes and catheters, dialysis, the use of plasma expanders, insulin infusers, vasoactive substances and hormones. The nursing literature on brain-dead pregnant women makes harrowing reading:

> Because of her pregnancy, she remained on her right side most of the time. When we placed her in any other position, the baby was distressed. As a result skin breakdown and pressure ulcers developed. She also had copious, foul-smelling, yellow secretions in her endotracheal tube, and we had to suction her constantly ... Her husband continued to visit every day. We could see the pain in his eyes as he watched his young wife's body decompose.[23]

The all-women nursing team, who were literally doing the doctors' dirty work, expressed their anger and distress at the extraordinary burden that had been placed upon them.[24] Having 'cared for' the woman for six weeks, her transfer to the operating room 'was like a funeral to us'.[25]

What may appear as requests by families to sustain a pregnancy are often a consequence of acute pressure from doctors who pursue agendas which are far from benign. The most outrageous example of this is the *Ploch* case. Initially, Marion's parents, who had only just learned that their daughter was pregnant, refused to give consent for her body to be ventilated.[26] However, after the meeting of the all-male ethics committee of Erlangen University, they were informed first that, '... on the evidence of comparable cases in the literature', the foetus stood a good chance of being salvaged alive and, second, that they would lose custody of any future child if they refused consent. Not surprisingly, they capitulated, though their consent was neither informed nor voluntarily given.[27] In the literature there was only one reported case in which a beating heart corpse had been successfully maintained for a period of more than three months. Yet, unbeknown to Marion's parents, to incubate to

---

21  Keller, E, *Reflections on Gender and Science*, 1985, New Haven: Yale University Press, p 185.
22  [1993] 1 All ER 821; (1976) 70 NJ 10; 355 A 2d 647.
23  Ascioti, K, Barber, M, Nettina, M and Santos, E, 'Sheila's death created many rings of life' (1993) *Nursing* 48.
24  *Ibid*, p 47.
25  *Ibid*, p 48.
26  The issue attracted media attention as they appealed to a mass circulation daily for help.
27  As told to *Stern* magazine.

certain viability the clinic's head doctor, Johannes Scheele, was preparing to establish a new world record. Tellingly, he talked about winning a 'first prize in the lottery'.[28]

Six months later, Dr James Jackson, chair of Maternal and Child Health Services in the Oakland case, won joint second. His comments reveal much about the status of medical knowledge and the legal and ethical constraints within which hospitals assume it is located:

> I personally think that if you put another one of these cases in the literature, the next time this occurs it almost compels (doctors) to go full blast, doing whatever they can do ... the next hospital faced with this decision would probably end up doing just what we did.[29]

At its most benign, what informs and underpins the decision to continue cardio-respiratory support beyond total and irretrievable loss of brain stem function is a heroic desire to wrest 'life' from death. The decision to suspend the formal processes and rituals of death, bereavement and mourning reveals much about the social status of the dead. Informed by early foetal rights discourse, not yet apparent in explicit legal sanction and buttressed by the institutions and ideologies of science, the clinical team which claimed the first live post mortem birth clearly believed they were under a moral duty to salvage the foetus.[30] Marion Ploch's doctor stated, 'there really isn't any question whether it should be tried or not ... we don't see any ethical reason simply to let the embryo (sic) die'.[31] Gerd Neubeck, a State prosecutor, insisted that to do otherwise would be a criminal offence.[32] His colleague, Hasso Nerlich, went further, initiating charges against Julius Hachetal for the curious offence of campaigning for illegal abortion. Hachetal's alleged offence was to have pressed for assault, poisoning and malpractice proceedings against Ploch's doctors.[33]

The medical literature is laced with attempts to legitimate these interventions by dismissing all arguments cast in the language of liberal autonomy on the grounds that death extinguishes all claims to personhood and self-determination. Yet moral agency is normally exercised after death in the sense of having directives carried out about the disposition of property and organs and the respectful handling of the body.[34] The fact that consent is

---

28  Anstotz, C, 'Should a brain-dead pregnant woman carry her child to term? The case of the "Erlanger" baby' (1993) 7 *Bioethics* 349.

29  Cited in *op cit*, fn 20, Singer, p 17.

30  See *op cit*, fn 6, Dillon *et al*, and fn 8, Field *et al*.

31  Cited in *ibid*, Anstotz, p 342.

32  *Op cit*, fn 8, Nelson, p 252, note 17.

33  As German abortion law presupposes a live pregnant woman the public prosecutor had little choice but to drop the charges.

34  However, there are examples of where a State interest trumps a right to refuse to have one's body used in a particular way. These include mandatory post mortems and public health requirements relating to the disposal of the body.

generally[35] required for procedures performed after death is ignored by Field *et al* who argue that:

> ... even a maternal refusal expressed before death does not, in itself, carry weight against the possibility of fetal survival. The mother is not harmed; no right of hers is violated, and great good can be done for another.[36]

In support of what they refer to as a 'straightforward instance of the medical rescue of the foetus from death', Field *et al* detail a long tradition of foetal rescue in Western society, from Asklepios, cut from his dead mother's womb by Apollo, to the Roman mandate of *Lex Caesaria*.[37] Chervenak and McCullough maintain, 'the brain-dead body is personless and devoid of the kind of interests that a living person has in his or her body. Thus we can find no strong objections to the incubator model'.[38] Dillon *et al* conclude that neither a Caesarean nor any other surgical intervention upon a dead body should be considered invasive and, therefore, should not require consent.[39]

Further, Dillon *et al* attempt to establish a beneficence-based relationship first between the dead woman and the foetus and second, between the doctor and the foetus. But, an ethical duty of beneficence implies not only a limited risk to oneself but, in this context, more importantly, a distinct gain to others. There is no systematic collection of clinical data on the outcomes of these interventions. The physiological maintenance of organ function for the benefit of the foetus remains entirely experimental. And, by definition, there can be no beneficence-based duty to subject oneself or a foetus to experimentation.[40] Premature delivery carries a risk of brain damage, haemorrhage and major lung disorder, further exacerbated in this context by the nature of the pregnant woman's illness or injury, the effects of oxygen deprivation and drug-related iatragenic damage.

Not surprisingly, in cases where the dead woman's family have sought to discontinue ventilation, former male partners, in a productive alliance with medical power, have marshalled arguments which the courts have translated into the rhetoric of foetal rights.[41] In the USA, the wishes of a progenitor and putative father, who is not the husband of the deceased, have prevailed over

---

35   The Human Tissue Act 1961 allows for the refusal of organ harvesting but, unless opposed by relatives, this can be done without the consent of the deceased.

36   *Op cit*, fn 8, Field *et al*, p 821.

37   See also Kantor, J and Hoskins, I, 'Brain death in pregnant women' (1993) 4 *Journal of Clinical Ethics* 308; Veatch, R, 'Maternal brain death: an ethicist's views' (1982) 248 *Journal of the American Medical Association* 1102.

38   Chervenak, F and McCullough, L, 'Clinical management of brain death during pregnancy' (1993) 4 *Journal of Clinical Ethics* 349.

39   *Op cit*, fn 6, Dillon *et al*, p 1090.

40   *Ibid*, Chervenak and McCullough.

41   Jordan, J, 'Incubating for the state: the precarious autonomy of persistently vegetative and brain-dead pregnant women' (1988) 22 *Georgia Law Review* 1103.

those of the next of kin.[42] In *University Health Services Inc v Piazzi*[43] a court granted a declaratory judgment, sought by a hospital, backed by a progenitor but opposed by a husband, that life support be continued for a pregnant woman at 19 weeks' gestation. The neurologist gave evidence that her body could be maintained for a further five weeks. Three weeks later the foetal heartbeat began to fade and the baby was delivered by Caesarean 14 weeks premature, weighing only a little over a pound, and died within 48 hours.

Subverting the trimester-based framework of rights elaborated in *Roe v Wade*[44] in *Piazzi*, the court established a State interest in preserving even non-viable potential life. In a tortuous and undisciplined judgement, it drew first on *Jefferson v Griffin Spalding County Hospital Authority*, where an application to stay a non-consensual blood transfusion and Caesarean section claimed by doctors to be necessary to save the life of a 39-week foetus was refused, and *Shirley v Bacon*,[45] which established a claim for wrongful death for the loss of a non-viable but 'quickened' foetus. These tangentially related cases were then placed in the context of a pregnancy exclusion clause in a natural death statute and the extension of homicide statutes to include a foetus which dies *in utero*. This allowed the court to conclude that the right to privacy, implicit in the 14th amendment, was extinguished by death. Thus, the adoption of the brain stem standard for the legal definition of death, intended to facilitate transplants and liberate families from emotional (and in the USA, financial) burden, was used as a reason to deny autonomy and prolong somatic life. In *Poole v Santa Clara County Kaiser Hospital*,[46] in a judgment which was similarly cursory and confused, the court issued an injunction restraining the parents of a brain-dead pregnant woman from discontinuing ventilation at 25 weeks' gestation. Instead, it granted the unmarried progenitor and putative father of the foetus the formal status of protector of the unborn by appointing him as its guardian *ad litem*. The biological investment of Marie Henderson's unmarried partner prevailed over the wishes of her next of kin who authorised doctors to disconnect the ventilator.[47] In the *Trisha Marshall* case a custody battle began between her parents and her partner. The issue was only settled when it was discovered that her partner was not the baby's biological father.[48]

---

42  *New York Times*, 26 July 1986, p 7; *San Francisco Examiner* 19, 22 June, 13 July, p B1, cited in *op cit*, fn 8, Field *et al*, p 822.

43  (1986) No CV86-RCCV-464 Super Ct of Richmond County, Ga.

44  *Op cit*, fn 3, *Roe v Wade*.

45  (1981) 274 SE 2d 457; (1980) 154 Ga App 203; 267 SE 2d 809.

46  (1986) Petition No 604575, Super Ct of Santa Clara County.

47  *Op cit*, fn 11, Hartouni.

48  *Op cit*, fn 20, Singer, p 11.

## POSTHUMOUS PREGNANCY: WHERE NEXT?

Legal opinion in the UK appears to be shifting against prolonging life where there is little reasonable prospect of recovery. However, the stage is set for posthumous pregnancy, even where the foetus is non-viable.

Since *Bland*, the High Court has sanctioned the withdrawal of artificial feeding and hydration in 12 cases, most recently in the case of a woman who was not in a persistently vegetative state according to the criteria laid down by the Royal College of Physicians' guidelines.[49] Further, there are clear *dicta* in *Re T*[50] and *Bland* which support the position that, where a living will has been executed, its content should be upheld by the courts. In response to the House of Lords' request in *Re C*[51] that the British Medical Association should elaborate a code of practice on living wills and proxies, a policy statement was published in support of 'limited legislation to translate the common law into statute and clarify the non-liability of doctors who act in accordance with an advance directive'.[52] It proposes that the validity of advance directives should be clarified, and the rights and duties of doctors, patients and relatives clearly delineated. Similarly, the Law Commission has advocated the extension of a legal right to 'die with dignity' in the event of terminal illness. However, it goes further in some respects than the BMA, in seeking to establish a right to nominate a proxy decision-maker to advise doctors in the event of future incapacity.

Specifically, the Law Commission proposes new legislation which would bring together all health, welfare and property decisions in its draft Mental Incapacity Bill.[53] Advance statements about health care made by a person with requisite capacity, intended to have effect at a time in the future when they lack that capacity, would be legally recognised. Decisions in the event of future incapacity could be made by a new donee of a 'continuing power of attorney'. What is problematic, however, is that the Law Commission attempts to re-enact key aspects of the first statutory recognition of advance directives, the California Natural Death Act 1976, a model adopted widely throughout the USA, by refusing to acknowledge fully autonomous choice in medical decision making during pregnancy.[54] In response to representations from the pro-life lobby, the Law Commission concedes:

---

49  See *Practice Note (Persistent Vegetative State: Withdrawal of Treatment)* [1996] 4 All ER 766.

50  4 All ER 649.

51  (1993) NLJ 1642.

52  British Medical Association, *Advance Statements about Medical Treatment*, 1995, London: BMA. See also reports of the British Medical Association conference (1995) *The Guardian*, 5 April.

53  Law Commission, *Mental Incapacity*, Law Com No 231, 1995, London: HMSO.

54  In 27 States advance directives include a clause which denies pregnant women the constitutional right to refuse life saving treatment. The attempt to exclude this right may be unconstitutional under *Roe v Wade* 410 US 113 (1973) which held that implicit in the 14th amendment is a right to privacy which can be interpreted as including a right to abortion in the first trimester of pregnancy. In the second trimester, the issue is constructed in terms of maternal health. Only in the third trimester does the State acquire a compelling interest in protecting maternal health.

By analogy with cases where life might be needlessly shortened or lost, it appears that a refusal which did not mention the possibility that the life of a foetus might be endangered would be likely to be found not to apply in circumstances where a treatment intended to save the life of a foetus was proposed.[55]

A woman's right to reproductive autonomy and bodily integrity is suspended by a presumption under clause 9 that a refusal cannot be valid where it endangers even *non-viable* foetal life:

In the absence of any indication to the contrary it shall be presumed that an advance refusal of treatment does not apply in circumstances where those having the care of the person who made it consider that the refusal (a) endangers that person's life or (b) if that person is a woman who is pregnant, the life of the foetus.[56]

But what this ignores is that when an advance directive is executed, the intention is to avoid futile, painful or degrading treatment which prolongs one's own life. Few women, in this context, are likely to ponder the likely array of non-consensual interventions on the pregnant body or the extraordinary end to their bodily existence made possible by the 'miracles' of modern science.[57]

The absence of any statement on viability in the Law Commission's proposals is curious in that in the UK, the courts have permitted women a narrow ledge of reproductive autonomy in contested abortion cases by neatly sidestepping the issue of foetal rights and translating the issue into the secondary reality of a clinical judgment on viability.[58] In *Paton v United Kingdom*,[59] although a husband's attempt to restrain his wife from terminating her pregnancy without his consent, under Art 8 of the European Convention on Human Rights, which extends the right to 'respect for family life', was rejected, the European Court was clearly concerned about the matter arising in the context of a viable foetus. The question of fathers' rights was left open in *C v S*,[60] in which a man seeking an injunction to stop his former partner having a legal abortion was denied a cause of action as next friend of the 'child' *en ventre sa mère* by privileging medical knowledge which denied viability.

---

55  *Op cit*, fn 53, Law Commission, para 5.25.

56  *Op cit*, fn 53, Law Commission, para 5.23–5.26; draft Mental Incapacity Bill, clause 9(3).

57  The same paternalist principle was adopted in the context of advance directives on death and dying in an influential 1988 report of a joint working party of Age Concern and the Centre of Medical Law and Ethics, King's College, London, again without comment or attempt at justification. See Age Concern Institute of Gerontology and Centre of Medical Law and Ethics, King's College, London, *The Living Will: Consent to Treatment at the End of Life*, 1988, London: Edward Arnold.

58  Sheldon, S, '"Subject only to the attitude of the surgeon concerned": the judicial protection of medical discretion' (1996) 5 SLS 95.

59  (1980) 3 EHRR 408 (EComHR). See also *Paton v Trustees of British Pregnancy Advisory Service* [1979] QB 276.

60  [1988] QB 135.

A late 1980s New York case shows the extraordinary officiousness of the US foetal rights lobby. Hoping to improve her chances of recovery, the partner of a pregnant woman in a coma sought guardianship in order to have her pregnancy terminated. Claiming to represent the interests of the non-viable foetus, third parties intervened in an attempt to have the Supreme Court stay the order.[61] Although the applicants lacked standing and therefore the challenge failed, the possibility that such a case could be brought before the courts suggests that any attempt at the legislative protection of the non-viable foetus is to be resisted.[62] Necessarily and inevitably, its already problematic aims and objectives will be subverted and extended beyond the limited context for which they were intended.

Issues of beneficence and potential viability were woven together in the tragic US case of *Re AC*, a misreading of which informed and underpinned the High Court decision here in the notorious *Re S*, Britain's first non-consensual Caesarean case.[63] Despite the objection of Angela Carder, her family and her doctors, George Washington Hospital sought a non-consensual Caesarean in an attempt to salvage a potentially viable 26-week foetus from the body of a terminally ill woman. The court held that the State had an interest in protecting the foetus, but could not impinge upon the pregnant woman's right to bodily integrity 'unless to do so [would] not significantly affect the health of the mother and unless the child ha[d] a significant chance of being born alive'.[64] All parties acknowledged that surgery would hasten her death, yet the operation was sanctioned by the court. Within two days both mother and child were dead. A death certificate recorded the Caesarean section as a contributory cause of death. The District of Columbia Court of Appeals reversed the decision by seven to one:

> Some may doubt that there could ever be a situation extraordinary or compelling enough to justify a massive intrusion into a person's body, such as a Caesarean section, against that person's will.[65]

Clinicians, if not lawyers, have clearly regarded brain death during pregnancy as sufficiently extraordinary and compelling to warrant such intrusion.

---

61  Meyers, D, *The Human Body and the Law*, 1990, Edinburgh: Edinburgh University Press, p 13.

62  See Sheldon, S, 'Multiple pregnancy and re(pro)ductive choice' (1997) 5 FLS 99.

63  (1988) 539 A 2d DC; [1992] 4 All ER 671. See Wells, and Fegan and Fennell, this volume.

64  The test was rejected as impossible to quantify by the British Courts in *Re F* [1989] 2 FLR 376.

65  [1990] 573 A 2d 1235, p 1297. That the operation violated personal integrity was supported by women's groups, religious groups, the American Medical Association and the American Civil Liberties Union.

# BLOOD TIES

In a different version of posthumous pregnancy, however, the interests of the reproductive male are constructed as compelling. In February 1997 the Court of Appeal overturned a High Court decision that Diane Blood should not be allowed to export sperm extracted from her dying husband's body without his consent. Her campaign of reproductive absolutism was so successful in mobilising public opinion that the Human Fertilisation and Embryology Authority (HFEA) was effectively constrained to set aside the very law it was set up to enforce. Public support for Blood's plight was expressed not only in tabloid column inches but also in donations by the public of over £20,000 towards legal costs. One of the most curious supporters of her campaign against the authority created to police the very legislation the Warnock Report gave rise to, was the author herself. Her report had expressed disquiet at the use of the gametes of the dead. Whilst it maintained that when one of the providers dies, 'the right to use or dispose of any embryo stored by that couple should pass to the survivor', the genetic material of a dead male provider is deemed worthy of greater protection.[66] 'The use by a widow of her dead husband's semen for AIH', the committee noted, 'is a practice which we feel should be actively discouraged'.[67]

Essentially, the Human Fertilisation and Embryology Act 1990 seeks to vest control over genetic material in the providers of gametes and embryos. The issue of a proprietary claim in UK law remains unclear because that control is mediated by a complex system of consents. Schedule 3 requires the provider to state in writing, at the time that the gametes are procured, the purposes for which this genetic material can be employed. Specifically, s 2(2)(b) provides that where there is consent to the storage of gametes or embryos the providers must determine what is to happen to them in the event of their deaths. A consent to the storage of any gametes or any embryo must 'state what is to be done with the gametes or embryo if the person who gave the consent dies or is unable because of incapacity to vary the terms of the consent or to revoke it, and may specify conditions subject to which the gametes or embryo may remain in storage'.

Sir Stephen Brown, president of the High Court Family Division, giving judgment in October 1996 conceded that, in the absence of written consent, the Human Fertilisation and Embryology Act 1990 prohibited posthumous treatment, and therefore the Authority acted reasonably in refusing Diane Blood an export licence.[68] In the Court of Appeal, counsel for Diane Blood

---

66 Warnock, M, *A Question of Life: The Report on Human Fertilisation and Embryology*, 1984, London: HMSO, para 10.12.

67 *Ibid*, para 10.9, note 1.

68 Blood's intention was to receive treatment in Belgium, where there are no consent requirements.

argued: first, that she had a right under European law to have access to medical treatment in Member States; and second, that artificial insemination by husband or partner is not regulated by the Human Fertilisation and Embryology Act 1990 and therefore written consent was not required. Counsel for the Authority conceded that, in most cases, the Act does not impose regulation on the AIH/P couple and Diane Blood assumed written consent was unnecessary as Stephen Blood was alive at the time when the coyly termed sperm 'samples' were taken. However, correctly, he conceded there was no exception to the rule that written consent was required for the *storage* of gametes.

By underlining the point that written consent was required and placing, as Ruth Deech put it, 'unusually strong' emphasis on the right to receive medical treatment in Member States under Art 59 of the Treaty of Rome, the judgment attempts to remove the possibility that the *Blood* case will establish a precedent.[69] Whether or not it does so remains to be seen.

But, more importantly, the *Blood* case, though hailed by many as a victory for women, does nothing to realign gender relations. Blood, a public relations executive, became a practised media performer.[70] Her presentation of herself was unsentimentally righteous and chaste. In both popular and professional discourse, Diane Blood's battle was represented in terms of persuading the HFEA to grant her the opportunity to conceive her dead husband's child. Sir Stephen Brown confessed, '[m]y heart goes out to the applicant who wishes to preserve an essential part of her late beloved husband'.[71] Interestingly, at the Court of Appeal the HFEA did not raise the issue of ethics, public morality, public policy or the interests of any child born as a result of such treatment. Instead, sympathy was expressed towards Diane Blood's stated desire to 'honour her late husband's wishes'.[72] The judgment was delivered on the day after what would have been the late Stephen Blood's birthday. Evoking his presence, she draped a banner bearing the words 'happy birthday' over his gravestone and told reporters, 'This is the nicest present he could have ... This was always my husband's wish as well as my own. And I am here to carry out his wishes'.[73]

Notwithstanding the consent provisions, the *Blood* case underlines the desire for a male presence to almost grotesque lengths. In this way it stands out in stark contrast to the furore in the early 1990s over the practice of

---

69  'Letters' (1997) *The Guardian*, 4 March, p 16.

70  Photographers were instructed to pose for her to take pictures outside the Court of Appeal.

71  Cited by Gerald Kaufman (1997) *Daily Mail*, 18 February. Paternity cannot be ascribed to the legally dead.

72  Court of Appeal, 14 January 1997, Lord Woolf MR, Henry LJ, Waite LJ; (1997) *The Guardian* 14 January.

73  (1997) *Daily Mirror*, 7 February, p 6. Pictures of Stephen Blood on his wedding day appeared in a *Daily Mirror* 'exclusive'.

surrogacy and the possibility of so called 'virgin births'.[74] In this context, the resistance to autonomous motherhood most graphically reveals the contested terrain of reproduction. However, as Millns observes:

> It appears that the spectre of the dead father figure is more readily acceptable than no father figure at all, or than a living parent who is in a same-sex relationship with the woman seeking treatment services.[75]

As Michael Thomson notes, the 'macabre, disembodied and spectral presence' of the father is prioritised over 'an embodied, corporal and supportive partner who happens to be the same sex'.[76] Certainly, the debates preceding the passage of the Human Fertilisation and Embryology Act reveal a deep hostility to the lesbian, single and unmarried. Anxiety about the absence of a male partner dovetailed into a moral panic about 'the family'. A House of Lords amendment introduced by Lady Saltoun which would have criminalised the provision of treatment services to the unmarried was defeated by just one vote.[77]

In the USA, two cases of sperm being harvested from men who, unlike Stephen Blood, were brain-dead, have recently attracted popular attention.[78] In the absence of a comparable regulatory authority, headlines were cloyingly sentimental: 'newlywed hopes to use sperm of dead spouse to start a family'.[79] Six months later, following a widow's request, sperm was surgically extracted from a corpse in the New York city mortuary. This operation generated little public attention, still less controversy.[80] While formally the issue is seen in terms of rights and property,[81] in practice medical decisions

---

74  (1991) *The Guardian*, 12 March; (1996) *The Guardian*, 19 October; (1997) *The Guardian*, 14 January 1997.

75  Millns, S, 'Making "social judgments which go beyond the purely medical": the reproductive revolution and access to fertility treatment services', in Bridgeman, J and Millns, S (eds), *Law and Body Politics*, 1995, Aldershot: Dartmouth, pp 97–98.

76  Thomson, M, 'Legislating for the monstrous: Access to reproductive services and the monstrous feminine!' (1997) 6 SLS 417.

77  Hansard, *HL Deb*, Vol 515, col 787 (1990) 6 February, cited in *ibid*, Thomson.

78  It is surprising how few cases have come to light given that sperm is easily harvested and stored.

79  (1994) *New York Times*, 5 June.

80  (1995) *The Guardian*, 21 January. The legal regulation of embryology and fertility treatment in the USA is far less rigorous than in the UK.

81  *Davis v Davis* (1992) 842 SW 2d; *Del Zio v Columbia Presbyterian Medical Center*, (1976) SDNY, 12 April; *York v Jones* (1989) 717 F Supp 421 (ED Va); *Hecht v Kane* (1993) 20 Cal Rptr 2d 275. In *Del Zio v Columbia Presbyterian Medical Center* a doctor destroyed sperm and the partner sued for conversion. The trial judge allowed the issue to go to the jury. In *York v Jones* a partner sued in tort for wrongful retention; again the question was allowed to go to the jury. In *Hecht* frozen sperm was willed to a partner. However, in the context of a wider dispute about the division of family property, adult children from a previous relationship objected and the sperm bank refused to release the 'legacy'. However, before the case went to appeal the parties agreed a settlement by which the new partner would receive 20% of the estate. The California Court of Appeal confirmed that sperm, ova and embryos were unique forms of property, and must be dealt with strictly in terms of the wishes of the testator. Therefore, to the extent that that sperm is property it is only so in the sense that the recipient is strictly bound by the testator's declaration of trust. The appellant was awarded 20% of the sperm

regarding appropriate femininity and fitness for motherhood determines which requests are acted upon.

Tim Murphy cites the extraordinary example of a 1993 Chicago case in which a hospital refused to act upon a request to harvest and bank sperm from a dying man so that his partner could be inseminated because of *his mother's* alleged drug use and inappropriate sexual behaviour.[82] The recent attempt by Ohl *et al* to formulate guidelines for US practitioners on sperm retrieval and storage is ostensibly informed by law's insistence on reproductive autonomy and consent. Yet doctors are urged to go further, to act as gatekeepers to the courts, specifically to seek, 'assurance of the well-being of any new life created'.[83] Clearly, this is narrowly defined, in that only one of the seven cases reviewed by the authors was gamete extraction thought truly worthy. Here:

> ... the wife and many family members gave a very consistent report that the couple had been planning to start a family in the next two months. We also received very convincing evidence that the family would assist in the new child's care to allow the wife to work to support the family.[84]

Elsewhere, the motives of the commissioning kin, even if the spouse, are subject to even greater suspicion and examination.

## FOETAL PROTECTION AND MEDICAL POWER

As new technologies such as artificial insemination, cryopreservation and in vitro fertilisation force us to acknowledge men as reproductive, sperm has become a locus of cultural value. Emily Martin's review of medical texts on menstruation and menopause exposes negative images of deterioration and dissolution. But in contrast, sperm production is described in terms of replenishment and renewal. She cites an extract from a text on male physiology:

> The mechanisms which guide the remarkable cellular transformation from spermatid to mature sperm remain uncertain ... Perhaps the most *amazing* characteristic of spermatogenesis is its *sheer magnitude*: the normal human male may manufacture several million sperm per day.[85]

Cynthia Daniels's account of the discourses around reproductive toxicity in popular and scientific media explores the personification of sperm, now

---

82  Murphy, T, 'Sperm harvesting and postmortem fatherhood' (1995) 9 *Bioethics* 380.

83  Ohl, D, Park, J, Cohewn, C, Goodman, J and Menge, A, 'Procreation after death or mental incompetence: medical advance or technology gone awry?' (1996) 66 *Fertility and Sterility* 889.

84  *Ibid*, p 891.

85  Martin, E, *The Woman in the Body: A Cultural Analysis of Reproduction*, 1987, Milton Keynes: Open University Press, p 48, Martin's emphasis.

accorded even a spurious consciousness.[86] Unlike menstruation, spermatogenesis, then, involves the production of something deemed valuable. In contrast, as Sheila Kitzinger observed two decades ago:

> ... awed by ... technology, it is not difficult to understand how a woman can feel she is merely a container for the foetus, the development and safe delivery of which is under the control of obstetric personnel and machinery.[87]

In common with other non-consensual interventions, posthumous pregnancy offers a superb symbolic representation of the medical model of childbirth, which pathologises pregnancy and demands institutionalisation and high technology interventions. In this fantasy of ectogenesis the pregnant body is abstracted as a foetal ecosystem, transformed into a field of medical operations.[88] The clinical team which claimed the first prolonged mechanical and pharmaceutical parody of pregnancy, chillingly described its task as the management of an 'intra-uterine environment'.[89]

The legal status of the foetus in the USA and the UK is bedevilled with anomalies and inconsistencies through which medical power is legitimated and extended. The courts have systematically sought to avoid the question of when life comes into existence and at what point it becomes worthy of legal protection. Instead, different branches of the law have elaborated doctrines of foetal rights tentatively and in isolation, each informed by different sets of assumptions and directed at different objectives. Law consistently and systematically fails to protect a pregnant woman's interest in her foetus, seeking instead to protect the woman and foetus from third parties and each other.[90] In both jurisdictions the juridical status of the foetus can be acknowledged retrospectively if it is injured *in utero*, but subsequently born alive.[91] In a substantial minority of States in the USA, moreover, the time-honoured proposition that the foetus has no essential juridical status has been undermined. By conflating the foetus and the child, while ignoring the

---

86   Daniels, C, 'Between fetuses and fathers' (1997) 22 *Signs* 579.

87   Kitzinger, S, *Women as Mothers: How They See Themselves in Different Cultures*, 1978, New York: Vintage Books, p 74.

88   See Stychin, this volume, p 224.

89   *Op cit*, fn 8, Field *et al*, p 820. Against the advice of *op cit*, fn 6, Dillon *et al* support of the maternal cadaver was prolonged for the purpose of mitigating the cost of neonatal intensive care. Costs for maternal care were $183,081, and neonatal care $34,703.

90   Wells, C and Morgan, D, 'Whose Foetus is it?' (1991) 18 JLS 431.

91   In *Bagley v North Hertfordshire Health Authority* [1986] NLJ Rep 1014 where medical negligence caused a stillbirth, Simon Brown J held that a claim for grief, sorrow and loss of society was barred because there had not been the death of a child. Even in the USA, claims for wrongful death are more concerned with compensating prospective parents than attributing legal personality to the foetus. In England and Wales the Congenital Disabilities (Civil Liability) Act 1976 confirms liability for injuries sustained *in utero* but protects women from coercive interventions by establishing only a prospective, contingent right. By embracing a doctrine of derivative liability any claim founded on the negligence of the pregnant woman is frustrated. The exception under s 2, which allows a woman to be sued if the negligence is negligent driving, is informed by the legal requirement that drivers hold third party insurance.

implications for the woman who is pregnant, courts have sanctioned both the prenatal incarceration and the postnatal prosecution of women labelled as recalcitrant. Women's perceptions of their best interests have been disdained and overridden by doctors, lawyers and judges. Surgical procedures including Caesarean sections, cervical suturings and *in utero* blood transfusions have been authorised with little argument, publicity or protest.[92]

In the USA, the most recent attempt to compel a pregnant woman to submit to coercive intervention confirms that *Re AC* was a turning point in US women's campaign for reproductive freedoms. In 1994 Tabita Bricci, a Pentecostal Christian from Romania, insisted upon a vaginal delivery even though she was informed that the foetus was not receiving sufficient oxygen through the placenta and would either die or be born with brain damage unless delivered by immediate Caesarean section. The Illinois Appellate Court upheld the first instance decision to refuse to interfere; the Illinois Supreme Court and the US Supreme Court declined to hear further appeals.[93] However, where antenatal conduct escapes regulation, the sanction of postnatal prosecution remains. Increasingly, in a war of attrition against women's struggle for empowerment and control, it is the criminal law which is invoked. In October 1996, in South Carolina, Cornelia Whitner was sentenced to eight years' imprisonment for child abuse after giving birth to a baby addicted to cocaine. In Iowa, Junyce Green has been charged with manslaughter after giving birth to a premature addicted baby who died within two weeks. A Wisconsin woman, Deborah Zimmerman, has become the first woman in the USA to be charged with the attempted murder of her foetus by poisoning it with alcohol via the placenta.[94]

In Britain the issue of foetal personhood is of sufficient public importance to warrant a recent Attorney General's Reference on transferred malice.[95] Coke's time-honoured definition of murder states that a victim must be 'a reasonable creature *in rerum natura*', consistently interpreted as meaning that a child must be totally expelled from its mother's body and have an existence independent of her.[96] The Court of Appeal confirmed that the attacker of a woman whose child was born alive but who subsequently died of injuries inflicted *in utero* could be guilty of murder. An intention directed at the pregnant woman can thus be transferred to the foetus.

Since *Re S*, the UK courts have consistently and systematically refused to elaborate the question of foetal rights. The consequence of eschewing rights talk, however, is that women are subjected to a form of surveillance and

---

92  See de Gama, K, 'A brave new world? Rights discourse and the politics of reproductive autonomy' (1993) 20 JLS 116, pp 116–22.

93  As in so many cases which have gone to law, the child was born safe and well.

94  *Op cit*, fn 86, Daniels, p 584.

95  *Attorney General's Reference (No 3 of 1994)* [1997] 3 All ER 936; [1996] 2 All ER 10.

96  *R v Poulton* (1832) 5 P&C 25; *R v Sellis* (1837) P&C 850; *R v Handley* (1874) 13 Cox CC 79.

control far more pernicious than the criminal law. In the seven cases which have come before the courts so far, non-consenting pregnant women have been forced to submit to Caesarian sections on the grounds of incompetence or treatment for mental disorder.[97]

# RIGHTS AND RELATIONAL AUTONOMY

In posthumous pregnancy respect for dignity, bodily integrity and self determination is surrendered to a medical adventurism which attempts to legitimate itself by reference to paternalism and necessity. Technology, law and the obsessions of the pro-life lobby mean that the prospect of joining the 'undead' is no longer the stuff of legend or horror movies. The disaggregation of brain damage and somatic death implicit in the legal definition of brain death describes not an empirical reality but a social category. Law has permitted doctors both to elaborate their own definition of death and to put it aside so that the pregnant body can be maintained in what is claimed to be the interests of even a non-viable foetus. While the practices and rituals of death and dying give meaning to relationships,[98] the relationships revealed by new technologies are no longer those between pregnant woman and foetus, but between medicine and foetus.

Motherhood as ideology and practice fosters a vision of connection and continuity which feminist legal theory is now beginning to explore. Thus, Robin West's starting point is that women are not essentially separate from others.[99] Women are distinctively connected, materially, through pregnancy, penetration, menstruation and breastfeeding, and existentially, in moral and practical life. However, drawing on the insights of radical feminism, West exposes a fundamental contradiction: the blurring of physical boundaries which these processes describe may be a source of oppressive rather than moral worth.[100] She concedes: '... pregnancy connects us with life ... but that connection is not something to celebrate; it is that very connection that hurts us.'[101] While feminist critiques rightly challenge liberal legalism's shiny ideological adjuncts of equality, neutrality and universalism as gendered, an engagement which seeks to invest law with insights drawn from the politics of experience may in some contexts be coercive and profoundly oppressive. Posthumous pregnancy, as the ritualised repudiation of female worth, flags

---

97   For a detailed discussion of cases from *Re S* to *Re MB* see Wells, this volume.

98   Hertz, R, *Death and the Right Hand*, 1960, Aberdeen: Aberdeen University Press.

99   West, R, 'Jurisprudence and Gender', in Bartlett, K and Kennedy, R (eds), *Feminist Legal Theory: Readings in Law and Gender*, 1991, Oxford: Westview.

100 Firestone, S, *The Dialectic of Sex: The Case for a Feminist Revolution*, 1970, New York: Morrow.

101 *Ibid*, West, p 214.

up contradictions in feminist attempts to expand the legal self by constructing a relational model of autonomy grounded in connection and interdependence. This model begs many questions. The most fundamental and pressing is how and by whom are our relationships to be constructed and, then, privileged? Fathers and those who claim to represent the interests of the foetus will clearly seize the opportunity to elaborate the new jurisprudence. It is ironic that it was Diane Blood's extraordinary appeal to a relationship, specifically a biological relationship between a dead man and a future child, which provided the support which secured her legal victory.

There is little to suggest that a feminist construction of connection and continuity would be accepted in the courtroom. But, even if it were, as appealing as the notion of relational autonomy first appears, as an agenda for action, it difficult to see how it can avoid collapsing into paternalism. Instead, feminism needs first, in Rosalind Petchesky's words, to 'recuperate' notions of self-ownership, not as a description of real lived experience but as 'a rhetorical strategy for political mobilisation and defining identities' in a way which is capable of challenging the pernicious biologism of medical and scientific discourse.[102]

---

102 Petchesky, R, 'The body as property: a feminist re-vision', in Ginsburg, F and Rapp, R (eds), *Conceiving the New World Order: The Global Politics of Reproduction*, 1995, Los Angeles: University of California Press, p 387. Compare this to Stychin's proposal for the elaboration of a concept of autonomy grounded in embodiment, this volume.

# CHAPTER FIFTEEN

# I DON'T WANT TO BE A BURDEN!
# A FEMINIST REFLECTS ON WOMEN'S
# EXPERIENCES OF DEATH AND DYING

*Hazel Biggs*

## INTRODUCTION

It is not immediately obvious that there exist any entirely feminist perspectives on death and dying or, if they exist, how they might relate to medical law. Death happens to people from all walks of life and people of all ages, and as a consequence it appears to be universal, apparently transcending social class, ethnicity, sexuality and gender. Yet when death occurs, it impacts not only upon its immediate victim but also on anyone who is associated with its victim, and the ways in which it is experienced are coloured by the characteristics of the individual who is encountering it. Women are uniquely involved with deaths that occur at the extremes of the usual span of human life; it is they who primarily care for the elderly within our society and they who must experience miscarriage, abortion and neonatal death in a way which is specific to their gender.

Gender is a defining feature of the social identity of each of us and this is no less significant in dying than it is at the moment of birth. It is arguable that the impact of gender at the time of birth affects the perceptions of those who are participants and observers of the new-born child. People will offer congratulations and respond to new parents and their child in particular ways according to the gender of the infant. Often boys are described as fine strong sons, whose crying is seen as demonstrating how vigorous they are, while girls are considered pretty and fragile creatures who cry because they are distressed and need comfort.[1] In a similar way, the gender of the dying person, and of those who care and are bereaved, shapes the experience and understanding of all concerned in life's final event.

This feminist perspective will be developed through an analysis of the experiences of women and the ways in which they perceive, are involved in, and react to, death and dying. These perceptions are themselves shaped by the roles society expects women to play in relation to death and dying. Specifically, the role women play as primary carers for the dying, impacts upon their experience and perceptions of death and dying. The caring role is

---

1   Brooks-Gunn, J and Schemp Matthews, W, *He & She: How Children Develop their Sex-Role Identity*, 1979, London: Prentice-Hall, pp 59–61.

not unique to women, but many feminist authors have contended that women experience it more acutely than men.

Robin West outlines the distinctions between men's and women's propensities towards physical, psychological and emotional connectiveness with others and uses her analysis to conclude that this leads women to be more caring and responsible towards others.[2] Her discourse accords with that of Carol Gilligan who has articulated the theory that care, responsibility, and relationships which focus on the particular needs of others, are fundamental to women's moral development and therefore shape women's life experiences.[3] This analysis of death and dying does not, however, rest upon an essentialist construction of an enduring femininity, or a single model of womanhood, which suggests that women are predisposed to be carers.[4] Rather, it is concerned to explore contemporary issues related to death and dying by examining women's experiences of death and dying from contemporary, historical and ethnographical perspectives. In this way it may be possible to make the connection between feminism, death and dying, and also to provide some insight into the present groundswell of public, political and legal opinion which favours reform of the law concerning euthanasia and assisted death.

The discussion will take the form of an examination of issues related to death and dying as they have touched women generally, through their unique contemporary, historical, and ethnographic experiences. Women's experiences of death, dying and caring in different cultures and at different times, exhibit features which are reflected in modern everyday life. When located within this context, these experiences are indicative of the inherent dangers that legal reform permitting euthanasia and assisted death may present for women.

Women are peculiarly affected by the changing political emphasis on health care and social support. State provision of welfare is being selectively reduced at a time when the average age of the population is steadily increasing. Recent cuts in welfare impact crucially upon the elderly who are now required to provide for more of their own care, either through contributions during their working lives or by the clawing back of assets they have accumulated. Women generally live longer than men and therefore are available to care for their menfolk, but are often left to care for themselves when they become infirm. As a consequence, women are nearly twice as likely

---

2    West, R, 'Jurisprudence and gender' (1988) 1 *University of Chicago Law Review* 14.

3    Gilligan, C, *In a Different Voice*, 1982, Cambridge, Mass: Harvard University Press, pp 159–60.

4    See: Held, V, 'Feminism and moral theory', in Kitty, E and Meyers, D (eds), *Women and Moral Theory*, 1987, London: Rowan & Littlefield; Fuss, D, *Essentially Speaking: Feminism, Nature and Difference*, 1990, London: Routledge; Laurentis, TD, 'Eccentric subjects in feminist theory' (1990) 16 *Feminist Studies* 115; and Brooks, DL, 'A commentary on the essence of anti-essentialism in feminist legal theory' (1994) 2 FLS 115, for a critical overview of essentialism.

to die in communal homes as men and must provide a greater economic contribution to their care over a more prolonged period.[5] The indignity of dependence coupled with the financial burden to children and the State may be sufficient to encourage many to consider euthanasia as an alternative.

In Britain, actively taking the life of another amounts to homicide (murder or manslaughter) under the criminal law, and assisting a person to commit suicide is also proscribed.[6] Most Western jurisdictions uphold similar prohibitions on euthanasia while some have permitted assisted death in limited circumstances. In 1996 the Northern Territories of Australia passed legislation permitting medically assisted suicide. Four patients were helped to die under the Rights of the Terminally Ill Act before it was successfully challenged in the Supreme Court and subsequently repealed. In Holland euthanasia is openly practised, subject to procedural guidelines,[7] but is not legally authorised, while Switzerland and the German Republic also allow assisted suicide in very strictly controlled circumstances. Earlier this year the Supreme Court in America heard two cases concerning whether or not patients in New York have the right to choose to die by assisted suicide. It concluded that no such constitutional right exists, and that New York's prohibition on assisted suicide does not violate the equal protection clause.[8] Presently the State of Oregon has legislation, which was passed in 1994, permitting physician-assisted suicide. However, a federal court has subsequently held the principle to be unconstitutional. This ruling is now under appeal.

There are a variety of ways in which British law could be reformed in order to permit euthanasia. Euthanasia could be taken outside of the scope of the criminal law so that its practitioners, while being procedurally accountable, would not be subjected to criminal sanction. Another option would be to create a new criminal offence of mercy killing which would strictly define the circumstances to which it applied and carry its own penalties.[9] Alternatively euthanasia could be made the object of a special

---

5   Statistics taken from Office of Population Census and Surveys, *Mortality Statistics, General: Review of the Registrar General on Death in England and Wales 1992*, 1994, London: HMSO, Table 7, demonstrate that 25% of men died in their own homes compared with 19% of women in 1992, and that 13% of men die in communal establishments as opposed to 25% of women.

6   Section 2(1) of the Suicide Act 1961 prohibits the aiding and abetting of another person's suicide.

7   The guidelines have been incorporated into s 10 of the Disposal of the Dead Act 1990 and require that a report is submitted explaining the circumstances of the assisted death which must then be verified by the coroner who will decide whether to prosecute under the Criminal Code. Reporting the circumstances of such a death does not of itself preclude criminal prosecution.

8   *State of Washington et al v Glucksberg et al* and *Vacco et al v Quill et al* (1997) US LEXIS 4038.

9   This suggestion was considered by the House of Lords Select Committee on Medical Ethics (1993–94) HL 21–II, para 260, but no recommendation was made to this effect. The *Government Response to the Select Committee Report* endorsed this position, 1994, Cm 2553, London: HMSO.

defence to the crime of homicide,[10] or the mandatory life sentence for murder could be abolished to enable judges to exercise discretion in sentencing those who have participated in euthanasia.[11]

Those who advocate changes to the present law concerning euthanasia argue that reform is necessary in order to give people the right to avoid the perceived indignity of protracted dying or unwelcome prolonged life, and enable individuals to exercise personal autonomy until the very end of life. Support for the legalisation of euthanasia and assisted death is growing,[12] and it is evident that many of the loudest voices calling for legal reform belong to women.[13] This chapter is concerned to determine the impact of women's experiences as carers on their attitudes towards death, dying and euthanasia, and the potential impact that any permissive legal change might have on women as a group.

## WOMEN'S EXPERIENCE OF DEATH

The authors of *Death, Gender and Ethnicity* argue that 'the ways in which a society deals with death reveal a great deal about that society, especially about the ways in which individuals are valued'.[14] The inequalities that exist between people in society are no less relevant during the dying process or at the time of death, and these shape individual experiences of death, dying and bereavement. The value placed on the experiences of women in this context reflect the general regard for women within society and this is clearly demonstrated by observing situations where women have unique encounters with death and dying. Examples of these unique situations include: infanticide; abortion; and miscarriage, stillbirth and neonatal death. In these contexts, women are more directly involved with death and dying simply because of their gender, and their experiences are distinct from those of men, even though men may share in the involvement.

---

10　Helme, T and Padfield, N, 'Setting euthanasia on the level' (1993) 15 *Liverpool Law Review* 75.

11　The 1994 House of Lords Select Committee on Medical Ethics strongly supported this course of action, at para 294, but it was rejected by the government, which favoured the status quo.

12　Helme, TM, 'Euthanasia around the world' (1992) 304 BMJ 717.

13　Some examples include Sue Rodriquez, who challenged Canadian constitutional law in *Rodriquez v AG British Columbia* [1993] 3 WWR 553, Annie Lindsell (1996) *The Sunday Times*, 8 September, who sought constitutional change in Britain, and Christine Taylor-Watson, who called for people to be allowed to choose the time of their demise: Driscoll, M, 'After a good life why can't we choose a good death?' (1995) *The Sunday Times*, 15 January.

14　Field, D, Hockey, J and Small, N, 'Making sense of difference: death, gender and ethnicity in modern Britain', in *Death, Gender and Ethnicity*, 1997, London: Routledge pp 1–2.

In Britain infanticide is a crime which can only be committed by women. It is narrowly defined by the Infanticide Act 1938 which stipulates that it occurs only where a mother deliberately kills her own child within 12 months of its birth and while 'the balance of her mind was disturbed by reason of her not having fully recovered from the effect of giving birth to the child or by reason of the effect of lactation'.[15] As a crime, infanticide is unique in that it can only be committed by a woman who is suffering from an abnormality of the mind. Yet infanticide has not enjoyed such a singular status throughout history. It has been tolerated by societies that have accepted it as a means to control population growth, as a religious sacrifice, or out of economic necessity, but it is a practice which has had a profound impact upon the women whose infants are its victims.[16] There are also many historical and contemporary examples of female infanticide which appear to characterise the undervaluing of new female life endemic in some cultures.[17]

Abortion remains a controversial subject which impacts physically and emotionally on the women who experience it, about which much has been written and said which does not require repetition here. In a perverse way however, it has been suggested that the abortion debate has in some measure been responsible for feminists failing to acknowledge the needs and grief of women experiencing the third of these categories, miscarriage, stillbirth[18] and neonatal death.[19] The emotional consequences of elective termination of pregnancy are habitually stressed in the medical manuals and particularly in pro-life literature, yet Germaine Greer believes that:

> The exhaustion and depression which follow spontaneous abortion are immeasurably greater than the unhappiness which follows an unwanted and terminated pregnancy, but women usually get no more sensitive treatment than being told to run off home and try again.[20]

The traumatic impact of miscarriage, stillbirth and neonatal death upon the women who experience them have, until very recent times, been largely invisible in statistics of mortality and morbidity. In Britain this appears to be a hangover from pre-industrial society when high rates of infant death were the expected norm and a child was not recognised as a member of its community

---

15 Section 1(1) of the Infanticide Act 1938.

16 McCormick, CP, *Ethnography of Fertility and Birth*, 1982, Oxford: OUP, p 129; Ellison, M, *The Black Experience: American Blacks Since 1865*, 1974, London: Penguin, pp 18–19; Greer, G, *Sex and Destiny: The Politics of Human Fertility*, 1984, London: Picador, pp 159–96.

17 Examples include the Inuit society described in Brody, H, *The Peoples Land: Eskimos and Whites in the Eastern Arctic*, 1975, London: Penguin, pp 192–93; and ancient India and China referred to in Weir, RF, *Selective Nontreatment of Handicapped Newborns: Moral Dilemmas in Neonatal Medicine*, 1984, Oxford: OUP, p 3.

18 Miscarriage and stillbirth are often clinically described as spontaneous abortion.

19 Lovell, A, 'Death at the beginning of life', in *op cit*, fn 14, Field *et al*, p 47.

20 *Ibid*, Greer, p 195.

unless and until it had been baptised.[21] Those who failed to survive long enough to be 'churched' were not acknowledged as ever having entered society.[22]

During the industrial revolution the families of women who worked in the mills were usually dependent upon the woman's income for survival. As a result women had no choice but to continue working throughout their pregnancies and if they miscarried they would often do so on the factory floor.[23] Those babies that were delivered alive would be placed in the care of nurses who, unable to feed them, would pacify them with laudanum while their mothers continued to work. It is reported that across Europe tens of thousands of babies died each year at the hands of these so-called angel-makers.[24] Women gave birth to life and other women ended that life.

In modern times a higher value is placed on new life, presumably because there are today relatively few births and modern medicine and technology encourages the expectation that pregnancy and birth will produce a perfect outcome. Yet it is reported that in the United Kingdom approximately 7,000 babies are born dead or die in the neonatal period every year,[25] and these losses are still 'largely unrecognised and undervalued'.[26] Society's failure to recognise the significance of such early deaths is reflected in the system of registration of births and the mechanisms available for disposal of the dead child, whereby 'the grief of women whose children have died either *in utero* or around the time of birth is made illegitimate through bureaucratic and ritual procedures which deny the social identity and meaning of the dead child.[27]

Arguably the position regarding the removal of the products of conception and the bodies of stillborn babies has improved in recent times. The position concerning miscarriages is complex, since these can occur at any time from conception until the legal age of viability is reached; hence the nature of the products of conception will differ according to the gestational age, as will the attitudes and needs of the mother. Stillborn babies were traditionally buried in

---

21  Hertz, R, *Death and the Right Hand*, 1960, New York: Free Press.

22  However, ceremonies of baptism were generally held when the child was scarcely a few days old.

23  *Op cit*, fn 16, Greer, p 192.

24  Hewitt, M, *Wives and Mothers in Victorian Industry*, 1958, reprinted 1975, Westport: Greenwood Press.

25  Rajan, L and Oakley, A, 'No pills for heartache: support in pregnancy loss' (1993) 11 *Journal of Reproductive and Infant Psychology* 75.

26  *Op cit*, fn 19, Lovell, p 35.

27  *Op cit*, fn 14, Field *et al*, pp 6–7. Until the 1970s certification of stillbirth consisted of a 'Certificate of Disposal' with no space for the baby's name. Today the legal definition and registration of stillbirth is linked to the legal age of viability of 24 weeks' gestation in the Stillbirth Definition Act 1992; prior to 24 weeks certification of neither birth nor death is required. Kohner reports, however, that 'a medical certificate may be given to acknowledge the baby's existence', see Kohner, N, *A Dignified Ending. Recommendations for Good Practice in the Disposal of the Bodies and Remains of Babies Born Dead Before the Age of Legal Viability*, 1992, London: Stillbirths and Neonatal Death Society.

the coffin of an unrelated adult, particularly if they were pre-term, but today more women, and their partners, are given the opportunity to see and hold their offspring, and increasingly provision is also made for burial, although this appears to be organised on an *ad hoc* basis depending on the policy of the hospital and the wishes of the parents.

Despite these recent improvements in medical recognition of the impact of neonatal death, miscarriage and stillbirth remain a taboo subject within society at large. When a baby dies in the neonatal period, its parents have usually been able to identify with it and mourning is expected and accepted. But if a child is lost through miscarriage or stillbirth, its social identity may be denied, as may the needs of its parents to grieve for its existence and loss. Alice Lovell describes the process whereby birth and death occur virtually simultaneously in the hospital maternity unit as being treated 'as if one cancelled out the other'.[28] This is probably due, in part, to the legal emphasis on definition and gestational age which requires registration and certification at some stages of gestation but not others. However, these definitions fail to take account of feelings of bereavement, and it is these feelings which shape many women's understandings of these deaths and the perspectives they bring to their understanding of death in more general contexts.

The division of labour and the allocation of roles associated with the care of the dying are also influenced by gender. People's experiences of death are constructed by the roles assigned to them by society and their relationships with the individuals concerned. In the care of the dying, as in all areas of social life, it is usually women who assume the role of primary carer. Therefore women and men tend to experience death differently because they generally contribute differently to the processes of dying and react differently. Societal and individual attitudes towards care is one manifestation of the gender distinctions which arise in the field of death, dying and bereavement. Women's experiences of caring for the dying influence their perceptions of death and dying and their attitudes towards their own care which can be examined by interrogating the shifting emphasis of care and control over dying throughout history and across cultures.

## WOMEN AS SOCIETY'S CARERS

Until the 18th century, death was predominantly an area of female control. Women tended to be responsible for all aspects of caring for the dead and dying, as they were for all aspects of birth. The angel-makers clearly demonstrate that responsibility for death can be an integral part of caring for, as Germaine Greer asserts, 'the crimes of the angel-makers were hardly

---

28   See, *op cit*, fn 19, Lovell, p 38.

recognisable as infanticide. Mothers had to work, children had to wait and laudanum was merciful'.[29] From the 18th century onwards, however, as part of a general trend towards medicalisation, death and the processes associated with it became increasingly 'de-feminised'. Men were involved in, and had control of, medicine and therefore were responsible for the overseeing and administering all medical processes, including dying.[30]

However, women continued in the subordinate role of informal carers and therefore retained control of many of the more menial tasks relating to death. An example of this is to be found in Coventry where it is reported that women, described as handywomen, acted as both layers-out of corpses and midwives up until the 1920s.[31] Today these tasks fall to the nurses caring for the dying, who are still mostly female, although funeral directors, predominantly male, may also be involved after the death has occurred.

Throughout history women have been unpaid 'lay' carers for the dying and chronically ill.[32] This is particularly marked in the domestic arena where caring 'flows out of the customary responsibilities' assumed by women.[33] Women are also regarded as 'front-line' carers within the institutional health service. As a result it is predominantly women who do the mundane work associated with death and dying, performing both practical and emotional roles whether they act as employed or voluntary carers. This is evident in the work of Michael Young and Lesley Cullen, who performed a detailed study of 14 people who were dying of cancer, and their carers.[34]

All the patients in the study had a variety of carers and all but two, who lived entirely alone, had at least one carer residing with them. Of the 12 who were cohabiting, one lived with an unmarried female partner and eight lived with a relative. Five of these relatives were spouses (three were female), one lived with her mother and two were cared for by a daughter. Many families shared care responsibilities but there was always a principal carer and in all except two cases these were women.

Young and Cullen comment on the gender typing of roles in the sick room and see this as a reflection of the gendering of care within society as a whole. They also investigated the reasons given by family members for not participating more in caring for their relations. The most common reasons given were participation in full-time employment and living some distance

---

29  See, op cit, fn 16, Greer, p 192.

30  Witz, A, Professions and Patriarchy, 1992, London: Routledge.

31  See, Adams, S, 'A gendered history of the social management of death and dying in Foleshill, Coventry, during the inter-war years', in Clark, D (ed), The Sociology of Death, 1993, Oxford: Blackwells , pp 149–68.

32  Ungerson, C, Policy is Personal: Sex, Gender and Informal Care, 1987, London: Tavistock.

33  Jordan, B, Value for Caring: Recognising Unpaid Carers, King's Fund Project Paper, No 81, London: King's Fund, p 16.

34  Young, M and Cullen, L, A Good Death: Conversations with East Londoners, 1996, London: Routledge.

away. These reasons were offered most commonly by male relatives which confirmed the suggestion that society views women, and particularly female relatives, as the most appropriate carers. Yet, society's expectations of women as carers can be culturally and historically specific, as are women's experiences of death and dying, and this can be demonstrated by reference to specific historical, ethnographic and anthropological material.

Llewellyn and Hoebel, in their seminal work on the Cheyenne, detail the attitudes of this particular society to its women and the role of women within the community.[35] Traditionally labour was divided on the basis of gender; it was the women who were responsible for the bulk of the domestic chores and for the caring roles:

> ... a woman used to do all the housework. When we moved from one place to another, as we did frequently, she would take down the tipis, carry them and all other household things to the place we were going and when we arrived our destination, she would not only set up the tipi but see to all other household affairs, such as cooking, gathering wood and so on. She went into the woods, cut down trees and brought the wood on her back to the tipi. A man could not do these things because others would laugh at him if he did so: these were woman's work. A man did nothing but look after the horses. He would also go hunting, procure game and when needed go to war.[36]

The sexual division of labour has been observed in countless communities and societies[37] and is reflected in the gendering of caring previously described. The various tribes of native Americans provide a graphic example of how women come to be defined in terms of the role they are expected to play within particular societies. Here it fell to women to perform the domestic chores such as cleaning, preparation of food, and manufacture of clothing. The woman would also cater for her husband's needs and raise and care for the children. Her role, and consequently her usefulness to the community, was defined in terms of her husband's and her family's needs. She was the primary carer in the same way as are women in modern Western society.

However, if something happened to the family of the native American woman, her role in the community would be immediately redefined. Her responsibilities towards the tribe as a whole were clearly understood: she represented a burden since she no longer had anyone to care for and nobody to provide for her. This was graphically illustrated in the film, *A Man Called*

---

35  Llewellyn, K and Hoebel, E, *The Cheyenne Way*, 1941, Oklahoma City: University of Oklahoma Press.

36  The words of Red Eagle, a Cheyenne Indian, quoted in Bonnerjea, B, 'Reminiscences of a Cheyenne Indian' (1934) *Journal de la Société des Americanistes* 27.

37  See, for example, Mansell, W, Meteyard, B and Thomson, A, *A Critical Introduction to Law*, 1995, London: Cavendish Publishing, pp 77–88.

*Horse*,[38] which is based on eyewitness accounts of the rituals and lifestyles of the native American Indians in the mid-19th century.[39]

The action was set in the North West Territory of America where an English Lord, played by Richard Harris, is captured, along with his horses, by native Americans. Naked from bathing, he is brought to his knees, given the name Horse and led by a noose to the Indian village. Once there, he is presented to the old woman who is to be his owner. She checks the condition of his teeth, feeds him hay and allows children to ride upon his back. As time passes Horse observes the customs and rituals of the tribe and eventually comes to be accepted as a man who earns the right to marry the daughter of his former 'owner'.

Inevitably, however, tragedy strikes. Horse's wife and her siblings are killed when another tribe attacks. This leaves the old woman without a family to care for. Horse watches as she cuts off her finger to symbolise her loss and then, through his own grief, realises that she is desperate for his recognition:

> Oh my God ... You've got nobody left to provide for you ... You'll give everything away ... You'll scavenge for offal ... With winter coming you won't last a month ... I will be your son!

Devoid of a family to care for, the old woman had nothing of benefit to offer the community. She would simply be a drain on their precious resources, a burden to the rest of the tribe. The traditional law dictated that in this situation she must distribute her belongings amongst the other women, destroy, or at least vacate, her tipi and live on whatever leftovers she could scrounge for as long as she could. Because of her age and frailty she would soon succumb. She was valued by her society for as long as she was able to fulfil her role as carer and homemaker, but once this function ceased to be required, neither was she.

A similar attitude has been noticed amongst the Inuit, where anyone who was perceived as burdensome to the community or otherwise just not pulling their weight in some regard, would be abandoned on the ice floe. Every member of this society would have to perform their allotted tasks and be able to keep up with the nomadic wandering of the group: 'readiness and ability to move is the key to living in the north. In this kind of society the highest possible degree of mobility represents a maximising of economic efficiency.'[40]

If an individual threatened this economic imperative, the rest of the community would simply walk away and leave them, usually while they

---

38  I am indebted to my colleague Per Laleng for suggesting the relevance of this title.

39  Produced by Sandy Howard, directed by Elliot Silverstein, screenplay by Jack De Witt and based on a story by Dorothy M Johnson. A CBS Fox film with acknowledgments to the documentation of George Catlin, Carl Bodmer and other eyewitnesses of the period as preserved in the American Museum of Natural History, the Library of Congress and the Smithsonian Institute.

40  Brody, H, *Living Arctic: Hunters of the Canadian North*, 1987, New York: Faber & Faber, p 101.

slept. Elderly women whose families no longer needed them were frequent victims of this treatment, but it was by no means exclusive to females. Troublesome men who perhaps had broken the law or simply refused to work to the required standard would also be abandoned to nature, although they would often be strong enough to track the group and later rejoin it.

These ethnographic examples help to demonstrate the caring roles assigned to women in different cultures and the value placed upon women and their labour within many communities. Frequently women are expected to be primary carers within a community, but once circumstances or age redefines their role, their value is diminished, as the Inuit and Cheyenne demonstrate. The experiences common to many women in modern Western society reflect the attitudes prevalent in the ethnographical material presented here. In particular, those women who feel they have nothing left to offer society once they are no longer required to care for others can experience a desire to withdraw from society in order to avoid becoming a burden when they need to be cared for themselves. This desire may be satisfied if euthanasia were readily available.

Dying and death can be 'a disruptive and destabilising force', which 'opens out personal and social relations to critical reflection'.[41] As a result of women's acquired perceptions about death, dying and their own value to society, attained through their experiences as carers, many approach their own demise with anxiety and trepidation. Such fears may result in a wish to avoid becoming dependent on receiving care from others and, in Britain, these fears are being fuelled by demographic changes and economic pressures in the welfare system. Concerns about the consequences and costs of care have raised awareness of issues related to death and dying and specifically the merits and demerits of euthanasia and assisted death which are not specific to women but may be of particular relevance to some women.

## EUTHANASIA AND ASSISTED DEATH

Although death is, in clichéd terms, a part of life and happens to everyone, in modern society it is increasingly outside of the ordinary experience of most people. Death and dying are today removed from the private domain of the family home to the clinical hospital environment where death is experienced as a medical event. Illich explains how death, and our perceptions of death, have altered over time:

> We have seen death turn from God's call into a 'natural' event and later into a 'force of nature'; in a further mutation it had turned into an 'untimely' event

---

41  Hallam, E, 'Death and the transformation of gender in image and text', in Field, D, Hockey, J and Small, N, *Death, Gender and Ethnicity in Modern Britain*, 1997, London: Routledge, p 108.

when it came to those who were not both healthy and old. Now it has become the outcome of specific diseases certified by the doctor ... The general force of nature that had been celebrated as 'death' had turned into a host of specific causations of clinical demise.[42]

Simultaneous with the changes to our expectations about death the average life expectancy in the United Kingdom has increased by 25 years during this century, and in the 37 years between 1951 and 1988 the number of people aged 80 and over nearly trebled, increasing from 0.7 to 2.0 million.[43] These statistics can be attributed to the advancement of medical science and applauded in many respects, since many people now have the opportunity to live for months or years longer than would have previously been possible. However, the downside is that the number of people suffering disabling, chronic, and terminal disease has also risen[44] and 'the ageing of the population alone means that the overall number of new cancer patients will increase at an estimated 0.5% a year over the next 20 years'.[45]

In the same period that has seen this huge increase in the longevity of the general population, euthanasia and assisted death have become the subject of intense public debate. Opinion polls suggest that public support for euthanasia has increased from approximately 50% in the 1960s to around 75% in 1992,[46] and that this is largely due to fears concerning prolonged dying and being kept alive inappropriately. The words of two people dying from cancer clearly illustrate the point: 'I hate pain. I'm not sure I have a fear of dying. It's the manner and the possibility of a lot of pain'[47] and 'I'm not afraid of dying, it's the method of dying. The only thing that worries me is that I don't want to last too long when the pain is too bad.'[48]

Lord Alport, speaking in the parliamentary debate following the *Report of the House of Lords Select Committee on Medical Ethics*,[49] suggested a reason why euthanasia is gaining public support. He argued that today, 'owing to advances in medical technology, life for an increasing number of people is nasty, brutish and long'[50] in contrast to a time when life was generally nasty, brutish and short, but nonetheless sacred. Life appears less sacred when it has

---

42   Illich, I, *Limits to Medicine*, 1995, Harmondsworth: Penguin, p 199.

43   'Age sex structure of the population', *Social Trends*, 1990, London: HMSO, Table 1.2, p 24.

44   Grundy, E, 'Future patterns of morbidity in old age', in Caird, FI and Grimley-Evans, J (eds), *Advanced Geriatric Medicine*, 1987, Bristol: John Wright.

45   *Review of National Cancer Registration System*, Series MBI, No 17, 1990, London: OPCS.

46   See *op cit*, fn 12, Helme.

47   The words of the patient identified as Janet, in *op cit*, fn 34, Young and Cullen, p 128.

48   The words of the patient identified as Harold, in *op cit*, fn 34, Young and Cullen, p 128.

49   1993–94 Parliamentary Session, Vol 1, 1994.

50   Hansard, Parliamentary Debates, House of Lords, Debate on Select Committee on Medical Ethics, Vol 554, No 83, col 1374, 1994 (9 May). These comments can be contrasted with those of Thomas Hobbes who argued in *Leviathan*, 1997, London: Norton, p 213, that '... the life of man [is] solitary, nasty, brutish and short'.

exceeded its natural span and its quality has been degraded. At such a time death can appear more attractive, particularly when the alternative is to become increasingly burdensome to those who care.[51] At this point it is interesting to draw comparisons between the Cheyenne and Inuit women who are cast out of their communities when nobody needs their care, and the increasing numbers of people, mainly women,[52] in modern Western society who live out their final days in the seclusion of institutional nursing homes.

The euthanasia debate is not polarised simply in terms of to die or not to die but more of how, where, and when to die? Many people fear a slow lingering death because such a death tends to be associated with a gradual loss of control and dignity. Ronald Dworkin identifies the crucial link between death and dignity which he believes emphasises '... how important it is that life ends appropriately, that death keeps faith with the way we want to have lived'.[53] Conversely the process of dying over an extended period of time can be seen as providing 'a chance to be able to come to terms with dying and with yourself, other people, to sort things out in your life over a period of time; to round off your life'.[54]

This is an argument which is also advanced in favour of euthanasia since, if available, it could facilitate the opportunity to make financial and emotional preparations for the inevitable death as well as avoiding unwelcome suffering. In some cultures it is considered inherently dignified to be able to select the time, place and manner of one's dying, and arguments in favour of euthanasia are frequently advanced on the basis of promoting dignity in dying:

> If the patients themselves wish it, I don't think we should begrudge anybody to have a dignified exit from life, and no way do they die with dignity and no one can make me believe otherwise. The trouble is, until you experience it, you don't believe it.[55]

'Until you experience it, you don't believe it' is a phrase which goes to the root of this analysis. The woman who expressed this view had cared for her husband throughout his extended terminal illness, and in spite of his repeated wish to die by euthanasia which his professional carers were unable to fulfil. The desire to die before medicine finally allows nature to take its course is not uncommon. A study, which was carried out to determine why people might seek this, demonstrated that 25% of their respondents would prefer to die or to have died sooner, and the primary reasons given were the wish to maintain

---

51  See Seale, C and Addington-Hall, J, 'Euthanasia: why people want to die earlier' (1994) 39 *Social Science and Medicine* 647.

52  See above, fn 5, which graphically illustrates the different experiences of men and women.

53  Dworkin, R, *Life's Dominion*, 1993, London: HarperCollins, p 199.

54  Kfir, N and Slevin, M, *Challenging Cancer – From Chaos to Control*, 1991, London: Tavistock, p 53.

55  See *op cit*, fn 34, Young and Cullen, p 135.

control until the end of life and to avoid the perceived indignity of dependence.[56] Control of pain was a crucial reason given by the respondents to the survey, but in making the link between women's experiences as carers and euthanasia it is not only physical pain that should be considered. Often it is impossible to separate the distress caused by physical pain from the 'psychic suffering' and 'potential disfigurement of the personality' described by Dutch doctors who practise euthanasia.[57]

Those who have been involved in caring for the young, the old and the dying are more likely to experience this type of pain and this reluctance to become a burden to other carers. Hence many women's perceptions and tolerance of their own illnesses and infirmities are inescapably coloured by their experiences as carers. They know what is involved because they have been responsible for doing it, or have at least supported others who have done it.

It has been reported that the general health of widows declined after bereavement, particularly where they had cared for the deceased. A significant proportion of these women became ill and showed symptoms which mirrored those of the dying person for whom they had cared. Approximately 15% of them died of what has sometimes been described as 'a broken heart'![58] For widows, bereavement is often more than simply grieving for the loss of a loved one, it is also associated with a loss of personal identity:

... that bereavement can be seen as the loss of the self most closely corresponds to the experiences of widows whose self-identity derived from the man they married, whose name they took, whose domestic life they serviced and upon whose income they depended.[59]

As a consequence it is easy to postulate that euthanasia may be an option which appears more attractive to women than men, both for themselves when they need care and perhaps advocated by women who are carers and observe the futile suffering of those for whom they must care. An informal trawl of press cuttings and media reports reveals that an apparent majority of those advocating the need for a legal right to die for themselves are women.[60]

For example, in 1993 Canadian-born Sue Rodriquez made a constitutional challenge to the Canadian Criminal Code which, she argued, conflicted with the Canadian Charter of Rights and Freedoms because it precluded her right to die with dignity by assisted suicide.[61] She was concerned that, because the Criminal Code prohibits assisted suicide, she would be forced to endure a life

---

56  *Op cit*, fn 51, Seale *et al*.

57  'Euthanasia: what is the good death?' (1991) *Economist*, 20 July, p 21.

58  Marris, P, *Widows and their Families*, 1958, London: Routledge and Kegan Paul; and Marris, P, *Loss and Change*, revised edn, 1986, London: Routledge and Kegan Paul.

59  See, *op cit*, fn 14, Field *et al*, p 9.

60  See *op cit*, fn 13.

61  *Rodriquez v AG British Columbia* [1993] 3 WWR 553.

of undignified dependence if she chose to end her life at a time when the progress of her disease physically prevented her from ending her own life. The courts were sympathetic to her argument but nevertheless the majority decision in the Supreme Court failed to uphold a right to die by assisted suicide and stressed the opinion that such fundamental decisions should properly be taken by Parliament.

Chris Taylor-Watson was a British woman who publicly called for people to be allowed to choose the time of their demise while she was dying from a brain tumour:

> If I had my way I could say good-bye ... I could choose my time and be calm and collected about it. I have had a good life and I would dearly like a good death ... my last wish is to die with dignity.[62]

Annie Lindsell was a woman who suffered from motor neurone disease and who had witnessed the death of a loved one from the same illness. Before she died, she sought constitutional change to provide individuals with a legal right to die and to ensure that her doctor would not be prosecuted if he gave her a lethal injection.[63] Although she did not succeed in amending the law, she was told that her own doctor would not be acting unlawfully if he provided her with drugs to alleviate her distress, if this incidentally shortened her life.[64] Another woman inflicted with the same condition and calling for a similar change in the law is Margaret Sedgewick.[65]

In America Dr Jack Kevorkian has become something of a celebrity due to his 'quest' to assist those who seek death but feel unable to proceed alone. But it has been suggested that Kevorkian has inappropriately focused the attentions of his home-made suicide machine (*The Mercitron*) on women.[66] The disproportional impact of Kevorkian's beneficence on women has been discussed alongside an examination of his professional qualifications, the efficacy of the diagnoses of his female patients and the interpersonal relationships he had with each of them. It is posited that in some cases the women concerned were either misdiagnosed as terminally ill or only in the very early stages of a progressive disease, the implication being that Kevorkian has taken advantage of these women for some, unarticulated, motive of his own. By contrast the influential *British Medical Journal* has carried a report characterising Kevorkian as a medical hero because:

---

62  Driscoll, M, 'After a good life why can't we choose a good death?' (1995) *The Sunday Times*, 15 January.

63  Wilkins, E, 'Death on demand' (1996) *The Sunday Times*, 8 September; Dyer, C, 'Woman challenges euthanasia law' (1996) 313 BMJ 643.

64  Wilkins, E, 'Dying woman granted wish for dignified end' (1997) *The Times*, 29 October, p 4.

65  See Hendrie, C, 'Right – or wrong – to die?' (1996) *The Mail on Sunday*, 13 October, pp 42–43, and *Nothing but the Truth*, Channel 4, 13 October 1996.

66  Gutmann, S, 'Dr Kevorkian's woman problem: death and the maiden' (1996) *New Republic*, 24 June, p 1.

No one has demonstrated any discernible motives from him except that he believes his work is right. Greed for money is absent because he has charged no fees. Greed for fame, too, seems unlikely because he has shunned the media except to explain his position. And no one has accused him of sadism in ending the lives and, according to him, the suffering of his patients.[67]

It is true that initially women were disproportionately represented in the numbers of those that Kevorkian had assisted to suicide but it is possible to suggest reasons why that may be so.

Men who commit suicide tend to be impulsive and choose drastic methods which are likely to succeed. Women, on the other hand, tend to favour less dramatic methods: '... in western Europe hanging, drowning and the use of car exhausts have a predominance of male perpetrators, whereas self-poisoning is more frequently, though of course not exclusively, associated with women.'[68]

Women's motivation, particularly the wish to avoid becoming burdensome, means that they are more likely to make a considered response to their situation: a response which might take account of the need for time to prepare family and friends and the need to ensure that the method selected was foolproof yet clinical. Janet Adkins, Kevorkian's first 'victim', seems to typify this sentiment. Diagnosed as suffering from Alzheimer's disease, she is reported to have planned her death at a time which would be least disruptive to her family, avoiding spoiling Christmas, and which enabled her to arrange her own memorial service. She is also said to have 'arranged for a therapist to mediate final "closure" sessions with her family'.[69] The fact that Kevorkian has assisted more women than men may simply be indicative of the issues that are the focus of this essay; that women feel the effects of illness and of increasing dependence more acutely than do men. Or it may suggest that many women feel vulnerable and concerned at the prospect of becoming the cared-for rather than the carer because society appears to no longer value them once they reach this stage.[70] Legal change to permit euthanasia could be perilous for women in these circumstances.

## CONCLUSION

This study illustrates that statistically, women live longer than men and that often, because of their experiences as carers, they appear to be more vociferous than men in calling for the legalisation of euthanasia. The evidence

---

67  Roberts, J and Kjellstrand, C, 'Jack Kevorkian: a medical hero' (1996) 312 BMJ 1434.

68  Pritchard, C, *Suicide – the Ultimate Rejection? A Psycho-Social Study*, 1995, Buckingham: Open University Press, pp 55–56.

69  *Op cit*, fn 66, Gutmann, p 3.

70  Parallels may be drawn here with the examples from the Inuit and Cheyenne societies.

of Kevorkian's women also seems to suggest that women are often more desirous of avoiding becoming burdensome to those for whom they had cared. Yet if active euthanasia were to be permitted as a right, what is to prevent the endorsement of this *right* being translated into a duty? How long will it be before those who seek euthanasia in order to avoid being a burden lose the right to continue living until the natural end of their lives? The experiences of women in the Cheyenne and Inuit societies who were expected to withdraw from their communities once they had outlived their usefulness as carers, are indicative of the dangers which could flow from laws permitting euthanasia. The introduction of legal euthanasia could alter social and personal expectations of old age beyond recognition, changing it from a time for relaxation and quiet enjoyment of the twilight years[71] to a time for resisting pressure and the expectations of those who perceive that all useful life is over.

It can be difficult to refute the view that euthanasia should be every person's right, that it should be legally permissible in order to provide individuals with the opportunity to select the time, place, and manner of their dying as a means of preserving personal dignity. Such an argument is founded on the ethical principle of individual autonomy[72] which is given legal expression through the doctrine of consent. Consent can validate conduct and procedures which in another context may generate criminal liability.[73] However, the doctrine of consent can be problematic and imperfect, especially where there are doubts concerning the validity of a consent given or withheld. Factors such as the decision making capacity or the impact of outside influences on that person are frequently introduced in cases where the validity of a consent has been questioned, and decisions can be taken by others contrary to the expressed views of the person concerned.[74] In the light of this it is arguable that no reform of the law to legalise euthanasia could provide adequate safeguards to protect those who may be vulnerable to pressure to accept euthanasia for themselves. While it is incumbent upon feminists to uphold the principle of autonomy and individual choice it is important that the principle is not endorsed at the risk of placing pressure on those who may prefer to exercise their choice to live.

---

71  Although clearly this is a stylised and idealistic view which does not accord with the experience of many elderly people.

72  An accessible explanation of autonomy in the context of medical care can be found in Gillon, R, *Philosophical Medical Ethics*, 1994, Chichester: John Wiley, pp 60–66.

73  For example, many of the procedures performed on patients every day, such as physical examination and drawing blood with a needle, would constitute a criminal battery in the absence of consent.

74  *Re T* [1992] 4 All ER 649; *Re C (Adult: Refusal of Treatment)* [1994] 1 All ER 819; and *Rochdale Healthcare (NHS) Trust v Chowdury* [1997] 1 FCR 274 are just a few examples of cases on this issue.

# INDEX